KU-162-891

Great Military Disasters

Great Military Disasters

A Historical Survey of Military Incompetence

AGO. No.	CLASS No.
19679	355
DATE	CHECKED
13.12.90	

Geoffrey Regan

ACC. No.	CLASS No.
25463	355 REG
DATE	CHECKED
July '00	

R.G.S. GUILDFORD.
J. C. MALLISON
LIBRARY.

M. Evans & Company, Inc.   New York

Library of Congress Cataloging-in-Publication Data

Regan, Geoffrey.

(Someone had blundered)
Great military disasters: a history of incompetence on the
battlefield/Geoffrey Regan.

p. cm.
British ed. published in 1987 under title: Someone had blundered.
Bibliography: p.
Includes index.
ISBN 0-87131-537-8
1. Military history. Modern. 2. Battles — Europe. 3. Battles —
United States. 4. Command of troops. I. Title.
D25.R37 1988
904'.7 — dc19   87-33593   CIP

Originally published in Great Britain in 1987 by B.T. Batsford Ltd

Copyright © 1987 by Geoffrey Regan

All rights reserved. No part of this book may be reproduced
or transmitted in any form or by any means without the written
permission of the publisher.

M. Evans and Company, Inc.
216 East 49 Street
New York, New York 10017

Manufactured in the United States of America

9 8 7 6 5 4 3

To Mother

Contents

5

CONTENTS

List of Maps

Acknowledgements

I would not have been able to write a book of this size and complexity without the help of a number of people. I would therefore like to record my thanks to Professor R.F. Leslie, Professor V.R. Berghahn of the University of Warwick, Dr E.J. Feuchtwanger of the University of Southampton, Dr John Morrill of Selwyn College, Cambridge, Dr John Gooch of the University of Lancaster and Dr Ian Roy of the Department of War Studies at King's College, London. In addition the librarians of the Bodleian Library, Rhodes House and All Souls College, Oxford gave me inestimable assistance. To their number I must add the staff at the Institute of Historical Research, the London University Library, the library of the University of Southampton, as well as the willing staff of the Hampshire County Library service at Winchester, Fareham and Portsmouth.

I would like to acknowledge my debt to the following authors, whose work proved particularly useful in the writing of this book: N. Dixon (*On the Psychology of Military Incompetence*, Cape, 1976); D. Divine (*The Blunted Sword*, Hutchinson, 1974); R. Hough (*The Great War at Sea 1914–1918*, OUP, 1983); C. Hibbert (*The Destruction of Lord Raglan*, Longman, 1961); P. Young (*Marston Moor: The Campaign and Battle*, Roundwood, 1970); M. Hastings and S. Jenkins (*The Battle for the Falklands*, Michael Joseph, 1983); H.P. Willmott (*Empires in the Balance*, Orbis, 1982); J. Winton (*Convoy*, Michael Joseph, 1983); R. Fullick and G. Powell (Suez: *The Double War*, Hamish Hamilton, 1979).

For permission to reproduce two maps from Alastair Horne's book *To Lose a Battle* I am indebted to both the author and Macmillan, London and Basingstoke. For the map of Cadiz harbour I acknowledge the kind permission of the author Roger Lockyer and the publishers of his book *Buckingham*, Longman Group UK Ltd. For kind permission to use Peter Young's map from his book *Marston Moor* I am indebted both to the author and to his publishers Roundwood Press, Kineton, Warwick. For

8

ACKNOWLEDGEMENTS

the map of the battle of Aspern Essling I am indebted both to Professor David Chandler and to The Macmillan Company of New York, publishers of his *Dictionary of the Napoleonic Wars*. For permission to use two maps from T.B. Costain's book, *The Three Edwards*. I acknowledge the kind assistance of the author and his publishers, Doubleday.

Finally I must express my gratitude to two people in particular who have done so much, in their different ways, to make this book possible. In these days of micro-chip and word processor it is sometimes difficult for a non-technical author to know which way to turn in order to produce his typescript as clearly and efficiently as possible. How lucky I was in having the help of Mark East, Manager of the Educational Support Division of Micro Facilities, Hampton Hill, Middx. Mark was a tower of strength in helping me through my 'teething troubles' with my Macintosh computer and kindly let me use a laser printer to produce my finished script – one occasion when the presentation undoubtedly flattered the content.

The other person whose assistance was indispensable to me was Tony Seward, the Senior Academic Editor at Batsford, who bore with my stylistic excesses and moulded my work into more conventional channels. Always quietly supportive Tony lent me the encouragement I needed when things were not going well. His influence on me has been so great that I would acknowledge that any merits the book might have owe much to his help, while any errors are, of course, my own.

Preface

Professional incompetence is of concern both to those who suffer from it and to competent members of a profession who seek to maintain its standards. It is not in the interest of teachers, accountants, solicitors, marine biologists, or members of a hundred other callings, to shelter those who are not properly qualified for the job; equally, there is no reason why members of the armed forces should be specially protected. It may be argued that the difficulties inherent in the military profession impose stresses of an entirely different kind to those in other occupations. Whether or not this is so, if the pressures of high command are likely to make such enormous demands on the individual, then the greatest care must be taken to weed out those who are incapable of meeting them.

Since 1945, far greater attention has been devoted to officer selection and training. Yet this was not always so. At various times in the past, promotion to high command in the armed forces has depended, not on the possession of qualities which fitted the individual to command large forces of men and equipment in complex and stressful conditions, but instead on social criteria like noble birth or membership of the right class, caste or religious group. Mistakes became common because those who exercised command were, quite simply, not up to the job. It had never been thought important in their selection to consider whether they would make good officers or not, mere membership of the group being regarded as in itself a guarantee of ability. Ironically, it was in the United States, that haven of democratic values and of the career open to talent, that some of the worst appointments were made. In 1861 command of the Union armies went less to the militarily able than to those whose political support was most needed by the President. In appointing the influential Democratic politicians Nathaniel P. Banks, John A. McClernand and Ben Butler to field commands, Lincoln, in the words of T. Harry Williams, 'saddled the army with some prize incompetents'.

Although the qualifications required for the military profession have differed throughout history, able generals have always shared certain qualities essential to field command, and without these no amount of silver spoons or gold braid will disguise a booby. And boobies there have been in plenty, wearing the uniforms of all nations, commanding armies, fleets and air forces, sending men to unnecessary deaths in their hundreds of thousands. As in all professions, incompetents have been in a minority, and I am not attempting to claim that their failings are typical of the armed forces as a whole: an attack on the inefficient hardly threatens the majority who perform competently. Nevertheless, the part played by them has been out of all proportion to their numbers and can hardly be ignored.

It has been suggested that military history should strictly be the preserve of the military itself and that no one can study it seriously who has not experienced military service at first hand. If this were to be the case I would have to admit myself singularly ill-equipped for the subject. However, the study of religious changes during the Reformation is not restricted to the clergy nor the history of the Black Death to the medical profession. To accept such an argument would undermine the nature of history as an academic study.

My intention in writing this book is a relatively humble one, namely to illustrate a problem that undeniably exists and has existed throughout history. There is nothing original in the concept of military incompetence, any more than there is in the idea that where men establish professional standards and codes of behaviour, there will be those who, for whatever reason, fail to live up to them. Unlike Norman Dixon in his interesting and entertaining book, *On the Psychology of Military Incompetence*, I make no claim to a new interpretation of why military disasters take place. Dixon's concern is with 'generalship', which he illuminates by means of his own discipline of experimental psychology. While acknowledging that historical events are determined by many complex factors, of a political, geographic, economic, social or climatic kind, he rightly emphasises the influence that the mind of the individual human being can have. His concern is to identify a distinct personality type which is prone to reach incorrect decisions under the stressful conditions of military service. However, in order to identify this 'authoritarian personality', he needs to 'play down the other factors in order to focus more clearly upon possible psychological determinants' in the events which surround military disasters. He goes further, asserting that military incompetence follows certain laws. To him, 'good commanders remain pretty much the same. Likewise, bad commanders have much in common with each other.' Naturally this is the point at which military history and psychology diverge. Military historians are not concerned with general theories of military disasters, only with why particular disasters took place, when they did and where they did. Each occasion is unique. The psychologist examining the causes of military disasters aims to identify factors which contribute to them, in order that these may be minimised or removed altogether in the future. In order to do this it is necessary to postulate initial conditions and general laws such that, if they are present in a particular case, disaster may be anticipated. This approach is unhistorical and cannot help us to understand why on certain occasions men will overcome their psychological limitations and succeed while on others men with far fewer personality problems will fail.

As I have pointed out throughout the book, even the most able commanders have erred on occasions. Grant at Cold Harbour, Lee at Gettysburg and Frederick the Great at Kolin, all made errors which, judged in isolation, could have earned them the title of 'incompetent'. Why did this happen, if these men were masters of their profession? Most who have been soldiers would agree with the simple answer, that their profession is an extremely difficult one to master completely. However, to the historian the problem is never that simple. To speak only of Grant or Lee or Frederick might seem to suggest that responsibility for everything that occurred rested in the hands of these men alone. But this is far from the truth. History is never predictable and the historian's task is to discover the unusual or surprising event which made the difference, the factor but for which events would have followed the expected pattern.

As an historian rather than a psychologist or a soldier, I have attempted to view the subject in its entirety, presenting a comprehensive range of factors, one or more of which are generally involved in military setbacks. I realise that to do this must necessarily limit the depth of my approach but it saves me from distorting the picture by concentrating too heavily on any one feature, however seemingly crucial it may be. Since space forbids a full analysis of each of the many different factors which contribute to military incompetence I have simply illustrated each with a few short examples, leaving it to the reader to add his own from the apparently endless supply provided by the military histories of all nations.

In the first part of the book I have grouped the factors which contribute to military incompetence under three headings, depending on whether they originate in the activities of the field commanders, the planners or their political masters. Naturally there is considerable overlap between the sections and it would be wrong to lay down 'hard and fast' rules. I have also tried to draw on a wide range of examples: just as incompetence is no more a distinguishing characteristic of the military profession than of any other, so the history of the British Army is no more liable to provide examples of disastrous blunders than that of other nations. The problem is international. Although availability of sources has resulted in a preponderance of British examples my aim has been to balance these with examples from every age and continent.

Public confidence in the army command survived the many blunders of the Victorian age generally intact. However, the horrors of trench warfare in 1914–18 and the casualty lists which left scarcely a home in Britain untouched concentrated the public mind on the inadequacies of the high command. After 1918 the notion that the generals had been stupid and incompetent became fashionable. As a result, much more attention was paid to the physical and mental capacity of military commanders as the pressures of modern warfare imposed unprecedented strains upon them. This has resulted in many useful insights and in Section 1 of the first part of the book I have devoted considerable space to illustrating how the failure to appreciate physical and mental deficiencies has contributed to many military setbacks. Nevertheless, just as it was always a mistake to neglect these points, so also is it now wrong to overstress them. The individual commander of genius may count for a lot in war just as his opposite, the prize booby, may do disproportionate damage; yet any general is only as good as the men he commands, their training and equipment, the supplies and transport on which he depends, the intelligence services and a thousand other things which are needed to put an army into the field. So, in Section 2, I have examined the role of the military planners. Examples abound of generals failing because those on whom they depended failed them. Just as Carnot was the 'organizer of victory' and Barham the man who provided Nelson, Howe and St Vincent with the tools of war, others might just as accurately be seen as organizers of defeat. One need only consider the role of the First Duke of Buckingham in organizing the expedition to Cadiz in 1625. Whatever the failings of Viscount Wimbledon as a general, and they were many, it was clearly beyond any commander to make up the deficiencies of those who planned and supplied the expedition.

In the twentieth century the concept of 'total war' has relegated the individual field commander to the role of merely a single piece, however vital, in a gigantic jigsaw, of which the parts are infinitely varied. Industrial and agricultural workers become front-line soldiers in total war, just as do coal miners, merchant seamen, doctors, women machinists, transport workers and others too numerous to mention. Is failure by such people to be accounted military failure? Surely it is those who organize the whole national war effort who are ultimately failing the combat soldier at the 'sharp end of war' if they do not make certain that he lacks for nothing essential. Field Marshal, the Viscount Slim, remarked on one occasion that, 'there are no bad regiments, there are only bad officers'. There are, however, numerous occasions when both the soldier and the officer are victims of those who plan and administer the war.

In the third section of Part One I examine an aspect of military incompetence which is far removed from the sphere of influence of the field commander, but whose effect on him is nevertheless more profound than any other. This is the world of grand strategy, linked to the political aspirations of the state, It is the political leaders who will decide what kind of defence policy to adopt and, if the occasion should demand it, what kind of war the field army will be called upon to fight. In this respect their responsibility to the fighting man is very great indeed and their mistakes are paid for with his blood. I have been concerned to illustrate a number of ways in which these mistakes have manifested themselves. Fundamentally there are two ways in which politicians can influence the competence or otherwise of the military. Firstly they will determine, through financial allocations, the kind of army that the state requires, and secondly, through national strategy, what that army should be expected to do. If the first factor is not balanced by the second then military disaster is very likely to follow as in the case of Spain in 1898. Spain's parsimonious defence policy left her navy dangerously weak for the task of maintaining the security of her empire. Yet her policy towards the United States in 1898 was that of a first-rate power, prepared to back up her cause with war if necessary. Political control of the armed forces can result in a demand for inappropriate action from them, which may defy military logic because its aim is to fulfil an urgent political purpose. Such was the case with the battle of Goose Green during the Falklands conflict of 1982 or the British intervention in Greece in 1941.

In Part Two I have expanded the themes of the first part by examining a series of examples in some depth. When one adopts a narrative approach to individual cases it soon emerges that no one factor weighs more heavily than another. Certainly the psychological and physical condition of the main protagonists plays its part, but it is only one element in the causative process. While the headstrong nature of the 'Bloody Braggadocchio Byron' or the jealousy of Lord Eythin played their part in the Royalist disaster at Marston Moor, inconsistencies in Rupert's generalship counted for far more. While Braddock might be seen as an 'authoritarian' personality doomed to commit errors of judgement under the stress of battle, the greater fault surely lay with the army administration which demanded wholly inappropriate tasks of its commander and troops. If

Shafter was a physical wreck at San Juan Hill or Silvestre a mental one at Anual, these were merely symptomatic of the greater confusion and incompetence prevalent in the administration of their nation's armed forces. Norman Dixon devotes much space to an analysis of General Percival's performance at Singapore in 1941-2. Certainly he is right to question that general's competence, but at the same time a strategic approach to the problem of Singapore reveals that Percival's position in 1941 was virtually hopeless. Barring a complete change of heart on the part of Churchill he was never going to have the tools with which to conduct an effective defence of Malaya. His incompetence, if such it was, was merely the tip of an iceberg.

One of the prices the famous must pay for their fame, and the great warriors of the past are no exception, is to become Aunt Sallies facing a barrage of assaults on their reputations from initiated and uninitiated alike. From the former they may expect a toleration born of shared experience, an understanding from that 'band of brothers' which shared with them the trials and tribulations of military command. From the latter – journalists, historians, politicians and the general public – they will frequently be forced to endure criticism which is both ignorant and ill-informed. This can perhaps be borne more easily if it is obviously unjustified, and far removed from the realities of the battlefield. At least, in combating such criticism, they know that they can rely on their fellow commanders, their brother-officers, to close ranks with them.

It has never been my own intention to snipe at reputations or belittle the achievements of brave men. I have set out as a historian to illustrate the facts of military incompetence and to show that failure within the profession of arms stems from a wider range of factors than exist within any other profession. This being so, it is not surprising that incompetence has been so widespread – indeed, the wonder is that it has not been more so. The competent and the efficient have returned with their spoils, enjoyed their triumphs, their 'ticker-tape' welcomes, their mentions in despatches, their medals, their statues, their tombs in Westminster Abbey, and yet how many of them have had the humility to wonder at their good fortune? To reflect on how, given the slim dividing line between success and failure, their reputation could have collapsed as completely as did that of Redvers Buller or Ambrose Burnside or Ernest Troubridge? The conduct of warfare is beset with difficulties, often heroically overcome, but sometimes proving disastrous. This book is concerned with those cases where the difficulties proved too great for the participants to solve. Their consequences were terrible in terms of human waste and for that reason alone it is salutary that they should be recalled, and their lessons pondered.

PART ONE

—I—
The Commanders

In surveying a subject like military incompetence over a period of two thousand years or more, the historian must be aware of how much attitudes towards warfare have changed in that time. Delbruck pointed out two particular dangers: that of 'subscribing to an incorrect tradition' through a failure to discern the technical impossibility of what is being claimed, and of transferring 'phenomena from contemporary practice to the past, without taking adequate account of the differences in circumstances'.[1] Napoleon was aware that warfare was essentially dependent on equipment and believed he could learn little from ancient writers as their military equipment had been so different.[2] General Ulysses Grant also felt that 'historical luggage' could impede progressive thinking. This is what he said about some of his fellow Unionist commanders:

They knew what Frederick did at one place, and Napoleon at another. They were always thinking about what Napoleon would do. Unfortunately for their plans, the rebels would be thinking about something else. I don't underrate the value of military knowledge, but if men make war in slavish obedience to rules, they will fail. No rules can apply to conditions of war as different as those which exist in Europe and America. Consequently, while our generals were working out problems of an ideal character . . . practical facts were neglected.[3]

Even the idea of 'courage' has changed over the centuries, to accommodate situations of which ancient or medieval warriors could have had no experience. There has always been a distinct difference between physical and moral courage, and yet it would have been more difficult to explain this to a medieval knight than to a modern soldier. Medieval writers were much concerned to define what courage was. St Thomas Aquinas believed that it consisted of a firmness of mind in the accomplishment of duty.[4] It was a virtue which made a man intrepid in the face of every danger, but there was an important proviso: it must be free of rashness. Courage was to the medieval mind midway between audacity and timidity. It was very much an aristocratic virtue, a noble form of behaviour linked to race, blood and lineage. No one thought to call the English longbowmen at Creçy or Agincourt courageous.

Yet courage was expected to rise above personal ambition, and knights who were arrogant or rash – 'outrageux' – were not considered courageous. To throw away one's life to no apparent purpose was also not necessarily a valiant act. Henry of Ghent gave an example of a Frankish knight who, at the fall of Acre in 1291, when other knights were fleeing, threw himself into the midst of the Saracens and died fighting.[5] The feeling was that his inspiration had been recklessness or a desire for personal glory and was not therefore a truly courageous act.

There are occasions when too much personal courage is as harmful as too little. The Duke of Wellington once declared, 'There is nothing on earth so stupid as a gallant officer'.[6] This did not mean that he regarded courage as ridiculous but that it needed to be displayed in the right place and at the right time. To show how strongly Wellington felt, there was an occasion, during the Peninsular War, where he sent a colonel with a message to a brigade of German dragoons, ordering them to charge. The colonel, on his own initiative, joined in the charge and was severely wounded. It is reported that after the unfortunate man had recovered Wellington marked his disapproval by completely ignoring him.[7]

Having demonstrated that differences do exist it might be asked if it is possible to look at military incompetence at all other than in terms of the military norms of each successive age. The answer is, I believe, that it is possible to examine the subject across a broad period of history as long as one is careful not to act unhistorically, by using twentieth-century criteria to judge the military actions of an earlier period.

There are fundamental aspects of military conduct which would have been as readily understandable to a Roman as to a modern military historian. Probably tactical errors like a failure to carry out adequate reconnaissance or an inability to make the best use of the terrain are little influenced by changes in military thinking, while a commander who was stupid or cowardly would have been as obviously unsuitable in one age as in another.

I therefore intend to examine both the personal and tactical weaknesses of commanders over an extended period of history. In doing so I am aware that I shall have to be selective: I do not wish to give the impression that all of the failings were present in every age or that military incapacity was or is any more common than that to be found in other areas of life. It is not the nature of the consequences of military incompetence that marks the essential difference but the extent of the damage that may be caused. While an incompetent accountant might damage the finances of his customers, an incompetent surgeon be responsible for the deaths of a handful of patients or an incompetent pilot cause his own and the deaths of two or three hundred passengers, an incompetent military commander may count his victims in thousands or hundreds of thousands. His responsibility is an enormous one and it is reasonable that great care should be taken in the selection, training and evaluation of such a man. However, this has not always been possible. Frequently commanders have held positions of such power and authority that they stood above criticism.

The role of the commander has changed greatly since the Athenians undertook their expedition to Syracuse in 413 BC. For a long time his right to command depended on his possession of warlike virtues which were often reflected in the name by which he was known, like the medieval Richard the Lionheart, John the Fearless and Boleslav the Valiant.[8] Being a skilled warrior himself, he took his place in the thick of the fighting and by his personal example inspired his men. Yet he found that the increasingly complex demands of warfare required him to have a better overall view of the battle than he could possibly have from being in the fighting line. As a result he began to take up a position at the rear of the army, possibly on a convenient hill or high point, and frequently commanding the reserve. From his elevation he found that he was able to move his forces to where they were most urgently needed. This art of seeing the battle as a totality required a lot more of a commander than merely the possession of a strong sword arm; it required a tactical sense. The commander needed to know something more about his opponents than merely the numbers and composition of their army. As the amount of information he needed to make his decisions grew ever greater he came to rely on a number of subordinates, each delegated with tasks under his authority. Moreover, the growth of armies, particularly during the Napoleonic Wars, made it impossible for the individual commander to observe the entire field of battle, even from his high point, and he became dependent on his staff officers to communicate decisions to his combat officers. This served to further distance the commander from the fighting area and made his task of direction more intellectual and less emotional. He was no longer able to affect the outcome of a battle by his own physical endeavours.

Now he needed to possess new skills, far removed from those of the medieval warrior commanders. He needed to be able to manage not only fighting men but also all the other departments which became necessary to put a man into the battle line and keep him supplied with food, clothing, shelter, medical services and transport. As Dixon has pointed out, it was in playing the various roles involved in high command, sometimes incompatible with one another, that breakdown often occurred.[9] At one moment the commander might need to play the heroic leader, inspiring those around him with appeals to courage, loyalty and duty, while the next moment a problem arose which required a military manager or technocrat. It is not surprising that the individual commander sometimes succumbed to 'noise' in the system. His judgement became affected by interference from both internal and external sources. As most military decisions are made under conditions of stress, where the commander himself may not have slept for days and may be suffering from all kinds of physical and mental pressures, it is not surprising that errors occur. If his perception of the military situation becomes affected by more irrational considerations than rational ones then these errors may take on a greater significance.

In view of the complexity of twentieth-century warfare the control of a nation's armed forces has passed beyond the capacity of any individual commander. This means that the field commander needs to operate as part of a team of planners, working to individual strengths and pooling ideas to produce a cogent strategy. This has not lessened the task of the commander. On the contrary, he must now be able to receive, process and transmit information with machine-like efficiency, even though he is not a machine and is prone to breakdown as the demands exceed his capacity to meet them.[10] Thus the twentieth-century commander faces pressures of a psychological kind which are far removed from those of his warrior-commander predecessors.

OVERCONFIDENCE OR TIMIDITY

The first area of incompetence I wish to examine is that which stems from an unrealistic overconfidence on the part of a commander, in his own ability and that of his army. It is frequently associated with rash and impetuous decisions, displays of personal courage of a high order though of little relevance to the military situation, a serious under-estimation of the quality of the enemy forces, often stemming from ethnocentricity on the part of the leader, and military action undertaken purely with the intention of forwarding the commander's personal ambitions.

Clausewitz has called war 'the province of uncertainty' and it is the task of any commander to reduce this uncertainty as much as he can before committing his troops to action against an enemy. He can learn much from reconnaissance operations and from intelligence work but even when he has done this he must remember that there will still be more that is hidden from him. This uncertainty should save him from making the mistake of being too confident, preventing him from under-estimating his enemy, or committing his own troops impetuously. Examples of over-confidence are so common in military history that it is difficult to narrow the choice. Nevertheless, in the following examples the commander's confidence in his own ability and that of his men is allowed to overshadow the very real arguments against an encounter undertaken in haste. In both cases the outcome was disastrous.

The influx of Goths over the River Danube in 376 presented the Roman authorities with an opportunity to make useful allies against the Hunnish threat from the East. However, the treatment the Goths received from corrupt Roman officials drove them to revolt and they pillaged the countryside around the city of Adrianople, though they were unable to capture the city itself. In Constantinople, the Emperor Valens had assembled a powerful army while the Western Emperor, Gratian, his nephew, was marching with his forces from the west to help his uncle. It seemed only a matter of time before the two Roman armies combined and crushed the Goths. The latter entrenched themselves in a great circular or oval camp, ringed round by wagons, like the later 'laagers' of the South African Boers.

At this point the actions of Valens become difficult to understand. Having summoned Gratian to help him, and with his nephew and his army so close, he suddenly decided to attack the Goths on his own. Apparently Valen's intelligence reports numbered the Goths at just 10,000 and this may have persuaded him that it was disgraceful for him to remain passive while an army of barbarians smaller than his own 'laid waste a thriving province'.[11] The evidence would seem to suggest that Valens was jealous of his nephew and needed to win a victory to maintain his personal prestige. Numbering just 10,000, the Goths were surely no threat to him. Valens therefore decided to attack the Gothic laager. Delbruck records the evidence of Ammianus that Gratian had sent an officer, Richomer, in advance of his army to persuade Valens to wait until he arrived and not commit himself rashly. In spite of this sensible advice and the opinion of Victor, the 'Magister Equitum', that Valens should delay his attack, 'the fatal destiny of the Emperor prevailed, as well as the flattering views of the courtiers, who urged that they swiftly rush to battle, lest Gratian become an equal partner in a victory almost won already . . .'.[12]

However, Valens had under-estimated the enemy strength by at least 50% and also had not been informed that a major part of the Gothic cavalry was out of camp, foraging for supplies. Failing to send out proper patrols the Roman flanks were driven in when the Gothic cavalry returned and the Roman cavalry fled, leaving the infantry to be massacred. Valens was killed and less than a third of his army escaped from this quite unnecessary battle.

Pride, and a contempt for their Turkish adversaries only slightly greater than that felt for their own Hungarian allies, caused the defeat of the French crusaders at Nicopolis in 1396. Arrogantly insisting that they would drive the Turks out of Europe, they boasted that 'if the sky were to fall they would uphold it on the points of their lances'.[13] But the French knights were strangers to eastern warfare and should have listened to their more experienced Hungarian allies. The fact that they did not indicates that they suffered from an ethnocentrism which led them to seriously undervalue the military prowess of others. Viewing the Turks as such insignificant opponents, they felt no need to take account of their enemy's strength or intentions. They disregarded the appeals by King Sigismund for caution and relied instead on their own undoubted bravery. But their over-confidence was also apparent in their lack of discipline. On the march to the city of Nicopolis the 'frivolity' of the French knights and the pillaging of local towns and villages outraged their allies.

When King Sigismund held a council of war he told the French knights that he intended them to occupy the front line of the crusader cavalry but to be preceded into battle by Wallachian foot soldiers, who would clear the field of the rabble of peasant conscripts which always fought at the front of a Turkish army. These footsoldiers, he explained, were used by the Turks to absorb the pressure from the charge of Christian knights, so that when they tired they could be counter-attacked by the lighter Turkish horsemen. This was good military sense, gleaned from a long exposure to the Turkish way of warfare. However, the French reaction was predictably unreasonable. They declared that they had not come so far, and at such expense, to go into battle behind a rabble of cowardly footsoldiers. The Constable D'Eu declared, 'to take up the rear is to dishonour us and expose us to the contempt of all'.[14] As Constable he was entitled to the front place in battle: it would be a mortal insult to have anyone ahead of him.

When the Turkish vanguard was sighted Sigismund sent his Grand Marshal to plead with the French knights not to act rashly but to work in conjunction with him on a plan of battle. It seems that some of the French leaders like Coucy and Vienne were prepared to comply, but the Constable shouted that the King wanted to deprive them of the glory and keep it all for himself. Admiral Vienne replied, 'When truth and reason cannot be heard then must presumption rule'.[15] With that the Constable led the French contingent out to battle.

Although they were poor tacticians, there was no denying that the French knights were formidable fighters. Properly used they would probably have won the day for Sigismund. As it was the impact of their charge broke the first line of Turkish infantry but then came up against a line of sharpened stakes behind which the Turkish archers stood. Facing volleys of arrows the French somehow broke through by sheer strength and hard fighting. Even now it was not too late for them to pause and wait for the main Hungarian army to come up and complete the victory. Coucy and Vienne again urged this but by now there was little discipline in the French ranks and the Constable refused to halt. Contemptuous of the Turks, the French had not bothered to ascertain the strength or composition of the Ottoman army. D'Eu believed they had broken their main force whereas, had he listened to Sigismund's advice, he would have realised that he had only beaten the vanguard. It was now that the foolhardy crusaders found themselves surrounded by the full strength of the Turkish cavalry. What followed was a catastrophe in which the whole of the French contingent was either killed or captured. Sigismund commented later, 'We lost the day by the pride and vanity of these French; if they had believed my advice, we had enough men to fight our enemies'.[16]

The defeat of the crusaders at Nicopolis had been avoidable. Not all of the French leaders had acted without thinking, for Coucy and Vienne appear to have displayed sound military judgement. Unfortunately, the position of Constable guaranteed D'Eu leadership of the army and he belonged to a military type who believed in war by preconception. Clearly all knights were not impetuous or contemptuous towards the enemy, and the Hungarians had an understanding of Turkish methods which should have helped the French. The problem was that though Sigismund needed the French knights, the weight of whose charge was known and feared by the Turks, he was unable to subdue their pride and ambition and discipline them in the ways of eastern warfare, which they were too careless to learn.

Under-estimating the enemy A military commander who under-estimates his enemy makes a threefold difficulty for himself. In addition to the real enemy that he must face, for whom he will have made no adequate preparation, he must face the enemy he has imagined and prepared for, as well as the resistance of those of his staff and junior officers who do not share his views. Incompetence in this case usually stems from a categorisation of people in terms of stereotypes. This may be a common failing in everyday life but it is quite unacceptable in a military commander who needs precise information about his enemy if he is to prepare himself correctly. The underestimation of the Boers during the Second Boer War arose because, though white men, unlike the coloured opponents the British normally faced in Africa, they seemed unmilitary in both appearance and methods. But what the British overlooked was that these men were irregular soldiers, whose skills were not gained on parade grounds by drill but by a close knowledge of the environment. Their technique of firing from behind cover may have appeared cowardly to the British professionals but it was common sense to the Boer. Kitchener's revealing comment that, 'The Boers are not like the Sudanese who stood up to a fair fight. They are always running away on their little ponies . . .' tells us all we need to know about the attitude of the British professional commanders to these 'unsporting' opponents.[17]

It seems to be a fault of European states with long military traditions that, as a substitute for rational judgement, the belief is fostered that their soldiers are superior 'man for man' to the enemy, and that in close combat the use of the bayonet will be successful. Thus the British greatly undervalued the Turk as a fighting man before Gallipoli, while at Buenos Aires in 1806 General Whitelocke could not regard the Creole and Spanish troops as serious opponents.[18] In both cases, the enemy turned out to be surprisingly tenacious, possessing the advantage of fighting on his own terrain against an adversary far from home. Under-estimation of difficulties to be encountered resulted in faulty preparation and incompetent execution. Again, the quality of the Japanese as fighters was badly misjudged by the British in the Second World War and the curious idea was prevalent that their poor eyesight would prevent them from being effective pilots. At Pearl Harbour and over Singapore and Malaya the Japanese were to demonstrate the hollowness of this argument. As Dixon has shown, one cannot know one's enemy by stereotyping him. Contempt for 'Wogs', 'Japs', 'Chinks', 'Gypoes', 'Eyties', 'Dagoes' and so on serves only to cloud the judgement of an enemy's real capability. Such contempt for his enemy explains the conduct of John, Earl of Warrenne, towards his Scottish opponents at Stirling Bridge.

Rivers are merely one of the many kinds of natural obstacles that a commander has to face. In order to cross a broad stream he will normally need to find a ford but to attempt a crossing in the face of an enemy on the opposite bank is an action needing the most precise planning. The existence of a bridge does not necessarily make things easier, as Warrenne found on 11 September 1297, when approaching the town of Stirling in Scotland.

William Wallace's Scottish troops had occupied wooded hills over-

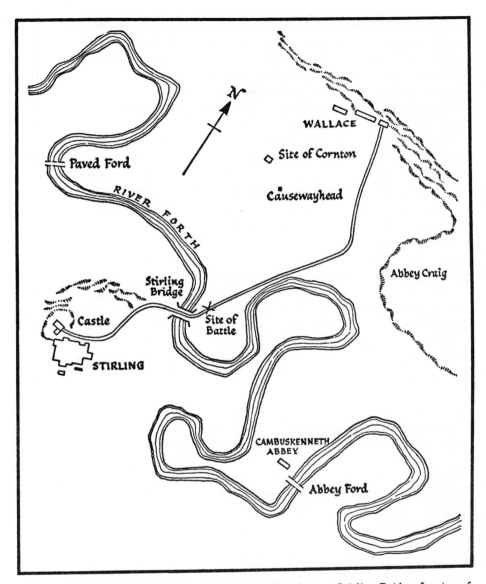

1. William Wallace had prepared a trap for the English near Stirling Bridge. In view of the fact that the English commander de Warrenne had several alternatives to crossing the River Forth by the very narrow wooden bridge he was greatly at fault for not taking one of them. His contempt for the Scots as warriors was not shared by his lieutenants but was enough to prompt him to cross a river in the face of strong enemy forces. He did this without any attempt to draw them off by making feints at either of the other possible crossing points.

looking the River Forth as it flows past Stirling. A single wooden bridge, wide enough for only two men abreast, crossed the river near the abbey of Cambuskenneth and led to steep slopes on which Wallace himself was stationed. As Warrenne approached with his troops he had already determined to cross by the bridge and attack the Scots' position, even though he had not carried out any reconnaissance and knew little of the difficulties his men would encounter.

The idea of moving thousands of men across a narrow bridge in the face of the enemy was an extremely ill-conceived one. It was pointed out to him that it would take eleven hours to move all the men across, during which time anything could happen. Sir Ralph Lundy told Warrenne that he knew of a ford less than a mile away, where the men could cross thirty abreast, but the commander refused to listen. His low opinion of the Scots as warriors was well known and, as Oman says, 'The wiser heads in the camp were filled with dismay at a resolve inspired by a foolish and overweening contempt for the enemy'.[19]

The English vanguard, led by Sir Marmaduke Twenge and Hugh Cressingham, now began to cross the bridge and form up on the northern bank of the river, overlooked by Wallace and his soldiers, many of whom were concealed in the woods. Showing strong discipline and patience, the Scots waited until at least a third of the English had crossed before attacking. Scottish spearmen seized the bridgehead to stop the main part of the English army from crossing, while Wallace attacked the trapped vanguard. Although Twenge was able to fight his way back, Cressingham, a hundred knights and several thousand English footsoldiers were massacred on the river bank, victims of their commander's incompetence.

Personal Courage As we have seen, the medieval writers differentiated between courage and recklessness. The commander requires a different kind of courage from that of the soldier in the front line of battle. Although he may be exposed to danger during the fighting, the commander's task is to suppress those factors which could distract him from his task of directing the battle. Clausewitz drew attention to this danger, particularly for the commander who had risen to supreme command through his personal exploits on the battlefield. Boldness may be a virtue but it can be misused.

The higher we go in the military hierarchy . . . the more necessary it becomes for this quality of boldness to be accompanied by careful thought to prevent purposeless acts of passion; for boldness on a high level becomes less and less a matter of mere self-sacrifice and more one of providing for the success and well-being of the whole army.[20]

THE COMMANDERS

At Flodden in 1513 all the Scottish leaders fought in the front ranks, like Landsknecht captains. They accused the English commanders of 'lurking in the rear' which was particularly unjust to the Earl of Surrey, who was 70, crippled by rheumatism and travelled in a coach. The English leaders had taken up positions from which they could survey the battlefield and actually perform the task that was expected of them, issuing orders and directing manoeuvres. On the other hand, the Scottish king, James IV, led his column into the attack and was killed at the farthest point of Scottish penetration, with all his personal retinue dead around him. Most of the Scottish leaders died in the fighting, so that an orderly withdrawal was impossible and a defeat turned into a disaster. Surrey may not have been as nimble as in his youth nor as apparently heroic as the knightly James IV, but he proved to be as competent a commander as his opponent was a rash, impetuous one. By risking his own life James was endangering not only the lives of his men but the welfare of his realm.

History records many examples of commanders forgetting their responsibility to command and becoming mere 'sabreurs'. Oman records the unusual fate of Montmorency and Condé, the leaders of the Catholic and Protestant actions during the French Wars of Religion.

At Dreux, by a comic and unique instance of righteous nemesis, each was taken prisoner by the other's army, because both chose to act as cavalry brigadiers rather than as responsible commanders-in-chief.[21]

At Revenna in 1512, the brilliant young French general, Gaston de Foix, sacrificed his own life in a futile pursuit of a beaten enemy. At Oudenarde in 1708, the French Marshal Vendome fought with pike in the front line of the French army instead of directing his forces from a position where he could see the development of the battle. Even as late as 1870 at the Battle of Vionville, the French commander, Bazaine, demonstrated his legendary courage by galloping up to the firing line, rallying wavering infantry, spending time personally siting two field guns and then leading a battalion of infantry into action, calling 'Allons, mes enfants, suivez votre maréchal'. He tried to be everywhere except where he was supposed to be. For over an hour no one led the French army as his panicky staff tried to find him. While nobody would question his personal bravery, he was clearly unsuited to the rigours of high command. This became even more evident at the great battle of Gravelotte-St Privat, where according to the French official historian, his conduct 'can best be compared with that of a simple soldier who abandons his post in the face of the enemy'. Throughout the battle the French Army fought without 'directing intelligence'. Bazaine's physical courage was no more valuable to it than that of the lowest infantryman; it was moral courage that was needed and he had none to give.[22]

Many of the worst commanders proved to have more literary than military skill.[23] In 1946 General Visconti Prasca published his memoirs, entitled *Io ho aggredito la Grecia* ('I attacked Greece') and his own arrogance seems to have revealed more than he can have realised. As Mario Cervi writes,

No civilian could so effectively have demolished the General Staff and its environment, the men at the top of the Italian military machine. However, certainly without intending to do so and perhaps without even suspecting it, he also demolished himself, perhaps chiefly himself. The book, though written in self-defense, does not succeed in covering up its author's colossal errors and irresponsibility.[24]

Visconti Prasca was an ambitious and scheming officer, who had risen to the command in Albania through the sponsorship of the under-secretary for war, Ubaldo Soddu. He was unpopular with the Italian General Staff because he often went over their heads and had direct contact with Mussolini. They rightly suspected that his aims were personal and that his ambitions were almost boundless. He saw the campaign against Greece as a triumphal procession with Greek resistance as minimal. By the time his troops had reached Athens he saw himself as a Marshal of Italy. He seemed to hypnotize Mussolini with his own enthusiasm for the war against Greece, which would consist of 'a series of rounding-up operations against the Greek forces'.[25] He spoke the language the Italian dictator liked to hear: not the careful and calculated planning of the military mind, but phrases like 'liquidate all the Greek troops', 'shattering blow', 'iron will'.

It was the intervention of Marshal Badoglio that threatened Visconti Prasca's plans. Badoglio considered that Prasca had far too few divisions for the campaign and suggested substantial reinforcements. However, Prasca did not want any more troops and insisted that five or six divisions would be enough. He found himself facing a dilemma. As a 57-year-old Lieutenant-General, low on the seniority list, he knew that if his command grew too big he would be superseded by a more senior officer. His enemy Roatta had hinted as much. In a conversation about the Albanian command, Roatta had exclaimed, 'But in the case you would become a full general-designate ahead of Rosi'.[26] In fact, Rosi was senior even to Roatta, so there was a danger that Prasca would leapfrog both of them. This, of course, was exactly what he was trying to do. Prasca wrote to his friend Soddu about the use of other generals.

From the operational point of view in present circumstances, there is no need for their presence, which would constitute an obstruction rather than a help, though all those sent by higher authority for any reason will be welcome . . . They will have their share of glory . . . That having been stated, I have reason to assume that there is a desire to use this participation of other commanders in the Epirus operation as a concealed but direct diminution of my responsibility as commander.[27]

Roatta was strongly opposed to the 'careerist' Prasca and wanted him replaced by Ambrosio or Vercellino but Mussolini was firmly behind the man who had so inspired him with a vision of Italian military might. He wrote to Prasca on 25 October:

Dear Visconti, you know, and if you do not I am telling you now, that I have opposed all attempts to take your command away from you on the eve of the operation. I believe that events and above all your actions, will justify me. Attack with the greatest determination and violence.[28]

The whole disastrous campaign was riddled with corruption and military ineptitude. Too much haste was apparent in every department because Mussolini was attempting a 'coup de main' before Hitler could intervene to stop him, and Visconti Prasca was trying to achieve a great victory before Roatta could rob him of the military command that would take him to the 'top of the military tree'. Prasca's ambitions required him to act before his troops were ready, to under-estimate the Greek threat so that he would be left in charge of the campaign and not superseded, to refuse reinforcements which would make his command too big for an officer of his rank and to exaggerate the efficiency of his own preparations and the fighting qualities of his troops in order to win the support of Mussolini. The outcome of this drive for personal advancement was a catastrophe for Italian arms and the loss of thousands of Italian lives in the cruel fighting of the Greek winter campaign.

Timidity and over-estimating the enemy A military commander carries an awesome responsibility. In wartime he may be directly responsible for the lives of thousands or hundreds of thousands of men and expensive equipment which may have imposed a crippling burden upon his country. As the sharp point of his nation's strategy his performance may mean the difference between defeat and victory in war and even determine the survival of the nation itself. It is hardly surprising that just as the stresses of command drive some men to behave rashly through over-confidence and a contempt for their enemy, so there will be others who show timidity and feelings of inferiority. The consequence can be military failure as disastrous as that stemming from impetuosity.

In warfare the evidence of failure is difficult to disguise. The dead may be left on the field of battle but they represent gaps in the ranks, statistics in newspapers and bereaved families. Lost or damaged equipment may mean the wasted lives of merchant seamen, losses in raw materials and foreign currency, wasted 'man-hours' in factories both at home and abroad. Losses of horses or vehicles may hinder transport while injured men are a burden on overstretched hospital services. Above all the casualties are a constant reminder to the commander of the part that he must play in the butchery of war. For him personally, failure may mean dismissal and the end of a career hitherto unstained by any hint of personal inadequacy. As a result, the anxiety he faces may make him prefer the safety of inaction to the dangers of doubtful action. He may rationalise this with the thought that not to fail is a safer option than risking everything in the hope of succeeding. He may even feel, like the Russian Grand Duke, that battles are hateful 'because they spoil the armies'.

During the American Civil War George McClellan was appointed by Abraham Lincoln to lead the main Union army, the Army of the Potomac, against the Confederate Army of Northern Virginia under Robert E. Lee. It was an unfortunate appointment, yet it is difficult to blame Lincoln for he was militarily inexperienced himself and tended to accept people at their own valuation until experience taught him otherwise. The 'Redoubtable McC', as the Confederates unkindly dubbed him, was in 1861 regarded as an aggressive fighting general. He was a brilliant martial figure, surrounded by a splendid staff, who gave every impression that 'things were happening'.[29] He was a good planner, indeed Lee considered him the best on the Union side, but he was chronically over-cautious and looked for every possible excuse to avoid battle unless he was assured of success. Early in his command he refused to assault the Confederate position at Munson's Hill because he insisted it was far too strong. Later, when the Rebels withdrew, it was discovered that their guns had been logs painted black.

For a while McClellan found a solution to his problems by recruiting the services of Pinkerton's Private Detective Agency to provide him with information about the enemy. This was an unfortunate decision, for the information which Pinkerton supplied was grotesquely misleading. It undoubtedly suited McClellan, who tended to create a situation in his own mind and believe that it was the real one, regardless of evidence to the contrary. Whether Pinkerton was simply incompetent or whether he was inclined to feed McClellan with information to match his preconceptions we can never be sure. What is certain is the damage it did to the Union cause.

McClellan exaggerated the numbers opposed to him as an excuse for not acting decisively. His strategy involved a great deal of planning which was quite unconnected with reality, but at the merest suggestion from Lincoln that he actually engage Lee in battle, McClellan retreated into his shell and began calling for reinforcements. In August 1861 he claimed the Confederates had four times his own strength and by March 1862 he accepted Pinkerton's report that Lee's army numbered over 80,000, when the truth was closer to 40,000. In June 1862, McClellan reported that 'the rascals are very strong', though his own force of 100,000 was being held up by Magruder's 23,000 Confederates. By October 1862 McClellan was claiming that Lee's army had reached the staggering figure of 150,000 men. At the same time a report published in *Harper's Weekly* included an estimate by Prince Napoleon, who had visited the Rebel camp, of their strength as 60,000 'ragged, dirty and half-starved' men.[30]

Even when McClellan was presented with the Confederates' entire battle plan, found wrapped round some discarded cigars, he moved too slowly to catch the separate parts of the Rebel army under Lee and Jackson. Believing he was only facing one part of Lee's army he acted uncharacteristically at Antietam Creek by attacking, though he kept a whole corps in reserve in case of defeat. Had he committed this force he would almost certainly have won a decisive victory. Nevertheless, he soon found reasons to justify his timidity: his men were tired, his transport disrupted and he needed reinforcements. Even so, he reported Antietam as a complete victory, which it was not. Not surprisingly Lincoln expected him to pursue what he assumed to be the beaten Rebel army and was shocked when he failed to do so. Visiting McClellan's camp Lincoln pointed to the vast extent of the army and asked a friend what he could see. The friend, surprised, said that it was the Army of the Potomac. Lincoln bitterly replied: 'So it is called, but that is a mistake; it is only McClellan's bodyguard'.[31] There was a clear lack of understanding between the professional politician and the professional soldier. Lincoln needed a fighter, not just a general who believed in out-manoeuvering his opponent. It is instructive that McClellan considered his greatest achievements to have been the occupation of the Confederate camps at Manassas and Yorktown after the Rebels had gone, because they had been won by 'pure military skill' and without loss of life. Lincoln could not see war in this way. He knew there could be no peace until the Confederate army was beaten, and that meant that men were going to be killed. T. Harry Williams suggests that the apparent caution of the Unionist generals in the early years of the war stemmed from their feeling that they lacked the strength to undertake the movements recommended by the

Jominian doctrine which had dominated their education at West Point.[32] However, Lincoln was no Jominian and in Grant he found a man of like mind who would fight an attritional war until the Confederate army was broken.

Originally appointed Commander-in-Chief after the Northern débâcle at First Manassas in 1861, in order to restore morale to the troops, McClellan managed only to emphasise Northern inferiority. So cautious was he in his movements that he produced uncertainty among his own men and a growing feeling among the Southern troops of their own superiority. By insisting that his men were always outnumbered he was able to make them believe that victory lay in avoiding defeat. Thus his own fear of failure was communicated to the troops. It says much for Lincoln's grasp of reality that he never allowed himself to fall into this trap. Of McClellan Cox wrote as follows:

The general who indoctrinates his army with the belief that it is required by its government to do the impossible, may preserve his popularity with the troops and be received with cheers as he rides down the line, but he has put any great military success far beyond his reach.[33]

McClellan was by no means the only Union commander who suffered from timidity or a tendency to exaggerate the strength of the enemy. At the beginning of the war Sherman was commanding Union forces in Kentucky; under the pressures of command he began to claim that he was outnumbered 5 to 1, though the two sides were in fact evenly matched. He even prevented George Thomas from advancing on the Cumberland Gap because he anticipated a Confederate attack in overwhelming numbers, when in truth the Rebels were heavily outnumbered. He was on the verge of a nervous breakdown and was relieved of his command and ordered to rest. On other occasions, Fremont, Rosecrans, Buell and even 'Fighting Joe' Hooker were guilty of exaggerating enemy strength.

Superstition and fatalism A belief that the outcome of certain events is pre-ordained is not one confined to primitive peoples. For a general such fatalism can often be the final resort of a mind so indecisive that it prefers to leave decisions to the operation of chance. In doing so there is the relief of feeling that the responsibility is no longer one's own. The incompetence which then occurs is not a product of misdirected action but of no action at all. An example from the ancient world illustrates the way in which superstition can materially affect the outcome of a battle.

By the summer of 413 BC the Athenian expedition to Syracuse was in difficulties. Its commander Nicias was a sick man and the command of the army was assumed by Demosthenes who had recently arrived with reinforcements. It soon became apparent to him that his only option was to raise the siege and evacuate his troops while he was able. When he confronted Nicias with this decision, the sick man pressed for a delay of a month to allow parties within Syracuse hostile to the Spartans to surrender the city to him. A month passed and all that happened was that enemy reinforcements arrived. It was clear now that the Athenians must leave in haste. When the expedition was on the point of sailing away there was an eclipse of the full moon (27 August 413 BC): the troops declared that this was an ill omen and refused to embark, urging the general to await a better day. According to Thucydides, Nicias 'was somewhat over-addicted to divination' and agreed to wait 'the thrice nine days prescribed by soothsayers'.[34] As Fuller says, this was a suicidal decision and the Spartan general Gylippus now took the opportunity to hem the Athenians in the Great Harbour by blocking its mouth with a line of triremes and merchant craft chained together.[35] The Athenians now attempted to break out by land but each of their divisions was caught in turn and wiped out. Of the 50,000 soldiers and sailors who had been sent by the Athenians against Syracuse no more than 7000 survived and these spent their days in quarries, while Nicias and Demosthenes were executed.

A recent example of fatalism on the part of a commander is that of Vice-Admiral Zinovy Petrovitch Rozhestvensky during the voyage of the Russian Baltic Fleet to Tsushima in 1905. Richard Hough summarises Rozhestvensky's problems:

For the man who led them, the voyage was a ceaseless struggle against the incompetence and perfidy of his subordinates, the corruption of his superiors, the antagonism and mockery of the world; culminating in the greatest sea battle of modern times. Yet even in the worst moments of agony and despair, neither the admiral nor his fleet could escape the twists of ironical farce which beset them on their voyage. . . .[36]

Rozhestvensky was presented with the task of sailing 18,000 miles to meet an enemy who had already defeated a naval squadron stronger than his own. His best battleships, of the *Suvoroff* class, reflected the limitations of Russian shipbuilding. As Hough writes,

To a Russian designer, perfection was only achieved by afterthought. With the *Suvoroff* class this resulted in an alarming top-heaviness which meant that the lower secondary armament could not be used in any sort of sea, and that all but two feet of the main belt of armour plate was submerged when they were normally loaded. This affected not only their speed, but also their stability, and the danger of their capsizing was so grave that Rozhestvensky received a signal a few days after he had left ordering him to strip unnecessary weight from decks and superstructure, even to the extent of avoiding hoisting all but essential signals from the yards.[37]

This was hardly an encouraging start. If the signal flags were a danger to a battleship's stability what would the Japanese shells and torpedoes do?

Although space does not allow us to follow Rozhestvensky's voyage in detail, it is instructive to look at just a few of the many problems which confronted him and eventually so weighed him down that he consigned himself and his squadron to fate. For one thing, there was no Russian base anywhere on the 18,000 mile journey and he was to be dependent for coal on pre-arranged meetings at sea with the German Hamburg-Amerika line. On his journey through the Baltic and North Sea, his hysterical lookouts saw Japanese torpedo-boats in the most unlikely places and disguises. Added to low morale was a feeling that there was danger everywhere and that every hand was turned against them.

In the North Sea a 'full-scale attack by Japanese ships' turned out to be a British trawler fleet from Hull. Incredibly the Russian battleships fought the trawlers, damaging several and sinking one, as well as suffering hits which they inflicted on each other. Rozhestvensky narrowly avoided causing a war between Britain and Russia, and was widely condemned and ridiculed in the newspapers of the world.

Meanwhile, at the Admiralty in St Petersburg, Rozhestvensky's enemy Klado had decided that reinforcements should be sent to join the Admiral. Anything would do, however unfit and derelict it might be. After all, it would increase the number of targets the Japanese would have to fire at. Rozhestvensky had originally condemned these 'old tubs' as worthless and nothing more than a millstone, which would hold back the rest of the fleet. When the Admiral heard that these ancient ships were to be sent to join him he decided to do everything in his power to avoid the rendezvous. Having reached North Africa, one of the Russian ships became entangled with a submarine cable. When her captain cut it away it severed Tangier's communications with Europe for four days. And so the ridiculous saga continued.

In spite of his efforts to mould his fleet into a fighting unit he was constantly borne down by the inefficiency of his subordinate commanders. The fleet's repair ship, the *Kamchatka*, for example, apparently fired 300 shells in a battle with three supposed enemy ships, a Swedish merchantman, a German trawler and a French schooner, and later signalled to the flagship, 'Do you see torpedo-boats?' A general alarm was sounded throughout the fleet until the repair ship admitted it had used the wrong code and had simply meant, 'We are all right now'.[38]

The worst problem for Rozhestvensky was that he knew, and the best of his officers knew, that they would have been better advised to turn back and risk being called cowards. They were not cowards but they found it difficult to avoid appearing buffoons. To those who took their work seriously this was a heavy blow to morale. They would fight bravely when the time came but it would be futile because they were not trained to fight a modern naval battle. News that reinforcements were being sent under Admiral Nebogatoff was the final straw. Their present ships were not good enough. What was the use of sending unseaworthy hulks 18,000 miles to be sunk off Japan? To Rozhestvensky this was enough to bring on acute attacks of neuralgia which confined him to his cabin.

At gunnery practice Rozhestvensky, who had been renowned for his gunnery as a young officer, watched while his destroyers scored not one single hit on a stationary target. When the battleships joined in, his flagship managed just one hit, which was on the ship towing the target. A formation of destroyers, ordered to form line abreast, scattered in every direction because they had not been issued with the new code books. Hough describe the failure of the torpedoes.

Of the seven that left their tubes, one jammed, two swung ninety degrees to port, one ninety degrees to starboard, two kept a steady course but went wide of the mark, and the last went round and round in circles 'popping up and down like a porpoise' and causing panic throughout the fleet.[39]

For Rozhestvensky the final insult occurred when he received an order from St Petersburg telling him to destroy the Japanese Fleet, sail on to Vladivostock and there hand over command to Admiral Biriloff, who was travelling there by the Trans-Siberian Railway. Biriloff was known as 'the fighting Admiral' even though he had never been in action. It was too much for Rozhestvensky to bear and despair turned to a mindless acceptance of fate. He would fight when the time came but it would be a reflex action, for everything he did seemed destined to fail. He was even being pursued by Nebogatoff's squadron of old ships, which he referred to as an 'archaeological collection of naval architecture'.[40] When the Russian fleet encountered the Japanese at Tsushima, Rozhestvensky confined himself to just two orders, the first of which caused 'mystification and dismay' while the second caused 'a state of chaos'.[41] The complete destruction of the Russian fleet followed, much as Rozhestvensky knew it would.

PERSONAL INADEQUACIES

It has been said that much historical writing overlooks the fact that men have feelings, needs and physical senses. For the military historian it is most important to take these factors into account as it is frequently in the stress of battle that they become most influential. In explaining incompetence it is far from adequate to simply explain mistakes by resorting to the 'bloody fool' theory, in which idiotic 'Colonel Blimps' are responsible for everything that goes wrong. Under certain circumstances it is probable that everyone could qualify under this heading but it would not advance our understanding very much if all mistakes were simply put down to foolishness. Fools there have been in plenty, both in the military services and in other walks of life, but there is no clear reason why such people should make greater progress in a military career than in any other. It is therefore necessary to examine the various personal defects which, aside from stupidity, have contributed to military incompetence through the ages.

It is a problem of any system which depends on promotion by seniority rather than merit that men can achieve positions of considerable power and responsibility at an age when their faculties are no longer as effective as they were. This has been particularly true of the military profession. Examples of able but aged generals are legion (as, of course, are examples of young, fit but disastrously inept commanders). Nevertheless, what cannot be overlooked is the effect that age can have in intensifying defects of the mind which are already present; thus, thinking, memory, intelligence and the quality of the senses deteriorate with age, and it is the wise general who is aware of his own developing weaknesses. As warfare moves into a more technological era it becomes increasingly unlikely that the aged commander will be able to adapt to swift changes.

A military commander, often working under conditions of extreme stress, possibly deprived of adequate food and rest, and perhaps operating in a harsh climate, is prone to debilitating ill-health. As a result attention must be paid to the physical and mental condition of the commander in order to assess how much it influenced his decisions. Not all forms of ill health are likely to result in military mistakes but any situation where the decision maker is subjected to extraneous factors which may cloud his judgement may be suspected. Anything affecting his physical health, like disease, wounds, overweight, alcohol and drugs, may affect his judgement. There have been relatively few cases where the commander of an army has been obviously insane though our evidence on this tends to be restricted, particularly on medieval or ancient battles.

It may be thought unlikely that a coward would achieve a position of command in any military organization, but that would depend on how one defined 'cowardice'. There are examples of physical cowardice on the part of commanders throughout history but it is difficult to generalise about the characteristics that each showed. If by cowardice one merely meant the opposite of courage or bravery there is a danger that we would find it necessary to include the vast majority of soldiers who ever went to war. Confronted by danger there is a natural desire to run away from it. There have been cases of commanders who have appeared to simply lack the nerve to risk their lives or reputations in combat with the enemy. Admittedly these cases have been few but they do constitute an area of military incompetence. More common, though less easily definable as cowardice, are the cases where the commander has fled from the battlefield before the fighting was over or the day lost. Such panic has often resulted in a collapse of morale on the part of the army thus abandoned and a complete loss of direction in its efforts.

Insanity In view of the frequently strained relations between civilian and military authorities it may not be considered unusual for a politician to express doubts about the sanity of a military leader. However, it must be rare indeed for such an accusation to be literally true, as when David Lloyd George, then Britain's prime minister, referred to the Greek Commander-in-Chief during the war between Greece and Turkey in 1921, as 'some kind of mental defective'.[42]

General Hajianestis had been an able officer in his youth but his mental health had declined as he ascended the ranks, and by the time he became a general he was hopelessly ineffective and no more than 'a courtier wearing military uniform'.[43] His appointment to supreme command had been a political one for there is no possible way in which he could have been considered fit for military service. He conducted the Greek campaign from his yacht in the harbour at Smyrna and spent most of his time in bed, suffering from profound mental sickness. For much of the time he felt unable to get out of bed because he believed his legs were made of glass or sugar and were so brittle that they would shatter. On other occasions he lay perfectly still on the assumption that he was dead. With such leadership the morale of the Greek army plummeted. On the days when he felt well enough to rise from his bed, Hajianestis spent much of his time in waterside restaurants, issuing mad and contradictory orders to his staff.[44] In the circumstances his replacement was only a matter of time, but when it came it was already too late to save the Greeks. Ironically, General Tricoupis heard that he had become Commander-in-Chief only after he had been captured by the Turks.

To include the renowned Prussian General Leberecht von Blucher in a discussion of mental illness or indeed military incompetence may seem surprising and yet, according to Alfred Vagts, Blucher was

. . . almost seventy years old, a reckless talker, a wild gambler, and a psychopath, visited by severe fits of senile melancholy and fancies. Time and again Blucher believed that, on account of his sins, he was pregnant with an elephant produced by a French soldier, as he told Wellington. At other times he thought the French had bribed his servants to heat his room so hot from under the floor that he would burn his feet unless he jumped or walked on the tips of his toes.[45]

Blucher's salvation and Prussia's was that he was strongly supported by both Scharnhorst and Gneisenau, who were less concerned with imaginary elephants and more with the fighting spirit the old man was able to instil in his troops. Nevertheless, matters did not always go so well. When Blucher was incapacitated by his mental problems during the campaign of 1814, General York refused to accept an order from Blucher, when it was brought to him by his enemy, Gneisenau, because it was signed upside down. 'One sees, the old man is insane again,' he said, 'Therefore it is really Gneisenau who commands us; that we must not suffer.'[46] There is no doubt that the dissension within the Prussian leadership at this time contributed to the defeats of the Allies by Napoleon in February 1814.

Illness and physical incapacity Under the stressful conditions of command in battle leaders will becoming increasingly aware of their own physical and mental deficiences. The conditions in which they serve may be such that minor physical ailments are exacerbated by extremes of heat, cold, humidity and so on so that the commander loses the singlemindedness which is essential to making military decisions. Psychological stresses may become magnified until they break out in psychosomatic disease or mental breakdown. History records so many instances of commanders whose health, both physical and mental, has affected their competence that it is possible to include only a few here. Nevertheless, it is a fundamental point that a commander who forgets his physical limitations may well collapse even more dramatically than one who remembers the common humanity he shares with his men.

The health of few commanders has attracted the attention of historians in the way that Napoleon's has. Cartwright lists a number of fairly common ailments that Napoleon suffered throughout his life – migraines during times of stress being one.[47] It is unlikely that these impaired his military capacity in his early years, but by 1807 the cumulative effect of so many campaigns was intensifying them. His irregular habits, particularly his tendency to rush his food, contributed first to constipation and then to piles, of which the earliest mention was in 1797 when he was 28. Another product of his eating habits was a sharp pain in his right side, a gall-stone colic or indigestion, and later probably a peptic ulcer. None of this would have been unusual at the time but it assumes a greater significance where the sufferer is unable to give himself enough rest and freedom from stress.

After 1807, there is undoubtedly a decline in Napoleon's physical condition with a concomitant temperamental decline. As his body became fleshy and undisciplined, so also did his temper become less controlled. By 1812 his speed of thought had declined markedly, possibly as a result of increasing physical ailments. At Borodino he was suffering from not only a heavy cold but also a painful bladder complaint, dysuria, which made riding difficult. His urinary problems, which had shown up as early as Marengo in 1800 were severe by Borodino in 1812. Professor W.T. Ayer has suggested that they possibly had their origin in schistosomiasis, acquired during the Egyptian campaign in 1799.[48] Sometimes known as bilharzia, the disease is water-borne and many of Napoleon's troops suffered from it after their return. Under such physical pain it is hardly surprising that he made so many mistakes at Borodino. His victories during 1813 and 1814 showed rare qualities and yet his health was forcing him to rely more on his subordinate commanders, who had been given little command responsibility during his earlier years. At Dresden in 1813 Napoleon was exhausted and soaked to the skin. After the second day's fighting he retired to his camp, ate ravenously, vomited and aggravated his stomach condition, leaving himself unable to direct his troops effectively. At Leipzig Napoleon was still afflicted by the same abdominal pain but also by a lethargy and sleepiness that affected both body and mind. An early example of the latter complaint occurred at Jena in 1806 when a company of grenadiers were forced to form a square around the Emperor, who had fallen asleep. After Leipzig, Dr Hillemand was amazed to note Napoleon sleeping soundly instead of trying to take charge of his defeated army.[49] The onset of this lethargy is usually attributed to pituitary dysplasia. In his youth Napoleon had an overactive pituitary gland but by his thirties it had become exhausted and he suffered the effects of a failure of this vital secretion. At Waterloo Napoleon was suffering from prolapsed piles, which made it difficult for him to mount his horse, as well as sleepiness and lethargy. He had been in the saddle throughout the whole of 16 June and was completely worn out. Though only 46, he was prematurely aged and unfit. On the decisive day of 17 June he did not leave his bed until 8 a.m. and left much of the command work to Ney, with unfortunate results for him and for France.[50] Napoleon's competence as a commander had become an upredictable quality. He was still able to rise to great heights as at Lutzen and Bautzen but he was also liable to make mistakes which indicated a decline in his mental and physical capacities.

Physical exhaustion of the kind suffered by any commander in the long-drawn-out battles of the modern age is an inevitable product of lack of rest and sleep. However much a commander believes he can drive himself indefinitely he is mistaken, for his judgement will undoubtedly suffer. Hugh L'Etang points out the effects of sleep deprivation:

Visual disturbances lead to illusions and hallucinations. There are gross deviations in the awareness of time. Disorganisation of mental processes leads to a slowing of thought, impairment of concentration and incoherence. Furthermore there is an inability to correct errors for these are not even recognised.[51]

During the Seven Day's Battle between 26 June and 2 July 1862, Freeman observes that the failures of certain Confederate generals were the result of '5-day fatigue' and that they had reached the limit of their endurance. This was particularly true of General Thomas 'Stonewall' Jackson, a 'delicate' man physically, who apparently needed a lot of sleep. During his Valley Campaign he had suffered six weeks of continuous stress and was approaching the point of collapse from stress fatigue. Returning after an all-night ride to see Lee he had collapsed, suffering from a 'depletion of the adrenal cortex'. Under his Chief of Staff, Rev. Dr R.L. Dabney's, control Jackson's troops marched badly and without 'Stonewall' there to hurry them along with his usual 'Push on, men, close up!' a whole day was lost while he slept. The result was that he failed to support Lee at White Oak Swamp as he had agreed.[52]

Environmental hazards have contributed considerably to the poor performances of commanders in action, by exacerbating physical weaknesses. And if these weaknesses are compounded by the age and infirmity of the commander then the situation is doubly dangerous. The destruction of the British army in Afghanistan in 1842 is one of the tragic epics of British history. Yet the disaster had been avoidable and much of the blame for it has fallen upon the person of the commander, Major-General W.G.K. Elphinstone. Elphinstone has been described, possibly accurately, as 'the most incompetent soldier that was to be found among the officers of the requisite rank'.[53] However, Elphinstone was man enough to know his limitations and tried to persuade the Governor-General of India, Lord Auckland, that he was unfitted to the command through ill-health. Whereas on other occasions Ambrose Burnside and Redvers Buller had doubted their intellectual capacity for the highest command, Elphinstone's pleas was based on the fact that the climate in Afghanistan could be extremely trying for a fit man, let alone the physical wreck which he had become by 1842. There can be no justification for Elphinstone's appointment and whatever his later failings, and they were many, the initial error was made by Lord Auckland.

In 1842 Elphinstone was nearly sixty years old and very unfit. An observer commented at the time that he was being carried in a palanquin, 'in a shocking state of gout . . . one arm in a sling and very lame . . .'[54] Patrick Macrory describes him in his book *Signal Catastrophe*:

The plain fact was that disease had ruined his physique and crippled his mental powers. He had almost lost the use of his limbs. He could not walk; he could hardly ride. The gout had crippled him in a manner that it was painful to contemplate. . . . Among the general officers of the Indian Army were many able and energetic men, with active limbs and clear understandings. There was one – a cripple, whose mental vigour much suffering had enfeebled; and he was selected by the Governor-General to command the army of Afghanistan . . .[55]

The ensuing catastrophe is graphically described by Macrory and it seems unfair to blame Elphinstone for what happened, for he emerges as the most completely pitiful figure in the book. He was passive to the end and died of dysentery, as a prisoner of Akbar Khan. Of his 4500 troops and approximately 12,000 civilian non-combatants, mainly women and children, only one European, Dr Brydon, and a handful of Indian soldiers survived the dreadful return march from Kabul through the Khyber Pass. The final judgement must be that in Elphinstone Lord Auckland chose a man thoroughly unfit for the arduous duties required of him. Incredibly, Auckland tried to appoint as commander of the relief force Major General Lumley, an elderly gentleman who was recovering from a serious illness. Only the intervention of his doctors prevented him being sent to Afghanistan in an attempt to force the Khyber Pass, something never previously done even by Tamburlaine the Great.

Hugh L'Etang gives many examples of the medical problems of great commanders. He does not suggest that they were unusually prone to illness or disease but that their stressful occupation made their physical and mental deficiencies more significant. Not every type of illness led to inefficiency or incompetence yet there can be little doubt that some had a marked effect.[56]

Old Age Norman Dixon has shown that old age is far from being a complete explanation of military incompetence.[57] General Pomeroy Colley, considered one of the brightest intellects in the British Army, was only 45 when he completely mishandled his troops at Majuba Hill in 1881, while at Taginae in 552, the eunuch Narses was 74 and yet quite capable of conducting one of the most brilliant tactical battles of his age.[58] One could continue to find such examples without their really affecting the central issue. War is a physically and mentally exhausting activity and as senior military command is usually attained by promotion, generals have often been old when they achieved positions of great responsibility. Moreover, the ageing process has intensified both defects of the body and the mind, and 'creeping incapacity' has been particularly common in those who hold high military rank.

Hardening of the arteries of the brain produces characteristic manifestations like general loss of energy and of capacity to adapt to unexpected or awkward situations, impairment of the ability to concentrate, lapses of memory, periods of confusion and emotional unreliability and irritability. A commander who is suffering some or all of these effects is poorly equipped to meet the demands of modern warfare, particularly where a crisis may be prolonged and his decisions consequently subject to stress and sleep-deprivation.

At Jena in 1806, the ultra-conservatism of the Prussian military machine was partly a product of its aged commanders. The Commander-in-Chief, Brunswick, was 71 and a veteran of the Seven Years War. His senior adviser, von Mollendorf, was 82, while the younger generation was represented by Hohenloe and Schmettau both, 60, and Blucher, 64.[59] Yet it was probably in the Crimean War that the effects of ageing were most clearly seen in the commanders appointed. On the outbreak of war in 1854, Britain had 13 generals who had more than 70 years' service each, 37 who had served between 60 and 70 years, 163 with between 50 and 60 years, 72 with between 40 and 50 years and seven 'juniors' with less than 40 years' service. It was from such a collection of geriatrics that Britain had to select the leadership of her army. It is hardly surprising that those chosen included men who were suffering severely from the adverse effects of the ageing process. Lord Raglan, the Commander-in-Chief, was 67, and with the exception of the Queen's cousin, the Duke of Cambridge, all the other senior commanders were between 60 and 70, with the Chief Engineer, Sir John Burgoyne, the oldest at 72. According to George Maude,

There is an old Commander-in-Chief, an old Engineer, old Brigadiers – in fact, everything old at the top. This makes everything sluggish.[60]

Aged cavalry commanders have always faced the additional physical demands of riding a horse. During the Russian invasion of East Prussia in August 1914, the cavalry commander of the Russian First Army, the elderly Khan of Nakhichevan, lost contact with his own men and was later found crying in his tent, suffering so badly from piles that he could not ride his horse.[61] At the battle of Kolin in 1757, one of Frederick the Great's cavalry commanders was aged over 80. General von Pennavaire was known as 'the anvil' because he was beaten so often, and on that occasion his handling of the Prussian cavalry was so inept that it was swept from the field by the Austrians and swiftly led to Frederick's defeat.[62]

During the Peninsular War, the Duke of Wellington showed admirable tact in his relations with the 70-year-old Spanish General Gregorio Garcia de la Cuesta, Captain-General of Estremadura. This ancient worthy had been trampled by his own cavalry at Medellin and was unable to mount his horse. Bryant describes his extraordinary form of transport:

Cuesta . . . was now forced to travel in a vast, lumbering coach drawn by nine mules. As, however, he never inspected the ground or reconnoitred the enemy, but, like a true countryman of Don Quixote, based his actions on strong imaginative hypotheses that had little or no relation to reality, this constituted no handicap in his eyes. He regarded Wellesley with contempt as a pretender to the art of war.[63]

In their preparations before the battle of Talavera it seems there was no need of an interpreter between the Spanish general and Wellington because the old man's invariable answer to anything suggested to him was 'no'. In John Colborne's opinion Cuesta was 'a perverse, stupid old blockhead'. Wellington himself was a little kinder, referring to him as 'obstinate as any gentleman at the head of an army should be' and 'Cuesta is too old and has not the talents to conduct in due order the great and confused affairs of a battle.[64]

Poor relations between commanders Hoffman's planning of the Tannenburg and Masurian Lakes campaigns in 1914 was based partly on the knowledge that the commander of the Russian First Army, General Pavel Rennenkampf, would not come to the aid of General Aleksandr Samsonov, commander of the 2nd Army. These two generals hated each other ever since they had brawled openly on the platform of a railway station at Mukden during the Russo-Japanese War in 1904. Hoffman was right in a sense when he claimed 'If the battle of Waterloo was won on the playing fields of Eton, the battle of Tannenburg was won on a railway platform at Mukden'.[65] Hoffman's observation raises an important point, which is the relationship between subordinate commanders within an army. If the dispute between Rennenkampf and Samsonov is one of the most famous – and most fatal – of such disagreements, it is by no means an isolated one. During the First World War the Russian Army seemed to have suffered particularly from this problem. At Cholm Headquarters in Calicia, the Russian Commander Ivanov and his Chief of Staff Alexeyev quarrelled so badly over who should open telegrams first that two copies of each had to be sent. The result was that both of them issued orders, usually different ones, in response to the messages received. In another part of the front the elderly commander of the Guard Army, Bezobrazov, refused to follow orders from his corps commander Olokhov, with whom he had fought publicly at a station earlier in the war. Although he was removed from command he had so much influence with the Tsar that he soon regained it. In the summer of 1915 he quarrelled with the commander of 3rd Army, General Lesh. When ordered to retreat he declared that 'the Guards never retreat'. The result was that his troops were massacred and he was removed from command once again. The Tsar again intervened declaring that he found Bezobrazov a 'charming' fellow and quite the sort of man who should command the Guards. The outcome was that Bezobrazov was now appointed to command the whole Guard Army.[66]

Napoleon had problems with his subordinate commanders, who frequently fought amongst themselves. During the Egyptian campaign, Renier and Destaing quarrelled so fiercely that it led to a duel in which the latter was killed. At the battle of Auerstadt in 1806 Davout was betrayed by Bernadotte, who withheld support from him. Refusing to accept orders from Davout the 'prickly' Bernadotte marched his troops away from where his colleague, with 27,000, was battling with at least 50,000 Prussians. In the words of Vagts:

Napoleon took the manifold jealousies among his generals as a matter of military nature, though he constantly avoided recognizing its menace to victory, particularly when he was not on the spot. . . . Each marshal or general appears to have had far more enemies. . . . Conflicts intensified when one of the marshals was subordinated to another, if only for a short period, especially when their respective jurisdiction was not clearly outlined.[67]

On one occasion Murat and Ney agreed to a duel until the encouragement this would give to the enemy was pointed out to them.

The animosity between Lord Lucan, the commander of the British cavalry in the Crimean War, and Lord Cardigan, commander of the Light Brigade, is almost too well-known to need describing. Its effect on the efficiency of the British Army would have been easier to estimate had the other commanders not been almost equally incompetent. At the start of World War Two the French commanders Gamelin and Georges hated each other intensely, British officers observing that if they would only stop making war on each other and concentrate on the Germans the outlook might be more hopeful.[68] The examples proliferate.

Cowardice It is rare, though not unknown, for a man to reach an elevated position in a military hierarchy and yet lack those qualities which are essential in any soldier. Every soldier feels fear at some time or other and yet the primary object of his military training will be not to help him suppress the fear but to combat the sort of behaviour which his fear may give rise to, like panic or flight. It is unlikely that an officer who is unable to control his reactions to fear would rise very far in the profession, yet the stress of command, combined with the possibly difficult conditions to which he is subject, may lower his resistance. Indeed, it has been observed that the better the soldier the longer his sense of duty will make him resist the stresses that are wearing him down and the greater will be his consequent collapse.

Just as personal courage is so difficult to define, so also is personal cowardice. Among commanders it has rarely been given much publicity as the mere acceptance that it exists would tend to undermine confidence in the officer corps. Nevertheless, there have been occasions where the rightness of a commander's decision appears to have been affected by considerations of personal safety. Perhaps the most famous example in British military history concerns the behaviour of Lord George Sackville, commander of the British cavalry, at the Battle of Minden on 1 August 1759. Sackville refused four orders from his commander, Price Ferdinand of Brunswick, to charge the disordered French and complete the victory. Fortescue observes,

Sackville was presently superseded and sent home. There he was tried by court-martial and pronounced unfit to serve the King in any military capacity whatever – a hard sentence but probably no more than just . . . the courage of some men is not the same on every day; and it is possible that on the day of Minden Sackville's courage failed him.[69]

The case of Rear-Admiral Sir Ernest Troubridge is rather less clear-cut than that of Sackville, yet probably more revealing of the problems of high command. In August 1914, Troubridge was in the Mediterranean, flying his flag in HMS *Defence* as second-in-command to Admiral Sir Archibald Milne. Richard Hough describes Troubridge in this way: 'He was a big, fine-looking man, the epitome of a sailor, much liked but with not too much "up top"'.[70]

On 30 July 1914, Admiral Milne received a telegram at Malta warning him of the possibility of war and instructing him if possible to bring to action the German battlecruiser *Goeben*, which, with the light cruiser *Breslau*, was operating in the Mediterranean. The Admiralty made it clear that he was not to engage 'superior forces', except in combination with the French navy.[71] This was a misleading directive and was to have unforeseen consequences. Although two British battlecruisers, HMS *Indomitable* and HMS *Inflexible*, sighted the German warships they could do no more than shadow them as Britain and Germany were technically not at war. The German commander, Admiral Souchon, was heading for Constantinople and realised that when Britain's ultimatum to Germany ran out at midnight the British ships would be free to attack him. As a result he fled at full speed and managed to outdistance his pursuers. The only British naval force able to intercept him was the squadron of four armoured cruisers under Rear-Admiral Troubridge patrolling off the island of Cephalonia in order to guard the entrance to the Adriatic.

Troubridge had warships which could have at worst slowed down the *Goeben* and delayed her flight, perhaps long enough for the pursuing British battlecruisers to have caught up. At best, by skilful manoeuvering and use of torpedoes, they might even have been able to sink her. It was a difficult decision for any commander to have to face, particularly after the Admiralty had advised Milne against taking on 'superior force'. It was all a question of what constituted superior force.

Troubridge's four cruisers were by no means old or weak vessels as is sometimes suggested, HMS *Black Prince* and HMS *Duke of Edinburgh* were nine years old, while HMS *Defence* and HMS *Warrior* were only six. Each carried 9.2-inch guns and between them they had a broadside of some 8480 pounds against 8272 pounds from the *Goeben's* ten 11-inch guns. However, their armoured protection was a mere six inches against eleven inches for the battlecruiser. Moreover, the *Goeben* was some five knots faster and could probably have outmanoeuvered even four opponents. At the battle of Jutland in 1916 it is interesting to note that when the *Defence* and *Warrior* encountered the heavy guns of the German High Seas Fleet they were both sunk very easily. However, Troubridge had none of the advantages of hindsight to guide him.

On the night of 6–7 August, Troubridge received reports from HMS *Gloucester*, which was shadowing the German ships, and thereupon set a course to intercept them at 6 a.m. on the 7th. There was no indication that he was unwilling to bring the Germans to action. During the night he changed his mind after a conversation with his flag-captain, Fawcet Wray, which took the following form.

Wray: Are you going to fight, sir? because if so the squadron ought to know.
Troubridge: Yes, I know it is wrong but I cannot have the name of the whole Mediterranean Squadron stink.

Wray returned 45 minutes later and said that after due consideration he did not relish taking on the *Goeben*.
Troubridge: Neither do I, but why?
Wray: It seems to me it is likely to be the suicide of your squadron.

Troubridge: I cannot turn away now, think of my pride.
Wray: Has your pride got anything to do with this, sir? It is your country's welfare which is at stake.

Troubridge then apparently consulted his navigator to ask if, in his opinion, the squadron would be able to close in on the *Goeben* so as to use its 9.2-inch guns. The navigator replied that he thought there was no chance and so Troubridge called off the interception.

Wray: Admiral, this is the bravest thing you have ever done in your life.[72]

Few were to share Wray's verdict. The view of many was expressed in the phrase, 'deplorable and contrary to the tradition of the British Navy'. The Court of Inquiry set up by the Admiralty judged that Troubridge 'had a very fair chance of at least delaying *Goeben* by materially damaging her'. From 5 to 9 November 1914, he was tried by court martial on a charge that he did, 'from negligence or through other default, forbear to pursue the chase of His Imperial German Majesty's ship *Goeben*, being an enemy then flying'. He was defended by a brilliant KC and gained much by being able to cite the instructions sent by the Admiralty to Milne not to engage a superior enemy. The *Goeben* was the only superior enemy at that time in the Mediterranean and so he gained acquittal on this technicality. Nevertheless, his reputation could not be recovered. Whatever he claimed as justification for his action there is no doubt that he 'lost his nerve' at the vital moment and attempted afterwards to rationalise this perfectly normal but militarily unacceptable occurrence. As Lieutenant-Commander Peter Kemp wrote:

I think his culpability falls into a different category; virtually in sight of the enemy and turning away. Wray was quite entitled to make his representations to Troubridge; the fault lay in Troubridge listening to them and accepting them.[73]

Richard Hough makes it clear that, however brilliantly Troubridge was defended at his court martial, it is impossible to overlook the fact that when the moment came to engage the enemy he allowed 'a few pleading words from his flag-captain suggesting likely defeat' to persuade him to turn about and allow his quarry to escape. At his court martial Troubridge referred to a 'mental struggle between my natural desire to fight and my sense of duty in view of my orders', but this sounds unconvincing.[74] He chose to break off from an interception course not because of his orders but because he allowed himself to think of the consequences of defeat. Whether this was the physical cowardice of a commander fearing defeat and disgrace, or of a man fearing injury or death, or the moral cowardice of an admiral who could not face the responsibility of making a difficult decision, is not easy for the historian to ascertain. The aftermath of his inaction may be summed up in the words of Winston Churchill: 'For the peoples of the Middle East SMS *Goeben* carried more slaughter, more misery and more ruin than has ever before been borne within the compass of one ship'.[75]

TACTICAL INCOMPETENCE

War is a province of errors; the greater the pressure on an individual commander, the greater the likelihood that he will make mistakes. In fact, as Delbruck has said, strategy consists in making one mistake less than the enemy.[76] This may seem rather a negative way of viewing the commander's art yet it gives a truer picture of what really occurs in battle than an overview in which orders are seen as precise and troops carry them out as if on a parade ground. So much military history, particularly that which deals with pre-twentieth century warfare, with its limited facilities for communication, tends to rationalise events and construct a picture of a battle as an ordered activity rather than the confused mêlée it so often was.

Norman Dixon has argued that explanations of military ineptitude which rely on the notion that the commander was simply stupid are generally inadequate.[77] Certainly it would be surprising to find an apparently 'stupid' man elevated to a position of responsibility in any profession. Yet it is in the peculiar stresses that warfare imposes on the individual that the dangers lie, for a man like General Braddock may be the ideal soldier in peacetime and may reach an elevated rank by ability on the parade ground, and yet, in the confusion of the fight, may reveal dangerous characteristics of panic or passivity which could not have been anticipated. Almost all commanders, even the great captains of history, have periodic lapses which could be construed as incompetence. On certain days even Napoleon or Frederick or Caesar could be incompetent in their direction of military action. The important point is that they made far fewer mistakes than lesser commanders. For every Kolin there was a Rossbach and a Leuthen; for an Aspern there was an Austerlitz and a Wagram. But for some commanders there is little to remember them by but their stupidity.

British generalship in the Second Boer War ranks, along with the Crimean War and the Gallipolli campaign, as a high point in the history of British military incompetence. At Spion Kop Buller entrusted the command to Lieutenant-General Sir Charles Warren, who was perhaps the worst of all the incompetent generals present in South Africa. Farewell described him as 'preposterous'.[78] Warren's military views were simplistic and he had once confided to Lord Wolseley that the best way to beat the Boers was 'either by sweeping over them with very long lines of infantry attacking simultaneously' or 'by pounding away at them with artillery till they quailed'.[79] In crossing the Tugela, he had given way to 'certain fads and fancies'[80] which included spending 26 hours supervising the transfer of his personal baggage across the river. When he had originally crossed the drift Warren had faced a mere 600 Boers but in time he wasted in moving his own baggage a further 6000 moved into position against him. In Farwell's opinion,

It was unfortunate for the British that two generals such as Buller and Warren should have been placed in command of the forces on the Tugela. Both were, though for different reasons, indecisive; together their incompetence was compounded. Neither was particularly clever. Buller knew he was not; Warren was convinced that he was, and even when it was dramatically proven he was not, he ever kept a higher opinion of himself. Buller's mistakes were those of a simple honest soldier, determined to do his duty. . . . Warren's mistakes were those of an arrogant man caught in the net of his own absurd theories and deceived by his own conceit. . . . Buller was a blunderer, but Warren was a fool.[81]

Between them Buller and Warren decided to assault the hill known as Spion Kop, without a proper reconnaissance and against an enemy of unknown strength. No thought was given to taking the field telegraph unit that was available, with the result that Warren at the bottom never had any communication with his assault force. Sandbags had been prepared for use on the top but the order to take them was never given. Moreover, there were only twenty picks and twenty shovels to dig trenches for two thousand men. The result was that they were unable to entrench themselves and suffered heavy casualties from the Boers situated above them.

One of the most extraordinary blunders of the 1914-18 period involved the fall of Fort Douaumont at Verdun to a single German sergeant in 1916. Through apparent absence of mind the fort was occupied by a mere 56 gunners manning the 155mm and 75mm turrets under the command of a Sergeant-Major Chenot. In February 1916, the Governor of Verdun telephoned General Chrétien, the commander of the Corps in whose area the fort lay, and ordered him to re-occupy the fort and defend it to the last man. Chrétien agreed to do this and passed the order on to his staff. However, Chrétien was due to be replaced by General Balfourier and when the latter arrived the tired Chrétien assured him that the occupation of the fort was in hand and that he need not worry. In the words of Alastair Horne:

Under the stress of sustained battle, the best-regulated staffs sometimes break down. Errors that would otherwise be inconceivable arise. Such a one occurred now. Somebody on Chrétien's staff, perhaps a humble corporal-signaller, forgot to transmit the vital order for the re-occupation of the forts.[82]

Meanwhile, on 25 February the 24th Brandenburg Regiment had been ordered to advance to a position about 750 yards to the north-east of Fort Douaumont. With the 2nd Battalion was a section of Pioneers commanded by Sergeant Kunze, whose task was to accompany the forward troops in order to clear barbed wire and other obstacles. By chance Kunze's section of ten men found themselves close to Fort Douaumont and Kunze ordered them to follow him towards the fort. Finding themselves in the moat surrounding the fort, on the sergeant's orders they formed a human pyramid so that Kunze could climb into one of the gun embrasures. With just two companions Kunze explored the long tunnels inside the fort and then – alone – he found four French gunners manning the 155mm gun. These he arrested at gun-point but then immediately lost his way and also lost contact with his two companions. Marching his four prisoners ahead of him Kunze came out into the open air when, suddenly, the prisoners bolted back into the fort by another entrance. Kunze was about to open fire when he noticed a barrackroom where some kind of lecture was taking place. Underterred, he promptly arrested the twenty French soldiers there, only for a shell to hit the fort and extinguish the candles in the room. Showing great presence of mind Kunze slammed the heavy door and locked it from outside. He continued his exploration, arrested another French soldier and then, finding himself in what he assumed was the officer's mess, sat down to his first square meal for weeks. The arrival of three German officers, Radtke, Haupt and von Bradis now completed Kunze's work and the fort was captured intact.

The news of the capture of Fort Douaumont, the 'strongest in the world' was greeted with rapture in Germany and the French made every effort to play it down, talking of the heavy casualties the Germans had suffered, 'a whole autumn of grey-green leaves fallen on the snow', and how fierce the fighting had been.[83] The truth was ridiculously different. Yet the consequences were enormous. To the British it was the high-water mark of German progress on the Western Front and many German observers assumed it was the beginning of the collapse of France. The fort had been taken without a shot being fired and yet its recapture by the Moroccans on 24 October 1916, was said to have cost France 100,000 lives, a heavy price for absent-mindedness.

Forgetfulness and administrative muddle played their part when on 22 January 1824, British troops under Sir Charles Macarthy were attacked by an Asante army of 10,000 men near the village of Bonsaso in West Africa. The Asante encircled the British force, who began to run short of ammunition. The British civilian storeman, Brandon, brought up the reserve ammunition boxes from Cape Coast but when they were opened they were found to be full of biscuits. British resistance crumbled and Sir Charles and his entire force were overrun and killed by the Asante.[84]

Tactical conservatism The technology of warfare changed slowly in the medieval world and resulted in greater tactical conservatism than was apparent in the ancient or the early modern periods. There were numerous occasions where such conservatism contributed to military disaster. As we have seen, the commander who bases his tactics on preconception is in danger of being out-thought by an enemy possessing either a new system of warfare or new technology incorporating tactical innovation. This problem was seen in the clash between the established military caste, the mounted knights, and the professional footsoldiers, frequently of peasant origin, whose skill with bow, handgun, pike or halberd made them a match for their social superiors. The changes that were taking place were resisted by the social group that had most to lose by surrendering its traditional military preeminence. Most of the rulers in Western Europe would have agreed with the Emperor Frederick II when he said that, 'The adornment of the Empire and of our power especially lies in a multitude of knights'.[85] Even at the end of the thirteenth century it was a widely held view that 100 knights were worth at least 1000 foot soldiers.

In many medieval battles social factors unconnected with military training assumed undue importance. On fields such as Courtrai (1302), Morgarten (1315), Laupen (1339), Crecy (1346), Poitiers (1356), Sempach (1386) and Agincourt (1415), the tactical conservatism of the knights contributed substantially to their defeat. The incapacity of the French leaders at Crecy was notable.

The effectiveness of the English longbow should not have surprised the French knights. English victories at Dupplin Moor (1332) and Halidon Hill (1333) against the Scots had been won by a combination of men at arms and bowmen fighting in formation, while at Cadsand in 1337 the English archers had shown their superiority over Flemish crossbowmen. The French themselves had even suffered at the hands of English longbowmen in a number of encounters prior to Crecy, including the naval battle at Sluys 1340, and the encounters at Morlaix (1342), Auberoche (1345) and St Pol de Leon (1346). The military leaders of France had had ample opportunity to judge the dangers of the English way of war and to have tried to counter it. Yet at Crecy the leadership was so bad that it simply delivered up its army to be slaughtered.

Edward III's army of 12,000, two-thirds of whom were archers, had taken up a good position, on a gentle ridge with both flanks protected. However, the French commanders never considered the tactical possibilities of flank attack. Instead, holding to a tradition of knightly pre-eminence which the Swiss had already challenged at Morgarten and the Flemings at Courtrai, they placed their faith in the weight of their frontal attack. Unable to profit from the experiences of the recent past they were doomed to repeat their mistakes.

The French army under King Philip VI had a cosmopolitan flavour. As well as the nobility of France there was Charles, King of the Romans, the Counts of Namur and Hainault, the Duke of Lorraine and King Jaime II of Mallorca, as well as hundreds of German and Bohemian knights under the blind King John of Bohemia. The French array consisted of probably 12,000 mounted men-at-arms, with a vast number of footsoldiers, who were, however, of little value and counted for nothing in French tactics. More significant was the contingent of 5000 Genoese crossbowmen who preceded the knights into battle, led by their own commanders, Odone Doria and Carlo Grimaldi.[86] The French knights were contemptuous of such mercenaries and ignored their complaints that they were tired after eighteen hours of marching and that their bowstrings were soaked.

It was late in the afternoon, and approaching the hour of vespers (6 p.m.) as the disordered French army came into sight of the English. Oman asserts that Philip, acting on the advice of Alard de Baseilles, wished to make camp in order to allow the rear of his army to catch up so that everyone might rest.[87] However, the undisciplined French knights would not listen to him. According to Froissart's account,

... neither the king nor the marshals could stop them, but they marched on without any order until they came in sight of their enemies. As soon as the foremost rank saw them, they fell back at once in great disorder, which alarmed those in the rear, who thought they had been fighting. . . . All the roads between Abbeville and Crecy were covered with common people, who, when they were coming within three leagues of their enemies, drew their swords, bawling out, 'Kill, Kill'. . . . There is no man, unless he had been present, that can imagine, or describe truly, the confusion of that day.[88]

Before leaving Abbeville the French host had been formed into nine or ten divisions but so poor was the discipline that by the time they arrived at Crecy little sign of order remained. Despairing of being able to withdraw his army into camp, Philip decided to attack.

The Genoese crossbowmen advanced towards the English, followed by the first line of French men-at-arms under the Counts of Allençon and Flanders. The first volley from the crossbows fell short and was answered

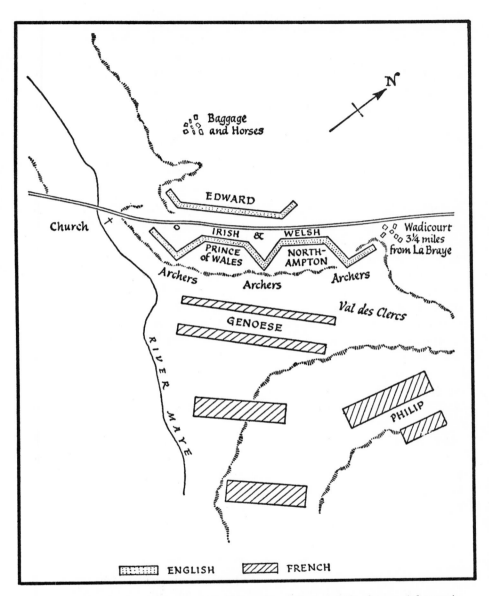

2. *The French assault on the strong English position illustrated the dangers inherent in matching feudal armies against tightly-organized professional troops. The French at no time tried to outflank the English force and their feudal nobility showed tactical conservatism by insisting on ill-coordinated charges in an attempt to come to close quarters with the English men at arms. The English combination of pike and bow was a tactical innovation which was to dominate battlefields until the development of efficient artillery and firearms a century later.*

by an overwhelming fire from the English archers. The Genoese panicked and tried to get out of range but could not break through the masses of French cavalry, who refused to make way for them. In anger at being held up by mere mercenaries King Philip called out 'Kill me those scoundrels, for they block our advance and serve no purpose!'[89] There now followed an incredible scene as the king's brother, the Count of Alençon, rode down the retreating Genoese. As Oman says,

This mad attempt to ride down their own infantry was fatal to the front line of the French chivalry. In spite of themselves they were brought to a stand at the foot of the slope, where the whole mass of horse and foot rocked helplessly to and fro under a constant hail of arrows from the English archery.[90]

Few of Alençon's first line came to grips with the dismounted English knights for most were brought down by arrows. Yet no attempt was made to clear the field before the second French line charged. This resulted in further confusion in which the blind King of Bohemia was killed.

Throughout the battle the French commanders showed no tactical understanding whatsoever. Each band of knights seemed to have the single idea of charging at the enemy head-on, with no thought of manoeuvre or flanking action. The only danger to the English occurred when some of Alençon's men-at-arms, avoiding the archers, managed to break into the division of the Prince of Wales, where they were beaten after a stiff fight. When the French had launched fifteen consecutive charges, the last of which took place after dark, they eventually withdrew having suffered enormous losses, including 1542 lords and knights killed, as well as thousands of footsoldiers.

The days of the feudal horsemen were numbered, for the longbow and later the handgun, combined with the pike, would give the advantage to the professional footsoldier fighting on the defensive. The French, however, clung to the traditional virtues of knighthood and the lesson they drew from their defeat at Creçy was the wrong one, that it had been the dismounted English men-at-arms who had triumphed, not the lowly archers. The result was that at Poitiers in 1356 King John II dismounted his knights and advanced these heavily armed warriors towards the English lines on foot. Again the English archers inflicted great slaughter though this time the battle was more of a hand-to-hand mêlée than at Creçy.[91] The French defeat resulted from their failure to co-ordinate bow and pike as had the English. The Austrians at Sempach in 1386 also experimented to their cost with dismounted men-at-arms against the Swiss.[92]

By the beginning of the fifteenth century the supremacy of the English archers was itself under challenge and what had seemed revolutionary in the early years of Edward III's reign was in danger of imposing on less able English commanders a stereotyped tactical system. However, the conservatism of the French nobility was at odds with the developing professionalism of other French commanders from lower social groups. At Agincourt (1415) the French revealed that they had forgotten everything learned so painfully during the early part of the war with the English, and attacked a well-entrenched English army made up mainly of bowmen. Further disasters were to follow at Verneuil (1424) and Rouvray (1429) before the French learned to cope with English tactics.

The most successful soldiers of the late middle ages, the English and the Swiss, had such a long sequence of success that there seemed to be no need for them to adapt their military systems to meet the changing needs of their times. They knew that what they did won them battles, so much so that an occasional defeat was assumed to be the result of faulty execution of their own system rather than any virtue on the part of their opponents. Thus, whereas their opponents were forced to evaluate themselves, the English and Swiss became ultra-conservative and succumbed to a changing military order.

At Formigny in 1450 the French used culverines to batter the English archers from a distance, while at Castillon in 1453 Talbot's headstrong attack was swept away by more than a hundred pieces of French artillery.[93] The longbow, so effective a weapon in the fourteenth century, was entering a period of decline, though it still had its supporters even in the seventeenth century.[94]

The supremacy of the Swiss during the fifteenth century, and their emergence as the preeminent mercenary soldiers, began to be challenged when the Emperor Maximilian introduced German landsknechts, who were infantry well-drilled in the use of the pike, and fought in the Swiss fashion. And this was only the first step in a process by which tactical organizations were developed to challenge the Swiss. During the Italian Wars of the sixteenth century it became obvious that the Swiss had in turn become imprisoned in the traditions of their great past. Soon the Spanish sword and buckler men were able to duck under the unwieldy Swiss pikes and come to close-quarters. The Stadiot light cavalry and the German arquebusier showed that the great age of the Swiss was ended.

The Swiss did not accept this process readily and their disastrous failure to adapt was demonstrated by their attempt to dislodge Colonna's imperial army from its entrenchments at Bicocca in 1522. Refusing to wait for their allies, the French, to set up their artillery, 8000 Swiss mercenaries forced their way through defensive hedges and trenches only to be shot down by the Spanish arquebusiers. Those that survived reached a deep ditch beyond which, on an elevation, stood German landsknechts. Oman describes what happened next:

Leaping into the deep excavation, the front ranks endeavoured to scramble up its further slope; but every man who made the attempt fell beneath the pike-thrusts of the Germans, who, standing on a higher level in their serried ranks, kept back the incessant rushes with the greatest steadiness. Three thousand corpses were left in the ditch before the Swiss would desist from their hopeless undertaking; it was an attack which, for misplaced daring, rivals the British assault on Ticonderoga in 1758.[95]

A belief in frontal assaults Much of the education and training of military commanders has been based on past experience yet those who have become too committed to tradition, in the face of modern developments both tactical and technological, have proved notably unsuccessful. Their failure to profit from past mistakes indicates an unwillingness to criticise those whom they have been taught to admire. Tradition may seem to offer certainty but, as Clausewitz has shown, war is the province of uncertainty.

To conduct a military action according to traditional tactics is to fight by preconception. This attitude is illustrated by commanders with a predilection for frontal assaults, usually against the enemy's strongest point. This tactic had the simple attraction of requiring little thought on the part of the commander and placing a total reliance on the quality and staying power of the troops. In the eighteenth century, such tactics required a body of obedient soldiers who could manoeuvre in well-ordered battalions and could advance unflinchingly upon the enemy. Drill had implanted in them a series of conditioned responses to orders, by endless repetition, so that they did not need to think at all. However, in some cases, as with Packenham at New Orleans or Burnside at Fredericksburg, it seemed to remove the necessity for thought on the part of the commander as well.

On 7 July 1758, General James Abercromby, commanding a force of 7000 British regulars and 9000 Provincial troops, was advancing to attack the French fortress at Ticonderoga, on the shores of Lake Champlain in Canada. The French commander, Montcalm, had a mere 3,600 men and supplies for only eight days. Nevertheless, he set about cutting down the surrounding trees and constructing a loop-holed breastwork some nine feet high, facing the north-west from which direction he expected the British to come. In front of the breastwork was a wilderness of branches and lopped tree-tops, making an advance in good order difficult.

However, impressive as the French efforts had been there was nothing there that should have greatly worried Abercromby. He had a number of options open to him. He could have attacked Montcalm's flanks, which were unfortified; or he could have brought up his artillery and battered the French breastwork to pieces; or he could have stationed his guns on a nearby hill, which overlooked the French position, and have raked it from end to end. He could even have starved his enemy into submission by cutting off his supplies from the north. It is rare in military history for a commander to be faced by such a range of options, any one of which guaranteed succes[96]. Abercromby, however, decided to accept none of these and, leaving the artillery at the landing stage with the boats, gave orders that the breastwork should be carried by a full frontal assault.

Neglecting every advantage, Abercromby personally retired some two miles to the sawmills, where the British had landed, and remained there throughout the battle, restricting his orders to the simple one of 'Advance and attack'. His officers carried out his instructions and formed up the British troops in impeccable order. Fortescue describes the British advance:

It was little that they could see through the tangle of fallen trees and dying leaves; possibly they caught a glimpse of the top of the breastwork but of not a white coat of the defenders behind it. On they came in full confidence, knowing nothing of the obstacles before them, when suddenly the breastwork broke into a sheet of flame, and a storm of grape and musketry swept the ranks from end to end.[97]

The troops showed remarkable courage, particularly the Highlanders who, brandishing their claymores, actually fought their way to the breastwork but could not climb up because no one had had the foresight to equip them with ladders. Some were hoisted up onto the ramparts but these were quickly shot down by the French defenders. For five hours the British infantry kept up the unequal struggle until at 6 p.m. the order was given to break off the attack. In all the British suffered nearly 2000 casualties against a French loss of 377. It was a staggering and completely unnecessary defeat which owed everything to 'the murderous incompetence and stupidity of Abercromby'.[98]

The First World War showed the clearest and most terrible examples of commanders whose tactical shortcomings and refusal to learn from past mistakes condemned millions of young men to die in frontal assaults against carefully designed entrenchments. The armies had outgrown the capacities of their commanders to use them. Dixon refers to them as 'saurians of a bygone age, huge in strength, massive in body, but controlled by a nervous system so sluggish and extended that the organism could suffer fearful damage before the tiny distant brain could think of, let alone initiate, an adequate response'.[99]

Attrition, in which each side sought to wear the other down until one or the other was unable to continue, through losses or a breakdown of morale, became a substitute for manoeuvre. For the attacking side, generally the British or French on the Western Front, the problem was to feed in soldiers at the point of contact faster than the defenders were able to destroy them. Ethics did not enter into it. A general was judged by his ability to maintain attritional advantage. At the Battle of Loos in 1915 the leadership was so inept that British losses were not balanced by either equivalent German losses or by ground gained.

After the first day's assault at Loos, General Haig decided that he needed the newly formed XI Corps under General Haking, consisting of two of Kitchener's 'New Army' divisions, the 21st and 24th, to make up for his heavy losses on the 25 September. Field-Marshal French, the British Commander-in-Chief, was unhappy at the idea of using such inexperienced troops, but Haig insisted that their very 'freshness' could be an advantage: 'with the enthusiasm of ignorance they would tear their way through the German line'. In Alan Clark's words, 'At its crudest, they didn't know what they were up against'.[100] Several times French tried to deny Haig the use of XI Corps but finally he relented on 25 September at midday.

Thus at the shortest notice XI Corps was ordered to the front and it was not until nightfall that they arrived behind Lone Tree Ridge. Neither division had been in France for more than two weeks and both were short of regular officers and NCOs. Moreover, their staff officers did not know the area they were in and had no large-scale maps to help them. Soaked to the skin and without hot food, the men were in poor condition before the attack even started, having been continuously on the move for eighteen hours. Nevertheless, their morale was high. They had been told they would simply be pursuing a demoralized enemy and that they would 'not be put in unless and until the Germans are completely smashed and retiring in disorder'.[101] Haig had no intention of keeping to this assurance and saw the attack on 26 September as a continuation of the previous day's battle.

In contrast to the opening attack on the first day of the battle, in which the assault by four divisions had been preceded by a four-day artillery bombardment and a discharge of gas along the entire front, the 21st and 24th divisions were not preceded by anything. In Alan Clark's words,

. . . the hapless 21st and 24th Divisions were expected to cross No-Man's-Land in broad daylight with no gas or smoke cloud to cover them, with no artillery support below divisional level, and attack a position as strongly manned as had been the front defences and protected by a formidable and intact barbed-wire entanglement.[102]

In Clark's view the attack of XI Corps was as futile and as foredoomed as that of the Light Brigade at Balaclava.[103]

At 10 a.m. a thin 'bombardment' of where the German positions were assumed to be took place, though the Germans suffered no casualties at all and their barbed wire remained intact. The firing lasted just twenty minutes and for the next forty minutes all was silent on the battlefront. At 11 a.m. the 21st and 24th divisions rose up from their positions and advanced in close formation, with their officers mounted at their head. The Germans were shocked at first by the sight of such dense masses of infantry but they held their fire until the British had formed up into extended lines and had begun their advance. The following extract is from a German account of the battle:

Ten columns of extended line could clearly be distinguished, each one estimated at more than a thousand men, and offering such a target as had never been seen before, or even thought possible. Never had the machine-gunners such straightforward work to do nor done it so effectively. They traversed to and fro along the enemy's ranks unceasingly. The men stood on the fire-steps, some even on the parapets, and fired triumphantly into the mass of men advancing across the open grass land. As the entire field of fire was covered with the enemy's infantry the effect was devastating and they could be seen falling literally in hundreds.[104]

The Germans could hardly believe the way in which the British troops marched doggedly towards them. Reaching the barbed wire, which was over nineteen feet across and four feet high, and armed only with hand clippers which were not strong enough to cut the thick wire, many men tried to scramble across it, while others tore at it with their bare hands. Others merely ran up and down the line trying to find a gap until they were shot down. Only after it was clear that there was no hope of breaking through did the remnants of the two divisions turn and retreat. So nauseated had the Germans been by the massacre that few fired at the retreating British troops. Of the ten thousand who had attacked that day no fewer than 385 officers and 7861 men had become casualties. The Germans suffered no casualties at all.[105] Neither French nor Haig can escape blame for this disgraceful waste of lives. In many instances in history troops have been committed to frontal assaults which have resulted in heavy losses but never has there been a more pointless sacrifice than that of the 21st and 24th divisions at Loos.

Failure to overcome terrain or elements The problem of the terrain over which an army must move and the effect that the elements have on both the terrain and the army is of great concern to any competent commander. It is obviously beyond his abilities to control the weather but it is not impossible for him to turn the conditions to his advantage or to prevent them being used against him. History records a number of examples where a failure to overcome these problems has resulted in military setbacks.

In 53 BC the Romans under Marcus Crassus suffered a major disaster against the Parthians near Carrhae in Mesopotamia. Before he had even invaded Parthia, Crassus was advised by Artavasdes, King of Armenia, to travel by way of his kingdom, as the Parthians were strong in cavalry but unable to operate effectively in the hills and mountains of Armenia.[106] Foolishly, Crassus rejected this advice and opted for the desert route through Mesopotamia though his army, consisting of seven legions and more than 4000 cavalry, faced great difficulty in supplying itself with food and water in a hostile country. One of his generals, Cassius, advised Crassus to rest in one of the Roman cities of Mesopotamia to give time to reconnoitre the enemy or, failing this, to advance on Seleucia, the Parthian capital, by way of the river Euphrates, which would provide water and guard one of their flanks in the event of attack.[107]

Rejecting this advice Crassus was persuaded by an Arab chieftain named Ariamnes to turn away from the river and head across the open plains. Soon the Romans were trudging through deep sand. Exhausted and thirsty, they fell victim to the 'Parthian tactics' of their enemies. Crassus was killed and with him much of the Roman force. Advancing on foot into a desert to confront an enemy force of cavalry was the height of folly.

The desert proved no kinder to General William Hicks in 1883. Hicks had spent almost all his career in the Indian Army and was on the point of retiring in 1883 as a colonel. Unexpectedly he was offered the chance to command an Egyptian army in the Sudan against the Mahdist rebels, with the rank of general. His army did not consist of very good material, many of the soldiers being survivors from Arabi Pasha's revolt, who were brought to the Sudan in chains. On the other hand, Hicks was hardly an outstanding officer either. After a few minor victories, he allowed his entire force of some 10,000 men to be drawn into the wastes of Kordofan, where they suffered from thirst and exhaustion. In terrain of which he had no experience at all he led his force in pursuit of tribesmen born and bred in the desert. The outcome was inevitable: except for 300 men the entire army was wiped out at El Obeid, as completely as 'Pharaoh's host perished in the Red Sea'.[108]

Far from the desert, in the mountains of Switzerland, the army of the Habsburg Duke Leopold II, consisting of some 2000 knights and 7000 footsoldiers, came to grief at Morgarten in 1315. The Austrian commander suffered the penalty for inadequate reconnaissance. He advanced into mountainous terrain with his cavalry in the van. His long column of mounted men followed the narrow track between the lake of Egri and the slopes of the mountain above. The Swiss had blocked the road ahead with a wall of loose stones, while the bulk of their forces, to the number of about two thousand hid themselves in the woods alongside and above the road. When the van of the Austrian army met the road block, which was defended by a small Swiss force, they halted but the rest of the column kept moving forward creating confusion in the narrow space. At that moment boulders and tree-trunks were rolled down the slopes onto the helpless riders and the Swiss burst from cover in a dense mass of halberd-men who struck the Austrians in flank. In Oman's words,

> The disaster was immediate and complete; the Austrian knights, packed in the road, had no space to turn their horses, and could not charge uphill – below them was the lake, behind them the road jammed by the rest of the army.[109]

Although Leopold managed to fight his way to safety nearly two thousand of his men, mainly the knights in the vanguard, died under the blows of the Swiss halberds or by drowning in the lake.

Leopold's defeat was the result of faulty generalship. His failure to reconnoitre the mountain path was inexcusable and his attempt to take cavalry into the mountains ill-advised. The Swiss had used the terrain to their advantage and Leopold had allowed them to dictate to him the way in which the battle would be fought.

Another commander who conceded to his opponents' command of the high ground and then marched into an ambush was the Byzantine Emperor Manuel I at Myriokephalon, in 1176. As his huge army, encumbered with a heavy baggage train and numerous siege engines, made its way into the mountains of the Sultan Dagh, his scouts reported that the Seljuk Turks were occupying the ridge above a pass through which the Byzantines must pass. It was an obvious place for an ambush yet Manuel decided to continue the march into the pass. When the mass of the army had entered the defile the Turks charged down on them, forcing the Byzantines into a dense mass like the Austrians at Morgarten. Unlike Duke Leopold, who fought his way to freedom, Manuel compounded his incompetence as a commander by personal cowardice and fled, leaving his army to its fate.[110]

The Danube proved no friend to Napoleon during his Austrian campaign of 1809. Crossing a broad river in the face of the enemy is a dangerous military manoeuvre, as Burnside found at Fredericksburg in

1862, but Napoleon was no Burnside. He had successfully negotiated such problems many times in the past and yet in crossing the Danube near the villages of Aspern and Essling in May 1809 he made elementary mistakes which cost him the battle. Having defeated the Archduke Charles at Eckmuhl on 22 April 1809, Napoleon decided that he must destroy the main Austrian army before it linked up with the Archduke John's troops in the south. Between him and Charles, however, was the river Danube, swollen by spring floods. Leaving large detachments under Bernadotte and Vandamme to guard against the Austrians re-crossing the river, Napoleon concentrated his attention on securing a bridgehead as soon as possible. However, the dangers were greater than he realized. So impatient was he to complete the destruction of Charles's army that he ignored warnings that unless careful preparation went into the bridging of the Danube it was likely to prove a disaster. As Chandler points out,

. . . not only would the enemy be in a good position upstream to float down fireships and other obstacles to smash the French bridges, the experts warned, but the Danube was also prone to sudden spates of floodwater in the late spring which might well prove equally fatal to the flimsy pontoons. These bitter lessons Napoleon was soon to learn for himself.[111]

The chief engineer of the army, General Bertrand, carried out a careful reconnaissance of possible crossing points and eventually decided on a spot near the island of Lobau, and preparations were made to build a bridge to the island. Because Napoleon was exhibiting signs of impatience, Bertrand built the bridge without protective palisades or flotillas of manned river boats, which would have headed off anything the Austrians floated downstream to damage the French structure. Assuming the Austrians were far away to the north, Napoleon saw little need for caution.

The plan drawn up by Berthier for the crossing to Lobau was 'hastily made and poorly prepared, being based on false assumptions and gross miscalculations concerning both the characteristics of the Danube and the dispositions and capabilities of the enemy army.'[112] Assuming that he would need to hunt down the main Austrian army Napoleon ordered that the French crossing be headed by swarms of light cavalry. These should have provided him with the information that he desperately needed, that the Austrians were entrenched nearby. As three French infantry and two cavalry divisions occupied the bridgehead, Napoleon began to worry that if the pontoon bridge to Lobau broke, his army would be split on either side of the river. Overnight the Danube had risen three feet, while 'water-borne missiles' – such as fireships and logs – continuously battered at his

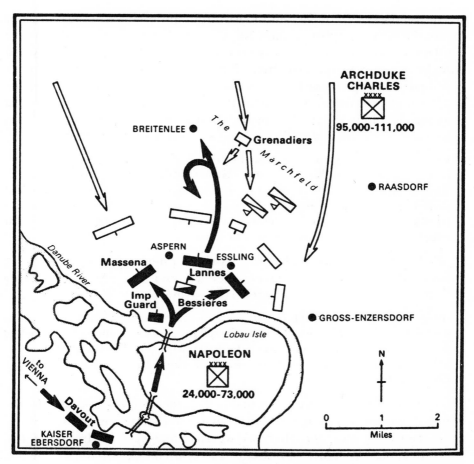

3. Napoleon's failure to locate the Austrian army meant that he attempted a crossing of the Danube in the face of overwhelming enemy strength. Only the superb fighting qualities of the French soldiers enabled him to evacuate his troops successfully to the island of Lobau.

leaking pontoon bridge.[113] He considered recalling his troops from the right bank but now the control of events was to be taken from his hands. The Austrians attacked. Had Charles realized the weak position Napoleon was in he could have destroyed the French troops on the right bank. However, caution was his undoing. For the first four hours of fighting less than 23,000 French troops were facing over 100,000 Austrians, vastly superior in guns and with the prospect of heavy reinforcements. Rarely in his entire career did Napoleon face such a catastrophe. Yet rarely also did his magnificent troops show such fighting qualities. Success or failure rested on the arrival of Davout's Corps from the left bank of the river. But again the bridge was broken and Napoleon realized that he would have to pull back his men from the villages of Aspern and Essling where they had fought so tenaciously. Casualties on both sides had been very heavy – a combined total of 46,000 killed and wounded – yet Charles had lacked the ability and determination to drive the French into the river, as he had seemed so often to be on the brink of doing. Kircheisen has been particularly scathing about Napoleon's conduct of the battle:

Although Napoleon's conduct must be said to have bordered on madness, in challenging fate, as he did, by venturing on a battle without knowledge of the Austrian positions, without securing his passage of the river, and without assembling his whole strength on the island of Lobau, yet the archduke's failure to make any further use of his victory is almost equally incredible . . . he might perfectly well have made an attempt to capture the island. . . .[114]

Field-Marshal Haig's plan for a British offensive at Ypres in 1917 disregarded both the terrain over which it would be fought and the likely effects of the weather. As Liddell Hart wrote,

A plan that was founded on faith rather than reason, both plan and faith were to be sunk in the mud of Flanders. Foch, himself the past exponent of 'faith-healing strategy', forecast the verdict when he deprecated the British offensive as a 'duck's march' and expressively remarked 'Boche is bad and boue is bad; but Boche and boue together–!'[115]

Haig adopted the plan in the face of many obstacles. He was advised by the meteorological experts that for an offensive in Flanders in the autumn he could hardly expect more than two weeks of fine weather. In saying this, of course, they were merely presenting a commander with the sort of data which must form a part of any military equation. No commander can control the weather but he can order his own actions in relation to known conditions. This is where Haig and the British High Command were culpable. To Liddell Hart, 'the Ypres offensive was doomed before it began', because the enormous bombardment planned by the British was destined to complete the destruction of the 'intricate drainage system' of that part of Flanders.[116] The ensuing mud was not simply the result of ill-luck, caused by unexpected rainfall. In fact, a memorandum had been sent from Tank Corps HQ to General HQ pointing out that if the bombardment took place the drainage system would be destroyed and the battlefield would become a swamp. This was no idle comment but based on information from the Belgian Government's 'Ponts et Chaussées' department, assisted by the best local opinion.[117] In fact, as early as 1915 the danger had been realised by engineers working in the area, which had only been reclaimed from marshland by the labour of centuries. Deaf to such considerations, on 22 July the British artillery, consisting of 3091 guns, including 999 heavy, opened a bombardment which continued until 31 July, firing 4.25 million shells valued at £22 million. This meant that four and three-quarter tons of explosive shells landed on every square yard of the muddy front. In neglecting this vital consideration the British were condemning their offensive to failure before it had started and thousands of men to unbelievable misery.

FAILURE TO COMMUNICATE

Good communications between a commander and a subordinate officer are vital, whether they take the form of a verbal message delivered by a staff officer, a letter, or signals by flag, telegraph or radio. The crucial requirement is that the recipient clearly understand the commander's intentions. There must be no room for misinterpretation.

The charge of the Light Brigade at Balaclava in 1854 is one of the most famous incidents in British military history and also one of the most obvious examples of military incompetence. Even in a war as poorly conducted as the Crimean, the charge stands out, though with such difficult men as Lucan and Cardigan in charge of the cavalry some sort of disaster was likely. The order sent by Lord Raglan to Lord Lucan was muddled. It read,

Cavalry to advance and take advantage of any opportunity to recover the Heights. They will be supported by the infantry, which have been ordered to advance on two fronts.[118]

For 45 minutes Lucan did nothing. He read the order as meaning that he should only advance when the infantry came up to support him and as yet he could see none. Raglan meanwhile was losing his composure. The earlier attack by the Heavy Brigade had disordered the enemy and a charge by the Light Brigade would have swept the enemy out of their redoubts. Why did not Lucan order an attack? As everyone waited the Russians began to drag away the British guns. Raglan ordered Airey to send another order. Airey scribbled these words on a piece of paper and gave it to his ADC, Captain Nolan.

Lord Raglan wishes the cavalry to advance rapidly to the front – follow the enemy and try to prevent the enemy carrying away the guns. Troop Horse artillery may accompany. French cavalry is on your left. Immediate. Airey.[119]

As Nolan sped away, Raglan shouted after him, 'Tell Lord Lucan the cavalry is to attack immediately'.[120] Lucan read the order but considered such an attack useless. Nolan was forced to pass on Raglan's last message that the cavalry should attack immediately. Lucan was both puzzled and angry. Where should he attack and what guns was Raglan referring to? Nolan pointed wildly, 'There is your enemy! There are you guns!'[121]

Raglan had overlooked the fact that from his elevated position he could see far more than the cavalry down in the valley. Lucan could see no redoubts nor any guns being taken away. His complete failure to keep himself informed of what was going on now contributed to a disaster. The only guns he could see were at the far end of the North Valley, where a mass of Russian cavalry were situated. Presumably this was what Raglan meant. And so Lucan instructed Cardigan to enter 'the valley of death' and the quite unnecessary 'Charge' of the Light Brigade entered the annals of military incompetence.

In the modern era of naval warfare communication between ships has been greatly simplified by the advent of radio. However, there have been occasions even in the twentieth century where it has been necessary to observe radio silence in order to keep the enemy from knowing tactical and strategic intentions, and this has meant, within a fleet or squadron, the use of flags or searchlights instead. During the First World War the work of Lieutenant-Commander Ralph Seymour, flag-lieutenant to Admiral Sir David Beatty, was particularly inept. In Beatty's own words, 'He lost three battles for me'.[122] Curiously, in spite of Seymour's incompetence and the fact that he was not even a signaller, Beatty insisted on retaining his services.

On 15 December 1914, the British Admiralty had advance warning of a major German sortie in the North Sea. British naval forces hurried to cut the Germans off and when the battlecruisers of Admiral Hipper began to bombard the coastal towns of Scarborough, Hartlepool and Whitby it seemed that Admirals Beatty and Warrender, with four battlecruisers and six battleships, had the Germans trapped. At 11.25 a.m. Commodore Goodenough's light cruisers encountered the light cruisers scouting for Admiral Hipper and a brief engagement took place. Hipper's main force was just 50 miles away when Beatty made a disastrous signals error. Assuming that two British cruisers, *Southampton* and *Birmingham*, were enough to deal with the German light cruisers, he wanted to use two others, *Nottingham* and *Falmouth*, with his squadron, so he ordered Seymour to signal by searchlight, 'Light cruisers – resume your position for look-out. Take station ahead five miles'.[123] No names of ships were mentioned and the wrong call-sign was used anyway. The result was that the captain of the *Nottingham* passed on the message to Commodore Goodenough in the *Birmingham*, who reluctantly broke off the action and resumed screening duties ahead of Beatty's battlecruisers, allowing Hipper to escape unscathed.

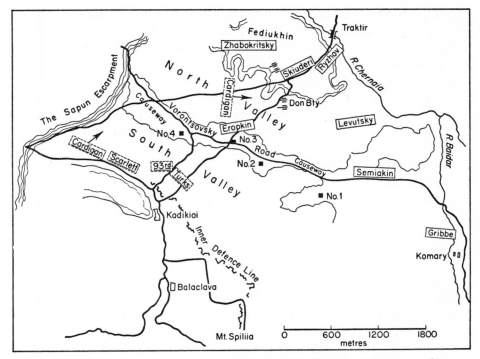

4. Imprecise orders from the British Commander Lord Raglan caused the famous Charge of the Light Brigade. Raglan made the mistake of using the phrase 'to the front' when in the confused fighting each of the British commanders faced a different front. Lucan and Cardigan were facing down the North Valley and presumed this was to what Raglan was referring. They assumed the reference to 'guns' meant the Russian guns, drawn up in the valley and on the Fediukhin heights.

When news of the dreadful casualties inflicted on the coastal towns by Hipper's ships reached Beatty, he demanded that Goodenough be dismissed at once. Jellicoe rightly refused, for the real failure was in Beatty's own ship. As Hough comments,

The true guilt for the ambivalent signal from the *Lion* points to Beatty's flag-lieutenant, Lieutenant-Commander Ralph Seymour, whose business it was to translate Beatty's intentions. He was the interpreter for his admiral who was deeply engaged in bringing his squadron into successful action and upon whom the whole future of the nation might rest. A flag-lieutenant's job was to select the wording and then the suitable flag, wireless signal, or morse message, to express it. It was Seymour who ought to have been sacked after the Scarborough Raid fiasco, not Goodenough.[124]

Seymour was not sacked and continued to work for Beatty at the battles of Dogger Bank and Jutland, during which his signalling was disastrous.

At Dogger Bank, although there were five British battlecruisers and four German, the signal was sent from Beatty's *Lion* 'Engage the corresponding ship in the enemy's line'.[125] No identification of British or German ships was given, with the result that *Lion* and *Tiger* ended up both firing at *Seydlitz* while no British ship fired at *Moltke*; *Moltke*, free of enemy fire, scored heavily on the British flagship, damaging her and forcing her to fall out of line. Nevertheless, the other British ships had a great chance of destroying the German squadron until more confused signals from the *Lion* caused them to slow down and concentrate on sinking the armoured cruiser *Blucher*. Beatty had signalled Admiral Moore on the *Tiger* to follow 'Course NE' in his pursuit of the enemy but this signal was left flying when the next one was raised which said, 'Attack the rear of the enemy'. The result was that Beatty's captains read the signal as 'Attack the rear of the enemy bearing NE'.[126] The only enemy bearing NE was the crippled *Blucher* and she was to the rear of the enemy squadron, so four British battlecruisers closed in on one crippled armoured cruiser, allowing Hipper's other ships to escape. After the action recriminations were widespread. Fisher blamed Captain Pelly of the *Tiger* for not firing at the *Moltke*, referring to him as a 'poltroon', while Admiral Moore was removed from his command. Yet the real problem was that Beatty's signals were just not clear enough and he must bear much of the guilt for not recognizing the weaknesses of Seymour and making certain that signalling was improved throughout his squadron.

WASTAGE OF HUMAN RESOURCES

Wars need to be cost-effective. At times in history miscalculations have taken place of the benefits to be gained from fighting, or the appropriate level and intensity of action that can be justified in terms of the rewards. Where wars have been fought over ideas it has proved impossible to balance costs and this may account for the extreme savagery of religious conflicts. Modern wars, notably the two world wars, have become irrational in that the costs incurred are so ruinous that victory is scarcely better than defeat. For the strategist and grand strategist, the costs may still be seen in terms of economic or political gains, but for the army commander the cost is almost always a human one.

Armies are made up of men and if they are not well treated they will not perform efficiently. They may be poorly fed and clothed as in the Crimea, or exposed to disease as in Walcheren or the West Indies. They may lack shelter from the elements or be exposed unnecessarily to hostile environments. In such cases, they become too weak, too ill or too mentally depressed to operate as proficient fighting units. One has only to consider the treatment given to the soldiers and sailors returning from Mansfield's expedition to Germany in 1624, from Cadiz in 1625 and from Ré in 1627. Thousands died of disease, exposure, starvation and general neglect, apart from those killed in action. Moreover, their Governments, made no effort to alleviate their suffering. Examples proliferate; medical conditions in Crimea in 1854 or in Mesopotamia in 1915 killed or incapacitated more men than enemy action.

T.E. Lawrence once wrote, 'To me an unnecessary action or shot or casualty was not only waste but sin'.[127] Yet there were always commanders prepared to sacrifice their men because they felt they were expendable. In Napoleon's phrase, 'A man such as I am is not much concerned over the lives of a million men'. Of the 600,000 men of the Grande Armée who followed him to Russia in 1812 no more than 10,000 were ever fit for action again.

Death and injury in war are not easily avoided. Every soldier knows that he risks his life in battle and high casualties are not necessarily a sign of incompetent command. Norman Dixon has shown that an unwillingness to risk casualties may be as militarily damaging as a stoical acceptance of them.[128] The problem arises when a commander begins to see his soldiers merely as units in a masterly game. It is a small step from here to the logic of attrition. As a substitute for tactical and strategical thinking, a reliance on mere numbers becomes a military option. If the attacker can feed more bodies into a sector than the defender can destroy then a breakthrough becomes possible. The defender then must improve his capacity to kill as part of the mathematical equation.

During the Franco-Prussian War in 1870, General Steinmetz ordered a frontal assault at Spichern. He commanded his men to use the bayonet only and suffered 62% casualties. It is said that the presence of Kaiser Wilhelm II at the front was responsible for much human wastage. Under the eye of the Emperor the German officers wanted not only to win but to win well and their men were sacrificed as a result.[129] During the Russo-Japanese War of 1904-5, General Nogi's attempts to take Port Arthur by 'human wave' frontal assaults have been condemned by one of his colleagues as 'insane'. Squandering his human resources in search of a quick victory the Japanese lost five times as many men as the Russians for no appreciable gain.[130] It was a startling anticipation of tactics to be seen again in August 1914. In the early months of the First World War it was the commanders of the French and German Reserve divisions who threw their men into the attack with a recklessness that reflected their own ambitions. The French Director of Artillery summed up this attitude when he announced 'Victory we shall gain with the breasts of our infantrymen'.[131] Once casualties had been incurred on a scale unparalleled in human history it was impossible to stop or the sacrifice would have been in vain. Defeat became unthinkable and had to be avoided at whatever future cost.

Space permits only a few examples to illustrate this vast area of incompetence. It must not be thought that the butchers were confined to a particular class of First World War generals only. Dixon notes such phrases as 'stupid, obstinate blimps', 'butchers', 'ossified brains' and 'donkeys' as applied to the 1914–18 generals and says himself that

Only the most blinkered could deny that the First World War exemplified every aspect of high-level military incompetence. For sheer lack of imaginative leadership, inept decisions, ignoring of military intelligence, underestimation of the enemy, delusional optimism and monumental wastage of human resources it has surely never had its equal.[132]

Quantitively Dixon is undoubtedly right but whether this is a result of warfare being fought on an unprecedented scale or because the generals were unusually poor is a moot point. The incompetent general commanding 100,000 men has a capacity for mischief far greater than he who commands an army of 10,000, though their faults may be the same. Where attrition was not pursued as a deliberate policy, as it had been at Verdun in 1916, human wastage was the result of the kind of stresses which could afflict the able general as well as the 'stupid, obstinate blimps'. As we have seen, though the degree of failure and its frequency is less in the cases of Ulysses Grant, Robert E. Lee or Frederick the Great, that does not mean to say that these commanders did not occasionally 'butcher' their men, nor that they should be absolved from the epithet 'incompetent' that is more frequently applied to Ambrose Burnside, Gregorio Garcia de la Cuesta or Redvers Buller.

During the Seven Years War Frederick the Great of Prussia achieved prodigies against the united powers of Austria, France and Russia, all countries with far greater populations and resources than his own. Nevertheless, in spite of a string of victories, Frederick suffered at Kolin on 18 June 1757, a stunning defeat at the hands of the Austrian Marshal Daun. For once his generalship seemed to be at fault and, in Christopher Duffy's words,

Kolin was, for the Prussian army, what the charge of the light brigade represented for the British in the nineteenth century.[133]

Although Frederick acknowledged the strength of the position that Marshal Daun had taken up, he made the elementary mistake of underestimating the qualities of his opponent. With his 35,000 men outnumbered by Daun's 53,000 he was under no necessity to seek battle.

In the words of a contemporary witness, 'The cause of our misfortune is chiefly owing to the great success the king of Prussia's arms have had in eight successive battles against the Austrians . . .'[134]

In spite of attempts by Prince Moritz of Anhalt-Dessau to disobey Frederick's orders for a frontal assault on a ridge held by the Austrians with 16 heavy cannons, the king overruled him and ordered the nine battalions of Moritz's infantry to advance up the Krzeczhorz Hill. The result was a massacre with the Prussian infantry 'climbing over heaps of their own dead and wounded' and the Austrian cannon cutting swathes through their well-ordered ranks. In all nearly 65% of the Prussian infantry became casualties. What had originally been planned as a flank attack, which is what Moritz had tried to carry out, Frederick had deliberately transformed into a bloody frontal assault against well-entrenched Austrian troops who outnumbered him heavily. The change of plan had been Frederick's but it was his brave soldiers who paid the price.

The two outstanding commanders of the American Civil War, Ulysses Grant and Robert E. Lee, were both guilty of wasting manpower on occasions. Although Lee had tended to 'shepherd' his troops in earlier battles, at Gettysburg he launched a frontal assault on Cemetery Ridge and suffered enormous casualties. Lee later accepted blame for the terrible casualties. As he said, 'I thought my men were invincible'.[135]

During 1864 the war had settled into an attritional struggle around Richmond. At Cold Harbour Grant's patience was exhausted. In the words of Fletcher Pratt,

The ceaseless vigilance, the strain of daily battles, was beginning to tell at Union headquarters, everyone's nerves were frayed. Grant gruffed at the adjutants; Meade took a perverse pleasure in making his staff uncomfortable, colonels hardly dared to speak to him, his voice 'sounded like cutting an iron bar with a hacksaw'. . . . As the result of some snarling exchange Grant swore that he would break through by main strength and ordered a general frontal assault for daybreak on June 3 – the only thing he ever regretted in his military career.[136]

The attack lasted just ten minutes and in that time the Federalists suffered 7000 casualties. If ever a battle had been planned in a fit of pique it was probably this one and Grant regretted it bitterly. The day after Colonel Upton, who had taken part, wrote to his sister

I am disgusted with the generalship displayed. Our men have, in many instances, been foolishly and wantonly sacrificed. Assault after assault has been ordered upon the enemy intrenchments, when they knew nothing about the strength or position of the enemy. Thousands of lives might have been spared by the exercise of a little skill . . .[137]

Great commanders make mistakes but they learn from them. Both Lee and Grant blamed themselves for the human waste involved in their attacks. However, it would never have occurred to a man like Major-General A.G. Hunter-Weston, commander of the British 29th Division at Gallipoli, that casualties had anything to do with him. On one occasion he said, 'Casulates, what do I care for casualties?' and just before landing his troops at Gallipoli he told them to expect 'heavy losses by bullets, by shells, by mines and by drowning'.[138] This was hardly the way to raise morale. After one bloody assault Hunter-Weston told the Brigade-Major of the 156th Scottish Brigade, which had just lost 1353 men, that he was glad to have 'blooded the pups'.[139] To John Laffin, Hunter-Weston was 'The Butcher of Helles'.[140] His frequent frontal assaults led nowhere for they had no fixed objectives. While he commanded at Helles the equivalent of three divisions were lost in attempting Achi Baba and Krithia, without a single worthwhile gain. He was for some reason averse to attacking at dusk, night or before dawn, and instead marched forward in broad daylight, so maximising his casualties.

In British military history 1 July 1916 stands out as the blackest day. By nightfall the British Army had suffered 57,470 casualties – an unprecedented figure – and yet it had not been a defeat.[141] No fewer than 12 of the divisions that took part in the Battle of the Somme suffered over 3000 casualties each.[142] So heavily did the 1st Hampshires suffer that there was no one left at the end of the day to describe what had happened to the battalion. Statistics, of course, tell nothing of the human suffering, and the more they are cited, the further we get away from the essential fact that men should have been treated as a scarce commodity to be exchanged in a miserly fashion and only for worthwhile gain. For 57,470 casualties the gain should have been enormous to balance the equation, yet it was minimal. Mistakes had been made but the greatest mistake of all was in being prepared to lose so many troops to gain such a small reward.

John Keegan describes the plan of attack.

The Fourth Army's eleven front-line divisions, of which six had not previously been in battle, were, on the cessation of the artillery preparation, and following behind its barrage fire, to leave their trenches and walk forward, on a front of about fifteen miles, for a mile and a half. In the centre of the front, a walk of a little less than that distance would give them possession of the German second line of entrenchments; on the northern sector, the walk to the German second position was a good two miles . . . the manoeuvre was to be done slowly and deliberately, for the men were to be laden with about sixty pounds of equipment. . . .[143]

As a preparation for the assault one and a half million shells were fired into the German positions during the previous week. This was an impressive total, yet of the 12,000 tons of shells fired only 900 tons were high-explosive. As a result the concussion on the German defenders was relatively trifling. As John Keegan points out, this meant that each ten square yards of front received only a pound of high explosive, or a square mile thirty tons. During World War Two Allied bombers dropped 800 tons of high explosive on each square mile of German positions in Normandy and yet most German defenders survived. Today NATO might use a tactical nuclear device on an area like the Somme front and yet some defenders would still survive.[144] The fact was that the German defenders in 1916 had not been wiped out and the whole assault was therefore based on a fallacy. Hunter-Weston, now promoted to Lieutenant-General and commanding VIII Corps, had told his men that all the wire had been blown away, even though they could see it standing intact, and that there would be no German trenches because they had all been destroyed.[145] When the defenders came to the surface and set up their machine-guns they found the British troops exposed in No-Man's Land. Within seconds of leaving their trenches British soldiers were being literally mown down by German machine guns. The 10th West Yorks were 'practically annihilated' in less than a minute. Those who did reach the German lines found that in many places the barbed wire had not been cut by the bombardment. Several battalions of the 29th Division were caught like this and machine-gunned as they tried to find a way through the wire.[146] Of the casualties, including 21,000 men killed, most were suffered in the first thirty minutes of the attack.

The disparity of casualties between Germans and British made the first day a total failure in terms of human wastage. Keegan shows that the German 180th Regiment lost 280 out of 3000 men on 1 July, while the British lost 5121 out of the 12,000 men attacking it.[147] With such an imbalance one is forced to use phrases like 'incompetence' and 'butchery'. Why did the High Command continue to thrust more and more troops forward into the killing fields? John Keegan suggests an answer:

... but the majority of battalions scheduled to attack did so, no matter what happened to those which had preceded them. There are a number of ways of explaining why this should have been so. Normal military sense of commitment to a plan was one reason, the spirit of contemporary generalship, schooled to believe in the inevitability of heavy casualties, another . . . . But most important of all was the simple ignorance of what was happening which prevailed almost everywhere on the British side of no-man's-land throughout most of the day.[148]

— 2 —
The Planners

In the foregoing chapter I examined the various ways in which incompetence revealed itself in the behaviour of individual commanders. Most of the faults were the product of personality defects which affected the tactical deployment of the forces they commanded. However, it is far too simple to see incompetence as purely an individual thing, the failure of a man promoted beyond his competence, or weakening under the stress of command. In most examples he merely represents the final stage in a planning process which may involve dozens of others, all equally likely to suffer from stress, ill-health, old age or timidity. It is therefore to the planners that I now turn.

Norman Dixon, drawing on the work of I.L. Janis, illustrates the factors which comprise 'group-think' and which may contribute to military incompetence.

Far from diminishing the chances of ineptitude, the group actually accentuates the effects of those very traits which may lead to incompetence in individual commanders. The symptoms of this process, which Janis terms 'group-think', include:

1. An illusion of invulnerability that becomes shared by most members of the group.
2. Collective attempts to ignore or rationalize away items of information which might otherwise lead the group to reconsider shaky but cherished assumptions.
3. An unquestioned belief in the group's inherent morality, thus enabling members to overlook the ethical consequences of their decision.
4. Stereotyping the enemy as either too evil for negotiation or too stupid or feeble to be a threat.[1]

In a militaristic society or indeed in a society during wartime, the group of planners represents an elite whose aim is to preserve the status quo. Dixon explains it thus:

We see it, in the case of the older European powers, as the natural product of a fundamentally jealous, class-conscious hierarchy whose nostalgia and basic conservatism ensure that the present must always bear the hallmark of the past.[2]

The conservatism that Dixon refers to often results in resistance to new ideas, technology and weapons. It has led to troops being supplied with inappropriate uniforms, weapons, transport and training. It has caused the condition of troops to be neglected with a consequent erosion of morale. It has resulted in the under-estimation of enemies through ethnocentrism and over-confidence as well as the over-estimation of enemy strength which has led to paralysis of military resistance. Through bad planning, the rejection of unpalatable information, obstinate persistence in the face of contrary evidence, the inappropriate choice of officers and the selection of unrealistic tasks, it had saddled the field commander with problems as great as those posed by the enemy.

The problems facing military planners have become far more complex in the twentieth century owing to the pace of technological change. The development of tanks and motor transport, of machine guns and automatic weapons, of submarines and aircraft carriers, or aircraft which can bomb cities, of rockets, radio and radar, has required an adaptability on the part of planners which is unprecedented. As D.C. Watt comments,

The effectiveness of national armed forces in the defence of their respective states and in the pursuit of the respective governments' political objectives depends on the degree to which the commanders and advisers can adapt and refine the manner in which they conduct war and the view of warfare which inspires the arming and training of their troops, to the changing technologies and circumstances of war.[3]

A state whose military planners make too little adaptation to the changing techniques of warfare will suffer the sort of defeat inflicted by Napoleon on the Prussians at Jena-Auerstadt in 1806. The Prussians, tied to the system which Frederick the Great had made so successful, suffered from a rigidity of tactics which the Napoleonic system found easy to overcome. On the other hand, a state whose planners indulge in too rapid experimentation may suffer from reaching a technological peak which other states, starting later and avoiding the early errors, soon overtake. The lauching of the *Dreadnought* in 1906 made every other warship obsolete. However, this affected Britain, which had the largest navy, more than any other state. It enabled Germany to threaten Britain's naval supremacy by building her own Dreadnought battleships. Although Britain, through a massive shipbuilding effort, managed to stay ahead in numbers, in quality the Germans undoubtedly had the edge, as they were to show at Jutland. D.C. Watt cites the example of the Italian air force.

In 1934 the Italian Air Force was the most advanced in the world. Marshal Balbo's bombing planes could outstrip the fighter aircraft of every air force. But in 1940 much of the Italian Air Force was obsolete.[4]

Perhaps the greatest problem which faces the military planners is to gain information from their political masters about the kind of war for which they should be preparing. Which states are likely to prove enemies and which allies? Do the politicians expect to be attacked or do they themselves wish to attack? Are they expecting a localised encounter or are they intending 'total war'? These and many similar questions need to be answered if the planners are to produce an appropriate military response to any given political imperative. However, whereas through much of history, political and military power has rested in the same hands, in the twentieth century the gap has sometimes been so wide that the military planners have been unable to operate effectively. The Suez operation of 1956 was an outstanding example of the breakdown that can occur between political and military authorities. The resultant fiasco owed much to the British Government's failure to define both the kind of war it wished to conduct and appropriate military targets in terms of its political aims.

CLINGING TO TRADITION

The British Admiralty has frequently been criticised for its resistance to new ideas and technology. David Divine quotes a memorandum by Lord Melville, the First Lord of the Admiralty, in 1828.

Their Lordships felt it their bounden duty to discourage to the utmost of their ability the use of steam vessels, as they considered that the introduction of steam was calculated to strike a fatal blow at the naval supremacy of the Empire.[5]

They clearly refused to entertain the possibility that steam power would be introduced by a rival navy, which would then inevitably challenge the supremacy of the Empire. According to Divine,

Of the twenty major technological developments which lie between the first marine engine and the Polaris submarine the Admiralty machine has discouraged, delayed, obstructed, or positively rejected seventeen. The eventual and necessary incorporation of these developments in the structure of modernisation has been achieved by individual and sometimes undisciplined officers, by political and industrial pressures, or – and most frequently – by their successful adoption in rival navies.[6]

For a nation whose very survival has frequently depended on the strength and effectiveness of her navy, Britain has repeatedly suffered in one vital area: naval gunnery. During the long years of peace that followed Trafalgar the Navy was rarely required to do more than patrol the seaways of the world, showing Britain's flag and upholding her prestige. It meant more, outside European waters, that the ships were smart and brightly painted than they were efficient fighting machines; that much was taken for granted. Gunnery practice, according to Marder, had become 'the Cinderella of all drills'.[7] If it was not convenient to fire all the practice shells they were usually thrown overboard. In fact, gunnery practice was actively discouraged by some captains in case the smoke dirtied the paintwork of the ship, or interfered with other social functions. Admiral Dewar recalled of HMS *Alexandra*:

. . . during the twelve-year stay of this ship in the Mediterranean the water-tight doors had been so worn away by constant polishing that they were no longer of use for the purpose for which they were intended. . . To enable all this bright-work to remain unsullied by rust all kinds of queer devices were resorted to. The captains of guns made large nightcaps of flannel to fit on the chases of their guns. . .[8]

The smartness of a ship enhanced promotion prospects for its commander and Marder reports that one admiral is said to have spent £2000 of his own money on paint and on beautifying his ship in order to earn his promotion.[9] Percy Scott describes the gunnery practice of the Mediterranean Fleet in 1896:

The quarter's allowance of ammunition had to be expended somehow, and the custom throughout the Navy was to make a signal, 'Spread for target practice – expend a quarter's ammunition, and rejoin my flag at such and such a time'. The ships of the Fleet radiated in all directions and got rid of their ammunition as quickly as possible. How the ammunition was expended did not matter.[10]

The Admiralty had no conception of the way in which technology was altering the nature of war at sea. One of the reasons why gunnery was considered so unimportant was the belief that encounters would take place at close range, certainly no more than 1000–1300 yards. Moreover, the idea was that after the bombardment the ships would close on each other and boarding would take place as in Nelson's time. When Sir John Commerell, soon to become Admiral of the Fleet, inspected the cruiser HMS *Northampton* he saw an officer not carrying a sword. When asked why the officer replied that he was the Chief Engineer and that there was not enough room for a sword in the engine room. 'What do you mean?' demanded Sir John, 'If the enemy has the good fortune to overpower us all on deck, how will you kill him when he comes down here if you have no sword?'[11] In fact, with guns now able to fire over 10,000 yards all this was ridiculously antiquated. The advent of the torpedo and the mine made fighting at close quarters dangerous folly. The French and Italian navies were making particularly good progress in the quality of their gunnery but the British lagged badly behind. In the bombardment of the

Alexandrian forts in 1882 eight British battleships fired more than 3000 rounds and secured a total of 10 hits, destroying a mere 30 out of 293 enemy guns.[12]

During the First World War the supremacy of the British fleet was consistently undermined by the deplorable gunnery of its main units. At the battle of the Dogger Bank, the first occasion on which Dreadnought capital ships clashed, the performance of Admiral Beatty's battlecruisers, nicknamed his 'splendid cats', was anything but splendid. In all, Beatty's five battlecruisers fired 1150 shells at Hipper's four battlecruisers, scoring a total of 6 hits or 0.5%. The hits scored on the *Blucher* must be disregarded as most of these were achieved at close range and after the rest of the German force had fled. The newest of the 'cats', HMS *Tiger*, performed particularly badly considering that she was the only ship fitted with director firing, scoring just one hit out of 355 heavy shells fired.[13]

The German gunners had done far better, even though Hipper's squadron had been outnumbered by the British and had been more concerned to escape than to fight. Excluding the doomed *Blucher*, the German battlecruisers fired 976 rounds and scored 22 hits or 2.1%. For Jellicoe, Commander-in-Chief of the Grand Fleet, these statistics confirmed his suspicion that Beatty's Battle Cruiser Squadron needed more practice. Hough points out that Beatty's ships had never practised at the sort of ranges common at the Dogger Bank encounter.

The bombardment of the Turkish forts at the Dardanelles in February 1915 showed the poor quality of many British gunnery officers. The British battleships were supplied with a seaplane spotter from HMS *Ark Royal*, Lieutenant Hugh Williamson. Unfortunately the battleship Williamson was spotting for, HMS *Cornwallis*, shot so badly that she was ordered to cease firing by Admiral Carden. Williamson was able to report, much to the Navy's chagrin, that during the morning bombardment not a single hit had been achieved.[14] The gunnery officers salved their wounded pride by blaming the airmen for misleading them. One view was that the naval men were accustomed to shooting at floating targets and could not adjust to stationary ones!

In the main fleet encounter at Jutland in 1916 British gunnery again proved poor. The British Grand Fleet mounted 48 15-inch guns, 110 13.5-inch and 104 12-inch, against the German High Seas Fleet with 176 12-inch and 24 11-inch. In both number and calibre of guns the British superiority was obvious. However, again the shooting of Beatty's battlecruisers was ineffectual, scoring just 26 hits out of 1650 shells fired. Jellicoe's battleships did rather better, achieving 98 hits from 2626 rounds.[15] However, though the Germans achieved rather less hits than the British, they succeeded in sinking three British battlecruisers, which raised two other important issues for the Admiralty: the quality of British armour-piercing shells in comparison with German ones, and the capacity of British ships to absorb punishment.

It might be thought that, with these examples before it, the Admiralty would have ensured that the gunnery of its major units had improved by the outbreak of the Second World War. Far from it. During the final stages of the pursuit of the German battleship *Bismarck*, the British battleships *Rodney* and *King George V* were able to close to almost point-blank range against a burning hulk. Even so the British shooting was dreadful. The two ships fired a total of 719 heavy shells at a helpless target and yet only a small proportion scored hits. Admiral Tovey was so exasperated that he told his fleet gunnery officer that he would have a better chance if he threw his binoculars at the *Bismarck*.[16]

Lest it be thought that the Admiralty was alone in resisting change, an example from the War Office should redress the balance. The story of the machine-gun illustrates just how unwilling the War Office was to adapt to the latest technology.

The French development of the *mitrailleuse* prior to 1870 attracted interest in Britain. A committee in 1871 concluded that the machine offered two advantages: firstly, it replaced manpower with machines and, secondly, it produced decisive defensive firepower.[17] Nevertheless, Britain did not adopt machine-guns on a large scale for another 45 years, and in 1914 the BEF went to France deficient in them. Many arguments were used against them: they were expensive, technically complex, heavy to move, used too much ammunition and were too defensive in an offensive-minded age. Sir John Adye, Director of Artillery, felt that the machine-gun had such limited powers and would be employed in such exceptional cases that it would simply be an encumbrance.[18]

During the Boer War, generals like Methuen, Gatacre, Warren and Buller, committed to frontal assaults with bayonets against entrenched opponents, failed to make effective use of machine-guns. In the Russo-Japanese War of 1904–5, Japan had triumphed through offensive tactics, manifested in frontal assaults pursued '*à outrance*'. The wasteful tactics of Nogi at Port Arthur were more influential than the lessons of the Boer War, in which defensive firepower had proved more effective. By 1914 the official War Office manual 'Infantry Training' stated that large numbers of machine-guns could not be permanently employed as they would destroy the army's mobility. Moreover, they should only ever be fired at critical moments in case they destroyed the 'advantage of surprise'. In 1914 Major General Altham declared that the 'Manchurian campaign has wiped out the mistaken inference from South African experiences that bayonet fighting belonged to the past . . .'[19]

As Director of Staff Duties in 1909 Sir Douglas Haig compiled the 'Field Service Regulations' in which he declared: 'Decisive success in battle can be gained only by a vigorous offensive' and 'Success in war depends more on moral than on physical qualities. Skill cannot compensate for want of courage, energy and determination.'[20] The British General Staff held firmly to a belief in the offensive, feeling that defensive warfare encouraged a defensive spirit, passivity and a decline in morale. However, not everyone felt like that, nor did everyone feel that superiority in manpower was essential to success in war. In April 1914 Captain J.F.C. Fuller wrote an article on 'The Tactics of Penetration', in which he postulated a penetration based on superior firepower, including the use of the machine-gun. However, as on so many matters, Fuller's was a lone voice.

During 1915, while battle raged on the Western Front and the machine-gun proved itself a valuable weapon, a dispute took place between supporters of the gun such as the Chief of the Imperial General Staff Sir Archibald Murray and its opponents, including Adjutant-General Sclater. Murray wanted far more men trained to use the machine-gun, pointing to the farcical situation that had been reached on 1 February 1915 when 890 machine-guns were idle in France for lack of men to operate them.[21] Even as late as November 1915, after the machine gun had slaughtered British troops at Loos, Sclater was still 'dragging his feet' in endeavouring to find 5000 men to train as machine-gun operators. It did not help that the British Commander-in-Chief, Sir Douglas Haig, had commented, in answer to a War Office Questionnaire, 'The machine-gun is a much overrated weapon, two per battalion is more than sufficient'. Kitchener cautiously increased that number to four. However, when Lloyd George became Minister for Munitions, he intervened to increase it to 64.[22] It was no more than was needed.

Such thinking dominated the British approach to the machine-gun in the period up to 1914. In the previous decade the War Office had ordered just eleven guns per year from Vickers and only Russian orders made it viable for the manufacturer to continue to produce them. However, when fighting broke out in August 1914, the War Office immediately panicked and began to order guns in an incoherent and feverish way. On 11 August 192 machine-guns were ordered, on 10 September 100, on 30 September 1000, and on 7 October a further 500.[23] Vickers were unprepared and were unable to meet the deadlines, producing just 1002 of the 1792. The fault lay not with Vickers but with the War Office, which had given the manufacturers no reason to expect such a demand. Once again a military revolution had been resisted by conservatives and both the nation and her manpower had suffered.

Resistance to new ideas The inter-war period saw a prolonged clash in British military circles between the supporters of the tank and its opponents, many of whom may be said to have possessed 'the cavalry mind'. The latter, clinging to the traditional role of the horse in warfare, had a baneful effect on the mechanization of British military forces prior to 1939.

In 1925, Field Marshal Earl Haig felt justified in challenging the thesis of Basil Liddell Hart's book, *Paris, Or the Future of War*. In this extract he states the outlook of 'the cavalry mind' very clearly:

Some enthusiasts today talk about the probability of the horse becoming extinct and prophesy that the aeroplane, the tank, and the motor-car will supersede the horse in future wars. I believe that the value of the horse and the opportunity for the horse in the future are likely to be as great as ever. . . I am all for using aeroplanes and tanks, but they are only accessories to the man and his horse . . .[24]

In 1919 the War Office in Britain faced the task of evaluating the lessons to be drawn from the four years of fighting. There was little to be learned from the static, attritional battles of 1915–17 except the obvious fact that no one could win a war like that. Equally obviously the two most important new weapons, the aeroplane and the tank, could bring a new mobility to warfare and banish the horrors of Verdun, the Somme and Passchendaele. However, the tank of 1919 was a flawed tool which needed development. It had shown what could be done if sufficient funds were available and if tacticians could devise ways of using it effectively. But the end of a long and expensive war is not the best time for the military to burden the population with taxation for research. And so, in the cutbacks of 1922, the size of the British Army was reduced to 126 infantry battalions, 20 cavalry regiments and just 6 tank battalions.[25]

The preference for horse over tank was clear yet it was based on entirely faulty conclusions. Even in 1914 the cavalryman had been obsolete and this process had been operating from at least as far back as the Franco-Prussian War. With the tremendous improvement in firepower, with machine guns, with infantry rifles able to fire fifteen times a minute and at a range of two miles, the cavalryman was too large a target. As a concentrated mass regiments of cavalry were particulary vulnerable to artillery fire. Nor was this the only factor, for in 'total war' it was vital that every part of a nation's armed forces should justify the cost in money and in man-hours expended on it. Cavalry were not cost-effective. In 1914

Russia's obsession with cavalry had imposed an enormous strain on her railway system, by requiring a quite disproportionate amount of rolling stock. Forty trains had been needed to move a cavalry division of 4000 men and 12 guns, whereas the same number of trains could move 16,000 infantry with 54 guns.[26] Moreover, a horse needed 12 pounds of grain every day and the transport of fodder tied up much of the railway system. Even the more modest British cavalry in France used more tonnage to ship their horses and fodder than was sunk by German submarines.[27]

The role of the British cavalry between 1914 and 1918 had been to wait for the infantry to break through the enemy's line so that they could pursue him to destruction. Two distinct problems faced them. In the first place there were no permanent breakthroughs and secondly the terrain was frequently impassable to horses. The idea grew therefore that the cavalry could co-operate with the newly developed tank. At Cambrai in 1917 the idea was put to the test – and failed. Some three hundred tanks duly broke through the German defences, while five cavalry divisions awaited their chance 'to exploit the gap'. Even though the tanks managed to advance four miles it was impossible for the horses to penetrate the broken terrain, the barbed-wire fences and the still-active machine-gun positions. A further year passed before the experiment was tried again on a grand scale. At Amiens, on 8 August 1918, the entire Cavalry Corps was assembled to break through the eleven mile gap forced by 604 British tanks. Its achievement was minimal and, in David Divine's words, 'ludicrously disproportionate to its four-year demands upon the national war resources'.[28]

The success of the cavalry in Allenby's Palestine campaign was a dangerous piece of evidence from which to generalise. Desert warfare had always suited mounted troops and the terrain in Palestine allowed a mobility quite impossible in Europe. It seemed a small accomplishment on which to base the survival of the cavalry for a further twenty years 'in a splendid obsolescence'.[29] Dixon explains why the horse continued to hold its place in the military scheme of things long after it had lost its traditional preeminence:

Upon reflection, it is hardly surprising that the horse became the *sine qua non* of the military life. For a thousand years man had found in it enormous advantages. There was nothing better for transportation and load-hauling. Horses raised morale and enhanced egos. Horses took the weight off feet and enabled people to go to war sitting down. When they lay down you could hide behind them. When it was cold you could borrow their warmth and when they died you could eat them!

Because of the traditionally rural origins of so many Army officers and military families, horsemanship in the context of sports like hunting became one of their preferred leisure activities. Since such sports as polo, pig-sticking and, in an earlier age, jousting not only act out symbolic aspects of real warfare but are also associated with a higher social class, there is little wonder that they should find so much favour with those who chose the Army as a career. All in all, it is not surprising that the cavalry became the branch of the Army with the highest status. Nor is it surprising that they should have become the most vehement in denunciation of the tank, which was seen as an 'intrusive junior rather than an heir apparent'.[30]

Although tanks had contributed in no small way to Haig's break-throughs on the western front in 1918, and although Fuller's 'Plan 1919' envisaged an even more central role for tanks in achieving deep penetration, tank production was ended immediately after the armistice.

The flood of new ideas which the war produced did not please everyone. Any flood threatens to wash away things that have stood for many years and ideas can be especially destructive of tradition. The Chief of the Imperial General Staff, Sir Henry Wilson, was determined to resist any such threat and the military establishment took its lead from him. Captain Basil Liddell Hart, one of the most progressive military thinkers of the century and an expert on the strategical and tactical use of tanks, became a particular target for the hostility of the military establishment. In the 1922 Military Essay Competition, Liddell Hart's essay was rejected by the judges, though it was later published in the *Army Quarterly*, from which it was translated into German and became a basic text for the German General Staff. Significantly, the winning essay was on the subject of the limitations of the tank.

The fate of Major-General Fuller was no less unfortunate for the military future of Britain. Fuller's writings on mechanized warfare were severely criticized by the General Staff. When Lord Caval expressed the view that officers should not write books, the echoes of Lord Cardigan can be heard. Dixon points out that his successor as C.I.G.S., Field-Marshal Montgomery-Massingberd, criticized Fuller's books even though he had not read them. He feared they would make him too angry if he did. In the face of such entrenched opposition Liddell Hart commented,

If a soldier advocates any new idea of real importance he builds up such a wall of obstruction – compounded of resentment, suspicion and inertia – that the idea only succeeds at the sacrifice of himself: as the wall finally yields to the pressure of the new idea it falls and crushes him.[31]

By 1929 obstructionism had prevented the development of Fuller's experimental armoured force: in that year Britain's military priorities are clearly reflected in Army expenditure on petrol for tanks and motor vehicles at £72,000, and fodder for horses at £607,000.[32] General

Edmonds commented to Liddell Hart, 'Any tank which shows its nose will in my opinion be knocked out – the wars you and Fuller imagine are past'.[33] In 1936 the poverty of War Office thinking was strikingly demonstrated when the new Master-General of the Ordnance, General Sir Hugh Elles, who had been the first great tank commander of the First World War, said that he had changed his mind about tanks: he now thought that they might be of some use though they would obviously occupy a secondary position to what they had done in the past.[34]

The rise to power of Hitler in Germany forced the War Office to review the tank question and to invite Vickers to supply designs for a new medium tank. Through the work of Sir John Carden, Vickers were able to produce two variants on the same design, the A9 light tank and the A10 heavy tank. However, the War Office was dissatisfied and declared that the A10 lacked sufficient protection for an infantry tank, though by what standards they judged it is difficult to be sure, for the General Staff had not yet agreed on the tactical employment of tanks. The year was 1936, two years from Munich, and Britain possessed just 209 light tanks and 166 medium tanks, all totally obsolete.[35]

The appointment of Hore-Belisha to 'create a small but highly-trained Army' armed with the best modern equipment saw the beginning of reconstruction within the War Office. However, in spite of the advice of Liddell Hart and the work of Gort as C.I.G.S., it had all started too late. The War Office had no clear policy on the sort of tank needed for the British Army, whether the cruiser tank or the infantry tank. The Germans had stolen so many marches on the pedestrian British military planners that when the time came it was to be Guderian and Rommel, the true 'heirs' to the British tank experts, who were to demonstrate the art of armoured warfare.

In 1939 the first contingent of the B.E.F. was sent to France with just one under-strength tank brigade, consisting of only two battalions, one equipped wholly with Mark 1 infantry tanks, and the other half with Mark 1 tanks and half with Matildas. Both tanks were heavily armoured though slow-moving vehicles and both were severely under-armed: the Mark 1 had just a machine-gun and the Matilda a 2-pounder gun which was unable to fire high explosive shell.[36] The rest of the only British armoured division arrived, in an incomplete state, in time to be shattered along with the French on the Somme. The division had arrived in France without its normal infantry and artillery components and in its two brigades two-thirds of the tanks were light ones armed only with machine guns.

David Divine summarises the effects of War Office conservatism:

It is at least necessary to point out that Britain – though not the War Office – had invented the tank and Britain – though not the War Office – had invented the tank strategy that presently and brutally swept the British Expeditionary Force out of France and broke the power of France for a quarter of a century.[37]

INTELLIGENCE FAILURES

A strategy based on an unrealistic appreciation of one's own military strength and an under-estimation of that of the enemy is fraught with danger. In October 1940 Mussolini launched an invasion of Greece against the wishes of some of his senior generals, against the advice of his main ally, Hitler, and in the face of military intelligence reports that Greek resistance might be stronger than expected. Why he did this has little to do with military reality and stems more from his jealousy of the German dictator. Mussolini had responded angrily on hearing of Hitler's occupation of Rumania. 'Hitler always faces me with a *fait accompli*. This time I am going to pay him back in his own coin. He will find out from the papers that I have occupied Greece.'[38] Surrounded as he was by sycophants, there were few men honest enough to tell him how mistaken he was. In Mario Cervi's words, Italian military policy was based on 'improvisation and pique', rather than the appraisal of experts.[39] Mussolini claimed that he had long been thinking about the invasion of Greece and that long-term planning had gone into it. Cervi comments wryly, 'the long preparation for the war dated back to a moment of pique forty-eight hours previously'.[40]

When Mussolini asked his military advisers about the state of mind of the Greek population the Foreign Secretary, Ciano, replied, as he knew he must, that it was 'indifferent to everything, including the prospect of our invasion'.[41] Mussolini was thus reassured. Visconti Prasca, commander of the Greek operation, now gave the Duce an account of the Italian invasion force.

The theatre of operations will enable us to carry out a series of rounding-up operations against the Greek forces – estimated to number about 30,000 men – which will enable us to occupy Epirus in a short time, ten or fifteen days. This operation – which might allow us to liquidate all the Greek troops – has been prepared down to the most minute details and is as perfect as is humanly possible. . .[42]

Prasca estimated that in the invasion area of Epirus the Italian superiority in manpower would be 2 to 1, and added that the Greeks 'were not people who liked fighting'. Mussolini was swept along by Prasca's enthusiasm and told him that he should not try to limit his casualties. Prasca certainly had no intention of doing that, for he had ordered his battalions to attack continously even if they faced divisions.

In Athens, the Italian Minister to Greece, Emmanuele Grazzi, could hardly believe what was happening. He had reported to Rome the strength of the Metaxas regime in Greece and that Greek military preparations meant that they would sternly resist an Italian invasion. How this justified men like Ciano in speaking of 'the indifference of the Greek people to all events that might take place, including an invasion by us', is difficult to understand. What is clear is that the plan for the campaign was based largely on erroneous information, from whatever source, that there were substantial anti-British and anti-Metaxas politicians in Greece who would welcome an Italian invasion. It is true that some Greek politicians were being bribed by the Italians but these hardly comprised a force capable of disrupting Greek resistance.

The Greek campaign stemmed entirely from the fact that Mussolini had drawn a wrong picture of the military situation. When an intelligence report dared to suggest that Greek resistance might prove tenacious it was disregarded because it did not conform with the Duce's thoughts.[43] It was to be war by preconception.

The Duce felt that an Italian invasion of Greece would be welcomed by many dissident groups inside the country and that resistance by the Greek army would be short-lived. In both these expectations he was to be disappointed. The over-estimation of Italian strength was proclaimed in Prasca's statement that his attack on Epirus 'has been prepared down to the most minute details and is as perfect as is humanly possible'. The facts cannot bear this out. The Italian army was in many ways no more modern than the Greek and was deficient in tanks, armoured cars, artillery and motor transport. In fact each division of ten thousand men had just 24 lorries and no worthwhile anti-aircraft defence. In order to increase the number of divisions on paper, each had been reduced to two brigades rather than three as in the Greek Army. Moreover, a third of all Italian divisional strength consisted of Blackshirt battalions, poorly trained, poorly armed and by no means the equal of regular soldiers. Where Colonel Amioni had predicted that 1750 lorries would be needed to launch the attack, there were only 107 available. Italian tank crews were frequently forced to fight on foot because their tanks were only designed for good weather and were useless in the muddy conditions.[44] Even so Visconti Prasca still insisted that his plans for the attack on Epirus were a model of precision.

In spite of the fact that Italy controlled the skies with her 400 antiquated and inefficient aeroplanes, no attempt was made by the Italians to support their invasion with heavy air attacks on Greek positions. In view of the speed with which Mussolini was forcing the pace both Italians and Greeks responded slowly. Of the 15 Greek divisions, 12 of them only recieved call-up papers after the invasion had started. Such laxity would have been severely punished by a more able enemy. However, Prasca moved even more slowly than the Greeks. In the first two days the southern prong of the invasion force advanced just six miles, while in the north they did not advance at all. This enabled the Greek commander, Papagos, to organize strong resistance. To Mussolini's surprise the much maligned Greeks fought with a determination which showed that the planning of the Italian High Command had been quite unrealistic. Far from the preparation being 'perfect' it soon became apparent that it was a shambles.

As soon as any means of transport was available, whether warship, merchant ship or aircraft, men were put on board, often piecemeal, and off it went. Heavy arms, radio transmitters, field kitchens, blankets, baggage, medical equipment, ammunition, transport animals and vehicles, however, followed as soon as possible by the appropriate means of transport. Consequently, when the men landed, they had only their light arms and personal equipment and ammunition.[45]

Greek victories now showed Mussolini the emptiness of Prasca's boastings and he was replaced by General Ubaldo Soddu. Unfortunately, Soddu's main interest lay in composing film music,[46] to which he devoted his attention while in Greece, and had to be removed on grounds of ill-health, with the command then going to Cavallero.

Just as the war in Greece was to be a testing-ground for the Italian army so it was also to be for Mussolini's ministers and party leaders. These the Duce sent to Greece as 'volunteers' to inspire the soldiers with Fascist qualities of 'toughness'. The ministers were put into senior military commands for which they were totally unfitted, while the work of the civilian departments slowed down or stopped altogether. There were even cases of official documents being sent under fire into the Albanian mountains to be signed by a minister.[47] The politicians, meanwhile, kept as far from the fighting as they could while those in the air force spent their time bombing Corfu, which had no anti-aircraft defences. Each time an important party official took off it was necessary for a 'guard' of Italian aircraft to accompany him on his mission.[48]

Rejection of unpalatable information Commanders and military planners need to be able to penetrate the 'fog of war'. In Norman Dixon's words,

Acquiring knowledge involves the reduction of ignorance through the acquisition of facts, but ignorance is rarely absolute and its reduction rarely total. Hence reducing ignorance can be regarded as reducing uncertainty about a given state of affairs. It follows that an unlikely or unexpected fact contains more information (i.e. reduces more uncertainty) than one which is already expected. But an unexpected fact is less readily absorbed than one which was expected.[49]

For the commander or planner the quantity of information that any fact contains must not exceed the individual's capacity to absorb it. A mind unclouded by other information may have a great capacity to absorb, subject of course to intellectual capacity. However, the military commander is rarely fortunate enough to receive new information when his mind is clear and untroubled by conflicting demands on his attention. Moreover, if he is already satisfied that he has all the information he requires on which to base his decisions then startling new information will be regarded as unwelcome and therefore unreliable. It is then that unpalatable information is ignored and mistakes are frequently made.

During the Second World War there were numerous examples of this form of error, from the German breakthrough at Sedan in May 1940 to the Japanese attack on Pearl Harbour in December 1941 and the British airborne attack at Arnhem in September 1944. In each case the victim received significant warnings in the weeks and months before. There was no lack of information or intelligence data yet a failure of analysis took place. There was a belief that 'it could not happen here' and this allowed warnings to be overlooked or rejected.

In May 1940 the French High Command was committed to the dual strategy of an advance into Belgium to the Dyle Line to confront the Germans far from the French border, and the defence of the Maginot Line along the French border with Germany. At the 'hinge' of the French line, Gamelin, the French Commander-in-Chief, placed complete reliance on the impenetrability of the Ardennes forest. Along a hundred miles of the Ardennes, the French line was held by just four light cavalry divisions, some still equipped with horses, and ten mediocre infantry divisions, behind whom there were no reserves at all. Facing them, across the Meuse, was Rundstedt with 45 infantry and ten panzer armoured divisions.[50]

French belief in the impenetrability of the Ardennes was unfounded. Alistair Horne points out that between the sixteenth and eighteenth centuries the Ardennes had been penetrated at least ten times by invasion forces while, astonishingly, during the 1938 French military manoeuvres an attack by General Pretelat exactly paralleled the German attack of May 1940.[51] Using seven divisions, including four motorized and two armoured, he broke through the forests and completely overran the defenders. The results were so shocking that it was decided to suppress them in order not to damage morale. The complacent Gamelin merely observed that it could never happen in a real war because reserves would have been available to parry the blow, though he seems to have forgotten his own words when it came to supporting the weak divisions at Sedan. The British CIGS, General Ironside, added his weight to a growing body of opinion that believed that the Germans might try to attack through the Ardennes but Gamelin refused to be convinced.

By 1940 aerial reconnaissance was playing an increasingly important part in military intelligence and the Germans had used it to observe the weaknesses of the Meuse defences. Gamelin, on the other hand, had made no effort to detect the massive concentrations of German armour in the Ardennes. He had built up a scenario in his own mind and was unwilling to accept any unpalatable information which might challenge his decision to concentrate his forces in Belgium. The French military intelligence, the Deuxiéme Bureau, was progressively building up a picture of German intentions which was quite different from Gamelin's. From the end of March they had monitored a growing interest on the part of German intelligence in road conditions along the Sedan-Abbeville axis, which could only presage heavy military commitment to that area.

Moreover, French intelligence had managed to locate all the German panzer divisions and the three motorized divisions and all indications pointed to the Ardennes as their target. Any reader of Guderian's book *Achtung-Panzer* would have realised the strong possibility that with Guderian in charge of armoured forces a concentration on a weak point, like that at Sedan, was almost a certainty. From Swiss sources the French learned of the construction of eight military bridges across the Rhine between Bonn and Bingen, again indicating that the spearhead of the German attack was not intended either in the south against the Maginot Line or in the north against Belgium. The French military attaché in Berne even informed the French commanders that he had strong evidence to suggest a German strike at Sedan, beginning some time between the 8th and 10th May. However, with all this accumulation of evidence suggesting Sedan, Gamelin refused to alter his view that the main German strike would come in Belgium. In the event the Germans struck the French line at its weakest point and achieved a decisive breakthrough. For all the warnings the French High Command received they were unable to take effective counter-measures. So determined were they to keep the fighting as far away as possible from the soil of France that they had closed their minds to the enemy's intentions and could only think in terms of a re-run of the German Schlieffen Plan of August 1914.

Again, in spite of the atmosphere of tension existing between the

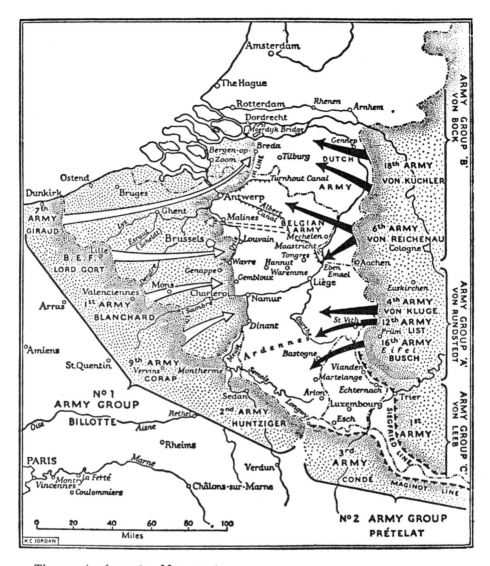

a. The opposing forces (10 May 1940)

5. The French High Command failed to respond to overwhelming evidence which indicated that the Germans intended to break the French defences at Sedan. Gamelin was convinced the German attack would come through Belgium. The result was that at the weakest point in the whole French line the Germans were able to achieve a decisive local superiority in men and equipment.

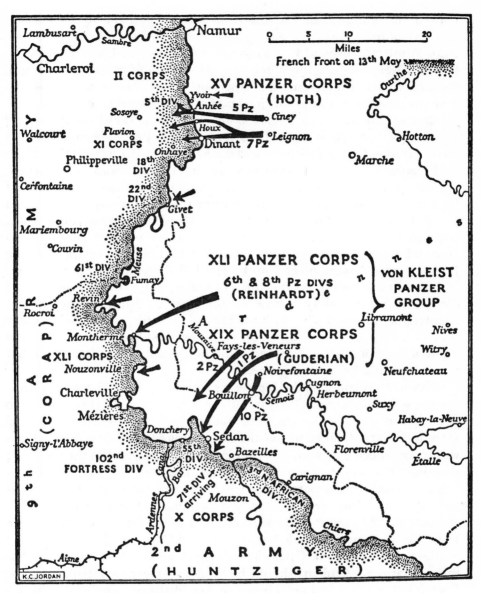

b. The Meuse crossings (12–13 May)

United States and Japan, the American base at Pearl Harbour was taken completely by surprise by the Japanese airborne attack of 7 December 1941. Admiral Husband E. Kimmel, Commander-in-Chief of the U.S. Pacific Fleet, was playing a relaxing game of golf with his colleague General Short, while some 96 American vessels lay at anchor in the harbour. It was a Sunday morning and for most people a day of rest, with servicemen off duty and a relaxed air apparent everywhere. How this could have been so is difficult to understand. Pearl Harbour was an obvious target for the Japanese, and the British attack on the Italian Fleet at Taranto had demonstrated how easily success could be achieved. Already there had been an accumulation of intelligence reports of Japanese naval activity, yet the assumption was that the target would be in South-East Asia. When Kimmel had asked his operations officer, Captain Charles MacMorris, what the chances were of an attack on Honolulu, the captain replied, 'None'.[52] Incredibly the approaching Japanese planes were picked up by the US Army's radar station near Kahuku Point, on the northern tip of Oahu, only for the report to be dismissed by the duty officer at the Shafter Information Centre, Lieutenant Kermit Tyler, with the immortal words, 'Well, don't worry about it'.[53] To Tyler the 'blips' on the screen just had to be an expected flight of B-17 bombers. His mind could not accommodate the possibility that they could be anything else.

Within thirty minutes the Japanese planes were over 'Battleship Row' and the war had started. Thirty minutes may not seem long in comparison with the months of intelligence failures in both Washington and Honolulu that had failed to give the Americans a lengthier warning, yet it would have been long enough to get interceptor planes into the air rather than have them destroyed on the ground. Lieutenant Tyler's incompetence was only a tiny part of the whole picture but in its effects it was enough to cost hundreds of lives and millions in lost *matériel*.

Space hardly permits a detailed account of the failures at Arnhem in 1944. For this one cannot do better than read Cornelius Ryan's *A Bridge Too Far*. In the case of 'Operation Market Garden' it was essential that the area around Arnhem should be relatively clear of German forces. Certainly planning had been based on the likelihood of – at the most – second-rate opposition. Indeed, when General Bedell-Smith warned Montgomery of the possible presence of German panzer divisions, the British commander ridiculed the idea saying there was more to fear from the terrain than the Germans. Yet, just 48 hours before the operation was due to start, SHAEF (Supreme HQ, Allied Expeditionary Force) received reports from Dutch sources of two German panzer divisions, 9th and

10th, in the area of Arnhem. How serious a threat could these pose? The planners believed that both divisions had been badly cut up recently and were reforming and being re-equipped with tanks. It was unlikely that they were operational.

It was photographic evidence which brought the matter to a head. Specially equipped photo-reconnaissance planes had made a low level sweep over the Arnhem area and when he received the results, Major Brian Urquhart found five photographs which showed the unmistakeable presence of German tanks in the area. He quickly took them to Lieutenant-General Frederick Browning, head of British First Airborne Corps, and pointed out the evidence of German tanks. Browning's reply is very similar to Tyler's three years earlier, 'I wouldn't trouble myself about these if I were you'.[54] The tanks, he believed, were not serviceable. So earnest did Urquhart appear in his belief that the tanks were real and operational that he was visited by the corps medical officer and advised to go home and rest. Clearly the planners were committed to the operation regardless of any evidence to the contrary.

Montgomery considered Arnhem a 90 per cent success; others thought it a disaster. Of the ten thousand airborne troops involved, only 2163 were rescued, 1130 were killed and over 6500 captured, half of whom were wounded. The Germans admit losses of 3300.[55]

Obstinate persistence in the face of contrary evidence If the ultra-conservatism of some military planners after 1918 obstructed the development of some of the technology which emerged from the First World War, there were others who made the mistake of predicting the end of traditional warfare and its replacement by terrifying aerial bombard-ments aimed at destroying the morale of the civilian population. In 1921 Air Marshal Sir Hugh Trenchard, a supporter of the idea of independent strategic bombing, declared that 'the next war could be won by bombing alone, by destroying the enemy's will to resist'.[56] An Italian general, Giulio Douhet, announced in the same year that the next war would be decided in a matter of days through lightning strikes by bombers. And both agreed with the notion that the bomber would always get through. In the event they were completely wrong, but in Trenchard's case the truth did not emerge until Britain had committed as much labour to the production of heavy bombers as was allotted to the production of the whole equipment of the Army. In the words of John Lukacs,

To predict the future along a simplistic line, as the ever-growing continuation of the present (or, rather, what seems to be the present) may be even more wrong than simplistic reliance on the past . . . the expected mass-bombing attacks on cities at the start of the war did not happen. We have also seen that air fleets were not decisive: German air power was unable to force Britain to surrender. Later, with less excuse, those American and British strategists who believed that a bombing offensive would break the Germans were even more wrong.[57]

The idea that the bomber would always get through was based on First World War thinking, in which anti-aircraft and fighter defence were in their infancy. Moreover, if all available resources were devoted to making certain that your own bombers got through, there would be nothing left with which to counter the threat from enemy bombers.

On the outbreak of war in 1939 Bomber Command was quite unprepared for a major bombing campaign. Too many British bombers were either obsolescent or inferior to their contemporaries in other countries. In view of the prevailing theory that the bomber would always get through, a view strongly held in Britain as well as abroad, it is extraordinary that when they were needed Britain did not have any planes capable of inflicting devastating damage on Germany. Even the modern Whitleys, Hampdens and Wellingtons were relatively innocuous. In the event, it was the Stuka dive-bombers rather than the German heavy bombers which dominated the campaigns in Poland, Norway and France.

In 1939 the RAF had been prepared for a programme of precision daytime bombing, in which terror attacks on civilian targets had no part. On one occasion when it was suggested in the House of Commons that Britain set fire to the Black Forest with incendiary bombs, the Secretary of State for War, Sir Kinsley Wood, replied in a horrified voice, 'Are you aware that it is private property? Why, you will be asking me to bomb Essen next'.[58]

Early British daytime raids against German warships at Wilhelmshaven resulted in heavy losses at the hands of German fighters. Already the idea that the bomber would always get through was being proved wrong. The British bombers were not able to defend themselves, being too lightly armed and far too slow. The result was that Bomber Command was forced into accepting night-time bombing, although it was not until Hitler attacked France on 10 May 1940, that the 'phoney war' ended. Bomber Command was now authorised to strike at targets in the Ruhr: 'significant successes were reported and powerful conclusions were drawn from them'.[59] However, on Christmas Eve 1939, photographic evidence was produced of two of the main German oil plants, at Gelsenkirchen. These plants had apparently been attacked twice, first by a total of 163 British bombers which has dropped 159 tons of high explosive bombs, then later by 134 bombers dropping a further 103 tons of bombs. The photographs showed that no damage at all had been inflicted.[60]

By early 1940 a change was taking place in thinking on the bombing campaign. In their report 'On Air Bombardment' the Chiefs of Staff were beginning to accept the idea that German morale could be damaged by air attack. Paragraph 15 stated,

The evidence at our disposal goes to show that the morale of the average German citizen will weaken quicker than that of a population such as our own as a consequence of direct attack. The Germans have been under-nourished and subjected to a permanent strain equivalent to that of war conditions during almost the whole period of Hitler's regime, and for this reason also will be liable to crack before a nation of greater stamina.[61]

It would be interesting to see what evidence was available at this stage to justify the belief that the German nation lacked stamina. It was an absurdly chauvinistic theory on which to base strategical decisions. The Chiefs of Staff then recommended that the next six months should be devoted to the destruction of the German synthetic oil plants, though a secondary aim should be the lowering of enemy morale, particularly in industrial areas. Interestingly, Hitler did not share the British belief that a country could be defeated by an air force alone and remarked to the Italian Foreign Minister, Count Ciano, that 'the experience Germany had gained in the air war against England indicated that it did not pay to bomb purely civilian targets'.[62] It would appear that Hitler's grasp of psychological warfare was greater than that of the Chiefs of Bomber Command. Winston Churchill was never totally convinced by claims that bombers could destroy 80% of German production, yet his pugnacity made him want to hit back in the only way he could at that time and that was through bombing raids. Lukacs makes the important point that Churchill's strategy was 'Erastian', in that he hoped to win the war in a way which would avoid the massive bloodletting on the continent which had marked the First World War.[63] If bombers could achieve victory without the need for Britain to commit mass armies to the fight then he would support them with everything he had.

Further damaging evidence of the ineffectiveness of night-time bombing was produced when, between March and July 1940, Bomber Command undertook the task of destroying the battlecruisers *Scharnhorst* and *Gneisenau* in harbour at Brest. In total, 1723 aircraft from Bomber Command dropped 1962 tons of bombs. Though the German ships were stationary, just nine bombs struck their targets, inflicting serious but not fatal damage.[64] Photographic investigation by Lord Cherwell of the midsummer raids on the Ruhr revealed even more startling results. Only one bomber in every ten actually got within five miles of the target and the bombs that those ten per cent dropped fell within an area of 75 square miles around the target.[65] This was a bad result and indicated that Bomber Command was not producing results commensurate with the investment in men, money and labour that the nation was making. They had failed to evolve a doctrine and training-system for night-time raids, had defective bomb sights and their navigational devices were clearly inadequate. Calder points out that in the bombing raids of 1940–41 more British fliers died than German civilians.[66]

On 19 May 1941, Trenchard presented Churchill with a memorandum on bombing policy. Although he was no longer on the active list, Trenchard's influence was still considerable in Bomber Command. In his view,

Absolute priority must be given to the long-range bombers for this work . . . as also for the planes and the necessary materials for this branch of the Air Service. The training of these bomber crews must be given priority over the training of crews for Coastal Command aircraft, Army Co-operation squadrons, the Fleet Air Arm, Photogaphy and Fighters, and this priority must be maintained despite the pressure on the Air Force by various departments.[67]

In view of the success of British fighters against German bombers during the Battle of Britain this memorandum must be considered shortsighted. If priority was to be given to long-range bombers at the expense of fighters then Britain could never again turn back a major German aerial campaign. What Trenchard was suggesting was that Britain should bomb Germany more heavily than she herself could be bombed. He rejected the clear evidence from the success of British fighters in August and September 1940, that without control of the air strategic bombing is an impossibility. To build large quantities of bombers does not guarantee air supremacy, as the Americans were to discover to their cost in 1943 and 1944. Only long-range fighter escorts could guarantee that the bombers got into a position to deliver their blows. Sir John Dill realised the essential flaw in Trenchard's thinking when he wrote

. . . we must be clear that, before any overriding priority is given to the building of a bomber force to achieve this end, adequate provision must be made for the security of this country and of those areas overseas which are essential for the maintenance of our war effort.[68]

Nevertheless, the Chief of the Air Staff, Sir Charles Portal, was in agreement with Trenchard that German morale was vulnerable and that the Royal Air Force could break it alone. Thus terrorisation became the definite policy of Bomber Command. The role of the army would be to mop up after the bombers had done their work.

Churchill was far less convinced by this sort of argument than American experts like General H.H. Arnold, who wrote in mid-1941 that his visit to England

... left me with the impression that by air alone we might bring Germany so completely to her knees that it might be unnecessary for the ground forces to make a landing ... Air power and air power alone could carry the war home to central Germany, break down her morale, and take away from her the things essential to combat ... Modern war has completely changed the old concepts.[69]

This view was, in Lukacs's words, no more than 'adolescent projection' and reflected the shallowness of American thinking at this time.[70] In October 1941, on the other hand, the British Prime Minister cautioned the Chief of the Air Staff against this kind of false optimism.

Even if all the towns of Germany were rendered largely uninhabitable, it does not follow that the military control would be weakened or even that war industry could not be carried on. The Air Staff would make a mistake to put their claim too high.[71]

However, in addition to destroying German morale, Bomber Command believed it could also destroy Germany's capacity to make war, by wrecking the German oil system, their transport and their industry.

Churchill came to believe that, far from destroying morale, civilian bombing could actually stiffen resistance as it had in Britain in 1940. In spite of three years of area bombing, designed at destroying cities, killing civilians and damaging German output, there is no evidence that the German will to resist was weakened. David Divine has shown that although Bomber Command never had the 4000 bombers they considered necessary to destroy German morale, the later bombers they received were much larger and carried more bombs than those in use when the figure of 4000 was specified.[72] Moreover, the entry of the United States into the war enabled the Allies to maintain daylight and night-time bombing continously, killing some 300,000 Germand civilians and injuring 780,000. However, even these enormous figures represent just 1.5 per cent of the civilian population and it should also be remembered that two-thirds of all Germans never suffered bombing of any kind.[73]

The failure of the strategic bombing campaign is evidenced by the fact that in spite of the heaviest bombing, production of war materials in Germany continued to increase up to 1944. In January 1945 30 new U-boats were built – a record for the entire war – even though the German shipbuilding yards had been subjected to saturation bombing.[74]

UNSUITABLE EQUIPMENT

As early as 1781, William Lloyd, a self-confessed 'military adventurer', challenged the prevailing interest in Prussian discipline which dominated the armies of the time and raised a storm that was not to finally die out until the twentieth century. He suggested that the uniforms of his day were senseless and that soldiers should be dressed and armed according to the nature of their tasks.[75] This may seem obvious, yet rarely have soldiers been given clothing that is warm in winter, cool in summer, hard-wearing and comfortable and which does not make the wearer too conspicuous. Unsuitable uniforms have been the cause of military disasters as certainly as tactical errors on the battlefield.

In 1912 the French Minister of War, Adolphe Messimy, was determined to reform the French military uniform, to fall in with the British, who had adopted khaki after the Boer War, and the Germans, who had changed from Prussian blue to field-grey. During the Balkan Wars, Messimy had seen the advantage gained by the Bulgarian troops in their dun-coloured uniforms, and was eager to make French soldiers equally difficult to see. However, he had reckoned without the traditional pride of French soldiers in their red képis, red trousers and blue coats. This colourful display may have served a purpose in close-combat fighting, by instilling pride in one's regiment and army, but by 1912 it was simply suicidal. The extended range of infantry weapons meant that soldiers need never see each other at close quarters in battle and the development of trench warfare in the autumn of 1914 made it all the more important for troops to be inconspicuous. When Messimy proposed introducing grey-green cloth he was abused for wanting to clothe French warriors in 'muddy, inglorious' colours. The newspapers took up the cry and the *Echo of Paris* declared that to banish 'all that is colourful, all that gives the soldier his vivid aspect is to go contrary both to French taste and military function'. In Parliament Messimy was attacked by a former Minister of War, M. Etienne, with what almost became a battlecry for French conservatism, 'Eliminate the red trousers? Never! *Le pantalon rouge c'est la France!*' Messimy was beaten but, as he wrote, 'that blind and imbecile attachment to the most visible of all colours was to have cruel consequences'.[76] In the month of August 1914 alone, France suffered 206,515 casualties. By 1916 the red képis had been replaced by a steel helmet and the red trousers had gone also, in favour of a new 'horizon blue' uniform which was still not as good as British khaki or German *feldgrau* but was soon smothered in the mud of the trenches and so offered good concealment.

If the French were slow to adapt, the British had not been much faster.

In spite of the evidence of numerous colonial encounters in the nineteenth century that it provided too vivid a target, the traditional infantry red coat was maintained, and helped the Boer marksmen at Majuba Hill in 1881, just as it had helped the French and Indians on the Monongahela in 1755. Braddock's British infantrymen had more to complain about than simply the colour of their uniforms, which made them such easy targets. They also suffered from the most inappropriate costume for conducting warfare in American conditions. Whereas the French had learned to adapt themselves to the climate and terrain, often wearing moccasins instead of boots, and fighting stripped to the waist, the British suffered disastrous setbacks before they reached the same conclusion and introduced irregular troops on a large scale. Following the Prussian model the British infantryman wore a uniform with a stock of leather which held his neck stiff, and his head was pulled backwards by the queue, or stiff pigtail. In the words of John Laffin,

The stock, a high leather collar, was nothing more than an instrument of torture, for it cut into the neck and chin and prevented the soldier from bending his head. In hot weather it was abominably uncomfortable and in wet weather it successfully channelled water into the soldier's clothing. . . .
The queue led to one regiment being called the 'Hard and Tights'. The 'hard' and 'tight' referred to the colonel's instruction about the setting of the queue. It was said that he wished to make it impossible for a man to close his eyes when on guard. . . .
And in this impossible outfit the men were not only expected to march and fight, but actually did march and fight.[77]

The soldier's breeches were usually so tight that they could hardly bend and 'stood like automata of wood, mechanically arranged for some exhibition . . .'[78] The Grenadiers even wore a tall mitre-shaped hat, with a metal plate bearing the King's name upon it. When the sun glinted on this it provided a superb target for any sharpshooter to blow out the brains of the unfortunate wearer.

A soldier's main concern is to be warm in winter and cool in summer. The inadequate supply of winter clothing has affected numerous campaigns, like those of Charles XII in the Ukraine in 1708–9 and Napoleon in Russia in 1812. One of the worst examples of inadequate supply of suitable clothing by the military authorities was during the Crimean War in 1854. Although warm clothing was eventually sent from Britain it was not distributed and men were forced to improvise uniforms from whatever was to hand. The effect on the military efficiency of the British Army of the inadequacy of the clothing issue was to be seen in the number of deaths from exposure and injuries caused by frost-bite

Like Napoleon in 1812, Hitler and his staff miscalculated the effects of the Russian climate. This imposed extremes of both heat and cold, yet it was the Russian winter which did the most damage. Hitler had expected to complete his campaign before the worst weather set in and adequate supplies of winter clothing were not available. The German soldiers, in summer uniforms, suffered badly and Russian troops were far better equipped to survive the elements. Heinrich Haape describes the effects on the German Army.

Those Arctic blasts that had taken us by surprise in our protected positions had scythed through our attacking troops. In a couple of days there were one hundred thousand casualties from frost-bite alone; one hundred thousand first-class, experienced soldiers fell out because the cold had surprised them.

A couple of days later our winter clothing arrived. There was just enough for each company to be issued with four heavy fur-lined greatcoats and four pairs of felt-lined boots. Four sets of winter clothing for each company! Sixteen greatcoats and sixteen pairs of winter boots to be shared among a battalion of eight hundred men! And the meagre issue coincided with a sudden drop in the temperature to minus 22 degrees.[79]

Military footwear has always been of prime importance in the efficient fuctioning of any army. In modern times there is no excuse for failing to equip soldiers with comfortable and hard-wearing boots. However, this has not always happened. The shoes issued by Union contractors during the American Civil War were cut to a uniform shape for either foot and this caused numerous cases of foot-soreness and straggling. Many Confederate soldiers had no boots at all and marched barefoot. During the Crimean War there was a great scandal about the issue of boots that were far too small for soldiers in winter conditions and were of such poor quality that the soles fell off inside days. The Russian boots were far superior to the British and Evelyn Wood was not alone in acquiring a pair from a dead Russian soldier. It is difficult to read without a sense of horror of the issue of cardboard shoes to the Italian troops accompanying the German invasion of Russia, while expensive luxury leather shoes continued to be sold in Italian shops. In the severe winter of 1941 in Russia, the German troops found their boots far from adequate. Heinrich Haape describes the gruesome resourcefulness of the German soldier.

Now we had an opportunity to equip our men with more winter clothing. Kageneck ordered that the 73 dead Russians be carried to the village and stripped of their felt-lined boots and warm clothing.

But the bodies were frozen stiff. And those invaluable boots were frozen to the Russians' legs.

'Saw their legs off', ordered Kageneck.

The men hacked off the dead men's legs below the knee and put legs, with boots still attached, into the ovens. Within ten or fifteen minutes the legs were sufficiently thawed for the soldiers to strip off the vital boots.[80]

Inappropriate weapons Military men are sometimes blamed as planning for future wars by preparing to refight past ones. Yet it is from the past that their experience comes and the more important question is what they take from it and how they allow it to affect their judgement. The Austrian commanders of the 1860s looked back to the defeats at Magenta and Solferino in 1859 at the hands of the French and drew the wrong conclusion. Overlooking the fact that the Austrian Lorenz rifle outranged the French weapons, and by virtue of its curved trajectory created a gap in the zone of fire, they assumed that the bayonet charges of the French infantry were policy rather than necessity.[81] They therefore adopted the 'Stosstaktik', reducing the importance of fire-power and preventing the timely rearmament of the infantry. The 'Stosstaktik' emphasised the bayonet as the primary infantry weapon and demanded all-out offensive action.[82] The Prussians were impressed by the courage of the Austrian troops in the war against Denmark in 1864, yet noted their very high casualties. The Austrian planners were entering a military phase similar to that of the French prior to 1914, with an emphasis on morale rather than materiel. And just as the French suffered for their 'élan' and their 'cran', the Austrians were to suffer on the battlefield of Könnigrätz in 1866.

The view is often expressed that the Prussian 'needle-gun' gave Moltke's soldiers victory over the Austrians at Könnigrätz, and that but for the parsimony of the parliamentarians Benedek's troops could have had the gun as well. In fact, this is far from the truth. It was the Emperor Franz Joseph and the military leaders who opposed the innovation. The Prussian 'needle-gun', the Dreyse breech-loading rifle, had been known in Austria since 1849. It had many advantages over the muzzle-loader, as Hew Strachan points out.

The weight of the breech brought the centre of gravity in the rifle nearer the shoulder and thus enhanced its accuracy. It ranged up to 800 yards. But its main attribute was its rate of fire, which could rise to seven rounds a minute.[83]

In 1851 a commission headed by Feldzeugmeister Augustin carried out trials with twenty needle-guns and rejected them on the following grounds:

Although the needle-gun permits rapid fire as long as there is no stoppage, this does not constitute any real advantage, because rapid fire will merely exhaust the ammunition supply.[84]

Although some Austrian officers were impressed with the Prussian use of the gun during the war against Denmark, the Emperor declared that the bayonet was a more honourable weapon than the breech loader and so further testing was stopped.

There were other reasons why the Austrians failed to supply their troops with the best weapons available. The breech-loader was a more complex rifle than the Lorenz and the educational level of the average recruit was low. There was little time to train them in the use of modern equipment. However, a stronger reason was the wish by the ordnance experts that their monopoly should not be infringed by bringing in equipment from outside. The Vienna arsenal had introduced new machinery in 1862 and was now able to make 1000 Lorenz rifles a day. Any attempt by private firms or foreigners to challenge their monopoly was met by the stern charge that 'private firms have neither the expertise nor the capability to meet the requirements of the army'.[85]

It was the essential conservatism of the military that prevented Austria from having breech-loaders in 1866. A year earlier, parliament had voted 130 million florins for extraordinary military expenditure, yet no attempt was made to re-equip the infantry until it was too late. When war with Prussia became certain there was a desperate attempt to produce breech-loaders or buy them from abroad. However, it was too late and the 5000 Remington rifles ordered from Belgium arrived only as the war was coming to an end.

The early Austrian success over the Prussians at Trautenau on 27 June 1866 showed Benedek how little chance the 'Stosstaktik' would have had against the superior Prussian fire-power. The only alternative was for him to change his tactics at the last moment and hope to disrupt the Prussian infantry with artillery fire, before sending in the infantry with the bayonet. At Könnigrätz, however, this plan failed and the Austrian casualties at over 40,000, were enormous. The incompetence of the Austrian planners in not supplying adequate weapons had sent their army into a battle they had scarcely any chance of winning.

Inefficient weapons If the quality of British naval gunnery, at Jutland and elsewhere, was disappointing, that of the shells fired by those guns was even worse. In 1916 the design and testing of naval shells was the responsibility of the War Office's Ordnance Board. The British armour-piercing shell (AP) was designed to penetrate armour at any angle and explode inside the ship. This it had clearly failed to do on numerous occasions, at Coronel, Dogger Bank and Jutland. At an oblique angle the shells tended to break up or only partially break through the armoured protection. This saved a number of German ships from destruction during the most hectic phase of the fighting at Jutland. The advantage built into the British Dreadnoughts, in terms of greater hitting power, was lost while they in turn suffered, in Jellicoe's words, 'the accepted disadvantage in the protection of our ships due to the heavy weights of our guns and ammunition which reduced the total weight available for armour plating'.[86] Thus it was that three British battlecruisers were sunk and no German capital ship during the main fleet action at Jutland.

The Admiralty had been aware since 1910 that the development of naval gunnery meant that battles would be fought at long range. This meant that there was a need for a shell which would penetrate armour at a steep angle. The specification for an AP shell was drawn up and passed to the Ordnance Board for testing. However, the tests that were carried out were for impact at right angles and not the steep angle needed. When Jellicoe complained of this he was told that further testing would be too expensive and the matter was allowed to drop when he took up his command at sea. Vice-Admiral Sir Francis Pridham claimed that it was possible, as a result of the system of checking then used, for as many as 71–84 per cent of shells to be 'duds'.[87] This was an incredible situation. For far less than the cost of a single Dreadnought battleship a comprehensive testing system could have been developed before the war began, with a resultant saving in British ships and the destruction of many more German ones.

The bomber pilot never saw his victim and rarely saw his enemy, yet was involved in the realities of war as completely as an infantryman fighting hand-to-hand on the ground. He was forced to act in darkness and drop death from the skies onto both military and civilian targets, and yet he rarely saw, except through photographic reconnaissance, the effects of the weapon he carried. If he had, perhaps he would not have so willingly risked his life night after night in the skies over Germany. Few infantrymen armed with rifles which fired only intermittently and with ammunition that had as many blanks as live bullets would stand resolutely if they knew there was a good chance that their weapon would let them down when they needed it most. There had to be a level of mechanical reliability below which it was unreasonable to ask men to risk their lives. David Divine has commented,

. . . it might have been more dramatic to say that half the bomber sorties made with the General Purpose bomb (the major part of all sorties made by the command) were useless before take-off. From which common logic must argue that half the command's casualties were unnecessary.[88]

The Official Historian of the Strategic Air Offensive, Sir Charles Webster, wrote about the General Purpose bomb:

Between 1939 and 1945 Bomber Command dropped over half a million 500lb G.P. bombs and nearly 150,000 two-hundred-and-fifty pounders. Not only were these bombs often unsuited to the task for which they were used because of their general characteristics, which consisted of an unhappy compromise between strength of casing and weight of explosive, but they were also relatively inefficient and all too often defective weapons. Their charge-weight ratio was only about 27 per cent as compared with the 50 per cent ratio of the corresponding German bombs, the explosives with which they were charged were relatively ineffective and large numbers of bombs failed to detonate. It was not, however, until the end of 1940 that any serious remedial action was taken.[89]

As late as 1935 the Air Staff had considered 500 lbs the maximum size needed for a bomb, yet by 1940 this had been demonstrated to be an absurd underestimate. Towards the end of 1940 a 4000 lb General Purpose bomb was produced but this was even worse than its 500 lb predecessor, breaking up on impact and producing an inferior blast. The grim story continued with the Medium Capacity bombs, which also broke up on impact and failed to detonate in a third of all cases. The High Capacity bombs, or 'blockbusters' as they were nicknamed, had poor ballistics; the early versions were fitted with parachutes, and were almost impossible to aim. In contrast to the ineptitude of British bombing production the Germans had succeeded in developing a far more efficient weapon. David Divine points out that Britain possessed in Dr Barnes Wallis 'one of the most remarkable geniuses in this field that the world has produced',[90] and yet, even though, after Dunkirk, it was obvious that Britain could only strike directly at Germany from the air the incompetence of the planners at Bomber Command could not manage to produce a worthwhile bomb. The result was that thousands of lives were wasted carrying defective bombs to drop on Germany.

WELFARE FAILURES

Disease has been one of the soldier's worst enemies throughout history and it is the responsibility of those who plan military operations to protect their troops, as far as possible, from exposure to the conditions which give rise to it. Much neglect has stemmed from simple ignorance and yet recurrent outbreaks of fever in certain areas, the West Indies most notably, did not prevent both Britain and France pouring troops into the area during the eighteenth century to die there of yellow fever. In the nineteenth century, in spite of advances in medical knowledge, far too little consideration was given to the physical health of troops, so that casualties from ill-health frequently outnumbered battle casualties and sometimes decided a campaign.

The island of Walcheren, at the mouth of the River Scheldt, was one of the unhealthiest spots in Western Europe. In 1795 the French commander there lost five-sixths of his entire force to the local fever, while in 1808 another French officer, Monnet, lost 1500 of his garrison.[91] These facts were known to the British government when, in July 1809, a huge amphibious operation was launched with the aim of capturing the island and advancing up river to cripple French resources at Antwerp. Why no consideration was given to the dangers of disease is difficult to understand. After all, all the islands of the Scheldt were known to be unhealthy, their marshes a breeding-ground for malarial mosquitoes. Their inhabitants 'were medically reported on as being pale and listless, suffering much from scrofula, the children rickety, and all much deformed'.[92] Heavy floods in the autumn of 1808 appear to have aggravated the disease which the British troops contracted on their arrival the following summer. As T.H. McGuffie writes,

The hot, wet and steamy weather in August, with thunderstorms and thick white morning mists above the stagnant polder waters, helped to spread the sickness. Active operations had till then kept the troops in good heart, but when purposeful action was replaced by incessant labouring on useless fortifications sickness grew apace . . . The men turned listless, prone to yawning, and finally collapsed completely, suffering from intense thirst, from shivering and burning fits, and finally falling into complete prostration.[93]

The cause was known, for men tried every device they could to keep away the 'infernal mosquitoes'.

The medical services available to the British army were quite deplorable even by the standards of the time. A medical board existed, consisting of a surgeon-general, inspector-general and physician-general, yet these men had little contact with the army, had never served abroad and were generally far too old to show the urgency needed. To make matters worse, the medical staff sent with the expedition was far below strength and the Board was not even consulted until the Walcheren fever was well established.

The fever spread with alarming speed: between 6 August and 3 September the number of cases leaped from 688 to 8134.

The men fell by thousands and little was done for them . . . those being sent sick to England lay on the beaches in their filth and misery for ten hours or so waiting for carts to carry them down to the transports; and there appeared 'much want of exertion' even before the end of August, 'to meet the difficulties arising from crowded hospitals and the shocking places allotted as barracks for the troops'. Men died hourly, 'almost by the minute'. . . .[94]

The hospitals in England were overwhelmed by the number of cases brought from the Scheldt. By 10 October two-thirds of the remaining troops were ill; 8477 sick and just 5616 fit for duty, out of an original invasion force of more than 40,000.[95] Losses through sickness and disease were not unusual in the British Army and the level of losses in the West Indies was extraordinarily high; in Jamaica the death-rate was 12 per cent per annum in peacetime. However, the tragedy of Walcheren was that it was unnecessary. The largest force Britain had ever sent abroad 'shivered its way through mists and fogs to a water-logged grave or a fever-ridden future'.[96] And as a result the military value of the expedition to Britain was nil.

The army medical services during the Crimean War were so deplorable that they have rightly become notorious as one of the worst failures ever in institutional care. The incompetence was military as surely as was the order which sent the Light Brigade against the Russian guns at Balaclava or the British infantry to destruction at the Redan.

Though statistics become less reliable – indeed unattainable – the further one goes back in military history, there can be no doubt that soldiers have always been susceptible to sexual diseases, and in the two world wars the problem took on great significance. Young men had been taken from their homes, from their wives and girl-friends and sent to foreign countries where, in some cases, the opportunities for sexual satisfaction existed widely. It was absurd for the military authorities not to come to terms at an early stage with a potentially explosive problem. Officially, it was accepted that soldiers probably needed some sexual outlet but it was official army policy to discourage them from seeking it. Army chaplains had this unenviable task, yet ultimately the problem was a medical one. In the early years of the Second World War, the British authorities wisely bowed to the inevitable and allowed brothels to remain open on condition that the girls submitted to regular medical check-ups. In Tripoli matters were well-organized, as a soldier wrote:

The army, with its detailed administrative ability, was able to organise brothels in a surprisingly short time and a pavement in Tripoli held a long queue of men, four deep, standing in orderly patience to pay their money and break the monotony of desert celibacy . . . Brothels for officers were opened in another part of town. . . .[97]

However, the Chaplain-General soon intervened to close down the official brothels with the result that they simply re-opened without the girls having regular check-ups. General Montgomery added to the problem by closing brothels in Cairo, and later in north-west Europe, with the assistance of Canadian and American authorities. Other notable 'red-light' areas were placed 'off limits' in Naples and Bombay.

John Ellis views this action by the military authorities as misguided. They were giving way to the sanctimonious attitude of certain religious critics and the effects were disastrous.

In Delhi for example the army ran what was known as the regimental brothel, in a building near Hakman's Astoria. The entrance was rather like a cinema with a corporal in a glass booth to whom one gave the last three numbers of one's army number and 5 rupees. He then handed over a chit with a room number on it and one was led there by an Indian babu and given condoms. The girls were well paid, in Indian terms at least, and were medically examined once a week by members of the Royal Army Medical Corps. Unfortunately, certain do-gooders in England got to hear about this and raised a storm of protest. The official brothels were quickly shut down, but this merely served to drive the prostitutes on to the streets or into other illicit establishments. 'Within three weeks', according to Corporal John Bratt (RAMC) 'every bed in the previously almost deserted V.D. ward, and every bed that could be crammed onto the verandah outside, was full'.[98]

For the rest of the war the incidence of venereal disease was so high in all theatres of war that its casualties often exceeded those caused by the enemy. In the Middle East the annual battle casualties per thousand were 35.5 in 1941, 31.1 in 1942 and 22.5 in 1943, while for V.D. the figures were 41.2 in 1941, 31.4 in 1942 and 21.8 in 1943. In Italy the V.D. figures were particulary high, reaching 68.8 in 1945 at a time when battle casualties were a mere 9.8. In Burma in 1943 the V.D. figure reached an astonishing 157.9 against battle casualties of 13.9. Nor should it be thought that these figures for the British army were unusual. In Tunisia in 1943, the American white soldiers reached 33.6, while for black soldiers it was an amazing 451.3.[99]

These figures were alarming not for moral but for military reasons. Clearly the efficiency of an army cannot be maintained if self-imposed injuries – V.D. being regarded as such – reached such a scale. An average V.D. patient spent twenty days in hospital being cured, at a time when there was an acute shortage of soldiers and when hospital beds were needed for battle casualties. The American authorities saw condoms as a potential solution yet feared to offend public opinion at home. John Steinbeck expressed the problem clearly. He criticised the hypocrisy which maintained

. . . that five million perfectly normal, young, energetic and concupiscent men and boys had for the period of the War Effort put aside their habitual preoccupation with girls. The fact that they carried pictures of nude girls, called pin-ups, did not occur to anyone as a paradox. The convention was the law. When Army Supply ordered X millions of rubber contraceptive and disease-preventing items, it had to be explained that they were used to keep moisture out of machine gun barrels – perhaps they did.[100]

The failure by both British and American military authorities to come to terms with the sexual needs of their soldiers showed an aspect of military incompetence which is rarely taken seriously. If one assumes that it is impossible – let alone physically and psychologically undesirable – to deny men sexual outlets then it is incumbent upon the authority which is responsible for their welfare and which has invested time and money in training them, to ensure that their health is not harmed by sexually-transmitted diseases. An army's concern is with a man's physical and mental well-being rather than his moral welfare. After all, he is required to behave as a killing-animal, so that basic instincts are more relevant than socially acquired ones. The closing of the official brothels by the army authorities was an act of military incompetence for it threatened the physical welfare of its soldiers as well as the military strength of the nation.

Bad planning Winston Churchill, as First Lord of the Admiralty in 1914, has received praise from historians for the way in which the Royal Navy was immediately ready for action when war broke out. On 4 August 1914, every British vessel was stationed according to the plans drawn up by the Naval Staff over a lengthy period. From Scapa Flow in the Orkneys, where Jellicoe's Grand Fleet was stationed, to the Channel where three battle squadrons of pre-dreadnoughts were placed, the naval planners had made the North Sea into a 'marine no-man's land'. The British battleships would block exits to north and south, while light cruisers and destroyers could patrol the east coast from their base at Harwich. The British stategy seemed excellent. In the words of G. Callender,

So long as Admiral Jellicoe and the Dover Patrol held firm, the German Fleet in all its tremendous strength was literally locked out of the world. The Hohenzollern dreadnoughts could not place themselves upon a single trade route, could not touch the outer hem of a single overseas Dominion, could not interfere with the imports on which the British Isles depended, could not stem the swelling stream of warriors who came from every land and clime to save the cause of civilisation.[101]

However, the naval planners and Winston Churchill 'in their planning for every contingency' had made a number of errors, the worst of which is described by Richard Hough.

The first of these weaknesses, which could well have proved fatal, was the lack of suitably situated, fully prepared, and fortified bases on the east coast. That immense armada which Churchill proudly described silently and speedily slipping through the Straits of Dover into the North Sea was like an army stranded in the open country, without a fortification in which to restore and defend itself. The dreadnoughts' compasses would lead the Grand Fleet to Scapa Flow. But that general anchorage with its inclement weather, bleak hills and fast-flowing tides and currents was unprotected by a single fixed naval gun or even searchlight against surface attack, and lacked booms or nets to guard the entrances against surprise surface or submarine torpedo attack, or fast minelayers.[102]

The oversight seems incredible. Given the fact that the nation's security rested on the Grand Fleet, why had no consideration been given by naval planners to the security of that fleet?

The problem was that there had been a substantial alteration in Britain's strategic imperatives. For centuries Britain had faced a naval threat from the south, from Spain, France and even Holland. British naval bases tended to be situated on the south coast, at Plymouth, Portland, and Portsmouth. The naval dockyards in the Thames at Chatham were excellent but too far south to meet the new German threat from across the North Sea. The need for east coast bases had been raised at the Admiralty as early as 1903, and a decision had been taken to develop Rosyth, in the Firth of Forth. However, building work was plagued by friction between the Admiralty and the War Office, for defence of the base would be the Army's responsibility. In any case, it soon became apparent that Rosyth would be too far south for the Grand Fleet to operate an effective blockade on Germany and, with the increase in size of the main fleet, it would also be too small.

By early 1913 consideration was being given to two other sites, Cromarty and Scapa Flow. When the Admiralty asked for permanent defences to be built at Scapa Flow the cost, £400,000, was considered prohibitive.[103] After all, that was a fifth of the cost of a dreadnought. By the outbreak of war the situation was chaotic. Scapa Flow was undefended, Cromarty incomplete and Rosyth considered too small. All other bases were so far south that they were useless for stopping a German break-out to the north. The reason for this state of affairs was the offensive doctrine which then dominated thinking at the Admiralty. Money spent on shore defences was money which would not be available for building and arming dreadnoughts, on which alone the security of the state depended.

The success of the German submarine U-9 in torpedoing the three

British armoured cruisers *Aboukir*, *Hogue* and *Cressy*, created panic in the Grand Fleet.[104] Periscopes were seen everywhere. Jellicoe in his unprotected base at Scapa Flow felt uneasy. While shore defences were being built he decided to take the entire fleet of 21 dreadnoughts and 8 pre-dreadnoughts to Lough Swilly on the north coast of Ireland. By the sinking of three old cruisers the U-boats had driven the British out of the North Sea. Worse was to follow when the Germans laid mines off the coast of Ireland and succeeded in sinking one of the newest British battleships, HMS *Audacious*.[105] Beatty complained to Churchill of the absence of a base 'where we can with any degree of safety lie for coaling, replenishing, and refitting and repairing, after two and a half months of war'. For Beatty the navy had been knocked 'off its perch', by the incompetence of the planners.[106]

At the time he wrote these angry words Beatty and his battlecruiser squadron were in a loch on the Isle of Mull, guarded from submarines by picket boats and nets. In reality they were hiding: 'We have been running hard now since 28th July', said Beatty, and he did not know how long they could go on like that.[107] The need for repairs was growing and the absence of a base made these impossible.

The Germans were never able to capitalize on the errors of the naval planners because it is doubtful if they would have believed them possible. The idea that the British main fleet, preeminent at sea for a hundred years, could be forced away from the war zone, albeit temporarily, by the absence of a secure base, the fear of the U-boat and occasional sightings of seals, would not have occurred to German admirals who still held the British Navy in awe.

—3—
The Politicians

Relations between politicians and the military have become far more complex in the last hundred years, as both the nature of society and the technology of war have changed. Where in an earlier period political and military leaders were often one and the same, more recently the two have grown apart until in some ways their aims may have become mutually exclusive. Certainly in terms of budgetary allocations the demands of a defence minister must now compete with a large number of other departments which have emerged in response to changes in society. However, just as the politician and the service chief may have grown apart in one respect, in another they have grown so close as occasionally to be almost indistinguishable. The nature of 'total war' in the twentieth century has imposed strategic requirements on a state that no military mind can solve in isolation.

Michael Howard has described military strategy as a form of organized coercion, defensive or offensive, in which either force or the threat of it is employed to compel an adversary to abandon his preferred course of action or conform to yours.[1] However, in the present century the almost limitless resources of industrialised states have meant that nothing short of the complete destruction of the physical and moral resources of a state can bring it into conformity with the victor's wishes. This has meant that what previously lay within the realms of the military commanders, such as battles won on land and at sea, fortresses captured, prisoners taken, territory occupied, may well not be enough to achieve total victory. The elements of strategy which concerned the soldier, namely the maintenance of a logistical system to permit an army or navy to operate and the use to which that the military force is then put, are no longer the whole of the picture. Two new elements must be considered: the social and technological dimensions of strategy are twentieth-century concepts. As war has become more complex technologically it has become vital for states to participate in various 'races' – to build battleships, fighter planes, tanks, bombers, missiles and so on. By 1918, however, the social element of strategy had emerged as a consideration as vital as technological development. In the inter-war period the issue of civilian morale and the strategic bomber theories of men like Trenchard and Mitchell came to dominate British military thinking. If the bomber would always get through and if civilian casualties were on an unimaginable scale, could Britain maintain herself in war if civilian morale collapsed? In the event, civilians showed themselves stronger and more resilient than the military had expected. Under German bombing raids over British cities ordinary people displayed stiffened rather than weakened morale, and similar reports come from German and Russian cities. Since 1945 the social dimension of strategy has been in the ascendant and in spite of the expansion of the technology of warfare it has not been possible to overlook the importance of people at grass roots level. The success of the great guerrilla leaders like Mao Zedong has illustrated this and few clearer examples of it exist than the triumph of the North Vietnamese over the United States. In spite of the greatest display of technology in military history the Americans were unable to overcome a people whose morale survived intact.

Clemenceau once said that 'War is far too serious a business to be left to the generals'. While this comment contains a great deal of truth it can also be misleading. Certainly, war and politics go hand-in-hand and strategy is essentially concerned with the deployment of the military to achieve a political objective. However, politicians can sometimes be as ignorant of the nature of the military as the soldier is of politics. Political objectives must therefore be related to military capacity and in this respect it is vital that politicians work closely with their military advisers to avoid the pursuit of unrealistic strategic aims. Failures have tended to occur where politicians have ignored this lesson or have assumed a role as Commander-in-Chief during wartime which allows them to interfere with military decisions. Perhaps the prime example of this is Hitler during World War Two. Undoubtedly he was a gifted amateur strategist, better than Churchill whom he regarded as a 'dilettante'. His military gifts were intuitive and, it has to be acknowledged, occasionally blessed by remarkable luck. However, a gambler like Hitler cannot succeed indefinitely, particulary if he alienates his own generals, on whose professional abilities he is dependent for his 'intuitive' victories. If the mistakes were his, they were usually manifested much lower down the hierarchy, as is generally the case with military incompetence at the political level. Macksey at Narvik, Percival at Singapore, von Paulus at Stalingrad, Montojo at Manila, Stopford at Suvla Bay, Wavell in Greece all suffered as a result of inept decisions taken at the political level – the list is endless.

Contributions by politicians to military incompetence may take several forms. As with Hitler in the Ukraine, political decisions may alienate natural allies and even turn them into actual enemies. A parsimonious defence policy unconnected to a realistic strategic appreciation may result in military commanders being faced with impossible demands. Where a state has denied its military forces equipment commensurate with its tasks then the fault is a political not a military one. Britain came close during the Falklands Campaign to asking just a little too much of her armed forces, however professional they may have been. In an increasingly technological age, flesh and blood still count for a lot but it is possible to expect too much.

With the growing appreciation of the social element in strategy have come psychological as well as physical attempts to break civilian morale. Propaganda as a weapon was misused badly by the Germans in the First World War, though by 1939 Goebbels was able to impose a far stronger hold on the German population than his predecessors had. However, neither the Germans in 1914 nor Goebbels in 1939–45 succeeded in affecting civilian morale in enemy states. In fact, inept propaganda is likely to prove counter-productive.

Perhaps the most significant effect that politicians can have on military incompetence is through their interference with the activities of the generals, their jealousy of them, and their attempts to insist on military action for political purposes. As Howard has shown, the task of the strategist is to use the available military forces to achieve his political object. However, the military actions must be appropriate ones, commensurate with the strength available, and designed to contribute to the central political aim. 'Side-shows', for whatever political aim, can be disastrous and Winston Churchill was responsible for more of these than any other political leader of the twentieth century. Like a latter-day Chatham he scattered British forces, and lost many of them, on ill-advised operations which detracted from the central military aim. His despatch of the *Prince of Wales* and the *Repulse* to Singapore was a futile act of 'showing the flag' and gave little consideration to the strong likelihood that without air cover they would be lost. Such a gesture could in no way make up for the decades of neglect which had followed the building of the Singapore Naval Base. If Britain could not afford to send a fleet to Singapore then she did not need the base and therefore did not need Singapore either. To cram the island with reinforcements just as it was about to fall to the Japanese was reckless folly. So also was the political gesture which led to British involvement in Greece. The result was that Greece was lost anyway, Crete quickly followed, many British troops and all their equipment were sacrificed and the brilliant North African campaign was halted and then reversed by Rommel. It is easy to blame men like Wavell, Neame and Ritchie, but to do so ignores the fact that this was a political blunder more than a military one.

An appreciation of the social element in strategy occasionally prompts politicians to press for military action in order to boost public support for a war. This was tried in Vietnam, though rarely effectively. During the Falklands War, politicians pressurised commanders to achieve some sort of success to compensate for the continuing bad news of naval losses. This was understandable but misguided. The operation to capture Goose Green and Darwin was a success only because of the remarkable fighting qualities of the British troops involved. Facing odds of 4 to one it was possible that 2nd Battalion, Parachute Regiment could have been defeated and had this occurred it would have weakened public support for the war more severely than the catalogue of ship losses.

ALIENATION OF NATURAL ALLIES

Alliances are generally made because two or more groups perceive a common threat, and wartime necessity can create strange bedfellows. The alignment of Imperial Russia with democratic Britain and France in the First World War and that of totalitarian Russia with Britain and the United States in the Second are just two examples. The overriding need to defeat Germany in both wars was enough to make concessions possible between allies on apparently divisive issues. These were problems of grand strategy and decisions taken by political rather than military leaders; in each case the military situation was of such gravity that political compromise became possible. However, history records a number of examples of political leaders finding it impossible to compromise and thereby alienating natural allies, with unfortunate military consequences. Two examples, one ancient and one modern, illustrate this.

In the seventh century Arabian idol-worship was on the wane as Jewish, Christian and Zoroastrian missionaries made converts. Monophysite Christianity was particularly successful and had established itself on the caravan routes as far as Yemen. On the borders of Byzantine territory, desert tribes like the Banu Ghassan were entirely Monophysite. They frequently provided troops for Byzantine armies and had taken part in the Emperor Heraclius's decisive campaigns against Persia. However, they had suffered persecution for their beliefs from the dominant Orthodox Christianity of the Byzantine Empire.

The success of Mohammed in Arabia posed a threat to Byzantine rule in Syria and Palestine, for the religion of Islam was an expansionist one. To defend the Byzantine frontiers against the Muslims Heraclius would have done well to conciliate the Christian Arabs. Instead, he attempted to force on these Monophysites a new doctrine known as Monoenergism which would bring about a compromise between them and Orthodox Christianity.[2] The Monophysites rejected it and strongly resented his interference.

The Muslim capture of Gaza in 634 convinced Heraclius of a new danger. After his brother had been defeated in 635, he sent two further armies under Theodore Trithyrius and the Armenian Prince, Vahan, to face the Muslims in Palestine. On 20 August 636, the Byzantine army, which contained a large contingent of 12,000 Christian Arabs led by a Ghassanid prince, fought the Muslims in a blinding sandstorm at Yarmuk. During the fighting, the Christian Arabs, who were Mono-physites and resented Heraclius for threatening their religion, went over to the enemy and settled the battle. The Byzantine army was virtually wiped out and all of Palestine and Syria fell to the Muslims. Everywhere they went they were welcomed by the Monophysite Christians who hated the Orthodox religion of Constantinople. By failing to compromise on the religious question Heraclius had lost the support of the Monophysite Arabs who could otherwise have held the desert frontier against the Muslims.

Stalin's brutal collectivization of farms during the 1930s had alienated the peasants. By 1941 the popularity of the Soviet regime was low and many subject nationalities within the state opposed a regime which denied them self-determination. This information was passed to Hitler by Count Schulenberg, the German Minister in Moscow. He pointed out that the USSR was an ideal area for psychological warfare, with the Germans posing as liberators of national minorities like Ukrainians, Balts, Latvians, Lithuanians, Estonians, Azerbaidjanis, Turkestanis, Cossacks, Armenians and Georgians. Schulenberg felt this would weaken support for the Russian war effort and possibly provide recruits for German armies. In Ronald Lewin's words, 'All that was necessary was a soft hand and a soft word'.[3]

However, Hitler did not share this strategic concept. To him all Soviet populations were *untermenschen* or sub-humans, and it was a waste of time for Aryan Germans to attempt to win the support of murderous barbarian orientals. How wrong Hitler was appeared in the early days of 'Operation Barbarossa'. During the summer of 1941, vast sections of the Soviet army surrendered to the Germans, who were surprised to find Russian officers contemptuous of Stalin and his clique and prepared to take up arms against him. As Leeb's Northern Army Group drove into the Baltic Provinces they found that the civilians greeted them as liberators, with many men offering to join them against the Russians. In the south it was the same story, with Ukrainians and Cossacks only too eager to see the Russian forces beaten. The chance was there for the Germans to organize an anti-Bolshevist crusade.[4]

Hitler now missed his greatest chance of toppling the Soviet dictator. His firm plans to annex Russian territory, use the displaced population as slave labour and fill the depopulated areas with German colonists drove the Soviet peasants into a desperate resistance against the Germans, which Stalin skilfully manipulated by emphasising the idea of 'national' war. By playing on Russia's past resistance to Napoleon in 1812 and Alexander Nevsky's victory over the Teutonic Knights in 1242 he was able to unite the population behind the Russian war effort. Yet in 1941, of the five million Soviet prisoners held by the Germans it is estimated that two-thirds would willingly have fought against the Communists. Hitler compounded his error by decreeing that 'the Russian soldier loses all claim to treatment as an honourable soldier according to the Geneva Convention'. Many of those who had originally been willing to fight with the Germans were so alienated that they joined partisan units and harassed the German advance. The arrival of SS 'Einsatzgruppen' to round up the population for extermination or use as slave labour was the final reflection of Hitler's strategic miscalculation.

POLICY FAILURES

In establishing grand strategy a state needs to consider not only its own goals but the likely reaction of other states. Britain, before 1939, had to come to terms with her own decline relative to states like Japan, Germany and the United States. She needed to take account of the strategic goals of both potential enemies and potential allies. She also needed to consider her own economic weakness and the changing perceptions of her role in international affairs that were held by her leading statesmen. In a sense she was forced to slip some of the burdens of her history.

Britain's decline as a world power, both economically and militarily, was exacerbated by the weakness of her pre-1914 allies, France and Russia, the emergence of Italy and Japan as potential enemies, and the resurgence of Germany. Ironically, France in the 1920s seemed the strongest European power; yet this was an illusion, for her declining population, political divisions and economic problems meant that she would not be able to face a re-armed Germany without substantial military assistance from Britain.

The Anglo-French Entente that had triumphed in 1918 had been a military alliance and was not destined to survive long in the postwar world. British and French politicians held widely separate views on how Europe should be reconstructed, particularly in terms of accommodating Germany. France, having suffered two invasions in 44 years, was convinced that Germany should be permanently disarmed. In order to maintain her security France kept the strongest army and air force in the world, as well as constructing an alliance system on Germany's eastern frontier, to which Poland and Czechoslovakia were the keys. Britain, on the other hand, felt herself to be strategically over-extended and unable to bear the economic cost of her imperial and continental commitments. This meant that Britain was keen to redress the excesses of the Versailles settlement and by re-establishing a balance of power in Europe simplify her task of influencing events there.

In the 1930s Britain's strategic position became substantially worse. Expansionist policies pursued by Italy and Japan, combined with the advent of German re-armament under Hitler, raised the nightmare of Britain having to fight three major powers. Moreover, by 1934, with naval cutbacks like the scrapping of the battlecruiser *Tiger* and the four battleships of the 'Iron Duke' class under the Washington Naval Agreement it was doubtful if the Royal Navy could even operate a One-Power Standard, while the RAF was not one of the four strongest air forces. Worried as he was by Britain's apparent military impotence, the Conservative Chancellor of the Exchequer Neville Chamberlain was even more concerned that Britain should avoid bankruptcy, and in his view re-armament in the mid-1930s could have spelled financial ruin.

Yet it was not only financial reasons that prevented Britain rearming. As Christopher Layne has pointed out,

When Britain confronted the strategic threat of a resurgent Germany after 1933, these factors – Britain's presumed economic weakness, the abhorrence of the prospect of war by the British people and the fear of Britain's vulnerability to aerial attack – combined to exercise a dominant influence on the British response to the German threat.[5]

In 1934 the British Chief of Staff concluded that 'should war break out in Europe, far from having the means to intervene, we should be able to do little more than hold the frontiers and outposts of the Empire during the first few months of the war'.[6] This was an accurate assessment, but tight budgetary controls prevented Britain rectifying it through complete re-armament. As a result, from 1934 Britain was forced into a strategic policy of 'deterrence', based on a misapprehension of the destructive value of aerial bombardment.

The British decision to adopt a policy of deterrence was based on the experience of the end of the First World War, when Zeppelin and Gotha raids on London killed many people and showed the devastating effect of civilian bombing. Both Trenchard in Britain and Douhet in Italy spread the belief that in the next war strategic bombing of urban areas would prove irresistible and that active defence against the bomber was impossible. The conclusion reached by military leaders in Britain was that the only defence against such a terror weapon was the capacity to strike back just as hard. Thus Britain would purchase security at the cost of equipping her air force with heavy bombers, and this was a low cost compared with that of a large standing army. Chamberlain expressed British policy in these words:

> . . . our best defence would be the existence of a deterrent force so powerful as to render success in attack too doubtful to be worthwhile. I submit that it is most likely to be attained by the establishment of an Air Force based in this country of a size and efficiency calculated to inspire respect in the mind of a possible enemy.[7]

The British Chiefs of Staff did not agree. Only a large army, capable of intervening on the Continent, would deter an aggressor. In their view, both potential allies and potential enemies would view the British concentration on an air force as typical of Britain's desire to avoid a European commitment. Thus the value of the deterrent would be low. They pressed for the creation of a British field force as well as an expansion of the Navy to reach a Two-Power Standard in relation to Germany and Japan. However, their ideas were vetoed by Chamberlain on the grounds of cost. He insisted that the strategic bomber force would deter Germany from attacking Britain and the Low Countries. How Britain could assist countries like Poland and Czechoslovakia was more difficult to explain.

The re-militarisation of the Rhineland by Hitler in 1936 convinced the French that war with Germany could not long be delayed. Thus they tried to persuade the British that priority should be given to the creation of a sizeable expeditionary force to fight alongside the French army. In this they were doomed to fail. With the threat to Czechoslovakia and Poland in the east, it is surprising that Britain and France made little attempt to persuade Russia into joining an anti-German alliance. A possible reason was that neither of the western democracies had confidence in Russian military capacity, combined with this was the fear and hatred of

Communism prevalent among the ruling classes of Britain and France. In Christopher Layne's view,

It was not unreasonable for the British leaders, who certainly were well aware of Hitler's views, to accept them and believe that Britain's strategy would be to encourage Hitler in his Eastern aims, and to thus pit Germany and the Soviet Union against one another. . . . It appears that the real reason there was no Anglo-Soviet alliance in 1937, 1938 or 1939 was that the British Government perceived (probably incorrectly) that there were viable alternative policies for protecting Britain's security interests.[8]

The weakness of Britain's policy of deterrence was that it carried no credibility. German intelligence sources could keep Hitler informed of the RAF strategic bombing capacity and he was therefore well aware of the fact that Britain did not have the bomber force necessary to inflict really decisive damage on Germany's war effort. By the outbreak of war in 1939, no country, not even Germany, had such capacity. Thus deterrence failed to deter Hitler because it was not backed up by military reality. Britain had been unwilling to accept the economic consequences of financing rearmament, instead opting for the less costly policy of deterrence through strategic bombing. Yet how could her enemies regard her as a serious obstacle to their ambitions when she was also unwilling or unable to back up her policy with the bomber force that would deter them? The only policy that would have impressed Hitler would have been for Britain to commit herself to building up a large army, ready to fight alongside the French. This would have deterred Hitler from his adventures in Czechoslovakia and Poland because he could not then have risked a decisive Allied strike on his undefended western frontier. As it was, without any hope of substantial British military aid, France became committed to the defensive and Hitler correctly read the signs that the French army had lost its will to fight. The Maginot Line thus served more as a prison than a fortress for French hopes.

In 1938 Hitler's claims to the Sudentenland brought Europe closer to war than any previous crisis. It seemed for a while that Britain and France would support the Czechs by force but at the Munich Conference a deal was arrived at that postponed war for a year. Historians have been divided as to the wisdom of the continued appeasement of the German dictator. It has been shown that Germany was at her weakest in 1938 relative to Britain and France and that war in that year could have been a strategic disaster for her. Other historians, however, have pointed out the pitiful state of Britain's air defences in 1938 and feel that she would have succumbed to the offensive power of the Luftwaffe. The strategic decision taken by the Allies at Munich had enormous military consequences and the leaders of the two countries should have been able, through the reports of their military intelligence services, to reach a conclusion based on a knowledge of their own and their enemy's strength. If this was so, then any decision they took was their responsibility. If it was not possible, through a deficiency in intelligence work, then the responsibility rests elsewhere. There is at any event a strong case for arguing that the best chance of Allied success against Germany was in 1938 and not a year later.

It is a common misconception that the Luftwaffe would have inflicted heavy damage on British – and French – cities in 1938. In fact it was in no position to launch or sustain such an attack and was being developed as a tactical air force, designed to support fast-moving tank and motorized infantry units. Its concentration on dive-bombers and medium bombers showed that it was not German policy in 1938 to undertake the strategic bombing campaign that everyone feared. Ironically, they had not succumbed to the myth of the bomber in the way that the British had. The problem for Chamberlain was that he presumed that Germany would do what he most feared, and carry out terror raids on London.

German military strength in 1938 was a shadow of what it would be in eighteen months' time. At the time of the Munich crisis the German Army had 48 regular divisions, of which only three were armoured, four were light reconnaissance and four were motorized infantry. It lacked heavy artillery and had few reserves. It should also be noted that five of the divisions were Austrian and of a far lower standard than the German units. The three armoured divisions were equipped with the obsolete PKW I and II light tanks while the medium tanks PKW III & IV were available only in small numbers for combat testing. The bulk of the German Army consisted of 37 infantry divisions, little changed from 1918, with horse-drawn artillery and transport. In the event of a crisis Germany could be expected to mobilise eight reserve divisions and 21 Landwehr divisions, consisting mostly of elderly First World War veterans who possessed little training or modern equipment.

On the other hand, it would be a mistake to over-estimate the strength of the Czech army at this time, a 'paper' army which had not been tested in action. Of the 30 Czech infantry divisions only 19 were regulars, and the reserve divisions lacked modern equipment. The regular divisions may be considered as equal to their German equivalents and were equipped with excellent weapons. It is probable that behind the extensive fortifications the Czechs built on the Silesian frontier they could have held up the Germans for some time, but with the poor quality of their military leadership it is doubtful if anything further could have been achieved

In Williamson Murray's view the lack of an all-weather capability in the Luftwaffe would have reduced its ability to support ground operations, while the deficiency in armoured forces would have made a German campaign against Czechoslovakia very different from that fought against Poland a year later.[9] Casualties would probably have been higher, progress slower and victory more hardly earned. This would have encouraged Hitler's critics inside the German army, of whom there were many, to assert their more traditional views at the expense of younger thinkers like Guderian. Stolfi has pointed out the use made by the Germans of captured Czechoslovakia equipment and armament factories during the invasion of France in May 1940.[10] Had the Germans been forced to fight their way into Czechoslovakia it is unlikely that so much Czech equipment would have been captured intact or that they would have been able to take over a viable armaments industry.

So far this account has examined the problems of a Czech-German conflict for Hitler, yet in the event of a general war he would not have had the luxury of a single-front campaign. Even in the east, there was the problem of how Poland and Russia would react, while in the west he had to take into account that France, his most powerful enemy, was as well-equipped as he to fight in 1938. Britain, it must be admitted, was less well prepared and it was her attitude towards Germany that was to be decisive.

It has been a common fault of general histories to dismiss the potential of the French army too lightly, possibly because Hitler did so and was proved right. However, the German generals did not believe in Hitler's intuition and preferred to base their strategy on firmer foundations, like intelligence reports. It was difficult for them to believe that the nation which had fought with such determination in the First World War, and had triumphed, would not pose a substantial threat in any future war. They were soldiers, not social scientists or, as in Hitler's case, reckless amateurs. What Hitler saw in the French Army they did not see and what they saw in the German Army he refused to see.

Stolfi has challenged the myth of German armoured superiority in May 1940; it is probable that in 1938 they would have found the French mechanised forces formidable opponents. The French tank industry had begun mass production in 1936 and produced more tanks of 'greater size and complexity than the Germans'.[11] Stolfi points out that against a maximum German output of 100 tanks a month, including the use of the Czech Skoda works, the French by January 1940 were able to produce 150. There is no doubt that properly used the quality of the French tanks would have enabled them to achieve at least a stalemate in 1938 and probably far more. Only the acquisition of Czech tanks and production facilities enabled the Germans to create the four new panzer divisions which replaced the light divisions which had been unsuccessful in Poland, and in which 297 Czech TNHP 35 and 38 tanks were used instead of the obsolete PKW 1s.

The situation in the Soviet Union is also relevant. In September 1939, when Hitler invaded Poland, Stalin had completed his purge of the Red Army and was an ally of Germany. A year earlier, however, he was still in the process of reducing dissidence in the army, and the military strength of Russia was consequently small. Nevertheless, in 1938 he was not yet allied with Germany, and was not supporting her economy with large quantities of raw materials as he was after the Nazi-Soviet Pact. Even if Russia was no military threat to Germany, Hitler could not count on getting any support from her. In addition, Rumania was alarmed by the threat to Czechoslovakia and warned Hitler that if he continued his aggression he could expect no more Rumanian oil after October 1938.[12]

Whatever plans Hitler had for eastern Europe he could not overlook the fact that his main enemies were in the west. Germany's 'Maginot Line', the Westwall, was a 'complete sham', which had only been started in 1938 and by the time of Munich had just 517 bunkers – a year later the figure stood at 10,000 – but even these were militarily useless as their concrete had not yet set. In the absence of formal defensive positions it would be necessary to employ large ground forces on the French frontier, but in view of the potential strength of Czech opposition where were these to be found? It fell to General Adam to command the entire western front with just 5 regular divisions and although Hitler promised him a further 20 if war broke out with France and Britain, Brauchitsch immediately contradicted the Führer and said that only 8 could be made available in the first three weeks![13]

Hitler was a gambler and did not allow such problems to worry him. He believed the French army was weak for all its apparent size and that its will to fight was negligible. He was right and it was intuition rather than intelligence reports that helped him. He found in the French military leaders only passivity and fear. Gamelin and the French High Command had no intention of launching an attack on the Rhineland while Germany was occupied elsewhere. They were prepared only to occupy the Maginot Line and then 'looking through the loopholes of our fortifications . . . passively witness the enslavement of Europe'.[14] In spite of a numerical advantage in the west of 56 divisions against an estimated 8 German divisions, Gamelin apparently lacked confidence in France's ability to win a worthwhile victory.

Britain's chief concern in 1938 was with Germany's air power. Alistair

Horne in a footnote to his book *To Lose A Battle* explains the basis for British fears and their impact on the nation's strategy.

No doubt aided by the exaggeration of Udet, both French and British experts feared the Luftwaffe for the wrong reasons in 1938. While they remained blind to the potential tactical significance of its dive-bombers and fighters, they were hypnotized by the carnage that Goering's He-111s seemed poised to wreak upon the civil population. In Britain in 1938, the Imperial Defence Committee estimated that the Luftwaffe could drop 3500 tons of bombs on London within the first twenty-four hours of an attack, while the Ministry of Health was anticipating 600,000 killed and 1,200,000 wounded in the first six months. (In fact, during the whole of the London Blitz only 18,000 tons of bombs were dropped, causing a total of 90,000 deaths over a period of seven months.) The RAF, reckoning its fighter force to be below the minimum required for the defence of Britain in 1938, misled the Government (as indeed the exponents of strategic air power have been misleading governments ever since) on the capacity of carpet bombing to win wars, which in turn greatly influenced Chamberlain's determination not to face war over Czechoslovakia.[15]

Horne continues by pointing out that though London and Paris may have suffered air attacks the damage would have been minimal compared to expectations. In 1938 Hitler lacked the bombers to destroy civilian morale, as well as the panzers and Stukas to succeed in a *blitzkrieg* attack on France. With this in mind it can be more clearly seen how little the Allies had to gain by delaying the inevitable. Chamberlain may have believed he had achieved 'peace in our time' but his military advisers should have convinced him that he was flying in the face of reality. Churchill saw the situation clearly.

Moreover, the naval balance of power, traditionally vital to Britain, was remarkably favourable to her in 1938. Neither of the German battle-cruisers, *Scharnhorst* and *Gneisenau*, had been completed, nor had the great battleships *Bismarck* and *Tirpitz*. Germany possessed no heavy cruisers, no aircraft carriers, six light cruisers, seven destroyers and just 12 ocean-going U-boats. The German Naval High Command (OKM) doubted its capacity to protect the trade routes in the Baltic and the Swedish iron ore shipments. Even without the *King George V* class battleships, Britain possessed a far greater mastery over Germany than she was to enjoy twelve or eighteen months later.

In strategic terms the German economy was extremely vulnerable in 1938. Her supply of vital iron ore from Scandinavia could be disrupted as it had been in the First World War by British naval blockade. Although she was self-sufficient in coal, Germany's western coalfields, particularly those in the Saar, were close to France and could have become a target for

French military action. If Italy entered the war, she would herself become dependent on German coal. In fact, for Germany coal was a most important source of foreign exchange and it was in this way that she obtained her petroleum. The efforts to create a synthetic fuel industry in the 1930s had not succeeded in making Germany self-sufficient in oil products. Far from it, for in June 1938 Germany had only enough petrol stockpiled to cover 25 per cent of mobilization requirements, while the situation for aviation lubricants was even more desperate, with just 6 per cent of wartime needs. The problem with rubber was just as great, for in mid-1938 synthetic rubber production had provided, again, a mere 6 per cent of German needs. In terms of munitions, gunpowder production was only 40 per cent and explosives 30 per cent of the First World War maximum figure.[16] The message was clear and in the period between Munich and the outbreak of war in September 1939 Germany made enormous efforts to meet the demands of wartime.

The strategic situation in 1938 is summed up by Williamson Murray.

The striking feature of the 1938 military situation was the relative unpreparedness of all the European nations to fight even a limited, much less a major war. All were acutely aware of their weaknesses. For the Germans the problem was compounded not only by their military unpreparedness but by their economic vulnerability.[17]

France, although she possessed an overwhelming military superiority in the west, had leaders who were unwilling to exploit this advantage in the event of a German attack on Czechoslovakia. British leaders, not possessing such strength, faced a difficult military equation: should they strike the enemy while he was at his weakest or wait until they were at their strongest? In the event, time was no friend to the Allies. Germany made better use of the twelve months' delay and was a far more formidable enemy in 1939 than she would have been if Britain and France had supported the Czechs at the time of the Sudeten Crisis.

The British strategic policy of deterrence failed in 1938 because it was shown to lack both 'muscle' and 'teeth'. In another sense it also lacked 'heart'. The strategic bomber force of the RAF existed only in men's minds, to reassure some and to frighten others. Chamberlain did not believe in it sufficiently to risk war against Germany and once he had backed down at Munich its deterrence value had clearly failed.

British confidence in the French army was sufficient to support the belief that there was no need for a large British army to fight alongside it on the continent. However, for the French the unwillingness of the British to create a mass army undermined their confidence in British intentions and weakened the French response to German threats to Czechoslovakia.

Failure of a policy of deterrence Many wars begin with surprise attacks: the Japanese attack on Pearl Harbour is merely the most famous. The Middle East wars of 1956, 1967 and 1973 all began in that way, as did the Korean War and the Falklands Conflict. Yet in each case how surprising was 'the surprise'? Gerald Hopple has suggested that in the case of the Falklands the answer is 'not very'.[18] Argentina had been indulging in 'sabre-rattling' for some time and there had been an invasion threat as recently as 1977. Why war came in 1982 had more to do with certain 'reassuring but misleading political and/or strategic assumptions'.[19] These took the form of apparently accurate though really misguided views on the part of both Britain and Argentina of their own and their enemy's capabilities.

According to Richard Betts, in the event of a surprise attack like the Argentinian invasion of the Falklands it is not necessarily valid to assume an intelligence failure, for the fault is often a political one.[20] Surprises of the Falklands, Korean or Pearl Harbour kind result from periods of unresolved tension. The nation then 'surprised' has generally received sufficient warnings without having taken any action on them. Miscalculation of enemy intentions usually stems from false strategic assumptions on the part of the victim.

In the case of Britain in 1982 the political failure was a direct result of national defence postures. The evidence of Argentinian intentions was available but it was wrongly analysed and therefore the wrong responses ensued. To the British people it seemed a storm that had suddenly blown up but to the Argentinians the 'Malvinas' had long been an issue of national importance. To the British the islands were just an echo of empire but to the ordinary Argentinian they were as meaningful as 'the blue line of the Vosges' to the French after 1870. Except for regional experts at the Foreign Office, few people in Britain knew how strongly Argentina had asserted her claim to the Falklands, particularly since 1945. There had been numerous crises in the twentieth century, during which Argentina had claimed sovereignty: such as those in 1927–8, 1933, 1966 and 1976. In 1977 there had been a serious threat of an Argentinian invasion of the Falklands. A British ship had been fired on and a Royal Navy submarine was sent to the South Atlantic as a deterrent. Yet by February 1981 it seemed that a negotiated settlement might be in sight. The fall of General Viola and his replacement by General Galtieri changed all this. Renewed 'sabre-rattling' by the uncertain junta caused a breakdown in negotiations. Faced with the new threat the British Foreign Secretary, Lord Carrington, had to decide whether the situation required the presence of another deterrent force in the South Atlantic. In the event, he chose not to send one, for budgetary reasons and because he felt an Argentinian invasion was unlikely.

Intelligence sources did not agree with Carrington. They believed the evidence was more alarming than he did and that an Argentinian invasion could not be ruled out. On 29 March 1982, Lord Carrington publicly indicated that Her Majesty's Government was reserving its military options should a diplomatic solution not be forthcoming. Secretly the nuclear submarine HMS *Spartan* was sent to the Falklands but already it was too late.[21]

The British policy of deterrence had failed to prevent the Argentinians from invading the Falklands. The root of this failure was to be found in a series of incorrect strategic assumptions. Perhaps the most important was the belief that the Argentinians would not resort to force to take the islands. After all, the dispute was one of the longest running ones in the contemporary world, dating back to the 1770s, and Argentina had never previously resorted to arms. Certainly there had been threats but these were regarded as empty ones, products of the rhetoric of South American politics. To Britain references to the Malvinas seemed to be entirely for Argentinian domestic consumption, aimed at externalising discontent with policies at home. Oddly, Galtieri even encouraged this British interpretation by talk of reducing inflation through cutting back defence spending, with the Navy as the main target.

Britain made a second mistake in under-estimating the significance of the Malvinas for Argentina. The islands may have been a very distant colonial acquisition for Britain, but to the average Argentinian they represented a part of the homeland, loyalty to which was inculcated into all the people from birth. Intensity of feeling of this kind can be misleading but is generally a fair indication that the problem will not just go away. In the words of Lawrence Freedman, by early 1982 the British

. . . could offer neither compromise to Argentina nor a credible long-term commitment to the Falkland islands. The only negotiating posture left was prevarication.[22]

Gerald Hopple adds, 'Bluff and stalling were hardly ideal negotiating postures for preventing a blow-up when the other side felt as intensely as Argentina did'.[23] However, the junta was also guilty of misreading the situation, confusing Britain's 'reluctant, half-hearted and ambivalent' diplomacy with an unwillingness to resist unprovoked aggression, particularly against small states.[24]

Janice Gross Stein has stated that deterrence as a strategy involves consideration of at least five factors, and that decisions taken without regard to them are apt to result in failure.[25] In the first place, a state must clearly evaluate the interests at stake. Then, it is necessary to have precise information on the nature of the challenge to be deterred. Thirdly, a state must have a clear understanding of the potential enemy's intentions as well as of his view of the options available to him. The fourth factor is the credibility of the commitment to respond to enemy action and, lastly, there has to be consideration of what response to make if deterrence fails.

Britain's strategic thinking was 'abysmal'. She had continued to hold on to the belief that Argentina would never attack even when the evidence suggested otherwise. This kind of 'wishful thinking-derived assumption' was a dangerous one on which to establish a strategic concept.[26] Moreover, rather than adjusting defence requirements to the possibility of action in the South Atlantic as a viable option in the event of deterrence failure, Britain had produced the worst response by refusing to cede the Falklands and yet making no defence commitment to them. Britain, like France in 1940, was failing to ensure that her political objectives were strategically achievable with the military forces available to her.

Ideally, Britain should have committed forces to the defence of the Falklands but the economic realities of the early 1980s made this unthinkable. However, by the time the Foreign Office became alive to the threat of Argentinian military action it was already too late to attempt deterrence. Britain's failure to have a worthwhile deterrent force on station worked against her interests in two ways. Its physical presence was of course not available to deter the Argentine invasion force but also, and more importantly, it is very likely that the absence of a deterrent force convinced the military junta in Buenos Aires that Britain did not really care about the Falklands enough to defend them and that an invasion would provoke no more than a token British reaction. In this respect the culpability of the British government is obvious.

Just as the British government failed to understand Argentina's emotional commitment to the Malvinas, so the junta failed to realise that Britain would fight over something about which she seemed not to care. Their mistake was understandable. Britain had already decided to withdraw the ice patrol ship, HMS *Endurance*, from Falkland waters and this would have meant the virtual abandonment of a deterrence role in the South Atlantic. Only the curious incident of the scrap metal dealers on South Georgia persuaded the Admiralty to let her remain. Otherwise, Britain never made Argentina aware of the possible risks she ran if she resorted to military means. Britain, in fact, had substituted a policy of bluff for real deterrence and when her bluff was called she was forced to respond on a scale and at a cost enormously higher than would have been needed to maintain an effective deterrent. The presence of a nuclear submarine in Falklands waters, and a clear message to the Argentinian junta that she was there and would be used if necessary, would have saved both countries from a war which need never have happened. To both the costs were enormous in men and material, all as a result of the incompetent operation of deterrence strategy.

Militarily, the Argentinians chose a bad time to escalate the crisis. Britain was in the process of running down her naval capacity for reacting to precisely the sort of operation the Argentinians were planning. The aircraft carriers HMS *Hermes* and HMS *Invincible* were, respectively, due to be retired and sold to Australia. This would have removed Britain's capacity to operate sea-based airpower. Moreover, plans for future carriers had been scrapped. The retirement of the last Vulcans would have removed long-range strike capacity. In turn, Argentina was due to receive new arms herself and the performance in the war of her Super-Etendards, equipped with Exocet missiles, shows what a difference that might have made. Another year or eighteen months would have left Britain without the capacity of launching an amphibious operation to land troops on a distant group of islands.[27] Still, hindsight does make strategic options appear to be simpler than they were at the time, and Argentina was justified in her assessment that the whole tenor of Britain's military thinking was to reduce commitments and concentrate on a European scenario, in which her role was to provide an anti-Soviet, anti-submarine force. Britain, in turn, probably felt that her 'gunboat' past had been safely stowed away with Drake's drum in historical mothballs.

CONFUSION OF MILITARY AND POLITICAL OBECTIVES

The fall of France in June 1940 and the evacuation of the British Expeditionary Force from Dunkirk removed any immediate hope of Britain striking directly at Germany. As a result, British strategic thinking shifted from the European theatre to the Mediterranean, an area of traditional British interest. In earlier wars, notably the Napoleonic and the First World War, the Mediterranean had been vital to British strategy, and from 1940 it took on that role again. It was to become the hub of British naval and military efforts after the entry of Italy into the war.

In view of Italian strength in the African theatre of war, with 300,000 troops in Libya and 200,000 in Ethiopia, the British commanders in the Middle East, Admiral Cunningham, General Wavell and Air Marshal Longmore, told London that they could only hold Egypt if they received reinforcements. In addition to their superiority in manpower, the Italian air force and navy was far stronger on paper than Britain's. On 16 August, the decision was taken to give priority to the Middle East on an ever-increasing scale. This concentration of her armed forces in Egypt forced Britain to make sacrifices elsewhere. In the Far East, promises to Australia and New Zealand of help in the event of a Japanese attack could no longer be honoured.

Britain was committed to holding Egypt for a number of reasons, not least of which was the prestige it represented in the whole Middle Eastern region. It had formed an important British military base for sixty years or more and its surrender was unthinkable. The attachment to Egypt was based on a complete misreading of Hitler's strategic intentions, assuming that his desperate need for oil would force him into attacking the Middle East. In fact such a move was not in Hitler's mind and his intervention in the Mediterranean area was simply a defensive response to British pressure on Libya and Greece. Certainly Germany was experiencing shortages of oil but these she was making good by obtaining stocks from Rumania and also from the countries under her sway.

British Mediterranean strategy in the early period of the war was quite unrealistic and lacked a sound awareness of military realities. Churchill's hopes of winning allies, particularly Turkey and the French in North Africa, were never well-founded. Weygand, ruler of French North Africa, may not have been pro-German but he was loyal to the Vichy Regime and would not have allied with the British unless their power had been overwhelmingly strong. The Turks, on the other hand, were militarily far too weak to be of use as an ally of Britain, and Churchill had more to gain from their neutrality.

The entry of Italy into the war offered Britain realistic military targets in Africa; if she could not hit directly at Germany she could damage German prestige by defeating her ally in Libya and Ethiopia, and victory in North Africa might eventually allow British troops to open a door to Europe by an invasion of Italy. Nevertheless, it was most important that Britain did not attempt to over-stretch her limited resources. However pressing the political arguments might be there were some decisions that would have to be reached on military grounds alone, otherwise potential disaster would be general, not local. Churchill's meddling in the military affairs of Middle East Command in 1940–41 contributed to four separate yet connected disasters: the Greek expedition, the fall of Crete, Rommel's recapture of Cyrenaica and the fall of Singapore. If there were failures at tactical level in each of the above cases there were far greater crimes committed by the political strategists, and the ensuing military failure was a product of their involvement.

On 28 June 1940, the Italian Commander-in-Chief, Marshal Balbo, was shot down by his own anti-aircraft defences. He was replaced by the much less able Graziani who immediately came under political pressure from Italy to launch an offensive into Egypt. Like Wavell on the British side, Graziani was short of everything he needed for an offensive: aircraft, anti-tank weapons, anti-aircraft guns, medium artillery, medium tanks and vehicles of all kinds. Nevertheless, Mussolini was relentless and ordered him to advance whether he was ready or not. According to Count Ciano, 'Never has a military operation been undertaken so much against the will of the Commander'.[28]

In September 1940, Graziani ordered his troops into Egypt, advancing as far as Sidi Barrani and then stopping to establish a chain of fortified camps, which were far too widely separated to support each other. Churchill impatiently 'prodded' his commanders to respond, disregarding the difficulties they faced.[29] Wavell, in particular, was under enormous political pressure from London. The Prime Minister clearly doubted Wavell's offensive spirit. He did not really understand this subtle and complex general who did not appear to revel in the war as he did. In October Eden was sent to Cairo to report on what offensive plans Wavell had formulated. To his surprise he found that the general was preparing an operation in the utmost secrecy.

Although intended only as a 'raid in force' Wavell's offensive succeeded in overthrowing the entire Italian Army in Cyrenaica. In view of the imbalance between British and Italian numbers this could not have been anticipated and, as a result, there were few support troops to exploit O'Connor's breakthrough. Also, Wavell and Lieutenant-General 'Jumbo' Wilson were far too distant to influence the fast-moving battle. On 7 December, O'Connor began his operation with just 25,000 men, though he had an advantage in tanks of 275 to 120, while his 50 'Matilda' tanks were almost impervious to enemy fire. O'Connor first attacked Sidi Barrani, which was taken in three days. However, Wavell in Cairo was unaware of just how great a victory had been achieved and wanted to recall the 4th Indian Division to send to the Sudan. The absurd situation was reached whereby Italian troops were running westwards in retreat while a large section of British troops was marching eastwards under orders to transfer to another front.[30]

The 7th Armoured Division continued its progress and by 22 January Tobruk had fallen. At this stage reinforcements were needed to exploit the breakthrough but these were held back in Egypt. In spite of an ever-diminishing assault force of tanks, O'Connor never let the momentum drop and by 5 February he had captured Benghazi and taken the whole of Cyrenaica. Unfortunately for O'Connor – and for Wavell – Churchill's

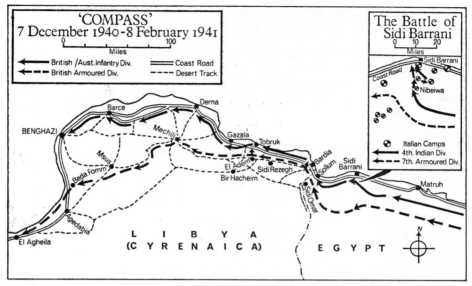

6. *The speed of O'Connor's advance took the Italians completely by surprise and promised the British complete victory in North Africa. However, after taking the whole of Cyrenaica, O'Connor was ordered to halt because Churchill needed his troops for the ill-fated Greek expedition. The arrival of German troops under Field Marshal Erwin Rommel transformed the situation and allowed Hitler to gain a foothold in North Africa from which he could threaten Britain's position in the Middle East.*

mind had turned towards his own personal hobbyhorse – a Balkan alliance against Germany. In the words of Liddell Hart, he was 'now chasing a different hare'.[31] All the military gains of professional soldiers were about to be frittered away by the gambling instincts of an amateur strategist.

In April 1939 Britain had guaranteed support to the Greeks in the event of a German attack. However, after the invasion of Greece by the Italians in October 1940, the Greek leader, Metaxas, was not eager to accept military support for fear of provoking German intervention. In fact, the Greeks were at least holding their own against Mussolini's incompetent commanders in Albania.

A.J.P. Taylor has described the decision to intervene in Greece as 'taken on political and sentimental grounds – Norway all over again'.[32] Churchill was trying to inspire Turkey and Yugoslavia to stiffen their resistance against Germany and put heart into all freedom-loving nations. However, such rhetoric availed the people of the Balkans little. There were times when Churchill seemed to be at odds with his own century. The primitive Balkan armies were no match for German professionals.

Nevertheless, Churchill was determined to support Greece at the expense of North Africa, as he informed the Chiefs of Staff on 6 January 1941.

It is quite clear to me that supporting Greece must have priority after the western flank of Egypt has been made secure. . . . We must so act as to make it certain that if the enemy enters Bulgaria, Turkey will come into the war. If Yugoslavia stands firm and is not molested, if the Greeks . . . maintain themselves in Albania, if Turkey becomes an active ally, the attitude of Russia may be affected favourably.[33]

As John Connell comments, 'this was extremely prescient'.[34] However, in other ways it was 'ivory tower' strategy. Churchill's comment that the securing of the western flank of Egypt had overall priority surely meant that until the Italians had been finally beaten in North Africa it would not be safe to plan other large-scale operations. Yet this is exactly what he asked Wavell to do, without strengthening his command, and by drawing troops away from their victorious advance through Cyrenaica. Churchill was making military decisions purely on political grounds, apparently strengthened by Foreign Secretary Eden's opinion that the Balkans could be held regardless of the situation in Africa. Connell comments that this sort of thinking

took too much for granted . . . within the exigencies of reality . . . such as weather, distance, the breakdown of vehicles, the lack of spare parts, the dribble of petrol from ill-designed cans, and the physical and moral exhaustion of men pressed beyond endurance. To call for complex operations on a vast scale, and simultaneously to demand the wholesale reduction of the minimum administrative, supply and communication facilities needed to maintain them was – to say the least – unreasonable.[35]

The Greek commander, Papagos, was surprised by the British eagerness to intervene in Greece. He felt it would be far wiser for Britain to concentrate on the conquest of North Africa before attempting anything else. However, Churchill ordered Wavell not to reinforce O'Connor, who was now reduced to just 50 cruiser tanks and 95 light tanks. Yet with this small force he managed to defeat the Italians at Beda Fomm and force the entire Italian army to surrender. The way was now clear through the Agheila bottleneck to Tripoli and despite their exhaustion O'Connor and the 7th Armoured Division were keen to race on and complete the overthrow of the Italian empire in North Africa.

At this stage the British advance was stopped on the orders of the Cabinet.[36] On 12 February, Churchill sent Wavell a long telegram praising the success of the troops but stopping any further advance. Only minimum forces were to be left in Cyrenaica and the largest possible force was to be assembled for despatch to Greece. It was hoped that at least four divisions, including one armoured, would be made available at once. All O'Connor's air cover except one squadron was to be withdrawn. Against the advice of two of his senior staff officers Wavell agreed to back the Greek operation. However, in this he was misled. He was advised that the Germans would be unable to reinforce the Italians in North Africa until April. Secondly, he understood that the Greeks would join the British forces in holding the defensible Aliakmon Line.

Political factors had caused the Greeks to change their mind and accept British aid. The death of Metaxas and his replacement by the more pliable Koryzis, had enabled Churchill to persuade the Greeks that it was in their interest to accept military help. But Hitler was not prepared to see the Italians defeated in Greece, with the possibility of British intervention on his weak flank while he invaded Russia. As a result, Luftwaffe squadrons were sent to Sicily from where they were able to shake the British hold on the central Mediterranean. And while Rommel prepared to intervene in Libya, Hitler got ready to invade Greece. British resources were fully stretched in Libya and East Africa and now Wavell, as Middle East commander, would have to face a new campaign in his command. On 7 March, with Wavell's agreement and the support of Cunningham, Longmore and the Chiefs of Staff, 50,000 British troops were landed in Greece. General Alanbrooke noted in his diary,

Are we going to have 'Salonika supporters' as in the last war? Why will politicians never learn the simple principle of concentration of force at the vital point and the avoidance of dispersal of effort?[37]

He later wrote,

I have, however, always considered from the very start that our participation in the operations in Greece was a definite strategic blunder. Our hands were more than full at that time in the Middle East, and Greece could only result in the most dangerous dispersal of force.[38]

Within a month the Germans had invaded the country and driven the British out, with the loss of 12,000 troops and all their equipment. According to Taylor,

It is difficult to believe that even a refusal to help Greece could have been such a grave blow to British prestige. The high hopes which had followed Wavell's earlier successes in Cyrenaica were dispelled. The British seemed to be back where they had started, obstinately on the defensive and with little prospect of ultimate victory.[39]

Meanwhile, matters had taken a very serious turn in Libya. The arrival of Rommel had transformed the situation, and with minimal forces – just 50 tanks – he was able to overrun the inexperienced troops who had replaced O'Connor's veterans. The defence of the Western Desert had been left to a skeleton force, an under-equipped and inexperienced Australian division and the so-called 2nd Armoured Division which had just one brigade of worn-out tanks, of which no more than half were serviceable at any one time. O'Connor himself had returned to Egypt for a rest and been replaced by Lieutenant-General Neame. Wavell himself on visiting the front had been alarmed by Neame's dispositions and by the wretched condition of the tanks. When the crisis developed O'Connor was sent to assist Neame but so swift was Rommel's advance that both generals were captured by the Germans on 6 April.[40] By 11 April the British had been driven out of the whole of Cyrenaica, except for Tobruk which was invested.

Churchill's attempt to establish a British foothold in Europe was unrealistic in terms of Britain's military strength. It had only been achieved by dangerously reducing the garrison in North Africa and by neglecting the claims of Singapore. The rewards in terms of a Balkans alliance against Germany were not worth the risks involved. Churchill should have known that Yugoslav, Turkish and Greek armies could never stand against a German army able to overthrow France in a matter of weeks. The reduction of British strength in Egypt was an open invitation to Hitler to gain a foothold for himself in North Africa. Just as the Germans had revitalised their Austrian allies in World War One into achieving a great victory like Caporetto, so the provision of an outstanding commander, German troops and equipment and air power, might just restore the morale of the Italians.

Churchill had always seen Egypt as the strategic centre of Britain's Mediterranean strategy. Yet by undertaking the Greek campaign he was allowing the Germans to replace the Italians as a real threat to 'the jugular vein of the British Imperial system – the Suez Canal'. In General W.G.F. Jackson's words,

Hitler had enough resources to make full use of an African foothold; Churchill had neither the resources nor practicable objectives to make any use of a British lodgement in the Balkans. It was hard to see what a four division expeditionary force could do in the face of List's Twelfth German Army with 18.[41]

In the final judgement it is the task of a Prime Minister's military advisers to tell him that his grand strategy is impossible for logistical reasons. There was no possibility of the British and Greek forces holding back the power of a German invasion. Without the British presence the Greeks would have been able to negotiate a settlement. There is an impression of blindness in the planning that led to four British divisions being offered for sacrifice on the altar of Churchill's ego. Even the much-vaunted British sea-power only sufficed to evacuate the main part of the British force and offer it temporary relief on Crete. British weakness on land was still far too great to challenge the Germans on the mainland of Europe.

Political interference in military affairs Political interference with the military is not a new phenomenon. In AD 408 the incompetent Roman Emperor Honorius jealously murdered his able general Stilicho, probably the only man able to hold back the threat of Alaric's Goths. Under similar circumstances in 454 Aetius, conqueror of Attila and the Huns, was murdered by the Emperor Valentinian, who had grown suspicious of his general's power. In both cases the military consequences for Rome were disastrous. Justinian's jealousy of his general Belisarius and his unwillingness to allocate him adequate resources for his campaigns was equally reprehensible. In the words of Ernest and Trevor Dupuy,

. . . probably most shortsighted of all Justinian's controversial conduct was his jealousy and mistreatment of Belisarius. No prince has ever been better served by a loyal subject than was the emperor by his great general. To prevent Belisarius (or any other general) from becoming too powerful, Justinian frequently hampered him by imposing divided command and by sending him on vast projects with totally inadequate forces.[42]

In more recent times generals have been forced to take military decisions on the basis of political rather than military criteria. The Duke of Marlborough was constantly under pressure from his political masters in England and the battle of Malplaquet in 1709 was fought for political rather than military reasons. The outcome was a pyrrhic victory which cost Marlborough and Eugene between 16,000 and 18,000 casualties against a French total of 12,000.

In the summer of 1864, during the American Civil War, the impatience of Confederate President Jefferson Davis had serious consequences when he replaced General Joseph E. Johnston with General John Bell Hood. Johnston was a shrewd commander who realised that Sherman's advance into Georgia might appear to have decisively split the Confederacy, but had in fact achieved neither the destruction of the Confederate army nor the capture of Atlanta. Until Sherman achieved one of these two things he was merely occupying space. In view of the imminence of the elections in the North it was vital for Lincoln that Sherman should achieve something decisive, as Grant was locked in an attritional struggle with Lee's army in front of Richmond and there seemed no likelihood of good news coming from there. For the South a stalemate in the war was the best they could now hope for and if Lincoln lost the election – as seemed eminently possible before the fall of Atlanta – then the Confederates might well achieve a negotiated peace. Therefore the crucial thing was to avoid a disaster in Georgia. This Johnston saw to be the wisest military option, and so he employed 'Fabian' tactics to avoid giving Sherman the chance of achieving any spectacular success. Sherman was operating on long and tenuous supply lines which could be constantly harassed, giving the Confederates an opportunity to relieve pressure on Atlanta.

However, Jefferson Davis believed that only military victory could win independence for the South, and battles would never be won if his armies avoided action. He felt Johnston lacked the qualities to beat Sherman by hard fighting and turned instead to the courageous but impetuous Hood. This change of command gave Sherman an opportunity he had despaired of ever having. Hood knew that he had been placed in command to fight and that was what he proceeded to do, carrying out two desperate assaults on the Federalist positions and suffering 13,000 casualties. He was now forced to withdraw inside fortified lines at Atlanta and withstand a siege. On 2 September, the city fell to Sherman, and news of the victory boosted Lincoln against his Democrat opponent, McClellan, who had based his campaign on the fact that the conduct of the war was a failure. The Confederates had lost Atlanta because Jefferson Davis interfered with the operations of an able commander who was temperamentally uncongenial to him.[43] Davis's own military training had convinced him that he had professional expertise in strategy, but in this he was deluding himself: he should have left the conduct of the campaign to the man on the spot.

On 25 May 1982, two Argentinian Super-Etendards, armed with Exocet missiles, took off on a mission to attack the aircraft carriers *Hermes* and *Invincible*. Unable to locate the carriers, one of the planes succeeded in sinking the 13,000 ton *Atlantic Conveyor*, which was carrying ten Wessex and four giant Chinook helicopters. Although by good fortune one Chinook was airborne at the time, the loss of the other three Chinooks, each capable of carrying eighty men at a time, was to have a severe impact on British strategy in the Falklands.

On the same day as the *Atlantic Conveyor* disaster, Brigadier Julian Thompson, at that time commanding ground forces, received instructions from Admiral Fieldhouse at Northwood that the commanders in Britain thought it was essential that now they were ashore British troops should engage the Argentinians immediately. There was an obvious target: the Argentinian garrison at Goose Green, 13 miles south of San

Carlos. Thompson was not convinced, viewing Goose Green as irrelevant to the main target, Port Stanley. Once that fell the defenders of Goose Green would be left with no alternative but surrender. He had intended to leave a small force to prevent an Argentinian flank attack from Goose Green while his main force set out for Mount Kent, overlooking Port Stanley. While the High Command in Britain were content for him to set out for Stanley they made it brutally clear that there was also to be a battle for Goose Green and that if he was unwilling to send a force there immediately they would find another commander who would.[44]

This order placed an unreasonable burden on Thompson. With his Chinooks lost in the *Atlantic Conveyor* it was already going to be necessary for the men to walk to Port Stanley – 'yomping' across the difficult terrain not from choice, which was the impression the media gave, but from harsh military necessity. With all hopes for a swift helicopter journey across the island dashed there was a danger that the men would exhaust themselves before they reached the battlefield. Now, to add to his troubles, and to ease those of the politicians, he was under orders to launch an immediate attack on Darwin and Goose Green. In the words of Max Hastings,

. . . the Goose Green affair was really the result of military impatience . . . British politicians needed news of some success after the losses of 25 May too badly to heed the caution they so often counselled on others.[45]

Thompson made one last attempt to persuade High Command at Northwood that the Goose Green operation was irrelevant, but without success. Available intelligence reports suggested that Goose Green was held by just one weak Argentinian battalion; in that case 2 Para – 450 men – under Colonel H. Jones should be strong enough to take the settlement, supported by three 105 mm guns, which was all that could be lifted into position in time. Had Colonel Jones complained that the artillery support was inadequate – which it was – he might have enabled Thompson to avoid the Goose Green operation, but Jones, on the contrary, was eager to go ahead. Scorpion and Scimitar light tanks were also ruled out as petrol was short and the terrain might prove too difficult for them. It would have to be an infantry action pure and simple.

As 2 Para approached Goose Green their progress was observed by Argentinian observers on the high ground; in response, General Menendez, the Argentinian Commander, heli-lifted reserves from Mount Challenger to the settlement of Darwin. The Argentinian reaction may also have been prompted by a BBC report that morning announcing that 2 Para was within five miles of Darwin. At a stroke the Argentinian garrison was increased from 500 to 1400, including some good quality troops, well dug-in. The British troops were now heading for an encounter with an enemy which outnumbered them three to one. It was only when the British managed to capture a Land Rover wth three Argentinians in it that they discovered they were facing more than just the expected weak battalion.[46]

In fact, the Argentinian garrison fought with determination throughout the battle, belying a description of it as 'demoralised and unmotivated'. It poured heavy artillery and mortar fire down on the paratroopers as they moved down the isthmus. In the words of Max Hastings,

Even a conscript enemy could feel formidable firing with unlimited ammunition from well-prepared positions, while the paras were suffering severely from the limited supply of ammunition inevitable among an attacking infantry force.[47]

Nevertheless, the sheer professionalism of 2 Para eventually triumphed, though at a tragic cost. Colonel H. Jones was killed in the battle for Darwin Hill and in all 17 men died, while 35 were wounded. The Argentinians lost 250 dead and missing and about 150 wounded. The most astonishing result from 2 Para's point of view was the enormous haul of prisoners: well over 1200 – three times their own total strength!

The intelligence failure which resulted in 2 Para being sent into action against such odds was the result of a breakdown in liaison between London and San Carlos. The Ministry of Defence knew of General Menendez's full order of battle and his transfer of troops but had not informed Thompson in time for him to reinforce the paratroopers.[48] The outcome could have been disastrous and would have crowned a confused operation fought for no strategic reason comprehensible to military commanders. As Max Hastings saw it,

The attack on Goose Green reflected haste and underestimation of the enemy by those who set it in motion, redeemed only by the brilliant performance of 2 Para. With the possible exception of South Georgia, the battle was the one instance in the campaign of 'backseat-driving' from London. The politicians and service-chiefs, deeply alarmed by the losses in San Carlos, demanded urgent action from the land force for political as well as military reasons . . . this episode was a classic demonstration of the risks and complications which can set in when a military operation is being conducted to serve an urgent political purpose.[49]

The heroism and superb fighting qualities of British troops had been placed at the service of politicians – a great responsiblity which should not have been abused. By demanding an operation like Goose Green regardless of difficulties, however, they risked failure and the lives of many soldiers.

FAILURE OF THE PROPAGANDA WEAPON

The value of propaganda in warfare was not fully realised until the twentieth century. Before 1914 soldiers were not much concerned with why they fought; it was enough that they were ordered to do so. The justice of one's cause was self-evident. However, with improvements in communications and information technology it began to be important that neutral countries in particular were convinced of the justice of the belligerents' war aims. It might be vital in establishing future alliances or at least for gaining war materials, trade or even the use of port facilities. In 1914 the great non-belligerent power was the United States of America, and both the Entente Powers and the Central Powers used propaganda in an attempt to win American support. In every way the German propaganda campaign turned out to be a catastrophic mistake, an object lesson in how to alienate neutral opinion. It is interesting to see the master-propagandist of the Second World War, Joseph Goebbels, in summing up his general philosophy, showing how much he has learned from the failures of his predecessors of 1914.

'The fundamental principle of all propaganda', he declared, was 'the repetition of effective arguments'; but those arguments must not be too refined – there was no point in seeking to convert the intellectuals. For intellectuals would never be converted and would anyway always yield to the stronger, 'and this will always be the man in the street'. Arguments must therefore be crude, clear and forcible, and appeal to emotions and instincts, not to the intellect. Truth was unimportant and entirely subordinate to tactics and psychology, but convenient lies . . . must always be made credible. In accordance with these general directives, precise instructions were issued. Hatred and contempt must be directed at particular individuals. . . .[50]

In contrast, the German propagandists of 1914 tried to appeal to intellectual opinion in neutral countries, chose imprecise and often lofty arguments which had no impact, and were generally unaware of the credibility gap that developed between what they claimed and what they did. They allowed the British to force them into a defensive posture which was unconvincing, and they failed to exploit their own items of propaganda value.

As a militaristic society the Germans overlooked the fact that most of the world was civilian in outlook. Their rage at the activities of Belgian *franc-tireurs* (civilians who shot at the German invaders) seemed ridiculous in face of their own violation of Belgian territory and their atrocities there. Their policy in Belgium was like that of the Emperor Caligula, *Oderint dum metuant* (Let them hate us as long as they fear us), yet their attempts to justify their military action appeared weak and self-

yet their attempts to justify their military action appeared weak and self-pitying, always concerned with real or imagined slights. The ugly face of Prussian militarism was never far below the surface, and as a result their propaganda effort remained unconvincing in comparison with the British and French claims to be fighting for the freedom of small countries and for democracy. On 5 August, Moltke claimed that Germany was fighting for her life, 'and all who get in the way must take the consequences'.[51] The German condemnation of the *franc-tireurs* was turned against themselves when the British emphasised the heroic role of the American *franc-tireurs* during the War of Independence. While to the Germans such civilians were criminals, to democratic societies they were heroes.

During the Boxer Rebellion of 1900, Kaiser Wilhelm II told the Germans in the force sent to relieve the Europeans in Peking to behave like the Huns of old. Clearly there was no racial connexion between the Germans and the Huns but the name stuck and so was born the image of the bull-necked, spike-helmeted German 'Hun', enemy of civilization, destroyer of culture and stock character of cartoons and films. The Germans could not understand how this idea of them had grown up and made the error of taking it seriously and attempting to defend themselves against it. Ninety-three eminent German scholars, including Gerhardt Hauptmann and Max Planck, issued a manifesto entitled *Es is nicht war* ('It is not so').[52] However, by trying to answer Allied charges of atrocities they merely gave the allegations more publicity. Meanwhile American journalists who accompanied the advance of the German armies through Belgium, like Richard Harding Davis, Will Irwin, Irving Cobb and Harry Hansen, wrote articles that contained searing indictments of German actions. Throughout Belgium there are today cemeteries bearing witness to the number of innocent civilians murdered by German troops. (For example, anyone who approached within 200 yards of a plane or a balloon whould be shot.) Against this the German government issued bulky, pedantic reports rejecting accusations of atrocities by German troops. Incredibly they were published only in German and were not translated into any foreign languages, presumably on the assumption that the neutral world spoke German.

The Germans failed to make a convincing defence of their invasion of Belgium and against the accusations of atrocities committed while they were there. It was all very well for writers like Thomas Mann to speak of the German people as

the most industrious, the most earnest, the best educated race in Europe. Russia stands for reaction, England for selfishness and perfidy, France for decadence, Germany for progress. German Kultur will enlighten the world and after this war there will never be another.[53]

– the world just did not see it that way. Bethmann-Hollweg, showing more perception than most, commented that by frequently proclaiming her right to rule the world Germany tended to get on people's nerves. Not only that but the behaviour of her soldiers in Belgium gave a sharper and more frightening edge to the caricature of the typical German; no longer the clumsy oaf but now the blood-crazed beast.

As disciples of Clausewitz the German military leaders looked for a short, sharp war, in which terror could be used against the civilian population in order to bring pressure to bear on the enemy leaders. It was on these grounds that German soldiers shot civilians, burned towns, and eventually razed the great cathedral city of Louvain. In British newspapers the headlines proclaimed 'The March of the Hun' and 'Treason to Civilization'.[54] The Germans were making war not just on the Allies but 'on posterity to the utmost generation'.[55] Against this, reports in German newspapers of German soldiers subjected to unspeakable cruelties by armed monks and by Belgian women and children, merely aroused ridicule. The French writer Romain Rolland wrote a public letter to his friend Gerhardt Hauptmann, asking 'Are you descedents of Goethe or of Attila the Hun?'[56] The Kaiser, absurdly insensitive to the niceties of propaganda, wrote to President Wilson of the United States declaring that his heart bled for the sufferings of Belgium, caused by the 'criminal and barbarous action of the Belgians'. His generals had been forced to take the strongest measures against 'the bloodthirsty population'.[57]

It was not as if atrocities were entirely one-sided. The German government made no attempt to use the ample evidence of Russian atrocities in East Prussia. Apparently the military leaders did not want to give the impression that the situation in East Prussia was at all dangerous, nor that their 'war on two-fronts' was ill-advised.

In August 1915 the Allies scored a propaganda hit with the case of Edith Cavell. She was a nurse working for the Red Cross inside German-occupied Belgium. She had apparently been helping British and French soldiers to escape to neutral Holland and was found guilty by a German court martial. Sentenced to be shot, her death caused a wave of revulsion in the United States, so well exploited by the British authorities that those Americans who had previously doubted the atrocity stories were forced to reconsider. The Cavell case was immensely damaging to Germany and yet her government failed to fight back when a perfect opportunity arose. A few weeks after Edith Cavell's death, two German nurses in a Red Cross hospital in France were found to be helping German soldiers to escape. Although they were executed by the French, the Germans made no attempt to exploit their deaths. The German view was that what they had done was in contravention of Red Cross rules and that the French had acted properly. Their courage could be admired but it was not a subject from which to make propaganda.[58]

Inside the United States, Dr Dernburg established a German Information Service, intending to put across the German case to the American people. However, his methods were clumsy in the extreme. His attempt to champion negroes against their white oppressors, amongst whom Britain and France as colonial powers could be numbered, was soon to be undermined by the German Government's objections that both Britain and France were using coloured troops in France against white Germans. In addition, Dernburg's campaign to win over America's 20 million population of German origin missed the point that many had left Germany in the first place to escape from the shadow of Prussian militarism and anti-liberal tendencies. Against German complaints that the British economic blockade was an inhuman outrage, the activities of the German submarines were far more decisive in moulding American opinion. The sinking of the *Lusitania*, the *Sussex* and then, in February 1917, the opening of unrestricted submarine warfare, completed the failure of German propaganda efforts in the United States.

The incompetence of Germany's own propaganda efforts caused their authors to underestimate the impact of British 'atrocity propaganda'. From as early as August 1914 Britain realised the value of winning the support of neutral opinion, in particular that of America, and as the war dragged on and a resolution seemed unlikely the friendship of the United States assumed even greater importance.

PART TWO

— I —
The Expedition to Cadiz (1625)

In planning, preparation and execution the expedition to Cadiz in 1625 was as poor as any military venture ever launched from Britain. Its weaknesses were so manifold that its failure is less surprising than the fact that it took place at all. It was the brainchild of George Villiers, the First Duke of Buckingham, who held the office of Lord High Admiral of England for a decade after 1618; during this period no less than four disastrous expeditions were launched to the Continent. Buckingham was a man impelled by personal ambition, who saw ends without the means of achieving them. His ambition far outstripped his resources, or the resources of the realm, and in his relations with Parliament, he overlooked the fact that his critics were also his paymasters.

A quarter of a century of peace had rusted the machinery of war in England and few foreigners regarded the English as a martial race. Indeed, Sir William Trumbull, Charles's ambassador in Brussels, reported that there the English were regarded as

... effeminate, unable to endure the fatigations and travails of a war; delicate, well-fed, given to tobacco, wine, strong drink, feather-beds; undisciplined, unarmed, unfurnished of money and munitions.[1]

Moreover, many people questioned the wisdom of an expedition against Spain at all, when the seas around England and even the coastal towns were not safe. Pirates swarmed in the Channel, preying on English shipping and terrorising ports all along the south coast.

The army of ten thousand which was assembled for the voyage to Cadiz was no better than an undisciplined rabble of pressed men, the dregs of society, untrained, unfed and badly clothed. Anyone more clear-sighted than Buckingham would have seen them for what they were, as far from being an army as he was from being an admiral. The Sergeant Major General of the Cadiz expedition, Sir William St Leger, informed him that 'the army, both by sea and land, be in a very miserable condition for want of clothes'. He added, in a letter to Conway, 'There are many that have not anything wherewithal to cover their nakedness'.[2] For months the soldiers had not been paid and many deserted or fell sick. At the end of August 1625 a new impressment of 2000 men was ordered and these were billeted on the farmers of South Devon. Trouble immediately broke out when the farmers discovered that the men had no money to pay for their food and the destitute soldiers took the law into their own hands, roaming the countryside looking for food, killing sheep and threatening violence. The Privy Council responded by issuing instructions to the Commissioners in Plymouth, to supply shirts, shoes and stockings to 'the poorer sort of soldier', and even trousers to those in dire need.

The whole subject of raising troops for foreign service needed attention. The aggressive foreign policy of Buckingham and the king placed a great strain on a system which had changed little since Elizabethan times and was riddled with corruption and inefficiency. Sir Edward Cecil, who was to command the Cadiz expedition, commented on his own levies that 'they were not to be accounted soldiers but the shadows of soldiers'. The levies of 1624 for Mansfeld's expedition had been described as 'gaol birds' and 'a rabble of poor rascals'. Those Buckingham took to Ré in 1627 were called 'the mere scumme of our provinces' by one of their own officers.[3]

When Sergeant-Major Leigh carried out a survey of 2500 men levied in 1625 for the Cadiz expedition, he found 200 defective, with 24 sick and 26 too old, being over sixty years of age. Four men were blind, one a minister of the church, one a raving madman, several were simpletons and a number were deformed or severely maimed. Clearly the system was being abused. One old and blind man was pressed simply because he had given evidence against the constable's brother, who had sworn to be avenged. A man of sixty, with eleven children, was pressed 'by the malice of Alderman Clearke'. Leigh found numerous examples of such malicious pressing but greed was a stronger motive. Even the Deputy Lieutenants of the counties were involved in corrupt practices.

Sir John Browne and Mr Henry Hastinges deputie lieutenants of the sayd country [Dorset] did release a miller an exstraordinarie stout man and tooke in his stead a boy of fifteene years of age, and as little as young, alsoe one other able man and for him took in a creature which when he stood upright on one of his leggs his other foote would reach but to the calves of it, one other man they sent which had not toase to his feet.[4]

The success of such an expedition as Buckingham envisaged required careful planning. The greatest need was to have a clear purpose and this was missing from the start. There was little information about the strength of the enemy forces and fortifications on the Spanish coast. Naval captains were ignorant about the currents, tides, bars and problems of pilotage around the intended target. The quality and suitability of the naval vessels, both as fighting machines and as transport had been overlooked and no consideration was given to the problem of disembarking the soldiers. Cecil emphasised from early on the importance of the quality of soldier needed rather than the quantity, particularly with musketeers. Moreover, it was most important that provisions of victuals and munitions were given priority. Cecil pointed out that failure in this area had been the cause of mishaps in earlier English expeditions.

. . . of all the exploits and undertakings of our nation, that none of them hath suffered (for the most part) more than through the negligence of provisions, as in victual, munition, boats for landing, and for receiving sick men to keep the rest from infection.[5]

However, in spite of the fact that all these matters were put clearly before the king and the Lord High Admiral, the expedition was allowed to sail, deficient in almost every way.[6]

Even the leadership was in doubt. It had been Buckingham's idea to strike against Spain by sea and it was assumed that he would lead, in his capacity as Lord High Admiral. Probably Buckingham intended to go, but first a bout of illness laid him low, and when he had recovered, Charles insisted that he should undertake a vital diplomatic mission to the Hague. So, retaining the pompous title of 'Generalissimo of the Fleet', Buckingham wrote to his friend Sir Edward Cecil, grandson of Elizabeth's great minister, and offered him first the position of Lord Marshal and subsequently the command of the entire expedition.

Cecil had the reputation of being a good officer, who had spent many years in the Dutch service, where he had absorbed the military principles of Maurice of Nassau. In a support capacity he would probably have proved an excellent choice, but this was to be his first experience of independent command. Moreover, amphibious operations were notoriously difficult and Cecil's ignorance of naval warfare was a major drawback. Only the support of a leading naval officer, like the Vice Admiral of the realm, Robert Mansell, could have overcome this disadvantage, yet in appointing the commanders of the expedition Buckingham selected men from the ranks of his friends and relations, irrespective of their experience in naval matters.

The Vice Admiral was to be the Earl of Essex who, though a brave officer, was eager to emulate his brilliant, if unstable, father's successful attack on Cadiz in 1596. Essex's irresponsibility during the next few months was to be a constant worry to Cecil. The Rear Admiral, the Earl of Denbigh, was married to Susan Villiers, Buckingham's sister. In fact, the six senior commanders were all soldiers, none of whom had experience of naval warfare.

After leaving the Netherlands, where sixty years of continuous fighting had honed the art of war to a fine point, Cecil was deeply shocked by the chaos he encountered on taking up his command at Plymouth. Here all was confusion. He wrote to Buckingham that the weaknesses of the fleet were, 'many, begotten out of so long a peace'.[7] The army was, if possible, even worse than the fleet. The ragamuffin soldiers had been billeted far and wide in an attempt to reduce trouble, so it had been difficult to assemble them all for training. Few understood how to use their weapons as these had been stored aboard the boats and the authorities refused to allow the men to have them in case they terrorised the local population in search of food.

The expedition had already cost half a million pounds and yet there were shortages in every department. There were examples of corruption, but more often the problem was simply inexperience. None of the Navy Commissioners had ever been called on before to prepare such a large undertaking and with the irregular flow of funds there was a very high incidence of wastage. As Cecil was aware, most of the troops had been pressed as early as April or May, even though they were not needed until well after midsummer. In the meantime, instead of being trained they merely sat about with nothing to do except contemplate the pangs of hunger in their bellies. Some deserted, others fell ill, and there was a constant need for replacements. Provisions rotted or were wasted.

As leader of the expedition, Cecil found it difficult to impose his personality on the other commanders and failed completely to mould his composite force into an effective unit. Yet few military leaders have been faced with such difficulties in defining their own role. Firstly, Cecil as a professional was aware of limitations in the preparation of both army and navy, but though he explained these to both Buckingham and to the king he was unable to effect any improvement. Perhaps he should have asserted himself more strongly. However, he owed his appointment in the first place to his friendship with the Lord High Admiral, and to have questioned the quality of Buckingham's preparations would have appeared ungrateful. A man of stronger character than Cecil would not have been so daunted, but he was accustomed to service, to loyalty and to doing his duty, and so, albeit unwilling, he accepted what he was given. He complained that he had found not one of the ten thousand men armed, and it had taken some time to recover their weapons from the fleet and have the rusty ones made good. In frustration he called for the punishment of the commissioners responsible for levying such 'rogues and . . . runawaies'.[8]

Cecil found himself hindered by two additional restraints. The king had instructed that he should be guided in all his actions by a Council of War, made up of the senior commanders and captains, and had also required him not to put the fleet at risk. A stronger man than Cecil would have known that, once at sea, his voice was law and that the king's instructions could guide his actions but never rule them. However, by adhering to the letter of the instructions Cecil was surrendering freedom of action and authority over his subordinates. They helped him to shirk his responsibility for making firm decisions and seeing them enforced.

Never before or since has an expedition set forth with so little idea of its purpose. Perhaps this was a reflection of the confused thinking of Buckingham and Charles, yet on 26 August 1625 the king had issued Cecil with a set of instructions, purporting to explain the aim of the enterprise, which was 'the protection and restitution of our dear brother and sister', meaning the Elector of the Rhineland Palatinate and his wife, Charles's sister, who had been driven from their lands by Spanish troops. In order to effect this 'restitution', Cecil's aim must be to weaken the king of Spain's trade,

. . . by taking and destroying his ships, galleys, frigates and vessels of all sorts; by spoiling his provisions in his magazines and port towns; by depriving him of seamen, mariners and gunners; by not suffering him to gather head from any port; by intercepting his fleets either going out or returning; and by taking in, and possessing some such place or places, in the many of his dominions, as may support and countenance our successive fleets.[9]

The instructions concluded with the following injunction:

Yet we do straitly charge you to have special care, principally to attend the surety and safety of our Navy, at all times, as the principal honour and bulwark of our Kingdom, the surety of your retreat and safety for the return of all our army.[10]

Such a responsibility could have worried any commander and Cecil wisely had a saving clause inserted which allowed him to execute any project which, though dangerous, had the support of the Council of War.

In order to understand the purpose of the expedition it is necessary to examine the instructions more closely. For example, if Charles had really intended to aid his sister and her husband, was an attack on the Spanish coast the most effective way to do it? Rusdorf, the Elector Palatine's agent in London, certainly did not think so. He argued that the ten thousand soldiers with the fleet could be more effectively used fighting the Habsburg troops on the Elbe or the Weser, assisting Christian of Denmark, rather than on the coast of Spain. On the other hand, there were different prizes to be won at sea and taking pride of place was the Spanish Plate Fleet on its way back to Spain from South America. What better way to convince the country of the effectiveness of Buckingham's foreign policy than to have the fleet return laden with enough gold to make Charles financially independent of Parliament? None of this was spelled out, though Spanish gold had been a traditional target during Elizabeth I's time. In that sense, this expedition cannot simply be seen in political terms but must be considered in the same light as some of the English expeditions of the last decade of Elizabeth's reign, as a semi-commercial venture.

If the instructions seemed wide ranging they were also remarkably unspecific. In the first place, what was the fleet's destination? It was to set sail eventually without anyone aboard, even Cecil, knowing precisely where it was going. This meant that no prior intelligence work was carried out to inform the commanders of the strength of coastal defences at the various Spanish ports which might be targets for attack. Instead Buckingham and the king visited Plymouth and held a council of war to try to decide where the fleet should go. No firm decision was reached, however, though San Lucar was considered a likely target. Before departing, Buckingham made it known that Cecil was to be made a peer of the realm as Viscount Wimbledon, presumably intending to strengthen his position in an expedition which contained various other peers.

Wimbledon's task was made all the more difficult since, as he did not know where he was going, he could not be certain whether the forces under his command were adequate for the tasks he had been set. No precise figures exist for the number of ships in the fleet, though Glanville in his journal refers to ninety vessels and six 'catches', having on board five thousand mariners and ten thousand soldiers.[11] Of the fleet, nine were great king's ships, which were heavily gunned, thirty were armed merchantmen, and the rest were Newcastle colliers, conscripted for the voyage which, as we shall see, were to give particularly poor service. Undoubtedly the strength of this fleet was more apparent than real. Wimbledon's flagship, the *Anne Royal*, was in fact the old *Ark Royal* used against the Armada, but renamed and renovated in 1608. Sir Michael Geere described the condition of his ship, the *St George*, considered by some 'the best of all the ffleet', in this way to his son:

. . . his Majestie hathe not a moore servisabler shipe in all his navey, but much wronged by reason of Rotten ropes & sayles & in all kyndes of stoares, viz, one shefte of our sayles, ware the owld Triumphes in the yere 88; and the other sute of sayles, which we had for our best, were the An Royals Cast sayles; our ffore shrowds ware the owld Garlands, which it semes served her many yeres, all, boothe sayles & ropes; starke Rattan oure store of new ropes; when we cam to make use of them & to open, the quoyles ware of divers pieces, & the best of them starke ratten, but fairly tard over. The shipe had nevar newe sayle made for her sence she was bult, lett all honest men Judge how his Majestie's service hathe been a bewsed.[12]

On 4 October the fleet was strengthened by the arrival of twenty Dutch ships, commanded by William of Nassau, bastard son of the great Prince Maurice. Of these, fifteen were to sail with Wimbledon, while five others patrolled the seas off Dover to ensure that neither the French nor the Dunkirk pirates took advantage of the absence of the English fleet.

As the day of departure grew closer, Wimbledon's depression increased. He wrote to the king on 4 October from his flagship, the *Anne Royal*, deprecating the departure of the fleet so late in the year and the fact that so much time had been wasted in the summer that they had no chance of surprising the Spanish ports, which would have 'all the intelligence that (they) can wish'. In his opinion, 'noe Navie . . . soe full of wants and defects was ever made more readie at soe short a warning'.[13] What is so astonishing is that Wimbledon, in this letter, anticipated virtually every mishap that occurred during the enterprise and yet allowed himself, by loyalty and a sense of duty, to undertake a mission which he knew was doomed to failure.[14]

On 3 October, Glanville tells us, articles of instruction were drawn up by Wimbledon for the guidance of the fleet. Due to one of the administrative muddles that was to dog the whole expedition they were not circulated to the individual vessels, an omission that was only discovered after the fleet had been driven back into harbour by storms. Even then it was only possible for rough, hand-written copies of the most important points to be delivered by rowing boat to a few selected vessels. The outcome was that many sea captains remained in ignorance on matters like places of rendezvous, Admirals' meetings and signals.

The fleet sailed from Plymouth on 5 October, only to encounter gale force winds. Essex, with his squadron, took refuge in Falmouth, but the bulk of the fleet re-entered Plymouth in indescribable confusion, with ships jostling each other in their eagerness to escape from the wind's fury. The scenes in the harbour were in fact a microcosm of the entire expedition, with no one able to impose discipline from above. Wimbledon's efforts were heroically futile, as he had himself rowed from boat to boat, bellowing instructions that were lost in the wind.

Three days later the fleet set sail again and was joined by Essex's ships. It was hoped that the fresh sea breezes would blow away memories of the months of dull routine in the south coast camps. However, Wimbledon was soon to have his force reduced when the king's ship *Lion*, with Vice Admiral Steward aboard, was found to be leaking and was discharged home. Why this had not been discovered before the fleet sailed is just one of the many mysteries that surround the preparation of the expedition. As if this was not enough, within three days the incompetence of the victualling and ordnance departments was starkly revealed. In Wimbledon's own words,

Manie shippes of the ffleet [were] but scantily victualled at our setting forth, which defect could not now be supplied, [1] pposed it to the Councell as a thing considerable how to take some present and seasonable course to make our victualls last the longer. And that to this purpose both the land and sea men might sitt from henceforth 5 and 5 in a mess, takeing onely the allowing formerly allotted to 4 men. . . .[15]

More bad weather struck the fleet, weakening ships already too weak for their purpose. *The Long Robert* capsized and sank with all hands, while a longboat from the *Convertive*, attempting to rescue survivors, was also lost. Wimbledon's flagship, the *Anne Royal*, suffered badly, with her mast loosening, her longboats swept overboard, her cannon breaking loose and smashing the woodwork, and sea pouring into the holds so that men laboured up to their knees in water to keep her afloat.

Ten days out, Wimbledon ordered a council of war to collect damage reports. The sea captains brought to him every complaint, real or imagined, that they could. Here was the occasion for Wimbledon to assert himself, but the sea was not his natural milieu, and he bowed to the superior knowledge of the sailors, overlooking the fact that few of the captains, particularly those who owned their own colliers, wished to risk their ships in what many felt to be a foolhardy exploit. Another king's ship, the *Dreadnought*, was said to be leaking badly but Wimbledon prevailed on its captain to stay with the fleet, which he did, albeit most unwillingly. A major problem was that during the stormy weather most of the ships had lost their longboats, which would make it difficult to disembark the soldiers if a landing was attempted. No pinnaces had accompanied the fleet, even though Wimbledon, before leaving Plymouth, had pointed out the absolute need for them in an amphibious operation. Moreover, victuals and water had been contaminated by seawater, and the gunpowder soaked. So depressing was the list of complaints that, as Wimbledon puts it, 'I was moved to abstaine from inquiring anie further how things now stood, lest while everyone sought to aggregate his own misfortunes, some discoyragement might thereby growe to the prejudice of the voyage. . . .'[16]

Some reports, however, could not be overlooked. It was now discovered that many of the muskets on board the fleet were defective, some of them grossly so, and had no touch-holes. In addition, the bullets supplied did not fit the firearms and the bullet moulds were warped. As if this was not enough, a serious argument over precedence developed between the sea captains and the lords who commanded the soldiers aboard each ship.

During the storms, contact had been lost with the squadrons of Essex and Denbigh, consisting of about forty ships. This was worrying enough, but on 19 October, approaching the coast of Spain, ten unidentified ships were sighted and Wimbledon ordered his fastest vessels to pursue them. An exciting hour-long chase ensued, with tension high on the English ships and everyone hoping that they had fallen in with the Spanish treasure fleet. How great was the chagrin when it was discovered that the 'flying enemy' were in fact part of Essex's squadron, who had carelessly failed to signal their identity as Wimbledon had instructed in his articles of 3 October.

With the coast of Spain in sight the time had come to decide the destination of the fleet. At a council of war on 20 October, the question of San Lucar, shelved at the earlier meeting with Buckingham and Charles, was again raised. Wimbledon informed the council of the king's instructions to make a landing on Spanish soil. As Lisbon had already been passed, the choice was really between San Lucar and Cadiz. To Wimbledon's astonishment, the sea captains who had supported a landing at San Lucar at the meeting with the king now declared that the entrance to that harbour would be too dangerous so late in the year.

Although he was prepared to accept their opinion he felt justified in asking why they had not made these objections to the king at Plymouth. They replied that it was now stormy and the depth of winter, while then it had not been. Exasperated by such logic Wimbledon could only bow to their greater experience of the sea. In 1627, when Wimbledon's diary was published, Admiral Monson seized on this point.

If the masters knew no more than the captains, I think they knew little, for I am informed few of the captains had any experience and skill in sea affairs . . . could the summer remove the bar and give them a safe entrance? Could the summer season give them more knowledge of pilot-ship than they had before coming thither? Or did they not know that winter was approaching when they were called to the council at Plymouth, for it could not be above twenty days more winter than it was when they were at Plymouth?[17]

THE EXPEDITION TO CADIZ (1625)

For a nation which, a generation before, had bred seamen to be the scourge of every sea and every enemy fleet, the captains she sent to Cadiz revealed just how low England's stock had fallen. Only Wimbledon's ignorance of naval matters saved him from knowing how badly served he was.

The council, having rejected San Lucar, decided to sail for Cadiz, with its safe anchorage at St Mary Port. In doing so it must have been in everyone's mind, not least in Essex's, that they were about to re-enact one of the most successful and famous actions of the Elizabethan period, the raid on Cadiz in 1596, an almost legendary episode, bejewelled with such famous names as Essex, Raleigh, Howard of Effingham and Vere. Eventually it was decided that St Mary Port, near the Bay of Cadiz, would be the safest point for landing troops, who could then march the twelve miles overland to capture San Lucar from the landward side.

The lack of prior intelligence work meant that the English had no current information on the state of defences along the Spanish coast. It was generally assumed that the port of Cadiz would have been strongly fortified after the ease with which it had fallen in 1596. This proved not to be the case and, had they known it, the city would have fallen to them with scarcely a struggle. From this point onwards Wimbledon and his forces moved as in a fog, with no clear plan and with no appreciation of Spanish reactions.

On 22 October, Wimbledon instructed Essex in the *Swiftsure* to hasten into the Bay of Cadiz, make for St Mary Port and anchor there, leaving enough space for the ships of other squadrons to come close in to the shore to discharge their troops. Without adequate reconnaissance it is hardly surprising that everything went wrong. The *Swiftsure* crowded on sail and headed into the bay, followed in a leisurely fashion by the other ships of Essex's squadron.

On the other side of the bay, nearest Cadiz itself, Essex sighted a squadron of twelve large Spanish ships at anchor, including the 1200 ton *Admiral of Naples*, with some fifteen galleys alongside. Here was his opportunity to emulate his father's exploits in this same bay thirty years before. Instead of carrying out Wimbledon's instructions, he headed straight for the Spanish ships, which cut their cables and tried to escape up a narrow channel leading to the town of Port Royal. Unsupported by any other English vessel the *Swiftsure* engaged the Spanish ships and the shore batteries of Cadiz. Wimbledon, entering the harbour, was warned

---

7. Wimbledon's failure to secure the Bridge of Zuazo enabled the Spaniards to reinforce the city of Cadiz while the English fleet was bombarding Fort Puntal.

THE EXPEDITION TO CADIZ (1625)

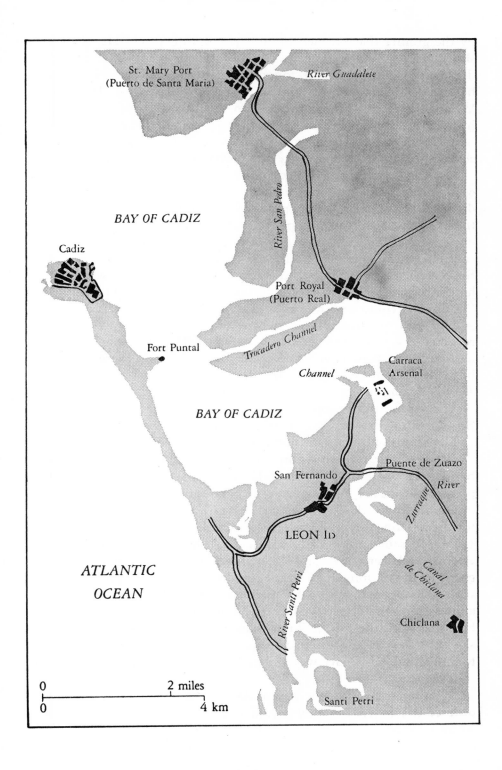

St. Mary Port
(Puerto de Santa Maria)

River Guadalete

River San Pedro

BAY OF CADIZ

Cadiz

Port Royal
(Puerto Real)

Fort Puntal

Trocadero Channel

Channel

Carraca
Arsenal

BAY OF CADIZ

Puente de Zuazo

San Fernando

Zurraque River

Canal de Chiclana

LEON Id

ATLANTIC
OCEAN

River Santi Petri

Chiclana

Santi Petri

0		2 miles
0		4 km

by the gunfire that his vice admiral was in difficulties. He ordered his ships forward to the rescue but many of the merchant ships and colliers deliberately hung back or fought faintly in spite of their admiral's bellowed threats, now lost amidst the sounds of gunfire. The fact that Wimbledon did not even know the names of his own ships can hardly have helped, nor the fact this was the first time he had commanded ships in battle, and that he thought they could move with the ease of cavalry squadrons rather than as leaky and barnacled leviathans.

Nevertheless, the Spanish could see only the numbers, not the quality of their opponents, and were content to make their escape. A moment of decision was at hand. By the purest chance Wimbledon had been given the opportunity of carrying out one of Charles's prime instructions, to destroy or capture Spanish ships, but he was going to lose it by being too cautious. Again his naval advisors gave him craven support. As the Spanish ships moved into the narrow creek Wimbledon was assured by his sea captains that they would be unable to escape from there and that the English could return later to destroy them at their leisure.

This was to prove disastrously wrong. Indeed, the whole episode reflected the incompetence of the captains. Had the entry into Cadiz harbour been made at ebb tide rather than at the full there would have been insufficient water in the creek for the Spanish to have effected their escape. Again one sees the consequences of poor planning and faulty reconnaissance. Why were the English unaware of the presence of the Spanish fleet? Precautions elementary in any age were being neglected.

The English fleet now anchored in the bay and Wimbledon summoned a council of war. The situation had changed and an overland journey to San Lucar would be impossible. However, the English were now to be presented with the chance of an even greater prize. It had never been the intention to attack Cadiz which, it was assumed, would be strongly fortified. However, at great personal risk, an English trader named Jenkinson sailed from Cadiz to the English fleet to tell them that the Spanish had been taken completely unawares and that the city was weakly garrisoned. An immediate attack could take Cadiz and provide Charles with a base on the Spanish mainland. However, Wimbledon again allowed himself to be swayed by the advice of the sea captains. They told him that until the fort at Puntal was captured the fleet could not rest safely, and as this concern had been uppermost in the king's instructions to him Wimbledon gave way and prepared a night bombardment of the fort.

As darkness fell, twenty Newcastle colliers, of shallow draught, were ordered to join five Dutch warships in the attack on Puntal, while three king's ships, which drew too much water to go close inshore, formed a second line. In the darkness there was confusion. The Dutch ships closed in and were met by a hail of fire from the fort but the colliers, disregarding orders, remained calmly at anchor. The Dutch took heavy damage, with two of their ships running aground to avoid sinking. At first light an irate Dutch admiral arrived on Wimbledon's flagship, denouncing the Newcastle captains for not supporting him. According to St Leger the colliers contained 'as ill captains as ever were in the world'.[18]

One suspects that a commander of stature like Drake, Hawkins or Raleigh would have known how to handle a situation like this. A few summary executions would probably have had the required effect. But Wimbledon was no leader and it was at moments like this that he proved it. His response to what amounted to mutiny was to have himself rowed from collier to collier warning the crews about their future behaviour and ordering them to support a renewed attack by the king's ships. With Essex leading the attack in the *Swiftsure* the colliers were at last forced into action of a sort though they again hung well back from the fighting. A few long shots from their guns proved more dangerous to Essex's squadron than to the fort and when one of them sent a shot through the stern of Essex's flagship they were ordered to stop firing. Perhaps they had made their point.

Under the heavy battering from the English ships the fire from the fort began to slacken and Wimbledon at last decided to land his troops to take possession of it, by escalade if necessary. Here was an opportunity for Wimbledon to assert himself on his accustomed dry land. Having directed Sir John Burroughs, another veteran commander, where to land the leading troops, he could only watch in bafflement as Burroughs disobeyed his order. Trying to take the fort at a dash, Burroughs landed his troops right under the walls with the result that the first boat was raked with musket fire from stern to stern, Captain Bromingham killed and others crushed by large stones hurled from the parapet onto the helpless soldiers and sailors beneath. A chastened Burroughs now landed the remaining troops where Wimbledon had originally intended, and the Spanish garrison surrendered. As a comment on the effectiveness of the English naval gunfire, it was now discovered that in spite of expending two thousand rounds of ammunition the ships had inflicted virtually no damage on the fort.

Wimbledon had captured Fort Puntal, but at a wholly disproportionate cost. In the twenty-four hours it had taken him to subdue the fort, the Spaniards had been able to re-garrison and re-provision the town of Cadiz, rendering it invulnerable to English attack. Don Fernando de

Giron, the Governor of Cadiz, had acted with great energy from the moment the English fleet was sighted. Many of his regular garrison were away with the Plate fleet and he knew he could not resist an attack unless he was immediately reinforced. He sent messengers to the local army commander, the Duke of Medina Sidonia, who rushed in troops from San Lucar and the surrounding towns. When the English had taken Cadiz in 1596 they had sent three regiments to secure the bridge of Zuazo, which connected the island of Leon, on which the city stood, to the mainland. Wimbledon, on the other hand, seemed to have learned nothing from the earlier English expedition and made no effort to fortify this bridge until too late. It was by this route that the Spanish were able to bring in reinforcements, while under cover of darkness galleys ferried supplies into Cadiz. All of this was taking place while the English and Dutch ships illuminated the night with their gun flashes, battering the fort whose defence undoubtedly saved Cadiz.

By Sunday morning Cadiz's garrison had been swollen to four or five thousand and Wimbledon saw that there was no hope now of taking the city by assault. In any case he had no confidence in his troops or their leaders. The expedition had failed from the moment he had been persuaded not to pursue the Spanish ships into the creek. Now all hope of surprise had gone. The bombardment of Fort Puntal had acted as a signal to raise the whole country and troops were on the march from Seville, Malaga, Gibraltar, Lisbon and many other towns, placing the English in danger of being trapped.

Ignorant of these developments Wimbledon continued the disembarkation of his troops at Puntal, until news arrived that an enemy force had been sighted at the Zuazo Bridge. Leaving Denbigh in charge of the fleet he issued orders for provisions to be brought ashore and for an attack to be planned against the Spanish ships in the creek at Port Royal. Then he marched off with eight thousand men towards Hercules' Pillars to try to cut off the Spanish force. After a six mile march, encountering no Spaniards, he concluded,

it seemeth that this alarm is false. But since we are thus forwards on our way, if you will, we will march on. It may be we may light on some enemy. If we do not, we may see what kind of bridge it is that hath been so much spoken of.[19]

Such naivety would be unbelievable were it not to be found printed in Wimbledon's later account of the expedition, along with the names of the other commanders who had agreed with his plan to go off on this 'wild goose-chase'.

The island of Leon, over which the English army were marching, was flat and marshy, given over mainly to salt production. Indeed, as they marched the soldiers may have seen the curious conical-shaped pillars of salt collected from the watery swamps that make up much of the island. The atmosphere on the island seemed impregnated with salt and brought on dreadful thirst for the soldiers, toiling in the heat of the Spanish sun. Their surroundings, almost surrealistic, were now to be the scene of a kind of grim farce.

While the troops were halted at Hercules' Pillars, Sir John Burroughs brought Wimbledon the news that none of his regiment had carried any provisions with them on the march or had eaten anything since landing. When Colonel Bruce pointed out that the same was true of his men, Wimbledon had no alternative but to send both regiments back to Puntal. Hardly had he recovered from this setback than there was news of a new sighting of Spanish troops. In fact it was another false alarm but without even attempting to check the accuracy of the report, Wimbledon ordered his men to march on towards the Zuazo Bridge.

Wimbledon can hardly have suspected that the bulk of his men were marching with empty knapsacks, having neither food nor drink. Why he was not informed earlier is just one of the many mysteries that surrounds the march to Zuazo. With night approaching and no Spanish troops in sight Wimbledon decided to camp for the night in an open field, near some deserted buildings belonging to the Duke of Medina Sidonia. At once the men began to complain that they were thirsty and hungry. When a report was brought to Wimbledon that a large store of wine in iron-bound casks had been found in one of the houses, in 'common humanity' he decided to allow the men to slake their thirst with some of it.

Orders were given for a butt of wine to be allocated to each regiment. The salty atmosphere, the raging thirst, the hot sun and the empty stomachs soon produced a not very surprising result. The army degenerated into a raging, drunken mob. The half-famished soldiers threw off all restraint and broke into the wine store, smashing open the casks. Discipline collapsed, with men firing wildly in the air, shooting each other and threatening any officer who tried to restrain them. When Wimbledon ordered the wine to be tipped away and wasted, men scooped it up in their helmets and then besieged the commander's room, threatening his life. For his protection Wimbledon's bodyguard had to fire into the mob. As Wimbledon later explained, 'I never did think myself to be in so much danger, for certainly the enemy with three hundred men might had routed us and cut our throats.[20] For the rest of that dismal night, the officers had to protect themselves from the attacks of their own men.

Wimbledon made many mistakes during the expedition but it is difficult not to sympathise with him on this occasion. Although the final responsibility rests with the army commander he should have been able to rely on his subordinates to do their jobs thoroughly. As Dalton points out,

An army containing nine colonels, a colonel-general, a sergeant-major-general, a Commissary General (Captain Mason), and endless captains and subalterns, ought not to have to depend on the commander-in-chief for filling their knapsacks with food.[21]

The incident with the wine was a bad misjudgement on Wimbledon's part but it was not the first and was not going to be the last occasion when English troops made the most of a supply of free wine. However, it simply added to the commander's profound disillusionment with his mission. As he told Buckingham,

I must confess it put me to some trouble and care, having to do with the command of the multitude in such a case, that even when they are sober they are incapable of order.[22]

The next morning Wimbledon decided that there was nothing to be done but to return to Puntal. His men were in no condition to meet the enemy, short of food as they were and obviously hung over. Leaving a hundred or so still drunk in the ditches, later to be butchered by the Spanish, the dismal army turned back and the road to Puntal was scattered with weapons and equipment as men lightened the burdens of the march. What Wimbledon had hoped to gain by this extraordinary promenade into enemy territory is difficult to understand. Presumably his intentions were defensive for he could hardly had expected the troops, of whom he was so scathing, to meet the Spanish in fair fight and beat them. But if his aim was to secure the Zuazo Bridge it was far too late to prevent reinforcements reaching Cadiz. If it was to secure his own evacuation there would seem to be little reason for his orders to land provisions and munitions at Puntal. It is unlikely that Wimbledon had any clear plans any more.

On his return to the flagship he met with further disappointment. Denbigh had, as ordered, prepared an attack on the Spanish ships in the Port Royal creek, to be led by Sir Samuel Argall. However, a delay of eighteen hours had followed this decision as many of the seamen from Argall's squadron were on shore and had to be recalled by beat of drum. At last fully manned, the English ships cautiously approached the creek only to find that in the time they had been allowed, the Spaniards, under the Marquis of Cropani, had prepared defences, sinking four hulks across the entrance and leaving room only for one boat to enter at a time. The great Spanish warships were drawn up in the creeks so that their full broadsides could play on any single intruder. Argall withdrew in frustration and took the bad news to Wimbledon on the *Anne Royal*.

Of the king's instructions little remained feasible except that relating to the interception of the Plate fleet. Wimbledon therefore ordered the re-embarkation of the men. Luckily, a number of shallops had been found at Hercules' Pillars and these considerably eased the transport problems.

That night it began to rain heavily and the soldiers, inadequately clothed and fed, and exhausted from their constant marching and counter-marching, spent their last night on Spanish soil in the open and in a pitiful state. The next day the fleet swept out of Cadiz Bay, 'as majestic and as harmless as when it had arrived six days before'.[23]

Rumours of war had crossed the seas even before the Spanish Plate fleet had left American waters; when it did sail it therefore took care to travel far to the south and then skirt the coast of Africa, entering Cadiz harbour a mere two days after Wimbledon had left. The English did sight eight ships and gave chase but they could not overtake them for their vessels were now 'foul and consequently ill sailers'. Perhaps it was fortunate that the English did not encounter the Spaniards for there was little in the performance of either soldiers or sailors to suggest they would have prevailed.

And now sickness broke out aboard many ships. The provisions were rotten and there was a desperate need for fresh drinking water. So on 21 October Wimbledon was forced to despatch twelve ships home carrying the horses and the sick men. Showing courage both admirable and futile he resolved 'to beate it out at sea in the continuance of this service'. But sickness was decimating the fleet and some vessels were unworkable. Lord De La Warr informed Wimbledon that the sickness was so widespread in his ship, 'that unles some of his sicke men were taken from him and other healthie Sea-Men give him in their steades, his companie was so weake thay could not man nor conduct the shipp but must let her drive in the sea'.[24]

The idea of moving infected men into areas free of infection was a remarkably unsound one. However, Wimbledon ordered thirty ships in the fleet to supply two healthy men each and receive two sick men in their place. Isolation of disease aboard ship was not unknown in the seventeenth century and in this instance Wimbledon acted with a startling lack of common sense. Aboard the ships conditions were appalling, with sick men lying below decks in total darkness through lack of candles; deprived of fresh drinking water, they subsisted on sips of foul beer. Sir Michael Greere wrote to his son that the food smelled so foully that, 'no dog in

Paris Garden would eat it'. [25] By 17 November it was obvious that further delay would spell the total ruin of the fleet and so, reluctantly, Wimbledon ordered a return to England.

Now the weather worsened and the fleet was scattered, with Wimbledon's flagship so badly damaged that it was doubtful if she could reach an English port. Eventually, on 11 December, she limped into the Irish port of Kinsale with six feet of water in her holds, carrying 160 sick men aboard and having already lost 130. She was followed by the *Constant Reformation*, without masts, and with a crew dying of thirst and starvation. Essex in the *Swiftsure* had made better time and arrived at Falmouth on 5 December, with several other ships from his squadron. And so through the winter months survivors struggled in along the south coast to discharge their wretched cargoes of human flotsam into the coastal towns. The vice-admiral of Devon, Sir John Eliot, gave an eyewitness account of the misery he saw.

The miseries before us are great, and great the complaints of want and illness of the victual. There is now to be buried one Captain Bolles, a landsman, who died since their coming in, and with much grief expressed the occasion of his sickness to be scarcity and corruption of the provisions. The soldiers are not in better case. They are in great numbers thrown overboard, and yesterday fell down here seven in the streets. [26]

Sir William St Leger described his own troops.

The state they now stand in is most miserable. They stink as they go, the poor rags they have are rotten and ready to fall if they be touched. The soldiers are sick and naked, and the officers moneyless and friendless, not able to feed themselves a week. [27]

The great expedition to Cadiz had ended. In Forster's words, it had been 'an attempt to fill the king's coffers by piratical foray on the wealth of Spain', [28] and as such it had failed. But who was really responsible for the failure? In attributing blame it is difficult to know where to start or when to stop, so great was the incompetence of all concerned in both planning and execution.

As Wimbledon had known from the start, the raw materials from which the enterprise was built were unsuited to their task. The soldiers were untrained, undisciplined and unwilling, with poor equipment and low morale, after waiting about in the coastal towns of Devon for most of the summer. Once the voyage began they found that their victuals were poor, the cyder foul and the provisions generally so bad that thousands of men were condemned to sickness, deprivation and death. The officials who supplied the fleet, like Sir James Bagg and Sir Allen Apsley, were seriously culpable.

The ships themselves were unsuited to such a voyage at such a time of year. Only weeks before sailing serious weaknesses had been revealed when several of them were outrun by pirate ships. Their hulls made them slow sailers, while their tackle was old and worn, some of it even dating from the time of the Armada. Their captains were cautious and possessed none of the fire that had inspired their Elizabethan forefathers. Their advice to Wimbledon had a disastrous effect on the commander's actions and contributed in a major way to the expedition's failure.

Wimbledon showed himself to be unsuited to high command. Although he was brave he was indecisive and failed to exert sufficient authority over his subordinates. He seemed to take the king's instructions too literally on occasions and allowed the sea captains too great an influence in the councils of war. There were occasions when he seemed to display little military competence or even common sense, yet he was unfortunate in having with him a group of commanders who shared Buckingham's favour though they lacked military ability.

Yet, while he did not accompany the expedition, the failure was chiefly Buckingham's. He had selected both the commanders at sea and the officials at home who had organised the fleet and provisioned it. His system of personal favouritism had ensured that those chosen had a vested interest in satisfying him as their pay- and place-master. As Lord High Admiral, he had no clear views on the purpose of the fleet and allowed financial and political pressures to sway him, so that it eventually became a pawn in his struggle with a difficult Parliament over finance.

The greatest tragedy of all was that nothing was learned from the fiasco. Neither Charles nor Buckingham sought the reasons for the failure and so were doomed to repeat them on the island of Ré. None of those who had provisioned the fleet were called upon to account for its deficiencies, nor did they lose the admiral's favour or patronage. No officer of the dockyard was asked to explain the condition of spars and sails or the foulness of the keels that made the ships so slow. Had it not been for the thousands of human wrecks stranded in coastal towns, forced to beg their way amidst a hostile populace, it might never have been thought that there had been a voyage to Cadiz.

—2—

The Battle of Marston Moor (1644)

The use of the term 'Cavaliers' to describe those who fought for the king in the English Civil War originated during the disturbances, late in 1641, between the London apprentices and the king's men led by the Lieutenant of the Tower, the 'bold and swaggering' Colonel Thomas Lunsford.[1] Where the close-cropped heads of the apprentices earned them the offensive title 'Roundheads', the king's men were abusively referred to as 'caballeros', signifying Spanish troopers, Catholic oppressors of Protestants, the hated national enemy. Only later did the word 'Cavalier' take on its more romantic associations.

However, it is as an adjective rather than as a noun that the word enters our investigation of military incompetence, for here 'cavalier' becomes less a definition of a man's status or politics and more a reflection of his attitude to warfare. Certainly those who had this spirit were courageous, yet so many of them were merely amateurs who rejected the professionalism of those who had served on the continent in the Dutch or Swedish service. Their dash may have carried them to victories on many fields yet, as the parliamentary armies became more professional, it became obvious that the cavalier spirit was not enough. It had, after all, its drawbacks. A thesaurus tells us that 'cavalier' can mean 'rash, incautious, imprudent, careless, giddy, reckless, wild, desperate, hot-headed, foolhardy, impulsive, over-confident', and it is interesting to see how often these qualities have been associated with military incompetence. It was at Marston Moor on 2 July 1644, in what was probably the decisive battle of the English Civil War, that the 'cavalier' spirit of one of the king's commanders, Sir John Byron, lost a battle which should have been won. His impetuous charge against the numerically superior cavalry of Cromwell destroyed the careful planning of his commander, Prince Rupert of the Rhine.

The prince, who was instrumental in raising the siege of York in July 1644, was far from being merely the personification of the 'cavalier spirit' that is sometimes presented. He was an experienced soldier even before he joined his uncle's forces in 1642 as General of the Horse, and his reputation for spirited leadership was firmly based on victories at Powick Bridge, Cirencester, Chalgrove Field, Bristol and Newark. As Peter Young has pointed out,

... Prince Rupert provided the bravura which gave the Royalist cavalry their undoubted dash. But, although an expert with sword and pistol and a gallant man to follow in a cavalry charge, the Prince was much more than a mere sabreur. During three years of imprisonment, at an age when nowadays a man of his status might have been at a university, he had made use of his time to improve his theoretical knowledge of the Art of War: military engineering, siege work, mining, all these subjects came within his view. . . .[2]

However, as Rupert moved towards York he was a man impelled towards battle by the belief that his king, Charles I, had instructed him by letter to seek out and destroy the enemy armies. This letter, sent by Charles on 14 June 1644, has been the subject of much controversy. Military historians like Peter Young have pointed out that in the letter there is no specific command from the king to fight a battle after York had been relieved.[3] The truth must therefore lie in Rupert's own interpretation of his instructions. Here is the relevant text from Charles's letter.

If Yorke be lost, I shall esteeme my Crown little lesse, unlesse supported by your suddaine Marche to me and a Miraculous Conquest in the South, before the effects of the Northern power can be found heere; but if Yorke be relieved and you beate the Rebelles Armies of both Kingdomes, which ar before it, then but otherwise not, I may possible make a shift, (upon the defensive) to spinn out tyme, untill you come to assist mee: Wherefor I command and conjure you, by the dewty and affection which I know you beare me, that (all new enterpryses laid aside) with all your force to the relife of Yorke; but if that be eather lost, or have fried themselves from the besiegers, or that for want of pouder you cannot undertake that worke; that you immediately Marche, with your whole strength, to Woster, to assist me and my Army, without whiche, or your having relived Yorke by beating the Scots, all the successes you can afterwards have, most infallibly, will be uselesse unto me. . . .[4]

The letter was written by the king at a time when he and his advisers were in a state approaching panic, with the parliamentary armies of Essex and Waller closing in on them. One of the king's advisers, Lord Culpeper, considered the letter a mistake, commenting 'Why, then, before God you are undone, for upon this peremptory order he will fight, whatever comes on't'.[5] Yet Culpeper was not alone in knowing Rupert's impulsive nature and the king is certainly at fault for sending such a confused document, knowing that it might drive his nephew into taking a desperate and ill-advised gamble. Charles believed that a successful battle against the parliamentary armies of Manchester, Fairfax and Leven would be necessary before York could be relieved. In this case the letter did require Rupert to fight to win the relief of the city. However, if the city could be relieved without a fight, which Rupert's skilful manoeuvering enabled it to be, then surely the king's instructions are that Rupert should move with his whole army to Worcester. Why then, having carried out the king's command to relieve York as well as achieving a great personal triumph, did Rupert stake everything, including the city of York, on such a risky encounter? This was the question asked by the Marquis of Newcastle and James King, Lord Eythin, who had been commanding the defence of York. In reply to them Rupert said that he had an absolute command from the king to fight the rebels. But did he really believe this himself or was he using the letter to bluff the unwilling commanders into supporting him? The historian can never know for certain, although Rupert's later actions suggest that he was seeking an encounter with the enemy while he possessed the psychological advantage, for as Peter Young has said, Rupert was a commander who had the habit of 'grasping the nettle'.[6] It is difficult therefore to avoid the conclusion that Rupert was deliberately exceeding his instructions by seeking battle and that he misled Newcastle into supporting him against his wishes by claiming that he had explicit orders from the king.

The three allied armies which had been besieging York, the Scots under Lord Leven, the Northern army under Lord Fairfax and that of the Eastern Association under the Earl of Manchester, comprised about 27,000 men, against Rupert's advancing force of no more than 14,000. Against such odds Rupert must have known from the outset that he would need the support of the York garrison before giving battle to the allies. His first task, therefore, was to bypass the enemy, force them to raise the siege and then link up with Newcastle's troops inside the city.

The allied generals were following the reports of Rupert's progress through Lancashire but had over-estimated his strength by some four thousand. As a result, on hearing of his arrival at Knaresborough, west of York, Leven decided he must raise the siege of the city, thereby abandoning his siege guns and a consignment of four thousand new pairs of boots, and move his entire army onto the moorland near Long Marston, to block the approach of Rupert's army.

Rupert, as a feint, sent a strong force of cavalry to face Leven's armies on Marston Moor, which the allies assumed to be Rupert's vanguard and therefore formed up in battle lines to await the arrival of his main body. Rupert, meanwhile, was moving rapidly north, crossing the River Ure at

Boroughbridge early on the morning of 1 July and marching into York from the north. This brilliant manoeuvre enabled him to link up with Newcastle's army in the city. On the other hand, it may also have given Rupert a feeling of overconfidence, for rather than resting his troops and attempting to weld a unified command with Newcastle, he decided to bring on an immediate battle with the three allied armies.

Unwilling to lose his momentum, Rupert sent Goring, who was General of the Northern Horse, into the city with a message for the Marquis of Newcastle, ordering the latter to join him, with the York garrison, ready to give battle the next day. This proved to be a major error of judgement on Rupert's part. He failed to understand the strain both the garrison and its commanders had been under during the siege, and his 'cavalier' treatment of Newcastle, a commander twice his age who had held unquestioned command over the North for two years, showed a fault in his own character. As Peter Young has said,

Rupert was not only a young man, he was a younger son, impecunious and touchy for all his victories and undoubted talent. Had he been as sure of himself in the council chamber as he was in the field, the armies quartered about York on the night of 1 July 1644 might have won the war for their king.[7]

The York garrison felt it deserved, if not fulsome praise, at least a few days of rest. The climactic feelings of relief that everyone must have felt on learning that 'the prince' had come to their rescue did not prepare them for the sudden anti-climax of knowing that they must march out against the enemy to risk their lives again so soon.

In fact, the York commanders, having endured so much, were piqued by Rupert's attitude, and James King, Lord Eythin, particularly so. King was a cautious Scot whose personal dislike of the prince stemmed from their experiences together in Germany. Rupert had been captured at the battle of Lemgo in 1638 because, some said, of King's dilatoriness. In response to this accusation, King blamed that day's defeat on the prince's 'forwardness'. Wherever the truth lay, there can be no doubt that King did everything he could to delay, if not actually prevent, Rupert's encounter with the parliamentary armies.

Newcastle, on the other hand, was a very different proposition. William Cavendish, Marquis of Newcastle, was an extremely wealthy grandee who had placed his resources at the disposal of the king. Though no soldier, he was a fine horseman and inspired loyalty among his many followers in the north. He was fulsome in his praise of Rupert, perhaps too much so. In his courtly letter of thanks to Rupert for the relief of York he may well have given the prince rather the wrong impression.

You are welcome, Sir, so many several ways, as it is beyond my arithmetic to number, but this I know, you are the Redeemer of the North and the Saviour of the Crown. Your name, Sir, hath terrified three great Generals and they fly before it. It seems their design is not to meet Your Highness for I believe they have got a river between you and them but they are so newly gone as there is no certainty at all of them or their intentions, neither can I resolve since I am made of nothing but thankfulness and obedience to Your Highness's commands.[8]

Rupert assumed from this that Newcastle was placing himself immediately under his orders, though this was by no means what the Marquis had intended. Indeed, Newcastle was so annoyed by Rupert's peremptory order to join him with the whole garrison that he threatened to resign. Persuaded against this action, he and King now tried to stall the prince from seeking battle straight away, in the hope that the differences between the parliamentary leaders would result in the break-up of the allied army without a fight, a not unlikely eventuality.[9]

The prince was told that the gates of the city had been blocked by earth and masonry during the siege, which would take a long time to clear. Moreover, would it not be better to wait until the 5000 reinforcements Newcastle was expecting from the North under Colonel Clavering arrived?[10] Rupert, however, insisted that he had a 'command from the king to fight the Scottish army whereso'er he met them'. Eythin was unconvinced by Rupert's reasoning and, according to Sir Francis Cobbe, he tried to persuade Newcastle not to commit the whole garrison to so dangerous an enterprise. He played on the fact that Rupert had 'insulted' the Marquis by his immediate assumption of command, But Newcastle's loyalty to King Charles was never in doubt. He swallowed his pride and prepared to follow the prince's orders, leaving Eythin to organise the infantry.

Wedgwood, drawing on Sir Hugh Cholmley's narrative, describes the mutiny of the York garrison which followed.

[Eythin] . . . with culpable irresponsibility, stirred up the irritation of the soldiers in York which it should have been his business to allay. He said, in the hearing of many, that he did not think the men should be expected to march until they had at least received all their arrears of pay. The opinion soon became a general mutter in the camp; many of the men believed that Eythin had positively commanded them not to march. By two o'clock in the morning there was a general mutiny; they would not move a step.[11]

While Newcastle, accompanied by his Lifeguard and a 'cortege of all the gentry in York', rode out from the Micklegate the next morning to join Rupert and his army at Marston Moor, Eythin was apparently prepared to let the footsoldiers continue plundering the enemy trenches outside the city. Why this was necessary when they had had the whole of 1st July to do so can only be explained by Eythin's determination to delay things so that Rupert would abandon the idea of a battle. In the event, he achieved the worst possible result, in that he delayed Rupert and yet did not prevent a battle, so that the Royalists were forced to fight at a disadvantage.

The parliamentary leaders, having heard of the king's success at Cropredy Bridge, news that had not reached the prince, believed that Rupert would now strike south into Lincolnshire to join his uncle's army. Therefore, in the early hours of 2 July, they decided to move south towards Tadcaster in order to bar the road to him. However, the appearance of Rupert's advance guard on the moor convinced them that they had made a mistake and they hastily sent messengers to recall their infantry, stretched out in straggling columns on the road south. They feared that at any moment Rupert might attack and in their depleted and confused condition defeat then seemed probable. However, confusion was not confined to the allied army.

When Newcastle and his mounted troops arrived on the moor it was approaching midday and Rupert found it difficult to conceal his frustration. 'My Lord, I wish you had come sooner with your forces', he told the Marquis, 'but I hope we shall yet have a glorious day'.[12] Newcastle informed the prince that the York infantry were still plundering the enemy trenches but that Eythin would soon get them in order. This news frustrated Rupert's plan to fall on the allied army, still assembling in disorder amidst standing corn and hedges and with little room to manoeuvre on ground turned marshy by the summer rain. He allowed himself to be dissuaded from attacking immediately by Newcastle, who promised that Eythin would soon be there with more than 4000 foot.

Rupert's decision not to attack as soon as Newcastle arrived was a decision he would later regret. Admittedly he would have had 3000 less foot but he would have encountered an enemy assembling in an air of panic, expecting every minute to be struck by a whirlwind of Royalist cavalry. Also, the prolonged waiting was taking its toll on Rupert's men, who had hitherto been marching 'on their nerves', with success breeding success. Waiting gave them time to think of just how tired they were.

The order of battle adopted by the allies was the best they could achieve under the circumstances, as troops took up position more or less in the order in which they reached the moor, with the Scottish infantry, who had headed the march to Tadcaster, being the last to return. By about 2 or 3 p.m. the allies had completed their preparations and by the time Eythin arrived at about 4 p.m., with 3000 foot and not the 4000 Newcastle had promised, it was to find the enemy confidently singing psalms.[13]

On the right of the allied army, facing Goring, was the horse of Lord Fairfax's Northern Army, some 3000 strong, under the command of his son, Sir Thomas Fairfax, who led the front line, with Colonel John Lambert leading the second. A third line, consisting of 1000 Scottish cavalry, poorly mounted on ponies, was led by the Earl of Eglington. In the centre it is difficult to determine the precise layout or command structure of the allied army, as there were six generals present, including three army commanders. Nevertheless, the infantry placed here contained a majority of Scots and cannot have numbered less than some 16–18,000.

On the left of the allied army was the cavalry of the Eastern Association commanded by Cromwell. He led the first line of cavalry, some 1500 strong, in person, while behind him was Commissary-General Vermuden with a similar force and a third line of over a thousand Scottish horse under David Leslie. The total strength of this wing, including musketeers, must have exceeded 5000. The enormous strength on this flank persuaded Rupert that he would need to strengthen his own right wing, where Byron had a mere 2600 cavalry.

As overall commander, Rupert would not be able to lead the cavalry as was his custom, and in selecting Byron he must have known that he was taking a risk. Byron's seniority in the royalist military hierarchy entitled him to such a command, yet his impetuosity and unreliability were well known: his headstrong charge at Edgehill in 1642 in support of Rupert had done much to deprive the king of a complete victory on that occasion. It is likely that Rupert was relying heavily on Sir James Urry, the Major-General of the Prince's Horse, to curb Byron's tendency to act without thinking. Nevertheless, so important was Byron's responsibility that the prince gave him explicit instructions on how to receive the charge of Cromwell's cavalry.[14]

It was common tactics at that time to intermingle musketeers with cavalry on the pattern established by Gustavus Adolphus of Sweden, and Byron's front line consisted of 1100 horse, with 500 musketeers, in platoons of fifty, placed between the regiments of cavalry. As a flank guard for Byron, Tuke's regiment of 200 horse was placed on his right. Behind the front line was a second line of 1300 horse, under Lord Molyneaux, containing Prince Rupert's own regiment. However, Rupert went further than this and improvised a 'forlorn hope' of musketeers under Colonel Thomas Napier, some 1500 strong, along the ditch which crossed the battlefield parallel with the Marston Road. These musketeers were intended to strengthen the junction of Byron's wing with the centre and particularly to break up the onslaught of Cromwell's cavalry.[15]

THE BATTLE OF MARSTON MOOR (1644)

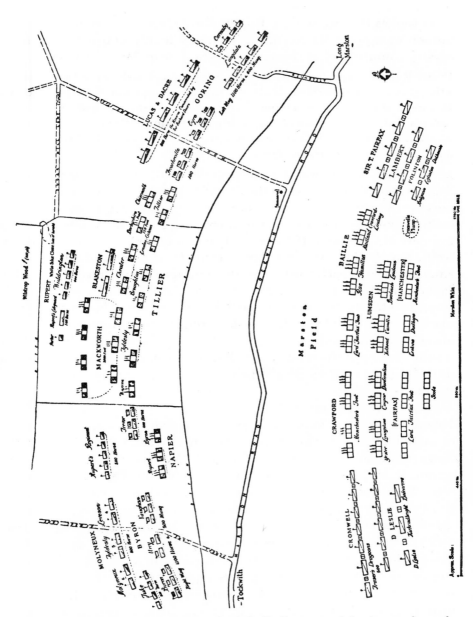

8. *Prince Rupert was aware of the strength of the Parliamentary left wing cavalry under Oliver Cromwell. He calculated that the musketeers under Napier would so disrupt Cromwell's cavalry as they crossed the ditch that Byron's right wing cavalry would have their best chance of success. Byron's failure to hold his position when Cromwell charged hampered his own musketeers and disordered his own horsemen as they crossed the ditch. The Royalist right wing was badly beaten and Cromwell was able to circle round the Royalist army and strike their left wing cavalry just as they had succeeded in driving Fairfax's troopers from the field. This decided the battle.*

As well as this precaution, Rupert also ordered up a small battery of cannon to support Byron, and gave him a highly unusual order for a cavalry commander, as the author of the *Life of James II* relates:

Prince Rupert had posted him [Byron] very advantageously behind a warren and a slough, with a positive command not to quit his ground, but in that posture only to expect and receive there the charge of the enemy . . . [who] . . . must necessarily be much disordered in passing over to him, as being to receive the fire of 700 musketeers in their advance to him, which undoubtedly had been very dangerous, if not ruinous to them.[16]

Byron must have found these instructions little to his liking. Cavalry depended for their success on shock, and to be stationary when the enemy horse arrived was to court disaster. Nevertheless, Rupert was skilfully making a virtue out of necessity in attempting to halt the renowned heavy troopers of Cromwell. If Byron had obeyed orders, Cromwell's cavalry would have faced concentrated musket fire from the cross ditch and from amongst the royalist horse where other musketeers were placed, as well as cannon fire from the guns placed on the hummock. In addition, his troopers, already disordered by such heavy fire, would have had to cross marshy ground and the ditch before re-grouping, depleted and with lowered morale, and then charging Byron's waiting squadrons. That would have been the moment for Byron to launch his own charge at a disorganised enemy with a good chance of changing the whole course of the battle.

In the centre Rupert had placed the infantry of both his and Newcastle's armies, to the number of about 10,000, under the command of Eythin. However, with the late arrival of that officer it is likely that the Sergeant-Major-Generals, Tillier and Mackworth, assumed that responsibility. The quality of these troops varied greatly, from the recently recruited Lancashire men, who threw down their arms in many cases at the first clash, to the veteran 'whitecoats', known as Newcastle's 'lambs', who were the best infantry on the field, and fought to the last.

On the left, Rupert gave the command to the General of the Northern Horse, George Goring, and to his Lieutenant-General, Sir Charles Lucas. As on the right, Rupert placed 500 musketeers on this wing to support the cavalry. Here the Royalists enjoyed a considerable advantage in terrain, which they were to put to good use. Rupert kept personal control of a reserve of 700 horse and was not, as some writers assert, commanding the right wing when Cromwell scattered it.

The arrival of Eythin's infantry at about 4 p.m., some six hours late, created disorder in the royalist ranks and it may have been this, or possibly the sight of Rupert's men preparing to eat, that convinced Leven that the right psychological moment had arrived to attack. Of the three allied commanders present, Leven was senior to Manchester and Fairfax who, as amateurs, no doubt deferred to the Scotsman's thirty years of experience in European warfare, particularly his service with the great Gustavus Adolphus. Leven could see that he outnumbered the Royalists substantially and, knowing Rupert by reputation, attributed his unwillingness to attack to some lack of confidence on his part.

In fact, Leven was probably right by this stage, for the strain of command must have been telling on the prince, particularly as he was having such a difficult time with Eythin and Newcastle. This was partly of his own making and might have been overcome if he had acted more diplomatically. When Eythin was shown Sir Bernard de Gomme's order of battle he was clearly dissatisfied with where his footsoldiers were to be placed.[17] He believed they had not enough time to reach these positions which, in any case, were far too close to the enemy. When Rupert offered to pull the army back, Eythin replied that it was too late for that and reminded Rupert that he had lost a battle in Germany by too much 'forwardness' and would do the same again here. Rupert showed admirable restraint in ignoring this taunt, and he and Newcastle now discussed what should be done so late in the day. Battle seemed most unlikely and the prince declared that he would attack in the morning. Newcastle asked if he was certain that the enemy would not attack first. Rupert arrogantly rejected this idea and in doing so fatally underestimated his opponents. So confident was he that there would be no fighting that day that Rupert told Newcastle to 'repose himself', which the Marquis did by smoking a pipe in his coach, on the edge of the field.[18] Rupert also ordered food to be brought from the city for the whole army, while he and his cavalry dismounted and began eating.

As Rupert relaxed his grip on the military situation, the initiative passed to the enemy. Leven was a far more experienced professional soldier than Rupert. Perhaps he had none of the prince's flair, but he had learned his craft and knew when his enemy had dropped his guard. In a storm of rain, which was bound to discomfort Rupert's musketeers, Leven ordered his cannons to fire, signalling the entire allied army to advance.

On the left Cromwell had been bombarding Byron's position for some while and the royalist cavalry, which had been in position most of the day and was eager to charge, must have pressed Byron to take some retaliatory action. Their cavalier spirit did not equip them to stand their ground and take casualties simply because the commander had a wider perspective on the whole field than they had. All they could see was that the enemy was taking toll of them without reply. Regiments often reflect the character of their commander and this was particularly true of the followers of the 'Bloody Braggadocchio Byron'. They needed little persuasion to disobey their orders and, at the sight of Cromwell's cavalry charging down towards them, charged out themselves to meet them. In doing so they disordered their own musketeers and provoked Tuke's flanking regiment into following their example.[19]

This was a disastrous mistake. Everything so carefully prepared by Rupert to disorder Cromwell's charge was now turned by Byron against his own men. It was they who were disordered in crossing the ditch and slowed by the marshy ground. Moreover, Napier's musketeers in the cross ditch had to move aside to let Byron's squadrons pass and the cannons on the hummock had to stop firing as they were masked by their own men. In the confusion the musketeers were easily cleared from their ditch by Colonel Hugh Fraser's Scottish dragoons, attacking from the flank. As a result of Byron's foolhardy action all the musketeers on the royalist right were wasted and when Cromwell's horse smashed into Byron's line in the marshy area and broke it, sending its scattered remnants fleeing from the field, there was no concentrated fire power to turn him back.

According to Cholmley, Rupert was 'set upon the earth at meat a pretty distance from his troops, and many of the horsemen were dismounted' when the fighting started.[20] In a matter of minutes, he gathered his reserve, consisting of his Lifeguard and Widdrington's Brigade, and rode towards the right wing in time to see Byron's troops shattered and his own regiment fleeing. Yelling above the tumult, 'Swounds, do you run, follow me', he managed to re-form them and lead them back into the fray, but they were beaten men following him through a sense of loyalty rather than with any hope of success. Their morale was broken and for this Rupert must bear some of the blame. He had led them, previously unconquerable, through Lancashire and on the triumphant march to York but had forgotten that they were merely 'flesh and blood'; once their ardour began to cool, aching limbs, rumbling bellies and nagging wounds would remind them of just how far they had come and how tired they were. They had been confident that morning when they arrived on the moor to watch the enemy assembling in ragged lines opposite them. But as the hours passed they could see the enemy increasing all the time, while their own reinforcements from the York garrison did not come. They were under a constant if desultory fire from the parliamentary cannon, which may not have caused many casualties but would have jarred nerves already growing sensitive under the strain of watching and waiting. There were even rumours of disagreements between their leaders and some said that the garrison had mutinied in York and would not come. And then, just when the order was passed round that there was to be no battle that day and men prepared to eat, they were shaken by the sight of the enemy bearing down on them. Under pressure Byron's judgement cracked and he led his troops out to meet the enemy as he had so often in the past. But this time he was meeting, in Cromwell, an opponent whose confidence was God-given and whose numerical superiority was decisive. Even the personal example of Rupert could do little to stem the rout of his right wing.

The cavalry on the allied right wing, commanded by Sir Thomas Fairfax, faced serious man-made obstacles to their front. In order to reach the moorland Fairfax would be forced to channel his cavalry through a narrow lane, described in Captain Stewart's account:

Betwixt them and the enemy there was no passage but a narrow lane where they could not march above 3 or 4 in front, upon the one side of the lane was a Ditch, and on the other side a Hedge, both whereof were lined with musketeers. Notwithstanding, Sir Thomas charged gallantly, but the enemy, keeping themselves in a body, and receiving them by threes and fours as they marched out of the Lane, and (what mistake I know not) Sir Thos Fairfax his new leavied regiments being in the van, they wheeled about and being hotly pursued by the enemy, came back upon the Lord Fairfax Foot, and the reserve of the Scottish foot, broke them wholly and trod most part of them underfoot.[21]

Having broken the rather disjointed charge of the allied right, the royalist commander on the left, Goring, led a counter-charge which drove the parliamentary cavalry off the field. Goring's men reached the ridge from which Fairfax had set off and found the right flank of the allied army completely open. Sir Charles Lucas now led the reserve cavalry in against this unguarded flank and spread panic through the right of the allied army so that all three of its commanders, Leven, Lord Fairfax and the Earl of Manchester, fled from the field.[22] Rumours of defeat spread down the road with them and in royalist Newark the church bells signalled a great victory for the king.

However, it was not to be. Seeing the disaster on the right, Cromwell had led his cavalry round the back of the royalist infantry so that they now occupied the position originally occupied by Goring's Northern Horse. Goring, at the top of the ridge, having with difficulty recalled many of his triumphant horsemen, could see a new opponent in Cromwell and that this time he would have to fight on disadvantageous ground and with greatly inferior numbers. As the two forces crashed together it was Cromwell's which proved the stronger; Goring's troop broke under the onslaught and scattered, with Sir Charles Lucas being taken prisoner.

In the centre, the heavily outnumbered Yorkshire infantry refused quarter and fought to the death until Sir Thomas Fairfax rode into the fray, beating up the weapons of his own men and shouting, 'Spare your countrymen'.[23] The whitecoat regiment of the Marquis of Newcastle fought virtually to the last man, overrun by allied cavalry, and were said by their enemies to have 'brought their winding-sheets about them into the field'.[24]

The battle, which had lasted some two hours, was said by some to be remarkable for the fact that all six commanders took to their heels and left the field before the end. This was true of Leven and Lord Fairfax and even Manchester for a while, though he returned later. On the royalist side, Newcastle and Eythin had done what they could to rally the troops but had not stayed with their doomed infantry. Rupert also had been in the thick of the fighting on the right but whether he really escaped by hiding in a bean field, as his enemies suggested, is uncertain.[25]

The outcome of the battle was that Charles lost both the city of York and the North of England. Newcastle, his main supporter in that area, left with Eythin for the continent, along with his whole staff and many prominent royalists. It was left to Rupert to try to rally the remnants of the king's army. Before Marston Moor the prince's reputation had stood equally high in both royalist and parliamentary camps, but this defeat was one from which it never recovered. For many now he would be branded as a 'hothead' who had fought an unnecessary battle, a commander as 'cavalier' in his treatment of his fellow commanders as he was impetuous in battle, and so careless that he had been surprised by the enemy attack while eating his supper.

This judgement was unfair. Rupert had made several errors of judgement during the campaign, none more, some would say, than by giving battle at all. However, his real failure was in his knowledge of men, and that could only be remedied by age and experience. He knew and mistrusted Lord Eythin, yet allowed himself to be persuaded into waiting for his arrival on the battlefield and then going over to a passive defence which was as dangerous to his uncle's cause as had been his previous eagerness to seek an encounter. Undoubtedly this delay materially affected the outcome of the battle. Similarly, he knew by experience Byron's weakness as an impetuous commander and yet placed him in a position requiring supreme patience and steadiness, qualities admittedly rare among the cavaliers. He must have known that if Byron disobeyed orders the result would be disastrous, for Cromwell's reputation as a cavalry leader was known to all, and especially to Rupert himself.

Colonel George Monck, who had already experienced the incompetence of Wimbledon's expedition to Cadiz in 1625, spoke with authority when he said,

War is not capable of a second Error; one fault being enough to ruine an Army; And therefore a General ought to be careful even of possibilities, accounting always that which may happen, to be as certain as anything which he doth most expect.[26]

Rupert made more than one error at Marston Moor. As we have seen, he interpreted the king's letter as no professional soldier should, reading into it what he wanted to read, as Culpeper obviously feared he would. Though no mere headstrong 'cavalier', like so many of the young gallants who surrounded the king, he still suffered from the audacity that oscillated between fault and virtue. His relief of York could only have been achieved by such audacity, but his decision to follow it with an engagement against a numerically superior army, which the shrewder and older Newcastle probably correctly felt would disintegrate after its failure to take the city, was merely foolhardy. Having taken the decision to strike, however, he then allowed lesser soldiers to persuade him against his nature to adopt a passive defence. To complete his discomfiture he even allowed himself to be taken by surprise by a 'plodding professional' like the elderly Earl of Leven.

—3—
Braddock on the Monongahela (1755)

'We shall better know how to deal with them another time', the dying General Braddock is reported to have said,[1] indicating that he thought he had learned something from the destruction of his column on the Monongahela River on 8 June 1755. However, historians have not shared Braddock's certainty; there have been numerous differing accounts of that day's fighting and just as many explanations of why the British met disaster. The view that grew up soon after the event emphasised the failure of British regular troops to adapt to New World conditions, where discipline and parade-ground training did not prepare the individual soldier to encounter the irregular tactics of both the French and the Indians.[2] Thus troops trained for the battlefields of Europe, where they were to encounter 'cumbersome armies of disciplined professionals engaging in elaborate, formalized manoeuvres, protracted sieges and open-field battles fought in rigid linear formations' had no answer to the frontier tactics which depended on 'small, mobile bands of woodsmen who used surprise attacks to create confusion, concealment to nullify enemy fire, and scattered, flexible alignments to reduce the effect of counter-attacks'.[3] As a corollary to this Old World versus New World view, there was much criticism of Braddock's leadership, and he was dismissed by some historians as simply a martinet, typical of the eighteenth-century British officer, bigoted, brutal and inflexible, contemptuous of colonials and Indians alike and unwilling to take advice from his subordinates. However, these traditional views have been challenged in recent years, particularly by Stanley Pargellis.

Pargellis approached the subject of Braddock's defeat as a problem in tactics. As he points out,

... Braddock and his staff, on the day of the battle, neglected to follow fundamental rules of war laid down in European manuals ... they 'messed up' their formations and never gave their soldiers a chance to demonstrate that Old World methods, properly applied, might have won the day. The fault lay in the quality of the leadership, not in the quality of the men.[4]

Pargellis therefore accuses Braddock of incompetence, not for his failure to apply the tactical principles of fighting on the frontier, but rather the tactical principles of European warfare, which he knew so well and which could still have prevailed. To support his argument Pargellis cites the standard military manual of the day, Humphrey Bland's *Treatise of Military Discipline*, which in several important instances Braddock neglected. However, Braddock knew 'Old Humphrey' virtually by heart and was a man who worked by the book. Moreover, all the accumulated wisdom of Bland's book could not alter the fact that the author had no experience of Indian fighting, so that most of his advice, particularly on conducting marches, related to the European sphere of warfare.

Such academic dispute, involving the use of stereotypes, is weakened the further it moves away from the people actually involved in the battle. Certainly, the eighteenth-century soldier was not trained to be an individual or to think of himself as an individual, yet however much drill was designed to replace the fear and uncertainty of the individual with the strength and certainty of the group it could not completely eradicate the characteristics which would make one man stand to the last while another ran. Just as individual soldiers were not absolutely equivalent units, nor were the formations which they comprised.

Thus, in assessing the failure of Braddock, one must consider the raw material he was given. To take up Pargellis's point, if Braddock failed because he neglected the European rules in which he was trained, is there any evidence to suggest that his troops would have performed any better if he had acted according to Bland's manual? If you do not train a soldier to think then you can hardly expect him to show initiative in a battle where his officers have either lost their heads or have been shot. And if the quality of the soldier is poor in the first place, through inadequate training, exhaustion or other physical deficiency one can hardly expect parade-ground precision when he is under fire from a hidden enemy.

The two regiments earmarked for service in North America were the 44th, under Colonel Sir Peter Halket, and the 48th under Colonel Thomas Dunbar. Both had been in peacetime country cantonments on the Irish Establishment, far from the actualities of war. They had been ordered to sail from Cork, each with a mere 340 men but equipped with seven hundred stand of arms, the aim being to bring them up to their full strength by recruiting in America. This was most unwise, particularly if the regiments were intended for immediate use, for the new recruits would have too little time to become accustomed to European practices.

On second thoughts it was decided to increase the British element in the regiments to 500, before they departed. This was by no means easy as service in the colonies was generally unpopular with British soldiers. As a result men had to be drafted in from other regiments, giving the latter opportunity to be rid of their own 'undesirables', with the result that the already weak cadre strengths of the 44th and 48th were further diluted by the inclusion of poor material from other regiments. In addition, once in Virginia, Braddock found it difficult to recruit men of the right quality, so some were drafted from the independent companies formed by that state, three of which were to accompany him on the march. By the time the troops assembled at Fort Cumberland, a third of each regiment was made up of American draftees.[5] These men were far from being the backwoodsmen of popular imagination and were more likely to have been the dregs of colonial society, men from the seaboard who had no knowledge of forests, frontier fighting or military discipline. Most of them were ready to run at the first sound of firing. It was a mistake on the part of the British authorities to think that good results could be achieved by sending second-rate troops, merely because they would not be called upon to face a well-trained European enemy.

Before Braddock's departure, the Duke of Cumberland had stressed to him that

. . . the Strictest and most exact Discipline is always necessary, but can never be more so than on your present Service . . . to prevent any Pannick in the Troops from Indians, to whom the Soldiery not being yet accustomed, the French will not fail to make all attempts towards it.[6]

This was sound advice, though it is unlikely that a man of Braddock's background would have erred in his application of discipline. Yet to expect each regiment to integrate as many as 50 per cent new members into its ranks and achieve the perfect cohesion necessary in a matter of a few weeks of intensive training was unrealistic. British infantry regiments which had served and were to serve with such distinction in European campaigns often had a year or more on the continent, in cantonments, before being committed to battle, in which time they were able to perfect the advanced elements of drill. Braddock's men, in spite of his considerable efforts, had little chance to achieve the standard which Cumberland expected.

It is significant that even though Cumberland knew that Braddock would be facing entirely new conditions in America, he still insisted on the quality which for eighteenth-century officers was an item of faith: discipline. It was the fundamental basis of military activity upon which everything depended. Cumberland was, in a sense, only expressing a truism, for adherence to a system of discipline has been the strength behind every successful military system in history. Yet discipline is not an absolute in that it can take different forms in relation to different moral codes and cultural norms. In military terms, irregular troops, whether Croats, Hussars and Pandours, or Abenakis, Hurons and Mingoes, have a discipline of their own, even if Braddock and Cumberland would not have recognised it as such. In fact, Braddock went further than some officers of his day would have done by modifying the ridiculously unsuitable dress of his men, which was too stiff, fussy and cumbersome for Indian fighting. In contrast, Captain Beaujeu, who led the French forces against Braddock, fought stripped to the waist, Indian-style.

Braddock's force had assembled at Fort Cumberland, to the number of about 2200 men. Of these 1400 were from the two British regiments, 450 were Virginian militia, (of whom Braddock had the lowest possible opinion, declaring that their 'slothful and languid disposition renders them very unfit for military service',[7]) one hundred were from the Royal Artillery, and there were also thirty sailors lent by Commodore Keppel of the Royal Navy. To this number one should add a small number of Indian scouts, concerning whose abilities Braddock was not as scathing as is often claimed.

The difficulties he experienced brought out the worst in Braddock. His executive skills were weak and as a strong disciplinarian he expected to be obeyed, though he was not able to communicate his wishes clearly and often substituted outbursts of temper for clear thinking. Even Washington, not generally unfavourable to Braddock, spoke of his ungovernable temper. 'He looks upon our country, I believe', he wrote, 'as void of honour or honesty. We have frequent disputes on this head, which are maintained with warmth on both sides, especially on his, as he is incapable of arguing without it, or giving up any point he asserts, be it ever so incompatible with reason or common sense'.[8] The picture that emerges is of a man lacking flexibility, which was to be a quality much in demand during his expedition.

On 10 June 1755 Braddock's force moved out of Fort Cumberland to begin its long march through the forest to Fort Duquesne. At the head of the column marched three hundred carpenters and pioneers, under Sir John St Clair, whose task was to clear a twelve-foot-wide road for the wagons, pack-horses and artillery to pass through. This made the march almost unbearably slow for the soldiers and gave them too much time to think. American recruits, who were from the eastern seaboard, had never been so far west, while to the ordinary English and Irish soldier who made up the British regiments there was nothing but the 'gloomy interminable forest' filled with unknown horrors.

After eight days' march, when the column had travelled no more than thirty miles, a report was received that 500 French reinforcements were advancing towards Fort Duquesne. It was obvious that unless the heavy baggage was left behind they might reach the fort before the British. Braddock, following Washington's advice, left the baggage with Colonel Dunbar, and moved on himself with 1200 men and a convoy now reduced to ten cannons, thirty wagons and some pack horses. Even now progress continued to be slow as the road builders flattened 'every molehill' and 'threw a bridge over every brook'. Braddock was failing to appreciate the vital importance of speed and surprise in frontier fighting and was allowing the French ample warning of his advance. In fact, they had no difficulty following the smoke of his camp fires, or the sound of axes as St Clair's work party cleared a path through the forest.

On 7 July Braddock reached the mouth of Turtle Creek, a stream which joins the Monongahela about eight miles from the fort. Here he expected the French to contest his crossing of the main river if they were going to oppose him at all. In fact, had he but known it, the French were in a state of great confusion, having heard from their scouts that the British numbered over three thousand, a force *'si bien sur leur gardes, marchant toujours en bataille'*[9], that efforts to harass them had been impossible. The French commander, Contrecoeur, had only a few companies of regular troops and would have to rely on a large contingent of Indians, many of whom lived in wigwams beside the stockade. He knew that the fort could not possibly resist a siege by so large an enemy force and decided he had only two alternatives: to surrender the fort with honours of war or to blow it up. However, two of his captains, Beaujeu and Dumas, disagreed and urged an attack on the British column. The Indians were not eager to fight, knowing themselves to be hopelessly outnumbered, but Captain Beaujeu called to them, 'What! Will you let your father go alone? I am certain of defeating them'.[10] He managed to persuade some 650 Indians to go with his 140 Canadian irregulars and 70 regular French troops to try to ambush Braddock near the river ford. When a message was brought to him that the British had crossed the Monongahela and were advancing along the trail by the river, Beaujeu declared

You see, my friends, the English are going to throw themselves into the lion's mouth. They are weak sheep who pretend to be ravenous wolves. Those who love

---

9. *Braddock had expected the French to contest the crossing of the Monongahela River near Turtle Creek. When this did not happen the British became overconfident and relaxed some of their precautions. Their failure to secure the hill marked 'S' on the map proved decisive.*

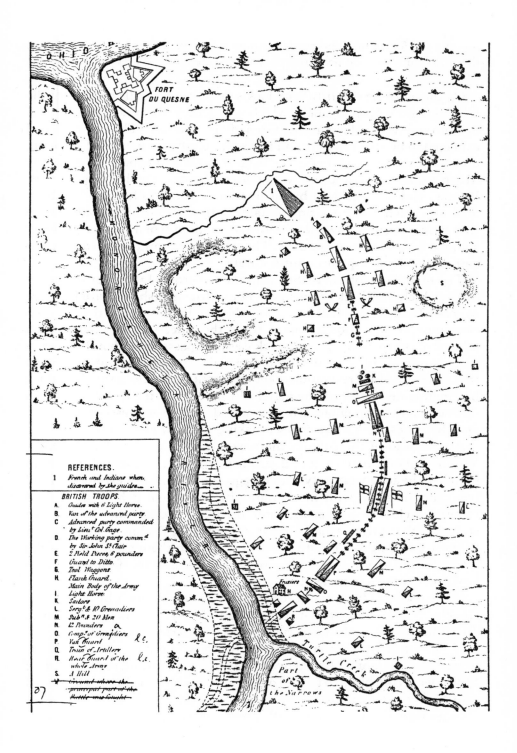

REFERENCES.

1   French and Indians when
    discovered by the guides.
    BRITISH TROOPS.
A. Guides with 6 Light Horse.
B. Van of the advanced party.
C. Advanced party commanded
    by Lieut Col Gage.
D. The Working party comm'd
    by Sir John St Clair.
E. 2 Field Pieces 6 pounders.
F. Guard to Ditto.
G. Tool Waggons.
H. Flank Guard.
I. Main Body of the Army
K. Light Horse.
L. Sailors.
L. Serg't & 10 Grenadiers.
M. Sub'n & 20 Men.
N. 12 Pounders.
O. Comp's of Grenadiers &c.
P. Van Guard.
Q. Train of Artillery
R. Rear Guard of the whole Army &c.
S. A Hill

their father, follow me! You need only hide yourselves in the ravines which line the road and when you hear us strike, strike yourselves. The victory is ours![11]

On the morning of 8 July Braddock's forces successfully completed the crossing of the Monongahela, which was done to the accompaniment of drums and fifes playing the Grenadiers' March. The general had expected to be attacked here and had sent his advanced force of 350 men, under Lieutenant-Colonel Gage, to clear the opposite bank if necessary. Much to his surprise there were neither French nor Indians present. Beaujeu had been held up by his unreliable Indian allies and had been unable to reach the ford in time. If fact, far from ambushing Braddock, he was simply rushing towards the British column when he unexpectedly collided with its advanced guard. The traditional view that Braddock was ambushed is consequently not accurate.

The main body of the British column had crossed the river in perfect order, which Braddock believed was bound to establish a moral advantage over any French or Indians who might be watching. It seems that the men were now in very good humour, while the officers congratulated each other that the main danger of attack was now passed and that the French would probably blow up the fort or evacuate it without a fight. It is likely that there was also a relaxation of the stringent precautions that Braddock had maintained so far on the march. From now on the forest was not as thick as many commentators have asserted and eye-witnesses refer to the fact that trees were more sparse, making ambush less likely.

At the head of the column there were Indian guides along with six Virginian horsemen to guard against surprise, while behind them marched the advanced party under Gage, the axemen to clear the path and two cannons along with their ammunition-wagons. Behind them, and rather too close one suspects, came the main body of the convoy, 750 strong, with the troops marching on either side of the line of wagons, and flanking parties thrown out right and left. With them came most of the artillery, four twelve-pounders on travelling carriages, four eight-inch howitzers and three mortars.

Some distance from the ford the path passed across a bushy ravine. Gage's advances group had just crossed this when there was a disturbance up ahead and the guides came rushing back. A curious figure, dressed like an Indian but wearing an officer's gorget, was seen rushing towards them.[12] It was Captain Beaujeu. At a signal from him and to the sound of Indian war cries, his men fanned out on either side of the British advanced guard, opening a galling fire from behind trees.

Gage formed up his men with great precision and fired a series of volleys at where he assumed the enemy to be, for by now he could hardly see a single one. Nevertheless this was undoubtedly the best British fire of the battle, and at the third volley Beaujeu fell, shot through the head, and many of his Canadian irregulars took to their heels. Captain Dumas now rallied the remnants of his force, while the Indians worked their way further round the British flanks, finding the redcoats easy targets as they stood in line. Gage's two cannons fired noisily into the trees but did little damage. This was like no battle that the British redcoats had ever seen and their confidence drained away as more and more of them fell to an unseen enemy. Eventually a rumour spread that the Indians were attacking the baggage wagons and had therefore completely encircled them. Discipline now gave way and they began to run back to St Clair's workers, sweeping them along with them towards the main column. The flank guards, under fire from Indians and British indiscriminately, abandoned the high ground and rushed back towards the milling crowds in the centre.

On what happened next there is no clear agreement, even among the eye-witnesses. Upon hearing the firing up ahead Braddock apparently ordered Halket to guard the baggage with the rearguard while the main body of troops under Burton were ordered to advance. Braddock himself rode forward, only to meet Gage's beaten troops retreating. Burton's men were advancing four abreast and as he tried to get them into line, the advanced guard collided with them, throwing everyone into confusion with soldiers massing together, in bunches twelve deep, firing anywhere. Many of the British casualties, some authorities think as many as half, were caused by the wayward firing of the frightened soldiers themselves. As one eye-witness reported,

The Confusion and destruction was so great, that the men fired irregularly, one behind another, and by this way of proceeding many more of our men were killed by their own party than by the Enimy, as appeared afterwards by the bullets that the surgeons extracted from the wounded, they being distinguished from the French and Indian bullets by their size. . . .[13]

One Virginia captain led his company to cover behind a fallen tree trunk; to his amazement they were raked by fire from the British regulars who mistook his men for the French. Some British officers, assuming the Virginians were deserting, stopped their own men from following their initiative. Braddock, fearing the collapse of discipline, roared at those men who had taken cover behind trees to return to their ranks; when some redcoats, showing unusual initiative, took cover themselves, they were called cowards and beaten back by the General's sword. The British regulars were far from being cowards, but as one said, 'We would fight if we could see anybody to fight with'.[14]

During the advance of the column that day, Braddock had inexplicably failed to occupy the high ground, particularly a hillock on the right flank. It was from here that some of the heaviest fire was coming and the wounded St Clair managed to point it out to Braddock before fainting. With fewer than a hundred men, Colonel Burton tried to storm the hill but was shot from his horse. On seeing their officer shot, his men immediately panicked and ran.

Braddock rode madly about, shouting at his men to form into small divisions and advance on the Indians to clear them at bayonet point, but to no avail. Washington, one of the few officers to emerge unscathed, had asked Braddock's permission to scatter three hundred men among the trees and fight the enemy Indian-style, but Braddock's reply was to threaten to run him through the body if he said anything like that again. 'We'll sup today in Fort Duquesne or else in hell', he is reputed to have cried.[15] Sir Peter Halket rode up from the rearguard to urge Braddock to let the men take cover. He had been with the 44th at Prestonpans when the Scottish Highlanders had driven the English from the field in panic and could see the possibility of the same happening here. However, his advice was cut short by a bullet and his son, going to his aid, was cut down also by a fusillade of shots. With his hat fixed to his head by a white handkerchief tied under his chin, Braddock himself was an almost unmissable target, yet for a while his life seemed charmed. Four horses were killed under him, but when he fell from the fifth it was with a bullet in his lungs.

The Indian scout Scarouady, one of the few to stay with Braddock's column, had recommended immediate retreat as he could see no advantage in the British simply staying to be shot by an enemy they could not see. However, it took Braddock three hours to reach the same conclusion, during which time no fewer than 60 out of 86 officers fell. With their officers gone and the general wounded, discipline collapsed and many troops fled from the dreadful scene. Washington tried to rally them but saw such fear in their eyes that he felt it would have been easier to stop the wild animals of the mountains.[16]

What followed was a total fiasco. The French were not prepared to follow up their victory in case Braddock was able to rally his still superior force and reverse the decision. Moreover, they knew that there was still a considerable force under Colonel Dunbar with the British baggage. What they could not have guessed was the disgraceful collapse of morale which had taken place and which was to result in Dunbar destroying his stores and munitions to prevent the French having them. Rarely was a defeat more surprising or more complete.

For our information on this battle we are forced to rely on the accounts of seven eye-witnesses and an eighth pieced together soon afterwards from reports of survivors. Of the eight reports, four – from Orme, Washington, Stephen and Gage – place the blame on the cowardly behaviour of the troops, while the other four – St Clair, Gordon, Gates and an anonymous letter from an officer in Dunbar's division – draw attention to weaknesses in the generalship as well as to the deficiencies of the troops.

Concerning the early part of the battle there is general agreement; about the activities of Braddock and the main body accounts differ. According to St Clair and Gordon, Braddock rode up at the head of the guns when he heard the firing ahead, with the main body advancing in great confusion. Gates wrote that the main body was advancing in column, thus inviting flanking fire, while another comment refers to 'men without any form of order but that of a parcell of school boys coming out of school – and in an instant, Blue, buff, and yellow were intermix'd'.[17] Clearly the discipline Cumberland had called for was missing and both Braddock and his officers had lost control. The flanking parties, so placed to prevent the enemy doing exactly what it did – namely enclose the British column on three sides – panicked and ran to join the scramble in the centre.

According to Pargellis, it would have been difficult with the formation Braddock adopted for his men to form into line as their double columns were separated by the line of wagons. In order to try to form up it was necessary for the men to advance along the line of wagons until they reached the end. While they were trying to carry out this manoeuvre, the amount of space available to them was reduced by the retreat of the advanced guard and so, deprived of room to form up, they panicked. They had not been taught to improvise or think for themselves. That responsibility had been their officer's, and in many cases he was already dead or wounded.

It is difficult to avoid the conclusion that someone had blundered. Pargellis refers to Bland's military manual, a book well-known to Braddock, which lays down clear instructions for a march through country where an ambush is to be expected. Bland states that if the vanguard is attacked the main body must remain where it is until a detachment has been sent forward to ascertain the situation. Only then may an advance be ordered. Bland continues with these words, 'An Officer's Character is hardly retrievable if surpriz'd without being prepared'.[18] Apologists for Braddock have pointed out that Bland had no experience of Indian fighting in preparing his manual. On the other hand Braddock had none either and therefore had no reason for not following

Bland's suggestions. Moreover, Bland had advised marching through wooded areas by platoons, as these smaller units were more manageable and more easily formed into offensive units. Again Braddock was at fault, for the formation he chose was so cumbersome that it was unable to form up at any point during the fighting. On a third point Braddock was culpable. Occupation of the high ground on the route of a march was a basic military tenet: to have left the hillock to his right unoccupied was a disastrous mistake. It seems that Braddock became over-confident so near to his target and led his men blindly into an 'ambush' the enemy had planned but had totally mismanaged themselves.

Braddock failed because he neglected certain fundamental principles of eighteenth-century European tactics; in doing so he would have been considered incompetent by contemporary standards. There was too little distance between the various parts of his column; his reconnaissance was faulty in that he had far too little warning of the enemy advance – even minutes could have been enough to have allowed his men to have moved into their well-ordered drill lines; his failure to occupy the high ground was an extraordinary error of judgement; the decision to march in column with the line of wagons dividing the main body in half seriously hindered its capacity to form up; the advance of the general and the main body to the sound of the guns was contrary to eighteenth-century practice and was tantamount to walking blindly into an ambush.

Nobody at any time doubted Braddock's courage and honesty but in the context in which he found himself he was quite unsuited to the command. He believed that courage was a substitute for thought, and discipline superior to common sense, but on the Monongahela he was to find that the individual soldier counted for more than he did in European fighting. Nevertheless, Braddock was not simply the martinet he has been painted. Many of his critics at the time were Americans who did not understand the disciplinary practices of the British army and resented them. No soft hand would have formed the composite ranks of the 44th and 48th into regiments and it was not entirely his fault that they found themselves facing a task that was beyond their capacity.

It is not on these grounds that Braddock must be judged incompetent. On his arrival in America he was aware of the dangers he would face in dealing with Indians and French Canadian irregulars. It had been stressed to him that it was important to employ Indian as scouts and that he must guard against surprise attacks, both of which he did. During the march to Fort Duquesne his camps were heavily guarded and as much as a third of his force was employed in flanking duties. Even the French were impressed by his precautions, as we have seen. And yet, having said all this, one is faced with the fact that when it came to a crisis he made every possible mistake. His apparently well-guarded column was taken by surprise, his flanking guards were driven in, his disciplined troops panicked, the high ground he had secured right along the march was now occupied by the enemy with terrible effect, his Indian scouts failed to save him and regarded him as an arrogant fool. Braddock was an officer with 45 years' experience in the army, yet he had never before been under fire. A parade ground is not a battlefield, and while Braddock's courage has never been in doubt, his capacity to think clearly in the stress of battle has. For Braddock, as a general officer, the battle on the Monongahela was the supreme moment of his life. It was what he had been trained for, and when the testing time came he forgot everything he had read of the campaigns of Marlborough and Eugene, Frederick and de Saxe.

Washington buried the general's body secretly and marched the entire army over the grave so that the Indians would never discover it.

—4—
The Commissariat and the Crimean War (1854)

Men are the raw material of any army: a general who forgets this is committing a crime not only against humanity but also against his own professional code. The logistics of battle, involving the movement of large numbers of men, stores, munitions, guns and animals in relation to the enemy, are designed eventually to place the soldier in the most effective position – well-armed, well-equipped, well-fed and, if necessary, well-mounted – to strike against the enemy. It is the task of the commander to ensure that his men are protected as far as possible from exposure to inclement weather, from deprivation of food and drink, from needless exposure to disease and from situations of morale-sapping boredom. If he fails in this respect, or if he feels that such ideals are not necessary for the common soldier, then he is contributing to his own downfall. Failures of this kind were so common during the Crimean War that it is impossible to do justice to the problem, yet the particular failure of the Commissariat can serve as an example of administrative ineptitude rare even in British military history.

British military administration developed from medieval practices and by 1854 suffered from an over-complicated system of rules and regulations, producing endless delay and procedural complexity. The control of transport and the supply of essential items such as food, clothing, fodder and ammunition were concentrated not in one but two separate departments, the Commissariat and the Ordnance, while the former was not even under military control but was staffed by civilians and controlled by the Treasury. In wartime the Commissariat was responsible for land transport and non-military supplies, like food for the soldiers, and forage for the horses and baggage-animals. This function was a direct outgrowth from the medieval practice of hiring wagons for use by the army and of contracting for food. In its manual of operations the Commissariat made the assumption that in wartime British troops would not be acting offensively but, being allies of the local population, would have no difficulty in finding local transport and supplies. Such a defensive mentality was a reflection of the effect that Wellington's Peninsular campaigns had had on all aspects of British military thinking. Its essential conservatism was to make the Commissariat quite unsuited to offensive operations, a fact which both Burgoyne and Raglan had noted in 1850.[1]

The Commissariat was staffed by civilians who were not subject to military discipline or to the authority of the Commander-in-Chief. The use of civilians in these 'support' areas did ensure that soldiers would be available to fight and not be tied up in non-combat duties. Yet it also meant that relations between civilians and the military were universally bad, with officers accusing civilians of not understanding military practices and of a fussy concern with paperwork.

The main weakness of the Commissariat was that it operated on an *ad hoc* basis, having neither a regular recruitment policy nor peacetime field training. Thus when a crisis developed and it needed to recruit commissary officers in haste the results were usually unfortunate. On 1st February 1854 there were just 178 commissary officers serving in British possessions worldwide, and 40 would be needed for the expected 10,000 men of the expeditionary force to the Crimea.[2] For the crucial position of Commissary-General, Sir Charles Trevelyan, Secretary to the Treasury, recommended William Filder, a retired officer of much colonial experience and a Peninsular War veteran; estimates of his age ranged from 64 to 70 and have divided historians far more than his performance in office, on which there is unanimity.

In spite of claims that the Commissariat officers sent with Raglan's troops were as 'capable' and 'intelligent' as were ever sent with any previous force, this was not saying very much, for they were hastily recruited men, some of whom had no previous experience. Filder later complained that he would have preferred one man trained in his job to ten police officers, referring to the Treasury's tendency to appoint officers from the Metropolitan Police, on no apparent logical basis other than a belief in their moral rectitude. When the expeditionary force was doubled from its original 10,000, there was no equivalent increase in Commissary officers and eventually only 44 went with the army, making lack of manpower a constant problem.

The system by which previous Commissary-Generals had depended on obtaining transport and supplies locally was hindered by the problems of conducting a campaign in the sparsely populated areas of the Crimea. As Wellington's Military Secretary, Lord Raglan might have been expected to have learned more from his great mentor than to winter in open country before Sevastapol. It would have been possible to have kept the majority of the troops in comfortable billets around the port of Balaclava, thus reducing transport problems to a minimum. It was not as if Raglan was short of advice, for Major-General Macintosh had warned that the ground in front of Sevastapol was extremely hard and unsuited to siege operations, while the winters there could be most severe and food and fuel short.[3] On 29 August, Burgoyne considered an attack on the city 'at the present time . . . a most desperate undertaking'. Land transport was short already, the weather was deteriorating, cholera had broken out at Varna, while manpower was insufficient and knowledge of the Crimea inadequate. On these grounds alone a winter siege of Sevastapol seemed unwise and Lord Raglan must carry some of the blame which attaches to the dismal performance of the Commissariat.

Commissary-General Filder did not officially hear from Lord Raglan that he intended to winter in the Crimea until 7 November. This disturbed Filder, who wrote to Sir Charles Trevelyan, pointing out his fears that the harbour at Balaclava was really too small for the needs of the army, while landing facilities at the wharves did not allow him to do more than keep pace with daily needs. Moreover, the road from the camp to the harbour was not made up and would become impassable in heavy rain. In short, he anticipated some of the disasters which were to strike, yet did nothing effective to deal with them.[4] He could expect little sympathy from the army officers, who felt that while their men did their duty they had a right to expect the comforts of food, warm clothes and shelter. As to the efficiency of Filder and his department, McNeill and Tulloch concluded in their report that the Commissaries had acted 'according to the measure of their ability and foresight', which begs a number of questions.[5] Certainly, there was much incompetence and whatever allowances are made for it, the fact remains that the department failed in its prime duty, which was to supply the troops in the field.

While the British soldier faced the Russians at the front he was also subject to an enemy he never saw and could not understand: the 'red tape' which delayed action until it was often too late, which forbade officials to issue lime juice or fresh vegetables, or to bake bread because regulations did not specifically authorise it. It was in this area that civil and military authorities clashed most strongly, with officers unable to credit the 'minutely-detailed regulations and lengthy procedures which bedevilled swift action'.[6] Everywhere there was evidence of inflexibility and of a rigid civil service mentality which no amount of urgency could persuade to alter procedures. Christopher Hibbert cites the following example, recorded by W.H. Russell.

The Medical Officer of the *Charity*, an iron screw-steamer docked in Balaclava for the reception of the sick, went on shore to see the commissariat official in charge of the issue of stoves.

'Three of my men', he told him, 'died last night from choleraic symptoms, brought on in their present state from the extreme cold of the ship; and I fear more will follow them from the same cause'.

'Oh! You must make your requisition in due form; send it up to HQ and get it signed properly'.

'But my men may die meantime'.

'I can't help that. I must have the requisition'.

'Another night will certainly kill my men'.

'I really can do nothing. I must have a requisition properly signed before I can give one of these stoves away'.

'For God's sake, then lend me some. I'll be responsible for their safety'.

'I really can do nothing of the kind'.[7]

Though the medical officer would not have understood it at that moment, what was taking place was not a clash of values but a clash of systems. The commissary officer felt that to give way in this one instance would have undermined the well-ordered system which he operated. He was tied by regulations which he felt unable to relax. The medical officer, concerned with the lives of his men, had an urgent need to cut through the regulations which seemed more concerned with property than with people. What he did not understand was the heavy burden placed on the commissary officer by the government, which held any official financially responsible for issuing articles not justifiable under his 'warrants'. At that very moment in London a lawsuit was in progress in which the Government was prosecuting a commissary officer for issuing stores beyond his 'warrant' during the Kaffir War in Africa.[8] Officials were not expected to use initiative or take responsibility beyond the circumscribed limits of the regulations. It was a system designed to discourage action. When a regimental officer had gone to Balaclava in search of vegetables for his men, he was told that departmental regulations prevented the issue of vegetables in quantities less than two tons. Christopher Hibbert cites the example of Major Foley de St Georges who, when trying to obtain a few nails, was challenged by the regulation that nails were only sold by the ton, but, undeterred, said he would have a ton and paid for them himself.[9]

The problems faced by the Commissariat at the start of the Crimean War were not only the result of individual apathy and administrative muddle, however, but also of a resistance to change which took its stand on the claim that what was good enough for the Duke of Wellington in the Peninsular War must be good enough for Lord Raglan in the Crimea. This was a remarkably short-sighted view, which overlooked the fact that

Wellington had been operating relatively close to Britain in friendly Portuguese and Spanish territory, and that anyway he had been particularly scathing about the incompetence of the Commissariat. It was clear to the leaders of the expedition, like Sir John Burgoyne, that they were unlikely to have any of the advantages of supply that Wellington had enjoyed, because their Turkish allies were quite unable to supply the baggage animals necessary. Even now, little was done by the Commissariat to remedy this defect because it was believed that the war would be over very soon and that long-term planning was therefore unnecessary.

By November 1854, many held the view that the Commissariat had completely broken down as a result of transport difficulties. The oxen and baggage horses were either dead or too weak to work and men were often forced to manhandle the supplies themselves. From lack of forage the regimental horses were dying at the rate of three a day, having already 'eaten each other's tails off'. The track which led to the harbour at Balaclava was deep in mud and was distinguishable only by the 'dead horses, mules and bullocks, in every stage of decomposition' which lined its path.

As a result of numerous complaints of inefficiency, in February 1855 Lord Panmure instructed Sir John McNeill and Colonel Alexander Tulloch to 'proceed to the Crimea in order to inquire into the whole arrangement and management of the Commissariat Department'. Additionally, they were to investigate the 'alleged delay in unshipping and distributing the clothing and other stores' sent from Britain.[10]

On 10 June 1855 McNeill and Tulloch sent their first report to Lord Panmure from Constantinople. They had not arrived until March, by which time conditions in the Crimea were much improved after the horrors of the winter, but immediately got to work by visiting the hospitals at Scutari, where they were told that the sick men arriving there were suffering from diseases attributable to diet. During the winter, they learned, the army had been supplied mainly with salt meat and biscuit, with a 'very insufficient proportion of vegetables'. It was consequently essential that supplies of fresh meat, vegetables and freshly baked bread be made available if the health of the men was to be maintained. It was no longer a matter of rules and regulations but of common sense and humanity.[11]

Their investigations soon forced them to some unpalatable conclusions.

The deaths, including those at Scutari and elsewhere, appear to amount to about 35 per cent of the average strength of the army present in the Crimea from the 1st October, 1854, to the 30th of April, 1855, and it seems to be clearly established that this excessive mortality is not to be attributed to anything peculiarly unfavourable in the climate, but to overwork, exposure to wet and cold, improper food, insufficient clothing during part of the winter, and insufficient shelter from inclement weather . . . much of the labour and exposure which the troops had to undergo was a consequence of the want of sufficient land transport, which it was the duty of the Commissariat to provide. . . . In like manner, the injurious consequences of defective cooking were . . . attributable to a deficiency of fuel, or of transport to convey it to Balaclava to the camp, both of which are matters affecting the Commissariat.[12]

In simple terms, the deficiencies of the Commissariat had made conditions for the men worse than was absolutely necessary and had contributed in a marked way to the appalling suffering they had undergone, both in the camp before Sevastapol and in the hospitals at Scutari.

The Commissioners were most concerned by both the quantity and the quality of the soldiers' diet. It was apparent that men were frequently reduced to half rations and occasionally received no food. On Christmas Day 1854 for example, Colonel Bell's men received no rations at all.[13] The Colonel then 'kicked up a dust' with a commissary officer and eventually some small portions of fresh meat were served out, but by that time it was dark and the men had no fires or means of cooking it. Salt meat and biscuit were generally available but these gave insufficient nutritional value to men working such long hours and in such conditions. Many of the soldiers could not eat the salt beef even when full rations were issued because 'the prevailing diseases were . . . affections of the bowels, in most cases connected with scorbutic tendency in the system; and not only the men, but the medical officers also, believed that those diseases were aggravated . . . by the continued use of salt meat'.[14] The result was that much salt meat was thrown away, sometimes hundreds of pounds a day by some regiments. Why more fresh meat was not made available is difficult to understand, especially when there was no shortage of cattle available in neighbouring states; in December, when only salt meat was issued, Filder admitted to having eight thousand head of cattle secured. He claimed that lack of adequate sea transport, difficulties in winter navigation and the delays caused by using the port of Balaclava prevented him from shipping them to the Crimea. Colonel Tulloch pointed out that sea transport was available and navigation difficulties on the journey from Constantinople were by no means insurmountable. Moreover, live cattle transported themselves once they arrived at Balaclava and could have provided much needed fresh meat in the camps on the heights.

On the issue of salt meat the Commissioners were particularly critical

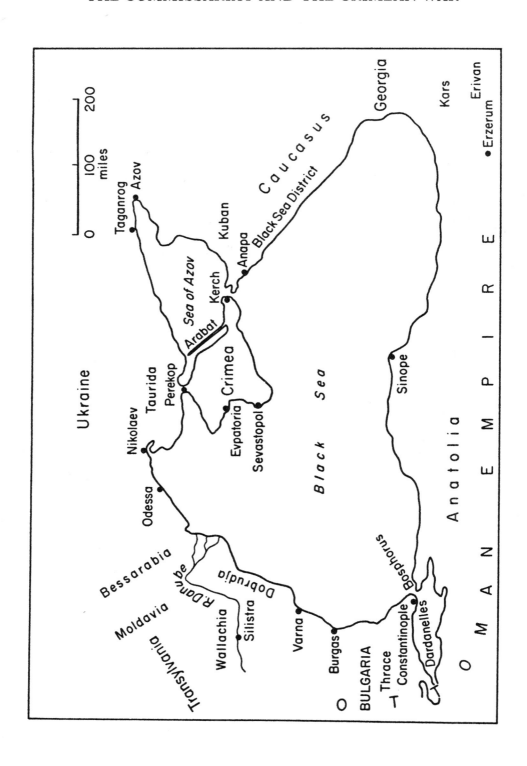

of Filder's efforts. It was well-known that where large armies were encamped there was generally a high incidence of diseases of the bowels and it was essential that every precaution should be taken to prevent this. Experience had proved that the use of salt meat in the diet increased both the number of those attacked by scurvy and the number of fatal cases. If one added to this the unusually difficult circumstances of the troops, the heavy work, the long hours, the winter season and the inadequate clothing and shelter, it was absolutely vital that 'no practicable means ought to have been left untried to protect the troops from the injurious effects of diet – one of the few conditions of the soldiers' existence which were absolutely within control'.[15] Instead of this, lives were wasted through sheer bureaucratic incompetence. It would have been more trouble for the Commissariat to issue fresh meat than salt meat, to bake fresh bread rather than distribute bags of biscuits, but it would have saved the lives of many and relieved the suffering of many more. Perhaps it was impossible for the civil service mentality to come to terms with the horrors that surrounded it, and it accordingly took refuge in its own ordered and regulated world, where casualties were just numbers on a sheet of paper.

Colonel Tulloch drew attention to Professor Christison's findings on the weight and nutritional value of the daily rations of a British sailor, a Hessian soldier and a British soldier in the Crimea. The nutritive weight of the sailor's rations was 28.5 ounces, the Hessian's 32.96 ounces, while the Crimean soldier's was a mere 23.52 ounces.[16] When it is also borne in mind that the soldier's salt meat was less nutritious than fresh meat and that in the Crimea he mainly threw it away because of the irritation it caused his bowels, and subsisted on rum and biscuit, it may be wondered how he survived at all. When it is also realised that, according to Professor Christison, an inmate of a Scottish prison, with no exposure to hard work or bad weather, recieved 25.16 ounces, including bread, vegetables, fish and milk, the plight of the British soldier is seen in stark relief.[17]

The Commissariat, it seems, could do nothing right. On 4 November 1854, 150 tons of vegetables were shipped on board the *Harbinger*, which left the Bosphorus without the correct documentation; when it arrived at Balaclava its captain could get no one to accept responsibility for the cargo, so it rotted, being either thrown overboard or consumed by roaming bands of French Zouaves. None of these vegetables reached the

10. *The problems caused by difficulties with sea transport were severely felt by the Commissariat. Although the Allies controlled the passage from Constantinople to Balaclava in the Crimea, port facilities in both places were atrocious. The lack of fresh meat, fresh bread and vegetables was felt to be the result of the breakdown in both land and sea transport.*

British troops at the front. From November to March there was insufficient fresh meat to maintain the health of the army, while the deficiency of vegetables aggravated the situation, most men having a monthly ration of two potatoes and one onion. While in Bulgaria, Lord Raglan had authorised the daily issue of two ounces of rice to each man, as a result of the prevalence of bowel complaints. However, on 15 November this order lapsed and through an oversight was not renewed, though Filder did point out that the supplies of rice were adequate but that he had no transport to carry it to the troops each day. Why Filder did not inform Lord Raglan that the issue of rice could continue if the men could fetch it themselves is difficult to understand, particularly as this was the only vegetable matter available to troops now increasingly subject to scurvy. When questioned on this, Filder informed the Commissioners that it was not the practice in the British Army to keep the Commander-in-Chief informed of the amount of provisions in depot and it was only at the end of January that Raglan took the initiative and began to inquire.

Had Lord Raglan been informed he could have discovered that instead of the salt meat, which many could not eat anyway, there was available at Balaclava and Scutari rice, potatoes, peas and Scotch barley, which would have been far more beneficial to the men's health and no heavier to carry than salt meat and biscuit. Filder had made it clear to Lord Raglan that it was not the task of the Commissariat to supply vegetables because 'according to the usage of the service' it was the men's own responsibility, and he was unwilling to do any more than was absolutely required of him.

Christopher Hibbert gives a graphic description of the harbour at Balaclava.

For days, for weeks on end, ships lay outside Balaclava waiting to come in and unload. And when they did so their crews, although well used to Eastern harbours, were appalled. Since the storm the ghastly pale-green waters were like a stagnant cesspool into which all imaginable refuse had been thrown. Dead men with white and swollen heads, dead camels, 'dead horses, dead mules, dead oxen, dead cats, dead dogs, the filth of an army with its hospitals', floated amidst the wreckage of spars, boxes, bales of hay, biscuits, smashed cases of medicines and surgical instruments, the decomposed offal, and butchered carcasses of sheep thrown overboard by ship cooks.[18]

One of the most controversial failures of Commissary-General Filder concerned the issue of lime juice. It had been learned centuries before that the scurvy which affected ships' crews on long journeys could be prevented by the issue of citrus fruit or lime juice. This was a well-established principle by the time of the Crimean War and the fact that so many British soldiers succumbed to scurvy was a national disgrace. On 10

December 1854 the *Esk* reached Balaclava harbour carrying 278 cases, containing nearly 20,000 lbs of lime juice, to be issued generally to the troops. In the previous month small quantities had been obtained from naval sources to help cure scurvy among the sick, but no general action had been taken to counter the rapid spread of the disease through the British camp. Fom the 10 December to the first week in February, the cargo of lime juice remained untouched on board the *Esk*, even though Filder knew it was there, because he did not consider it his job to inform the army of its arrival.[19]

The Commissioners reported that until April 1855 the troops had no bread and had to make do with hard biscuit. This was particularly unfortunate for the sick and for those with scurvy who could only eat the biscuit in great pain from their inflamed gums. Some bread was apparently available from private sources in Balaclava but at a price far beyond the ordinary soldier's pocket. The French had established bakeries and were supplying their own soldiers with fresh bread, which the British could easily have done according to Colonel Tulloch if the initiative had been present, for there were enough bakers in the regiments to make it a feasible project.

The issue of green coffee to the troops has come to symbolise the inefficiency of the Commissariat in the Crimea. Tulloch was quite clear in attributing this extraordinary blunder to Commissary-General Filder, who specifically requested that the coffee beans should be sent unroasted, even though it was pointed out to him the difficulties this would present for the men (Filder asserted that unroasted coffee beans were less prone to dampness and mould on the journey). The outcome was predictable. Unequipped to roast and grind the beans the soldiers often drank a foul concoction which was actually injurious to their health, according to their medical officers. The commander of the 1st Regiment commented,

A ration of green raw coffee berry was served out, a mockery in the midst of all this misery. Nothing to roast coffee, nothing to grind it, no fire, no sugar; and unless it was meant that we eat it as horses do barley, I don't see what use the men could make of it, except that they have just done, pitched it into the mud![20]

The men can hardly be accused of lack of initiative, some finding cannon-balls and empty shell cases to grind the coffee berries, while others were seen cutting up their dried meat into strips and using it as fuel to roast their coffee.[21] Ironically, in the stores at Balaclava there were some 2705 pounds of tea which required none of the complex procedures of preparation that the coffee did.

The Commissioners claimed that one of the causes of sickness in the army was defective cooking. During the march to Balaclava, and the crossing of the Alma, most men had lost their camp kettles and cooking equipment. Thus when they arrived before Sevastapol they were poorly equipped to cater for themselves, having just a small mess-tin each and needing to find their own fuel to light a fire. This was easier said than done. Quickly the available wood around the camp was used up and there was 'not a twig to be seen now as thick as any one's finger; all cut away and burned up'.[22] With snow upon the ground the men could not even dig up roots, while in wet weather few men had the experience to burn the green or wet wood. Those returning from spending all night on duty in the trenches, exhausted and frozen, were unable to cook anything hot for themselves without scavenging round for roots to burn, often only to be found at great distances from camp. Most men were too exhausted to undergo this further trial and made do with hard biscuit soaked in rum, possibly followed by raw pork.

Commissary-General Filder correctly pointed out that it was not the practice of the Commissariat to issue fuel to troops in the field, only in barracks, yet this was a new situation and little was to be gained from such inflexibility. The army should not have been wintering in the open and for that decision no blame attached to him. But once the decision was taken it was his duty to do everything possible to improve conditions for the men. The cold was intense, with ink freezing in bottles, toothbrushes needing to be thawed out before use, and soldiers on night working party returning with four-inch long icicles on their moustaches. One private soaked two shirts overnight and the next morning found them so frozen that he was forced to parade for kit inspection complete with wash-tub.

On the subject of firewood, Raglan was forced to overrule Filder by instructing him to provide fuel for the winter and, by a general order of 4 December, to issue it to the troops. However, although Filder had provided a depot of fuel at Scutari for the use of the army in barracks, he was most unwilling to comply with Raglan's order to issue it to the troops in the field. One can sympathise with Filder as one might with any overworked civil servant. Undoubtedly he was already overburdened with duties, certainly he faced difficulties with land transport and admittedly the area for landing stores at Balaclava was limited. Yet men's very lives were at stake and his insistence on precedent, particularly that of the Peninsular War, where troops in the field found their own fuel, was unforgivable in the context of the operations before Sevastapol. It was not until the 29 December that Raglan was able to persuade him to issue the fuel.

At the root of the Commissariat's problems was the deficiency in land transport. While the army had been in Bulgaria the problem had not been great but when it embarked for the Crimea nearly all baggage animals had been left behind. It was not until the end of October that about half of the regulated number arrived, and most of these animals had died by January when a second and smaller batch arrived at Balaclava. The conditions under which the horses and mules worked were appalling, with inadequate forage, exposure to damp and cold, and overwork. In the absence of the baggage animals it seems that the men, already subject to 'labour and exposure as great or greater than they could bear, without injury to their health' had to perform tasks of transporting supplies on roads ankle-deep in mud from the camp on the heights down to the harbour at Balaclava. The journey frequently took them twelve hours, during which time they were without food, shelter or rest. This absence of adequate transport exposed the troops to short rations, loss of their rice and a complete absence of other vegetable foods. Nevertheless, transport was still found daily to carry to the front immense quantities of shot, shell, cannon and platforms.

Filder had under-estimated the transport needs of the expedition. He was aware on arrival before Sevastapol that the resources he had were far below what he would need, yet he made little effort to improve matters, claiming to McNeill and Tulloch that he could not increase the transport in the Crimea because he could not feed any more animals.[23] This was a vicious circle of his own making, for the shortage of forage was a direct result of Commissariat incompetence. He had arranged a contract for the preparation of 800 tons of hay on the Sea of Marmara, at Buyook Tehakmedge. However, the contractors failed financially after producing between 600 and 700 tons, and when hydraulic presses were sent from England to compress the hay that was available for shipment, they were set up at Constantinople, fifteen miles from where the hay was, making it necessary for the hay to be somehow transported to the presses rather than vice-versa. The outcome was that the hay was not shipped, the horses died for want of forage and men consequently starved and froze.[24] In sheer frustration, Lord Raglan, having 'unceasingly and urgently' impressed on Filder the need to improve the transport system, finally sent army officers to purchase transport horses from Eupatoria, Constantinople, Smyrna and even Sicily.

In their second report to Parliament, completed in London in January 1856, McNeill and Tulloch concentrated their attention on the work of the Commissariat in providing clothing and blankets. They began by describing the extraordinary way in which the men were deprived of their knapsacks.

The British soldier usually carries in his knapsack clothing sufficient to admit of at least one change, but on landing in the Crimea, so great was the anxiety to advance rapidly upon Sebastapol, that authority was given to leave the knapsacks in the transports, and of this permission most of the corps appear to have availed themselves. Generally, therefore, each soldier had only a shirt, a pair of boots, and a pair of socks, loosely rolled up in his blanket; and even of these a great part was lost at the battle of the Alma, or during the march. This separation from the knapsacks could have produced but little inconvenience had it terminated with the march; but, unfortunately, they were left on board of the different vessels from which the men had disembarked, and these, being urgently required to bring reinforcements and supplies, were sent to the opposite coast, carrying the knapsacks with them. It appears from the evidence that, on the average, more than six weeks elapsed before they were recovered, and then, in many cases only after they had been plundered of a great part of their contents. The valises of the Cavalry, which were likewise left behind, shared the same fate, and the great majority of the troops were thus deprived, for a considerable time, of a change of clothing.[25]

The loss of the knapsacks had incalculable consequences for the ordinary soldier in the siege lines before Sevastapol, who had only the clothes he stood up in, these soon wearing out in the harsh conditions of trench life. Without his spare kit any man unfortunate enough to be injured arrived at the hospital at Scutari in a wretched and destitute state, caked in mud and verminous. In wet weather the men had no change of clothes and wore their sodden kit day after day, sleeping wrapped in a greatcoat and a single blanket on the muddy floors of their tents, with nothing to shield them from the damp ground. Tulloch later commented,

The destitution of our troops in this respect, as they landed, fever stricken and covered with filth and vermin, on the shore at Scutari, had excited the astonishment, and awakened the sympathy of all Europe. . . .[26]

Although large quantities of warm clothing were sent from Britain, the loss of the *Prince* on 14 November, with 40,000 greatcoats, boots for almost the entire army and 'everything that was most wanted', combined with the usual failures in distribution at the harbour of Balaclava, meant that it was slow to reach the men, who suffered appallingly during the month of December. Ironically, supplies of 'rugs' came in by each ship until they numbered some 25,000 by January, yet in spite of the fact that they were as useful as blankets for keeping out the cold and damp, only 800 were supplied to the troops and no one had the imagination or initiative to issue any more.[27] Of the thousands of paillasses shipped to the Crimea to protect the soldiers from the moisture of the ground, none were issued to the troops because straw and hay were lacking with which to stuff them.

By the end of November, 12,000 greatcoats had arrived safely at Balaclava, but at the time when they were most desperately needed, the months of December and January, when men were dying of exposure, over 9000 remained in store. The reason for this extraordinary decision by the Commissariat was the service regulation, established by Queen's warrant, that soldiers should not be issued with greatcoats more than once in three years. In spite of the desperate need of the troops, which must have been obvious even to Commissary-General Filder, no one saw fit to dispense with this restriction, or question why such great quantities of coats were being sent if it was not intended to distribute them.[28]

Deficiencies in the supply of boots and shoes will have a disastrous effect on an army even in the best of conditions. In the harsh conditions of a Crimean winter, men generally wore more than one pair of socks, and with the damp weather causing their feet to swell few of the available boots fitted. The Commissariat supplied boots of certain specified sizes but paid no attention to the fact that conditions might require them to adjust their requisitions to include more of the larger sizes, so that men frequently had to wear boots so small that 'women could scarcely have got them on'.[29] British soldiers, who had viewed with horror the stripping of corpses and grave robbing by their Turkish allies, began to lose their qualms as their own clothes began to disintegrate. Christopher Hibbert cites the example of Midshipman Wood, later Sir Evelyn, who paid a sailor ten shillings to find him some Russian boots from a graveyard.[30] He was very pleased with those he got, and his example was followed by many British officers, who preferred captured Russian boots to the British ones, which were of such a shamefully bad quality that 'the soles dropped off after a week's wear'.[31] The poor quality of the British boots was a consequence of the Commissariat's desire to keep costs low, and contractors had clearly economised, providing boots totally unfit for wet, muddy conditions. On 1 February the 55th Regiment, parading in 'one vast black dreary wilderness of mud', sank into the slime and the strain of pulling their feet out caused all the boot soles to be sucked off. The men apparently threw the boots away and marched to the front in their socks.[32]

In view of the vital importance of horses to both cavalry and land transport, little effort was made to preserve them from exposure to the harsh conditions. Individual measures by sappers and miners preserved their own baggage horses, but even though fairly moderate shelter could have saved many lives, the attitude of men like Lords Lucan and Cardigan remained hidebound. Lucan apparently referred to the idea of digging a pit for a horse to stand in out of the wind as consigning him to 'a grave', while sheltering a horse behind canvas was the 'act of a madman'.[33]

Cardigan, who asserted that he and his weakened troops would have had difficulty in carrying up all the barley needed for their horses, felt that this was a justification for bringing up none at all. While Cardigan stayed on his yacht for four or five days at a time, the survivors from his Light Brigade endured terrible hardships. Winter had come early and snow swept through the camp, freezing both men and horses. On 7 November, the Commissariat informed Cardigan that they no longer had the transport to bring forage the six miles from Balaclava to his camp and suggested that either he fetch it himself or else send all the horses down to the harbour for safe keeping. Cardigan refused both suggestions, insisting that the Light Brigade had a duty to guard against a renewed Russian attack, however unlikely. The result was that the horses were forced to subsist on one handful of barley a day, standing knee-deep in mud and with no cover whatsoever. In desperation they gnawed their straps, saddle-flaps, and each other's tails. When Cardigan ordered that no injured horse should be destroyed it condemned the starving horses to a lingering death, lying in muddy pits with no one brave enough to put them out of their misery. The bad relations between Lucan and Cardigan provided constant headaches for the Commissariat, with Lucan willing to spare 494 horses from the Heavy Brigade to bring provisions up from Balaclava to the infantry, yet unwilling to spare a single horse to carry anything to the relief of the ravaged Light Brigade, which Cardigan commanded.[34]

The shortage of nose-bags for the horses resulted in the animals losing half their barley at every feed. Incredibly, a large supply of nose-bags was on board the *Jason* in Balaclava harbour. No one would take responsibility for landing them and it was not until late January that these vital horse-stores were brought ashore. Similarly, horse medicine which had been demanded five months earlier was eventually discovered in January 1855, in the holds of the *Medway*.

The French 'Intendance Militaire' was an example of what was possible even in the middle of the nineteenth century. It had sub-divisions of medical staff, administrative staff (supplying clothing, forage and provisions), military workmen (carpenters, labourers etc), hospital attendants and transport corps. Spurred on by the example of French efficiency, things began to improve for the British, partly as a result of better performance by commissary officers now accustomed to their work, and partly helped by the improved spring weather.

Criticism of the Commissariat centred on the persons of Commissary-General Filder and his chief in London, Sir Charles Trevelyan. Filder, in particular, seems to have had an unfortunate capacity to arouse great hostility. Colonel McMurdo of the Land Transport Corps, for example, said, 'I never in the whole course of my existence met so disagreeable a coxcomb and so utterly impracticable an official as this little viper'.[35] Filder seemed to take it as a personal slight on his 'skill or ability' if he was ever found to be in need of help, and rejected French offers of stores, replying, in January 1855, that 'We are not now, nor have been at any time, in want of them'.[36] Filder was understandably attacked from many quarters, particularly over his extraordinary insistence on the issue of green, unroasted coffee. Even his own chief, Trevelyan, believed that he had committed a gross misjudgement in estimating that only 6000 transport animals would be required, when according to Commissariat procedures double that number was more likely. McNeill and Tulloch were scathing about Filder's failure to issue the 278 cases of lime juice for two months, during which time many of the troops were suffering from scurvy. The only possible conclusion was that Filder was incompetent, and Lord Palmerston commented that he was wholly unfit for his post. Yet to place all the blame on Filder is unjust. Had he received stronger backing from London, particularly from Sir Charles Trevelyan, things might have been better. Moreover, with a man of Lord Raglan's essential gentility, Filder was able to play the civil servant regardless of the consequences. It is difficult to believe that a stronger commander would have allowed him to exert such a malign influence on the welfare of the army. McNeill and Tulloch concluded that 'a man of comprehensive views might probably have risen superior to . . . disadvantages. . . .'[37]

Filder was quick to defend himself against the Commission's criticisms, alleging that he had been judged 'partly out of a misconception of the extent of my power and responsibility as head of the Commissariat'. Undoubtedly there was some truth in this, but the Commissioners can hardly be blamed when even the Commander-in-Chief was unaware of the Commissariat's ill-defined responsibilities. Much of the trouble originated in London, where Filder's superior, Sir Charles Trevelyan, exercised a 'baneful influence'.[38] According to Colonel Dunne, the destruction of the British army resulted from the mismanagement of the Commissariat by Trevelyan. Filder had reason to feel 'let down' by his chief, who admitted simply ignoring Filder's letters on several occasions, and that the Treasury acted only when 'later letters . . . became precise, pressing and urgent'.[39] Filder's requisition for 2000 tons of hay, for example, sent on 13 September 1854, was complied with eight months later, by which time the horses were dead. Hibbert describes the confusion in London:

Disastrous as the muddle was in the Crimea, in London it was a great deal worse. In the bewildering labyrinth of offices through which requisitions passed on their way to someone who could give them his attention, the chaos was stupefying. A list of urgent requirements might, for instance, pass through as many as eight different departments before it was even known whether or not the items needed could be supplied from stock. If they could not be supplied from stock there were long discussions and conversations, unrecorded arguments between contractors and officials, until a satisfactory price and date of delivery had been agreed. Everyone was satisfied, all commissions were paid and mouths silenced; and then weeks and perhaps months later goods of disgraceful inferiority were supplied.[40]

The furore which followed the publication of McNeill and Tulloch's reports prompted the Government to establish a Board of General Officers to review the reports and investigate the work of the Commissariat. The outcome, however, was little short of a 'whitewash'.

—5—
The Battle of the Crater (1864)

Among military commanders, the ability to achieve spectacular failure from positions promising success has fortunately been a rare one. One of those who possessed this perverse quality was General Ambrose Burnside who for a time in 1862 commanded the Army of the Potomac, during the American Civil War. Over six feet tall, square-shouldered and with a broad, handsome face, sporting a magnificent set of whiskers, Burnside was as impressive in appearance as any general could be. However, behind the smile there was an uncertainty and lack of confidence in his own ability which could prove to be disastrous at moments of crises. Nor was Burnside intelligent. Few commanders have risen so high upon so slender a foundation. He had not sought the army command in 1862 and had told Lincoln that he did not feel competent to take over from George McClellan, whom he admired. Lincoln had insisted, and it had taken the bloody defeat at Fredericksburg to prove to him the truth of Burnside's assertion.

In the summer of 1864 Burnside was commanding IX Corps before Petersburg. Ulysses Grant's drive to take Richmond had bogged down in trench warfare and many of the horrors of the 1914–18 conflict were anticipated in the bloody and futile assaults which broke on the apparently impregnable Confederate lines. Burnside's Corps occupied trenches only 130 yards from an enemy strong point, known as Elliott's Salient. This fortified position was all that stood between the Union forces and the strategic town of Petersburg.[1]

The trenches opposite Elliott's Salient were held by the 48th Pennsylvania Regiment, made up of volunteers from Schuylkill County, in the anthracite region of Pennsylvania. Over a quarter of the regiment had been coal miners in civilian life and its colonel, Henry Pleasants, had trained as a civil engineer, working on the Pennsylvania railroad in the 1850s, gaining experience of mining and tunnelling. When he overheard one of his men comment, 'That God-damned fort is the only thing between us and Petersburg, and I have an idea we could blow it up', he

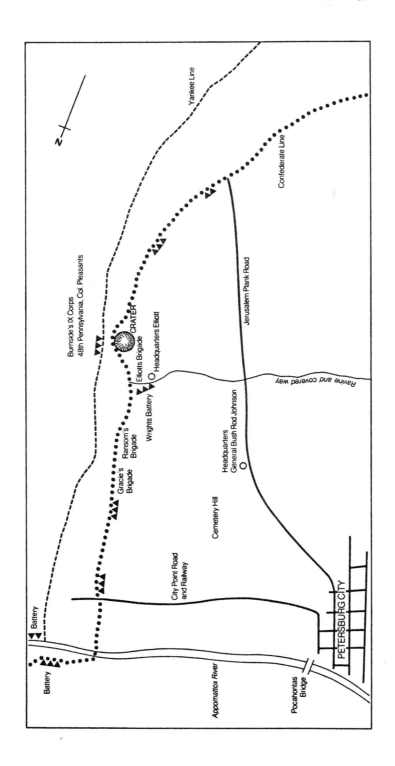

drew up a sketch of the surrounding terrain and presented a plan for a tunnel to the corps commander, Ambrose Burnside. The plan consisted of digging a shaft fifty yards behind the Union lines, to prevent observation by the Confederates, and then tunnelling five hundred feet under the Rebel position before blowing it up.[2]

It was such a daring plan that the Army Engineers dismissed it as impossible. But Pleasants was convinced it could be done. Burnside passed it on to his army commander, George Meade, who was far from convinced. Eventually the plan reached Grant himself and he concluded that the tunnel would at least keep the men occupied and save them from morale-sapping boredom.

However, in spite of having the support of the Commander-in-Chief, Pleasants found an almost total lack of cooperation from those who had the expertise to help him. Meade had promised him a company of engineers and any other help he needed but when he asked for it none was forthcoming. Burnside confided that neither Meade nor Major Duane, the Army's chief engineer, believed that the scheme was possible. Duane had called the whole thing 'clap-trap and nonsense', saying such a length of mine was impossible and men would be smothered for want of air or crushed by the falling earth. In any case, the Rebels would hear the work and dig counter-mines.[3]

Undeterred, Pleasants organised his men into shifts, with the non-combatant Harry Reese acting as mine boss, and began burrowing into the west bank of an abandoned railway cutting, well hidden from view. For lack of picks the 48th were compelled to dig with their bayonets at the outset, while hardtack boxes were converted into barrows for shifting the dirt, which had to be covered with bushes every morning to escape the eyes of enemy look-outs. Soon timber was needed to shore up the walls and ceiling of the tunnel. Again, none was forthcoming, and so Pleasants ordered his men to tear down an old railway bridge for timber and then re-activate an abandoned sawmill.[4] In spite of encountering wet clay which made the tunnel sink, and marl, which turned to concrete on contact with the air, Pleasants kept altering the angle of the tunnel, to ensure good drainage, and the digging continued. Technical problems, which had worried the army professionals, were soon overcome by Pleasants's inventiveness. For adequate ventilation, he installed an airtight canvas

---

11. The mine dug by Colonel Pleasants and the 48th Pennsylvania Regiment was a brilliant success. It offered Grant a chance to break the Confederate defences in front of Petersburg and materially shorten the war. The fact that it failed was due to the incompetence of Corps Commander Ambrose Burnside and the cowardice of Divisional Commanders Ferrero and Ledlie, who stayed under cover once the attack began.

door just inside the entrance to the tunnel. Beneath it ran a square wooden pipe along the floor of the shaft to the diggers at the end, who extended it gradually as the tunnel grew longer. A fireplace near the sealed door sent heated air up its chimney, creating a draught that drew the stale air from the far end of the tunnel and pulled in fresh air through the pipe, whose mouth was beyond the door. Inside, the tunnel was five feet high, four feet wide at the bottom and thirty inches wide at the top.[5]

After some two hundred feet of the tunnel had been dug, Pleasants needed to take precise readings to ensure it came up under the Rebel position. He therefore applied to the Army engineers for the instruments necessary to make accurate triangulations but was refused. In fact, Burnside had to obtain a theodolite for him by wiring a friend in Washington, who volunteered to lend him an old one.[6]

Peering over the top of the front line trenches, and under constant sniper fire, Pleasants took his measurements, and on 17 July 1864 he was able to inform Burnside that the tunnel, 510 feet long, was exactly 20 feet below the Confederate redoubt. Pleasants now proceeded to dig a 75 foot shaft across the end of the tunnel, to form a 'T', and filled this shaft with some four tons of explosive, in eight connected magazines. The engineers once again proved unhelpful, refusing him a galvanic battery and supply of insulated wire to set off the charge.[7] Undeterred, Pleasants spliced together two ordinary fifty-foot fuses, stuck one end into the powder in the 'T' shaft and ran out the rest one hundred feet down the main tunnel, from which position it could be ignited.

Although Grant had initially regarded this project as just a useful way of keeping the men busy, he now decided to give Burnside substantial support for the attack following the explosion of the mine. In view of this, it is difficult to understand how an assault which might have ended the war at a stroke could have been held up for weeks by the sheer cussedness of the army engineers. Perhaps Meade was content to see Burnside's plan fail. Nevertheless, when it became obvious that the tunnel could be dug and that Grant was prepared to support Burnside's assault on the Confederate position, Meade began to take the project more seriously.

The ridge behind the Confederate lines was not high and could be reached by a gentle, grassy slope. If the Federalists gained this they could go on to take Petersburg itself and this would ensure the fall of Richmond. Grant, knowing that Burnside's target was just half a mile away, decided to back the assault with everything he had. In order to force Lee to thin his defences in front of Burnside, he planned a feint attack north of the James River. Hancock's Corps, along with two of Sheridan's divisions, was accordingly moved across the James to create a diversion or even a simultaneous breakthrough. Grant's ploy worked perfectly and Lee moved five infantry divisions to Bermuda Hundred to block Hancock, leaving Beauregard with only three divisions to hold Petersburg.

While Pleasants and his men carried the gunpowder in 25 pound kegs down the tunnel, Burnside was making his plans to exploit the expected breakthrough. The explosion was timed for 3.30 a.m. on 30 July and was to be followed by an attack by the whole of Burnside's IX Corps, supported on the left by Warren's Corps and on the right by that of 'Baldy' Smith. To reinforce the effect of the mine, 80 field guns, 18 heavy 10-inch mortars, 28 light mortars and 18 4.5-inch siege guns were dug in opposite the Confederate position. Once the mine exploded Burnside's Corps was to go straight for the ridge without stopping for anything. Time was of the essence and the troops had to occupy the high ground before the Confederates could recover from their shock.

Up to this point Burnside's planning had been very sound and belied his reputation, earned at Antietam and Fredericksburg, of being a bungler. His corps was composed of four divisions, three of which had been in constant action and were war-weary, whereas the fourth was relatively fresh. This was an all-black division of some 4,500 men, commanded by General Edward Ferrero, and Burnside's decision that it should lead the assault was a perfectly logical one in terms of its numbers and its freshness. Accordingly, it was told its task, which was to fan out to the right and left of the crater and hold back counter-thrusts from the flanks, while the rest of the corps poured through the gap created. Ferrero's troops even underwent special training for leading the assault. However, it was at this stage that things began to go wrong. Purely military considerations were pushed into the background as politics reared its head.

Ferrero's division had up till then been confined to guard-duty, due to the prevailing view that the negro was unsuited to combat conditions. Sherman for one was highly suspicious of their quality as troops and when asked whether a negro was as good as a white man for stopping a bullet, replied, 'Yes; and a sandbag is better'. Burnside was determined to show that this view was mistaken. However, he had reckoned without the political sensitivity of his superiors. The use of black troops had been something of a gamble, taken to placate the abolitionists, and Meade was not prepared to sacrifice his reputation by sending these inexperienced troops into an assault which could turn into a massacre. He therefore ordered Burnside to choose one of his other divisions to lead the assault. Burnside furiously referred the matter to Grant, but the Commander-in-Chief eventually sided with Meade. In his evidence before the Committee on the Conduct of the War, Grant later admitted that this decision was a mistake, yet he knew that he could not ignore the political implications of using these black troops in such a dangerous operation.[8] From this moment the entire operation was doomed.

Burnside now faced the difficult job of re-arranging his plans in a mere twelve hours, only three of which were in daylight. All the training Ferrero's division had undertaken was wasted and the assault was now to be spearheaded by men who had virtually no preparation for their task. One cannot help feeling sorry for Burnside, but what followed was a performance as imcompetent as any in the war. As Bruce Catton remarked of IX Corps Commander,

. . . from this moment on he was as poor a general as a grown man can be, and both the army and the Union cause as a whole would have been much better off if he had taken to his bed, pulled the covers over his handsome face, and let someone else take charge.[9]

Instead of considering the merits of his three remaining units, he decided to consign the matter to luck by allowing the three divisional commanders to draw lots. The winner of the draw was General Ledlie, whose division was undoubtedly the weakest in the Corps, while Ledlie himself was quite unfit for command. It was generally considered that Ledlie's men were 'gun-shy' and only weeks before Burnside himself had described the whole division as worthless.[10] Why therefore he allowed them to lead the assault is not clear. One can only suppose that he was abandoning responsibility for what was about to happen.

General Ledlie was basically a coward and was known to his subordinates as a weakling. In an attack on 18 June, he had found a safe place to hide and, armed with a bottle, had abandoned his men as they fought to carry the Rebel trenches.[11] This seemed to be common knowledge to everyone except Burnside himself. The Corps commander was known for his loyalty to his subordinates but he was also a very poor judge of men. Even without specific knowledge of Ledlie's weaknesses he should have been able to judge the character of his divisional commander well enough to know he should never be entrusted with the vital task of leading the assault on 30 July. The problem was that by this stage Burnside was not acting entirely rationally himself.

Ledlie's division assembled at midnight and then advanced along the covered ways which led to the Union front trenches. In the darkness, their journey through the maze-like network of covered ways was a nightmare. Eventually they took up position and awaited the explosion which was timed for 3.30 that morning. Meanwhile, no-one had informed Ferrero's division that there had been a change of plan. The coloured troops assembled excitedly at the bottom of a ravine, out of sight of the enemy and forgotten by Burnside, who took up a position in a gun emplacement a quarter of a mile from the front line and quite out of touch with events. Meade was operating from even further back.

At the appointed time, Pleasants sent a man to light the fuse, but zero-hour came and went in perfect silence. Thirty minutes passed, then an hour, and still nothing happened. The first light of dawn was beginning to appear in the sky as Grant lost patience and ordered Burnside to launch his assault anyway, without the mine. Behind the Union breastworks, IX Corps had been standing to arms for more than four hours and the tension was draining the men's confidence.

Pleasants ordered his mine boss, Reese, to go down the tunnel to see what had happened to the fuse. With great courage Reese crawled four hundred feet down the tunnel only to discover that the fuse had gone out. Assisted by Lieutenant Jacob Douty, he relit it and ran. At 4.45 a.m. the explosion came. A brigadier with Hancock's Corps described the scene.

Without form or shape, full of red flames and carried on a bed of lighting flashes, it mounted toward heaven with a detonation of thunder [and] spread out like an immense mushroom whose stem seemed to be of fire and its head of smoke.[12]

Simultaneously 80 guns opened fire into the smoking remains of the Confederate position. The shock was so tremendous that Burnside's own troops panicked and ran and it took ten minutes for their officers to re-assemble them for the assault. It was now, just when time was of the essence, that an appalling discovery was made. The plans, so carefully worked out between Meade and Burnside, to flatten the parapets and abatis to allow the assault troops to spring out immediately in battle formation, had not been carried out.[13] Thus, in the early morning light Ledlie's troops found themselves at the bottom of eight-foot-high trenches, with no apparent way of getting out. Improvisation became the order of the day. One officer organised a ladder by jabbing bayonets into a log wall, and up this a trickle of troops clambered into the open. Others formed a stairway of sandbags but the compact mass of assault troops envisaged in the original plan never materialised. Far from attacking on a broad front, a brigade in width, closely supported by the second brigade, the Union troops emerged as a thin dribble, which moved uncertainly towards the smoking crater left by Pleasants's mine.

The sight that met their eyes was astonishing. One hundred and seventy feet of the Confederate line had simply disappeared, leaving an enormous crater, sixty feet across and thirty feet deep.[14] Ledlie's men, far from bypassing the obstacle and charging the ridge, seemed bemused by the experience and stood peering into the great hole. There were rebel soldiers buried to their waists in earth, others with only their heads or legs sticking out of the debris. Some of the assault troops began digging for survivors, while an officer, ordered his men to dig out a cannon. One Confederate officer, dug from the crater, told them that he had been asleep when the big bang came and awoke to find himself flying in the air.[15]

For some five hundred yards there were no Confederate troops manning their positions and yet vital time was lost through lack of leadership. From his position Pleasants could see that his mine had been a brilliant success and that victory was within Burnside's grasp. All he had to do was to order IX Corps forward to the ridge and Petersburg would be theirs. But time was vital or else Beauregard would reinforce the breach.

The engineers who were supposed to move ahead of the troops, clearing the obstructions, had not turned up. Moreover, Ledlie himself was in a bombproof shelter four hundred yards behind the lines drinking rum borrowed from a brigade surgeon.[16] Occasional reports were brought to him there and he issued orders to advance to the ridge but made no effort to emerge from his shelter to see what was happening. In fact, the whole attack had stopped while his troops, acting as rescue parties, salvage teams or merely as sightseers, clambered down into the crater and milled about like a flock of sheep. Not a vestige of military organisation remained as this aimless mob enjoyed the sensation of being in the open and free from enemy fire.

Burnside, from his position, had no idea of what had occurred other than that the mine had succeeded and a breach had been made. Without receiving reports from the front he simply ordered more troops forward. Potter and Willcox now led their divisions through the covered walkways, down the trenches wide enough only for two or three abreast, colliding all the time with returning couriers and injured men, and then into the front line trenches, where they then had to clamber up the bayonet ladders and sandbag stairways and over the eight-foot wall. The passage of over seven thousand men in this laborious way inevitably destroyed any remaining chance that the operation had of succeeding.

With the passage of over thirty minutes the Confederates had had time to recover and were now concentrating a heavy fire on the men in the crater. Of sixteen guns concentrated on the ridge the Union guns were able to knock out ten but the remaining six cut swathes in the exposed troops. No one exerted any authority over the thousands of men now crowded in the crater, many clinging to the almost sheer sides by fingers and toes, while others toppled forward and fell onto their comrades below.[17]

Meade had agreed with Burnside that the attack must be taken at a rush or it would fail. Up to five o'clock he though the assault would succeed, by six perhaps at the expense of hard fighting but by seven o'clock it had no chance. On this assessment there seemed no point in pushing more men forward in support of a plan that had obviously failed. However, there had been a total breakdown in leadership. Ledlie and Burnside were over four hundred yards from events, while Meade was above a mile. Grant was later to assert that Burnside should have been at the crater himself with the men but, as at Fredericksburg, he had preferred to operate from far back, in a kind of fog, sending out orders that bore no relation to events.[18]

His only order consisted of the word 'attack'. By 7.20 a.m. Meade had clearly lost his temper and demanded to know from Burnside what was happening. Burnside angrily accused Meade of 'unofficer-like and ungentlemanly' behaviour.[19] Meanwhile, the crisis developed. What had so far been a fiasco now became a tragedy, as men's lives were thrown away through sheer incompetence. Unaware that the attack had completely failed Burnside ordered Ferrero's coloured division to advance. At first Ferrero demurred, pointing out that there were already three divisions huddled together in the crater, but Burnside was insistent. Under arms since before dawn and many of them believing that their original orders still stood, the black troops charged forward with the intention of seizing the ridge. Ferrero, however, had no intention of going with them. He stopped off at Ledlie's bomb-proof shelter and shared his rum, consigning the command of his troops to his brigadiers.[20]

By this time the Rebel troops had reoccupied their trenches and opened up a withering fire on the advancing negro soldiers. Nevertheless, the latter desperately fought their way into the trenches and captured some. Reports were sent back to Ferrero, who casually ordered them to take the ridge, if they had not already done so. The whole situation had changed, yet no-one was on hand to appreciate it. Confederate mortars were dropping shells onto the troops trapped in the crater, who had no shelter and were so crowded together that they could scarcely move. A strong Confederate counter-thrust drove Ferrero's men out of the trenches and the killing began. 'Take the white man, kill the nigger!' was the cry from the Rebels, as Burnside's division streamed back to their trenches in complete rout.[21]

Grant now suspended the operation though Burnside still believed it could be reorganised. An infuriated Colonel Pleasants yelled at Burnside that his commanders were nothing but a bunch of cowards. Grant himself could not believe what had happened. As he told Halleck, it was 'the saddest affair I have witnessed in the war'.[22] Casualties in the coloured division alone were almost fifty per cent. Although the whole plan had been altered to prevent just such a massacre, through sheer stupidity it was allowed to happen.

At 9.30 a.m. Meade ordered the withdrawal of the men from the crater. This was easier said than done. Suggestions that a covered way be dug out from the Union lines to the crater were immediately rejected by Ferrero and Ledlie, yet there seemed no other way of evacuating the thousands trapped no more than a hundred yards away. A mass break-out would have involved heavy casualties and possibly affected the morale of troops on either side of IX Corps. Burnside was convinced the men would have to stay in the crater until nightfall.

Inside the crater the situation was intolerable. Those who could clung to its walls, hanging on by digging elbows and heels into the earth, and trying to fire their muzzle-loaders at the well-entrenched Confederate troops. More than ten thousand men were crowded into an area of less than a quarter of an acre and all the time they were subject to raking rifle fire and canister shot. In the searing heat of midsummer the agonies of thirst were added to their sufferings.

Shortly after noon the Confederates launched an assault against the trapped IX Corps in the crater. The issue was not long in doubt. Without adequate leadership and with morale at rock bottom, thousands of Burnside's troops took to their heels. Nearly 1700 men were captured and hundreds more killed. Along Meade's front that morning the Union Army suffered over four thousand casualties in one of the most futile operations of the entire war.[23]

Meade's anger was predictably turned against Burnside, whom he wanted court-martialled for incompetence. The argument between the two men prompted a staff observer to comment that their exchange of recriminations 'went far toward confirming one's belief in the wealth and flexibility of the English language as a medium of personal dispute'.[24] Grant showed more diplomacy by sending Burnside on an extended period of leave. At the Court of Inquiry which followed the fiasco Ledlie was rightly condemned and dismissed, though Ferrero mysteriously escaped the punishment he richly deserved.

However, it is with Ambrose Burnside that the fiasco at the crater is most associated. How fair the judgement of history has been is difficult to say. Burnside had found it hard to live down his humiliation at the hands of Lee in 1862; with his confidence gone and after his failure at Fredericksburg he should not have been entrusted with high command again. It was not simply the fact of defeat but the nature of it that was at issue. In adversity Burnside revealed aspects of his character which rendered him profoundly incompetent as a commander of men.

Ironically, the battle for the crater exposed some of the best and some of the worst characteristics of the military profession. The conception of the tunnel and its construction by Colonel Pleasants was brilliant. He overcame all obstacles, both natural and man-made, with a single-minded determination that was wholly admirable. He welded his men into a team that worked round the clock to achieve its target.

The courage of the coloured soldiers in Ferrero's division arouses a sense of wonder. Standing to arms for six or more hours, they were then flung into a situation of such abject confusion that all their weeks of preparation were of no use to them. Undaunted they bypassed the mayhem of the crater and actually seized Confederate trenches at bayonet point. Lacking any kind of coherent plan, and with their general far back in a bomb-proof shelter, they eventually succumbed only to a powerful counter-attack.

If vision and courage were not lacking, why did the 'crater' assault disintegrate into fiasco? The answer is both simple and complex. Mistakes were made of the most elementary kind, and qualities assumed to be present in commanders of high rank were missing. So much is clear. But why these things happened is far more difficult to answer. In the first place, Burnside had a reputation as something of a bungler. Perhaps it was deserved, but if it meant that his fellow commanders did not trust him he should not have been placed in a position of command. Meade had observed Burnside at some of his worst moments in 1862 and clearly felt he was incompetent. When he passed on Pleasants's idea for the tunnel Meade was prepared to dismiss it, as he would anything originating from Burnside. After all, his chief engineer had told him the plan was impossible. Nevertheless, after Grant had given it the go-ahead, he was prepared to let the mine be dug if only to keep the men occupied. What he was not prepared to do was to order his engineers to give it the priority it deserved, and so Pleasants had to fight not only the natural problems of digging the tunnel but all sorts of man-made problems, which delayed the completion of the work by some two weeks.

The problem of judging Ambrose Burnside is more complex. He supported the idea of the tunnel and did everything he could to help Pleasants. His plans for the assault, worked out with Meade's approval, were sound. Ferrero's was his best division and it was logical that it should lead the attack. Burnside, after all, did not share the views of some Union generals that the negro would not make a combat soldier. In fact, until just twelve hours before the assault was due to take place there could be little to criticise in Burnside's performance. The intervention of Grant, to support Meade's objection to the choice of Ferrero's division, was the turning point. Grant obviously believed he had sound reasons for ordering the change, but he left Burnside with far too little time to make alternative arrangements. Probably, a postponement of the operation would have been wiser. However, whatever decision was taken, it was Burnside's duty to try to implement his orders to the best of his ability. It can hardly be claimed that he did so. His casual approach to choosing a replacement division, by pulling straws, was disgraceful. He was widely known to consider Ledlie's division as worthless, and this must have cast doubt on the divisional commander. Even so, he allowed Ledlie to lead an assault which could have brought the war to an end.

During the twelve confused hours before the mine was fired the plans that Meade and Burnside had drawn up for flattening the Union breastworks to enable the men to advance in brigade-width order were simply overlooked. How Burnside could have missed this vital requirement is as difficult to understand as the fact that no one in the Corps, over fifteen thousand strong, drew it to his attention. With speed of the essence it was essential that the men should move smoothly into the attack and advance to capture the ridge, allowing nothing to distract them from their task. This made the presence of their commanders more necessary than usual. Grant later blamed Burnside for not being at the crater himself to see this done. The criticism may be justified but Burnside no doubt assumed that divisional leaders like Ledlie and Ferrero were with their men, and not skulking in a shelter, drinking rum. Had Burnside been more in touch with the affairs of his corps he would have known that this was not the first time that Ledlie had acted in this way. Burnside, who so clearly knew his own limitations, obviously did not know those of his subordinates.

Burnside resigned from the army and returned to his business interests in Rhode Island. Entering politics, he served three terms as state governor and died during his second term in the United States Senate. It is said that he recovered some of the geniality which the war and high command had drained from him. Nevertheless, his incompetence as a commander had cost his country dear in terms of lives lost. The fiasco at the Petersburg Crater would not have happened had he not revealed aspects of his character which were both childish and destructive. As one historian wrote,

There was no . . . intention to sacrifice but, if stupidity be culpability, few generals of ancient or modern times rank with Burnside in the guilt of manslaughter.[25]

—6—
The Battle of San Juan Hill (1898)

The campaign fought by American troops in Cuba in 1898 revealed weaknesses in every aspect of the national military system. A long period of peace at home and a policy of isolation from European affairs meant that there had been no attempt to keep abreast of contemporary European military practices, and in many respects the United States had actually slipped backwards militarily since the Civil War. As Captain Rhodes observed,

If the beginning of the war with Spain – a second-rate military power . . . found our country without accurate maps and statistical information of our adversary's military resources; lacking in carefully formulated plans of mobilization, concentration and operation; without magazine rifles, smokeless powder, and breech-loading cannon for our reserves . . . what must have been our loss in lives, treasure and national prestige had we been pitted against a first-class power?[1]

American unpreparedness for war was apparent in many ways. When war was declared against Spain on 21 April 1898, the Regular Army consisted of just 2143 officers and 26,040 enlisted men. In the same month the *Anuario Militar de Espana* gave a figure of 196,820 Spanish soldiers in Cuba – 155,302 regulars and 41,518 volunteers.[2] Consequently, the Americans would be forced to raise large numbers of raw troops who would then have to be organized, equipped and trained in great haste before being rushed into active campaigning. The condition of America's land forces in 1898 was described by Lieutenant-General Miles:

The army of 25,000 men . . . was not even sufficient to have properly guarded our sea-coasts, in the event of a war with a strong naval power.
   The militia, composed of the national guards of the several States, was, as a rule, inefficient, and, as a body, could be practically disregarded. Its arms and equipment were obsolete and unfit for troops fighting an army properly organised and equipped. . . . Small arms using smokeless powder had been manufactured for the use of the regular troops, but there was not a sufficient supply of these arms to equip even the small army called into service at the time of

its mobilization. Our field artillery, our siege-guns, and all our heavier guns were constructed for, and used, black powder. This in time of action proved to be a great disadvantage; and, in fact, the regiments of volunteers which were present with our army in Cuba had to be withdrawn from the firing line on account of the obsolete fire-arms with which they were armed, while the field artillery were subject to the same disadvantage.[3]

The pressure of public opinion was forcing the Army to act before it was really ready. On 30 May, Major General William R. Shafter was ordered to proceed to Cuba with all his troops and 'capture the garrison at Santiago and assist in capturing the harbour and fleet'. Shafter was a '63 year old, fat, gouty veteran, who looked like three men rolled into one'.[4] Physically he was quite unfitted to the command of American forces in Cuba. He had never previously commanded large forces in action and soon found himself overwhelmed by administrative problems. Arriving at Tampa in Florida on 1 June, Shafter found that 'the utter absence of anything resembling systematic management afforded a spectacle of military unpreparedness sufficient to make the most boastful American blush for shame'.[5]

The choice of Tampa as the port of embarkation may have seemed logical in terms of its geographical proximity to Cuba, but in every other way it was an unwise one. Tampa had only one pier and was served by a single-track railroad, down which all the supplies for the expedition had to come. Trains were queued up as far as Columbia, South Carolina.

The switching facilities were entirely too limited, and for miles the line was choked with freight-cars which could not be unloaded near the places where the regiments were encamped and the supplies needed. As the cars had no labels indicating their contents, consignments could not be found when wanted. . . . An officer seeking clothing would open a car only to find cannon or seeking bacon and beans would find shirts and shoes.[6]

The embarkation of nearly 17,000 men took four days, when eight hours at most should have sufficed. The fact that the men were due to land on a hostile shore and face possible combat immediately does not seem to have occurred to the authorities. 'Men, supplies and equipment were loaded into ships helter-skelter without regard to the order in which they might have to be discharged in case resistance was encountered during landing.'[7] So confused did the embarkation become that some regiments took matters into their own hands, commandeering transport and equipment meant for other units, and even fought on the pier to ensure that they got aboard one of the transports. Men of the 71st New York Regiment took over one train at bayonet point, thus depriving the 13th

THE BATTLE OF SAN JUAN HILL (1898)

Infantry of its transportation. Eventually nearly 10,000 troops were left behind for lack of transport.

By 20 June the expedition had reached Cuba and, on the advice of the leader of the Cuban rebels, General Calixto Garcia, Shafter decided to land at Daiquiri, eighteen miles east of Santiago. Why the Spaniards made no attempt to contest the landing is unclear. As it turned out, the disembarkation was possibly even more chaotic than the embarkation at Tampa. No plans existed for an amphibious landing and units were expected to come ashore as best they could, with or without equipment or food. The captains of the merchant ships chartered as transports refused to take their vessels too close to the shore, while others actually fled and had to be hunted down by naval ships. Lacking the means to transport the horses the expedient was adopted of simply dropping them overboard and encouraging them to swim ashore. Many unfortunately swam out to sea and were drowned before someone suggested roping them together and leading them from a boat.[8] The landing took days to complete. German military observers expressed the view that 300 determined men could have prevented the Americans landing at all.[9]

After some 6000 men had been landed at Daiquiri, Shafter began to march towards Santiago by the most direct route. On 23 June, Brigadier-General Henry W. Lawton, commanding the vanguard, captured Siboney, which then became the new base for the entire operation. The landings now continued at Siboney at night under navy searchlights with no attempt at concealment. The American soldiers seemed to regard it as a kind of holiday.

It was one of the most weird and remarkable scenes of the war, probably of any war. An army was being landed on an enemy's coast at the dead of night, but with somewhat more of cheers and shrieks and laughter than rise from the bathers in the surf at Coney Island on a hot Sunday. It was a pandemonium of noises.[10]

It was at this stage that the lack of discipline among Shafter's commanders began to threaten the expedition. The commander of the dismounted cavalry was a volunteer Major-General and Confederate Civil War veteran known as 'Fighting Joe' Wheeler. Accompanied by Colonel Wood, Lieutenant-Colonel Theodore Roosevelt and the 'Rough Riders', Wheeler was determined to strike the first blow of the campaign before the regular troops under General Lawton could do anything about it.

Under cover of darkness Wheeler rounded up one squadron from each of the 1st and 10th cavalry, a total of about 1000 men, and set off to attack the nearest Spanish force, at Las Guasimas. Lawton awoke in time to stop

Wheeler's men taking away a small dynamite gun on which 'Fighting Joe' was depending for artillery support, but otherwise he could do little but fume and wait. Wheeler had set off in the direction of Santiago at 5 a.m. and soon found himself in a very stiff fight with the rearguard of a retreating Spanish force. So hard-pressed was Wheeler's force that they were forced to send back to Lawton for infantry reinforcements. Lawton obliged, but by the time the infantry arrived the Spanish had broken and fled leaving Wheeler, Wood and Roosevelt masters of the field. As the Spaniards fled the incorrigible Wheeler was heard to shout with delight, 'We've got the damn Yankees on the run'.[11] This 'gallant action' as it was reported in the United States, cost 16 American lives and made Theodore Roosevelt a national hero. It also served to give the Americans an inflated view of their own prowess and resulted in their seriously underestimating their opponents.

Wheeler's action had been completely irresponsible and a serious row broke out between 'Fighting Joe' and Lawton. The latter threatened to put a guard on his troops so that Wheeler could not 'spirit them away' in future. Meanwhile the troops assembling at the village of Sevilla were experiencing great hardships. Though there was enough water, food was very limited due to the problems of the long supply line, and there was never enough fodder for the horses. Moreover, the area had endemic yellow fever and malaria, hot days, cold nights, and a variety of unpleasant and poisonous animal inhabitants, including tarantulas, centipedes and scorpions. The impatience felt by the numerous volunteer soldiers is clearly expressed by one sergeant:

There's Santiago, and the dagoes, and here we are, and the shortest distance between two points is a straight line; which is something everyone knows, and don't have to study strategy to find out. I am in favour of going up there and beating the faces off them dagoes. . . .[12]

On 28 June Shafter received the disconcerting news that 8000 Spanish reinforcements were approaching Santiago. In fact, the true number was nearer 4000 but it was enough to prompt him into taking immediate action. Sending Garcia and his Cuban irregulars to block the advancing Spanish force, he now planned to attack the city from the east. Two diversionary attacks were to take place to distract the attention of the Spanish commander, General Linares, and prevent him concentrating his forces against the main American strike at the San Juan Heights. At daybreak on 1 July, General Lawton's division, supported by General Bates's independent brigade, were to attack the fortified village of El Caney, some six miles to the north of the city, while at the same time

General Duffield and his Michigan Volunteers were to carry out a feint attack at Aguadores. Shafter expected El Caney to fall in less than two hours, whereupon Lawton would return to join General Kent's infantry division and the dismounted cavalry of General Wheeler in the attack on the San Juan Heights.

Sickness now began to affect the senior commanders. Wheeler was confined to bed and Sumner took over the command of the cavalry, while Shafter suffered from chronic gout and malaria, combined with the effects of heat and over-exertion. He was quite incapable of directing the battle from the front and made the mistake of assuming he could conduct it from an HQ located a mile east of El Pozo. Not surprisingly he soon lost contact with his scattered units. From a hill he was able to glimpse El Caney and San Juan Hill over the tops of the trees but was unable to see what was going on at ground level. He devised a cumbersome system of delegated authority whereby he used his staff officer McClernand at El Pozo to relay messages, while at the front his ADC, Lieutenant J.D. Miley, was to coordinate operations. In principle this arrangement may have seemed possible but in the heat of the battle it failed. Staff officers found themselves making command decisions, while small-unit leaders were forced to act entirely on their own initiative, without the direction of superiors.

At El Caney, Lawton had prepared his attack for 7 a.m. and was expecting 'an easy and well-nigh bloodless victory'. He had allowed two hours to capture the hamlet, which would enable him to march his men back to San Juan in time for the main assault, due to begin at 10 a.m. The four light field guns that Lawton hoped would batter the enemy blockhouses proved ineffective. They were built of a pattern already obsolete in 1898 and were far inferior to contemporary European guns. Lawton soon had reason to revise his timetable. The Spanish infantry, well entrenched and armed with Mauser rifles, put up stubborn resistance for over eight hours. Although numbering only 500 against the 5400 Americans who encircled them, they fought with a determination worthy of a better cause.

McClernand, meanwhile, was in a quandary. Lawton's failure to take El Caney had disrupted the entire plan. Should he defer the attack on San Juan or should he order Kent and Sumner to attack on their own? The dilemma was of Shafter's making. What was the point in Lawton committing a whole division to an attack on a worthless series of blockhouses which would fall to the Americans as soon as they had taken the San Juan Heights? When Shafter heard of Lawton's failure he immediately ordered him to break off the fight and join Sumner and Kent at San Juan. However, Lawton was not prepared to withdraw without achieving a victory and Shafter was forced to allow the futile struggle to continue until, at about 3 p.m., the Americans at last overran the El Viso blockhouse. The Spanish had suffered 235 casualties and 120 prisoners, while the American losses were 81 killed and 360 wounded.

The San Juan Heights commanded the eastern approaches to Santiago, and General Linares had fortified them. From the elevated position of San Juan Hill, 125 feet high and with brick blockhouses on the top, the Spanish defenders would have an admirable view of the area in which the Americans would have to deploy before their attack. Yet, incredibly, Linares had committed only 1700 men to defending this crucial area, with just 521 on Kettle Hill and San Juan Hill.

On the morning of 1 July, Sumner and Kent's divisions set out for San Juan along the difficult jungle path. At 8 a.m., with the sound of firing clearly audible from El Caney to the north, Captain Grimes had positioned his artillery at El Pozo and opened fire on the blockhouses and entrenchments just visible in the morning mist on San Juan Hill. The immediate outcome was not what the Americans had expected.

Congress had neglected to provide our artillery with the modern smokeless powder, and as the first great clouds of white smoke billowed forth from El Pozo, the Spaniards very naturally took them as a target for their own artillery. The cameras recording the 'first shot' were still clicking and an interested crowd of people from the regiments below was just gathering upon the hill to see what was going on, when the first answering shell sang over the battery and burst on the slope behind it, extinguishing a number of Cubans and wounding several Rough Riders who were in the farmyard below.[13]

It soon became apparent that Grimes's guns were doing no more than acting as a target for the Spanish guns and they were ordered to cease fire. For the lack of smokeless powder, the richest country on earth would now have to send its troops into battle without any artillery support.

As 8000 men struggled along the congested jungle road they took with them an inflatable hot-air balloon, from which Lieutenant-Colonel Derby made observations. In case the Spanish defenders had any doubts

<hr>

12. Lack of centralised command accounts for the confusion of the American attack on the San Juan heights. Shafter was too ill to command in person and tried to conduct the battle through a series of intermediaries, McClernand at El Pozo and Miley with the advance troops. Lawton's unnecessary assault on El Caney only added to the confusion by delaying the main assault on San Juan Hill. Grimes's artillery battery may be noted to the west of El Pozo. During the battle they caused as much damage to their own side as to the Spaniards.

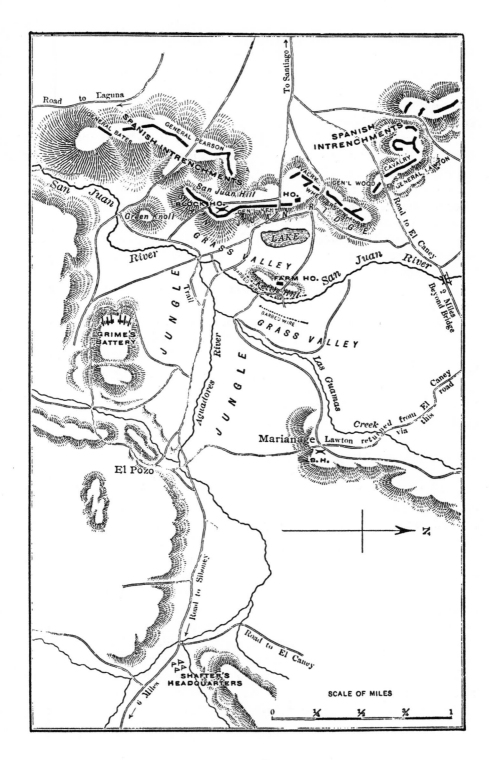

as to where the American troops might be the balloon served as a marker to bring down a rain of fire on the helpless masses below. Colonel Wood was unimpressed by Derby's 'aerial reconnaissance' and thought the balloon 'one of the most ill-judged and idiotic acts' he had ever seen.[14] Had Shafter carried out reconnaissance of the region west of El Pozo the balloon would not have been necessary. However, no one, from divisional commander to private soldier, had had a chance to examine the ground leading to the Spanish position or to assess the numbers of the enemy or the strength of their defences.

The congestion on the jungle path was severe. From El Pozo Hill, whence Shafter was trying to follow the advance, it appeared that 'the whole command was . . . swallowed up under a sea of green above which there arose only the delicate stems of the scattered palms and the majestic and swaying bulk of the balloon, accurately delineating the advance'.[15] The Spaniards responded by raking the area around the balloon with shrapnel. No one in the American ranks could return the fire or even see where it was coming from.

As the column approached the open meadow land below San Juan Hill, Sumner halted for an hour, perplexed by the problem of deploying his men in the face of such concentrated fire. Suddenly a voice was heard from on-high, 'Is there a general officer below?' In spite of the numerous casualties caused at ground level by the presence of the balloon, Lieutenant-Colonel Derby had remained unharmed. In fact, he had made an important discovery. There was a track leading off the main path which looked as if it would provide a second point of access to the meadow and greatly simplify the deployment of the American troops.

General Kent decided to move his division along this new trail and the lead was taken by the 71st New York Regiment, the only National Guard unit to take part in the battle. The choice of the 71st to lead the attack was a very bad one. Alone of the troops present the 71st had the disadvantage of using the old 'black-powder' rifles, which rendered the user an easy target for the enemy. Already somewhat shaken by their experiences on the jungle path, these part-time soldiers now found themselves leading the division along an unknown trail, under a galling fire and against an enemy of unknown strength. Men began to falter until they were bunching together, unwilling to go on. Some turned to run but fortunately Kent and some senior officers managed to quell the panic by ordering the men to lie down in the long grass and allow the other regiments to pass.[16]

Eventually the two divisions reached their assault positions beneath San Juan Hill. Facing them were barbed wire entanglements which the oversight in not bringing wire-cutters with them was to turn into an even more formidable obstacle.[17] Without any form of artillery support the only option was to take the hill by infantry assault. The unenviable task of ordering the attack fell to young Lieutenant Miley, acting for General Shafter. Sumner told him that the men could not stay in these exposed positions for long: they would have to attack or retreat. At 1 p.m., with no sign of Lawton's approach from El Caney, Miley authorised the assault.

The American infantry sprang into action and began hacking away at the barbed wire with their bayonets. In many cases this was futile as the wire was connected to tree trunks. Then salvation arrived in the shape of Lieutenant Parker and a battery of Gatling guns. Even this boded ill for the 71st New Yorkers, lying at the side of the jungle path. On seeing Parker's machine guns the men let out a great roar, whereupon the Spanish defenders poured a volley of fire into the area of greenery from which the cheering had come, which put many 'forever beyond the possibility of cheering'.[18]

Once in position, Parker opened fire and the effect was immediate. The Spanish defenders could be seen scrambling out of their entrenchments and running back towards Santiago. As the enemy fire fell away, the American infantry sprinted across the meadow and up San Juan Hill. Even now the artillery would not leave them in peace. From El Pozo Hill, the gunners had been unable to follow the fighting and had been forced to stay silent. However, on seeing the blue dots climbing the distant hillside it became clear that the time had come to join in. The artillery opened fire with disastrous results. As Captain Allen of the Sixteenth Infantry recorded:

The advance continued steadily and without a pause until we were on the steep slope near the crest, two-thirds of the way up, when our artillery fire coming from our rear became dangerous . . . Some shells struck the slope between me and the crest . . . there arose at the foot of the slope and in the field behind us a great cry of 'Come back! Come back!' The trumpets there sounded 'Cease firing', 'Recall', and 'Assembly'. The men hesitated, stopped, and began drifting down the steep slope. . . .[19]

One officer had the initiative to wave his hat at the gunners, whereupon they fired and wounded him. It took some time before the artillery could be silenced so that the advance could continue. One is left wondering how matters might have stood against a determined enemy, prepared to counter-attack and regain the hill.

Sumner's dismounted cavalry had meanwhile stormed Kettle Hill, which the Spaniards abandoned before the Americans reached the top. Once in possession of the San Juan Heights the assault stopped as the

Spanish defenders fell back behind strong defences on the outskirts of Santiago. In spite of a numerical superiority of 12 to 1 at El Caney and 16 to 1 at San Juan, the Americans found the Spanish tough opponents, far harder in fact than they had expected. The infantry was now exhausted, and without proper artillery support there could be no question of an immediate advance on the city. The Americans had suffered heavily for their successes: 205 men killed and 1180 wounded. To cope with these casualties the Army had advanced equipped with just three ambulances and no extra rations, or the means of finding any.[20]

It must be rare in military history for an army to have performed as ineptly as the Americans did at San Juan Hill and yet win the battle. In almost every area they had proved themselves unprofessional and incompetent. Shafter's illness undoubtedly had a serious effect on American efficiency. But why was a man weighing over 300 pounds, once described as resembling 'a floating tent', sent to command troops in such a hostile climate?

Shafter's mistakes were overshadowed by the even more numerous errors of his opposing commander, General Linares. Though his men fought with great courage it is difficult to believe that they had their heart in what they were doing. As professionals they were doing their job, but against the enthusiastic commitment of so many of the American soldiers it was never going to be enough. In view of the size of the Spanish army on Cuba – almost 180,000 men – it is incredible that Linares could concentrate so few for the defence of Santiago. The San Juan Heights were crucial to the defence of the city and yet he allowed the Americans to assemble sixteen times as many men as he had placed to defend San Juan Hill. Moreover, why did he have no counter-attack planned against the Americans once they took the San Juan Heights? He must have known the difficulties they would have in keeping troops supplied there. The overall impression is that there was a lack of commitment on the part of the Spanish High Command.

On the other hand the Americans did almost everything possible to avoid victory. Shafter's attack on El Caney, and the obsessive eight-hour struggle by Lawton's division, were futile and indeed counter-productive. Originally intended as a diversionary attack, Lawton allowed it to develop into a full-scale battle which prevented him reaching his appointed position for the assault on the San Juan Heights and consequently delayed that action by three hours. A holding action by a small force could have immobilized the Spanish garrison and still released the bulk of Lawton's division.

Shafter's plan of attack was too complicated and took no account of the difficulties of terrain that his troops would face. He had not carried out any reconnaissance and the use of the balloon was no substitute for careful prior preparation. All the technical developments of the last century or more seem to have been forgotten as thousands of infantrymen slogged their way through thick jungle, suffering silent death from unseen enemies, knowing nothing about the terrain they would meet and having no clear idea how they would assault the enemy positions.

The performance of the American artillery was deplorable. Using obsolete guns, 'black-smoke' powder which gave away their position, and having only the most rudimentary understanding of cooperation with advancing infantry, they proved a liability during the entire campaign. The result was that the American infantry found themselves having to attack well-entrenched defenders without artillery support. Even if his field artillery failed him, Shafter did not exploit all the possibilities available. He made no use of the naval guns which, from a range of 8000 yards, could have brought down a devastating fire on Santiago and the Spanish defences on the San Juan Heights. It was a distinct possibility that naval fire alone might have sufficed to force the Spaniards to surrender, thus saving the heavy casualties incurred in the assault.

Finally, Shafter failed completely to weld the 5th Army Corps into a unit. He failed to maintain discipline among the officers, particularly in not restraining General 'Fighting Joe' Wheeler, as well as the various volunteer groups, like Wood's and Roosevelt's 'Rough Riders'. Shafter was not fit enough personally to direct the campaign and the collapse of the command structure on 1 July would have been severely punished by a more active and able opponent.

—7—
Suvla Bay (1915)

When Field Marshal Sir John French decided to dismiss his Corps Commander, Sir Horace Smith-Dorrien, in February 1915, legend has it that he asked the future Chief of the Imperial General Staff, William Robertson, to carry out the unpleasant duty for him. Robertson, who had risen from the ranks, apparently carried it out in a direct manner by announcing to the startled Smith-Dorrien, 'Orace, you're for 'Ome'.[1] What Robertson's technique lacked in subtlety it made up for by being clearly understandable. In dealing with subordinate commanders any commander-in-chief needs to ensure that his orders are clearly expressed and that his intentions are understood. There are, however, many examples in military history of excellent plans failing not through any inherent deficiency but because of a breakdown in communications within the command structure.

On 7 August 1915, 22 British battalions consisting of over 20,000 men were landed at Suvla Bay in the Gallipoli Peninsula. Their task was to reach a line of low hills between two and five miles inland, unoccupied by Turkish forces. Opposing them was a force of only 1500 Turkish gendarmes under the command of a German cavalry officer, yet the British completely failed to achieve their objective. A commander of less refined sensibilities than Sir Ian Hamilton might perhaps have found ways of convincing the IX Corps commander, Sir Frederick Stopford, to get up from his bed, go ashore, and inspire some sense of urgency in his men: had he done so, the course of the entire war in the East might have been very different.

By July 1915 the Gallipoli campaign, which had promised to force Turkey out of the war, had settled into an attritional struggle. In order to break the deadlock a plan was devised for a new landing of British troops at Suvla Bay. This would relieve the pressure on the British forces at Cape Hellas and Achi Baba, as well as enabling a break-out from the Anzac bridgehead by Australian and New Zealand troops to secure the Sari Bair ridge in the centre of the peninsula. The combined forces from Suvla and Anzac would then cross the four miles to the Narrows and so secure the passage of British warships into the Sea of Marmara, which had been held up since March. Additionally, major Turkish forces would then be trapped between the northern British forces and the British and French troops in the south. The end of the campaign could be both swift and successful

The choice of Suvla Bay for a landing was an excellent one. It offered a safe anchorage for the warships and supply vessels, and was known to be very lightly defended by the Turks. With the advantage of surprise, the new IX Corps would be able to seize the semi-circle of hills which surrounded the bay about four miles from the sea, and then join the attack on Sari Bair being carried out by the troops from Anzac Cove. It was vital that the troops from Suvla should seize the isolated heights of Chocolate Hill, Scimitar Hill and Ismail Oglu Tepe, in order to prevent the Turks using them as gun emplacements to dominate the attack on Sari Bair. Taken as a whole the plan was a complex and brilliant one which demanded the most exact planning and the most vigorous leadership. In neither of these respects was it to be fortunate.

In coordinating the break-out from Anzac with the landings at Suvla Bay, there was a need for careful planning and speed. Once surprise had been achieved the Turks could not be allowed to recover. What was needed was a man who had both personal energy and a capacity to inspire his men. Hamilton was aware of the kind of man that he wanted to command the landings. But Gallipoli ranked low in War Minister Kitchener's scale of priorities. The result was that to command this vitally important operation there was assembled, according to the biographer of Sir John Monash, 'the most abject collection of generals ever collected in one spot'.[2]

On 15 June, while plans for the new landing were still at an early stage, Hamilton told Kitchener that the new commander of IX Corps needed to be a man of stiff constitution. Conditions in a Gallipoli summer were likely to be so severe that only the fittest officers would be able to stand up to them. Hamilton added that three essentials for the man chosen would be a good digestion, steady nerves and the capacity to get a good night's sleep amidst the stresses of command.[3] Hamiltion was hoping that Kitchener would send one of the experienced generals from France like Byng or Rawlinson, but there were problems. In the first place, Kitchener was not happy about asking Sir John French to release one of his best officers from what was regarded as the main front in order for them to be used in the Gallipoli 'sideshow'.

The second difficulty was tl · question of seniority. Lieutenant-General Sir Bryan Mahon, who was taking the 10th Division to Gallipoli, was senior to both Byng or Rawlinson, and could not be expected to serve under either of them. Hamilton had a low opinion of Mahon's abilities, describing him as 'quite hopeless'.[4] However, etiquette required that the Corps commander should be an officer senior to Mahon, and of the very few available generals only two, Ewart and Stopford, held the necessary rank. Hamilton regarded Ewart as quite unsuitable, in view of his considerable bulk, which would hinder him in the hot conditions, and so Stopford was chosen by default to command the vital Suvla operation.

The Hon. Sir Frederick Stopford, although only 61, was in very poor health and had been on the retired list since 1909. Before leaving for Gallipoli he had been so feeble that he had been unable to lift his own dispatch case into the train; on arriving he had hurt his leg, so that he was *hors de combat* from the outset.[5] He had seen service as ADC in Egypt and the Sudan during the 1880s and had been military secretary to Sir Redvers Buller during the early part of the Boer War, but had never commanded troops in battle. More of a military historian than an active commander, he proved to be an abysmal choice for such an important job. As his Chief of Staff he brought with him Brigadier-General Reed, a gunner with South African experience and a VC, whose experiences in France convinced him that no operation could succeed unless preceded by a lengthy bombardment. This attitude was quite unsuited to an operation which depended so much on speed and surprise. It boded ill for the success of the operation that Hamilton had little confidence in either man yet failed to make it clear to the War Minister that this was so. Incredibly, he gave Stopford an almost free hand to conduct the Suvla operation and waited forlornly at his HQ on the island of Imbros for news of its progress.

Of the officers who would command IX Corps it is enough to say that they were elderly men, possessing few of the qualities needed. They had gained seniority through length of service rather than ability. Only the enormous extension of the armed forces in 1914–15 could have justified calling them from retirement to lead men in battle, in some cases for the first time. The British official historian wrote of them, 'Some were men who would never have attained command in times of peace, and they lacked the power of inspiring the well-educated and enthusiastic young civilians who had flocked to the Army at the first call to arms'.[6] Major-General Hammersley, commanding 11th Division, had only shortly before suffered a nervous breakdown and was still far from fit. His total collapse on the first day of operations contributed to his division's failure to occupy their targets. Hamilton was particularly bitter with Kitchener: 'I know he is not capable of understanding how he has cut his own throat, the men's throats and mine, by not sending young and up-to-date generals to run them [the divisions]'.[7]

Although Hamilton had impressed on Stopford the need for urgency and the fact that Chocolate Hill and 'W' Hills 'should be captured by a major, forceful assault before daylight', he was dealing with a cautious man who was not prepared to risk failure by trying too much. Mahon had already told Stopford that the plan was too intricate and this, combined with the reports of his pessimistic Chief of Staff, who thought a preliminary bombardment essential, led Stopford to tell Hamilton that he could not guarantee to take the hills, but would try. Hamilton should have made it clear at this point that the hills were the main objective of the landings but he failed to do so. In fact, his final instructions to Stopford on 29 July were rather misleading:

Your primary objective will be to secure Suvla Bay. . . . Should . . . you find it possible to achieve this object with only a portion of your force, your next step will be to give such direct assistance as is in your power to the General Officer commanding Anzac in his attack on Hill 305. . . . Chocolate Hills and Green Hills are known to contain guns which can bring fire to bear on the flank and rear of an attack on Hill 305. . . . If, therefore, it is possible, without prejudice to the attainment of your primary objective, to gain possession of these hills at an early period of your attack, it will greatly facilitate the capture and retention of Hill 305.[8]

On 3 August Stopford replied to Hamilton with the following ominous message:

I fear that it is likely that the attainment of security of Suvla Bay will so absorb the force under my command as to render improbable that I shall be able to give direct assistance to the G.O.C. Anzac in his attack on Hill 305.[9]

This was a drastic watering-down of the original plan and Hamilton should not have allowed it to pass unnoticed. It clearly showed that Stopford did not really understand his role properly and had come to see the landing itself as the vital element in the operation rather than the advance on the hills. In fact, Stopford had passed on the plan to his divisional commanders without reference to the need for speed or urgency and had merely said that they should reach the hills 'if possible'.

Hamilton's obsession with secrecy was understandable in an operation depending so much on surprise, yet there can be little doubt that he took it to extremes. Stopford himself had only been allowed to know of the plans three weeks before the event, Hammersley a fortnight later, while it was the 30 July before the Brigadiers were briefed. Only a glimpse of the landing areas was given to the commanders for fear that the Turks would interpret increased interest in the area as preparation for a landing. When the 11th Division landed many of its officers had never seen a map of the Suvla area and scarcely understood what they were supposed to do. Those who did receive maps found that half had been printed with Turkish place-names, while the others contained simply the English translations, but none contained both.

The plans for landing the 34th Brigade under Brigadier-General W.H. Sitwell went disastrously wrong. It had originally been intended to land three companies on the extreme left of 'A' beach to clear Suvla Point and occupy the Kiretch Tepe ridge, while three other companies would land on the right of 'A' beach to occupy Hill 10. However, the destroyers carrying these troops anchored in reverse order, nearly one thousand yards south of the designated beach. This meant that the cutters carrying the men ashore approached from a difficult angle and two of them struck a reef. The heavily-laden men had to wade ashore over slippery rock and up to their necks in water, as well as facing Turkish fire. It was past midnight before the men completed their landing. The 11th Manchesters, designated to clear Suvla Point, found themselves nowhere near their target and hopelessly lost.

The battalion searching for Hill 10 found themselves on the edge of the Salt Lake and came under heavy fire from Turkish snipers, who found the white armbands worn by the British soldiers a useful target in the moonlight. No one seemed to know the whereabouts of Hill 10. At 2 a.m. Sitwell mistook a sandy hill four hundred yards to the south for the hill; however, his men now came under even heavier fire from the defenders of the real Hill 10. It was not until first light that Hammersley ordered the 33rd Brigade, sitting idle on Lala Baba, to support the 34th Brigade in their assault on Hill 10. Shortly after 6 a.m. the hill was at last taken and its hundred defenders driven off. However, no attempt was made to advance on Chocolate Hill, a mere two miles to the south-east, and this was not occupied for a further twelve hours. Everywhere the advance had stopped short of the high ground.

On the morning of 7 August, Brigadier-General F.F. Hill, command-

---

13. Against weak Turkish resistance the British landings at Suvla Bay completely failed to achieve their objectives. The incorrect landfall of 34th Brigade was the result of faulty navigation by the Royal Navy. The British failed to capture the vital highpoint of Tekke Tepe, one of the main objectives of the operation, even though it was unoccupied by any Turkish defenders.

SUVLA BAY (1915)

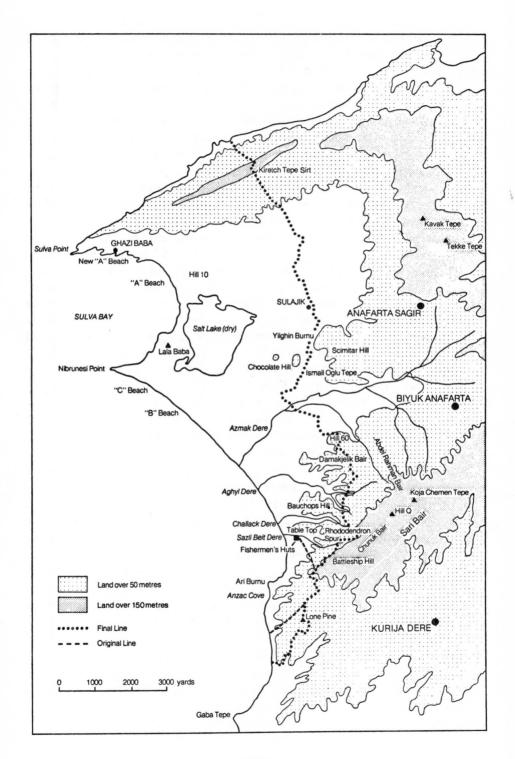

Sulva Point

GHAZI BABA

New "A" Beach

"A" Beach

Hill 10

SULVA BAY

Salt Lake (dry)

Lala Baba

Nibrunesi Point

"C" Beach

"B" Beach

Kiretch Tepe Sirt

Kavak Tepe

Tekke Tepe

SULAJIK

ANAFARTA SAGIR

Yilghin Burnu

Scimitar Hill

Chocolate Hill

Ismail Oglu Tepe

BIYUK ANAFARTA

Azmak Dere

Hill 60

Damakjelik Bair

Abdel Rahman Bair

Aghyl Dere

Koja Chemen Tepe

Bauchops Hill

Hill Q

Sari Bair

Challack Dere

Table Top

Rhododendron

Sazli Beit Dere

Spur

Chunuk Bair

Fishermen's Huts

Battleship Hill

Ari Burnu

Anzac Cove

Lone Pine

KURIJA DERE

Gaba Tepe

Land over 50 metres

Land over 150 metres

•••••• Final Line

- - - Original Line

0   1000   2000   3000 yards

ing 6000 troops of 31st and 30th Brigades, was bewildered to find himself at Suvla. His men had been aboard their transports for a month at Mytilene and awoke to find that they had been moved to this new area without the faintest idea why. Hill had been given no idea of the planned operation and had simply awoken to find his ships under fire. After visiting Stopford aboard HMS *Jonquil*, he was told to disembark his men at 'C' beach, as 'A' beach was still under fire, and there place himself under Hammersley's orders. Should Hammersley not be available he was to support the assault on Hill 10 or complete the capture of Kiretch Tepe. It had been assumed, unwisely as it turned out, that the bulk of 11th Division would have moved off the beaches by this time and would be occupying the high ground, according to the plan. As a result there were no preparations to receive a further 7000 men, and the 13,000 already ashore were in a state of utter confusion. To add to this, three more battalions of the 10th Division now arrived from Mudros, with Lieuten-ant-General Sir Bryan Mahon, who was the 10th division commander. He was instructed to land on a new beach and told that the six battalions of his division under Hill would revert to his command once he landed. This did not happen for five days. Hammersley, meanwhile, changed his mind and ordered Hill's men to attack Chocolate Hill instead of Kiretch Tepe. Mahon, on landing, sent two of his remaining battalions to join the 11th Manchesters on the Kiretch Tepe ridge. The 10th division was being committed in a piecemeal fashion and its commander was left with just one battalion of troops and absolutely no guns. It is no wonder that Mahon, the senior Lieutenant-General at Suvla, felt slighted.

Aboard *Jonquil* Stopford was pleased to have got his men ashore with such light casualties, though his complacency was ill-founded. Ashore chaos reigned. A German described the British landings as like 'a disturbed ant-heap'.[10] On Hill 10, General Sitwell would not budge in spite of every effort by his Staff Officer, Colonel Malcolm, who argued that Hammersley's orders had required the capture of Chocolate Hill and 'W' Hills. Sitwell was exhausted both physically and mentally and found excuses for his inactivity. His troops were too tired, they were short of water, they were badly disorganized, facing strong enemy positions, had suffered heavy casualties, needed time to recuperate. Many of these claims were true but in wartime one cannot expect the enemy to sit back and give one time to recover. Sitwell's orders had been to press on with the advance and this he should have done regardless of the consequences. His situation was made all the more ridiculous by a report from a young officer returning from a reconnaissance trip that there were virtually no Turks at all in the vicinity.[11]

For the attack on Chocolate Hill Hammersley ordered the troops to make an extraordinary 'advance' around three sides of the Salt Lake. This was because it was believed that the main Turkish fortifications faced south, whereas ironically they faced north-east, exactly the direction from which the British were advancing. Hammersley had somehow decided on a five-mile diversion in order to attack the only system of continuous trenches in the whole Suvla area. Meanwhile, the vital ridge of Tekke Tepe, one of the targets of the whole operation, was absolutely undefended by men or guns and could have been occupied at any time. The fact that the three brigade commanders, Hill, Maxwell and Sitwell, all remained behind at Hill 10 during the attack, only added to the confusion.

Major Willmer, a Bavarian cavalry officer, commanded the troops in the Suvla area. With no more than 1500 Turkish gendarmes, he was trying to buy as much time as possible in order to allow the Turkish commander Liman von Sanders to send reinforcements from Bulair. His trenches on the northern and western breasts of Yilghin Burnu (including Chocolate and Green Hills) were defended vigorously but eventually he withdrew to Ismail Oglu Tepe ('W' Hills). The British troops were exhausted after having captured Chocolate and Green Hills and no reinforcements were sent to help them drive the Turks away from 'W' Hills. It was not until the morning of 8 August that Hammersley heard of the capture of Chocolate Hill, but neither Stopford nor Hamilton learned even this much. The breakdown in communication within the British high command was almost complete.

Sir Bryan Mahon, facing Kiretch Tepe, was in no mood to be reasonable. He felt himself too senior an officer to command a mere division and yet he had already lost one of his brigades to the Anzac fighting and had now been further stripped of nine of his remaining twelve battalions. He was left with just 3000 men and no guns, all of which had been left either in Britain or in Egypt. Faced by no more than 700 Turks Mahon was too angry to realise the opportunity that lay before him.

In the chaos of the landings the planners had overlooked the need to supply the troops with water. In a temperature of 90 degrees in the shade, thirst (exacerbated by a staple diet of salt beef) took its toll on the British and Irish troops, many of whom were still suffering the effects of their anti-cholera injections. With Mahon threatening to resign in pique, his Irish soldiers had their minds on more mundane matters. 'We have the heathen Turks on the run, by-the-holy!', one said, 'why don't they sent us up some water?'[12]

In the Final Report of the Dardanelles Committee, the failure to supply water to the men at Suvla Bay came in for heavy criticism. Of the five water-lighters which had been expected on 7 August only two arrived and both grounded on a sandbank a hundred yards from the shore, so that their hosepipes were unable to reach it. It was almost twenty-four hours before water was available from either of them. Yet not until late afternoon on the 7th did Stopford take any action to rectify this glaring inadequacy. He contacted the Principal Military Landing Officer at 17.30 hours with the message, 'Water for troops essential to success of undertaking. None has been landed. Can you arrange that this be landed at 'A' beach?'[13] In the first twenty-four hours of the operation most of the British troops were without water throughout and many of Mahon's men were forced to abandon their positions on the Kiretch Tepe ridge to seek water on the beaches.

The Commander-in-Chief, Sir Ian Hamilton, received no news from Suvla other than Stopford's early statement that the troops had got a little way beyond the edge of the beach. By the morning of 8 August he began to suspect that something had gone wrong. He had received reports from both the Anzac and Cape Hellas fronts but nothing material from Suvla, where IX Corps had been ashore for twenty-four hours. Reports from the Naval Air Service indicated no strong Turkish forces in the area, so what was Stopford doing? Had the high ground been occupied, and if so, why had the Commander-in-Chief not been informed? Planning for the operation had been based on the assumption that there would be a maximum of thirty-six hours before the Turks brought up strong reinforcements from Bulair. At the most there could be not much more than six or seven hours left.

Perhaps Hamilton should have rushed to Suvla himself to force Stopford into action. But this was not his way. Instead he sent Colonel Aspinall-Oglander, the staff officer responsible for planning the oper-ation, along with Colonel Hankey, Secretary of the Committee of Imperial Defence, to see what was actually happening. At once a series of delays and mishaps occurred which reflected little credit on the Senior Service. Aspinall and Hankey had to wait three and a half hours before the Navy could supply them with any kind of transport from Imbros; finally a trawler was used, and took two hours to cover the 19 sea miles to Suvla. With the fate of the entire campaign depending on speed and urgency this was apparently the best the Navy could do.

In the meantime, at Suvla, the naval spectators were standing by in anguished frustration at the pitiful progress being made on land by IX Corps. Although Chocolate Hill and half of Green Hill had been taken by dusk on the 7th, all the encircling hills remained in the hands of the Turks. Moreover, at least half of IX Corps had not even been used. It seemed to onlookers that the military plan had collapsed. Commodore Keyes visited the *Jonquil* and tried to instil some urgency into Stopford but without success. Stopford instead elected to congratulate 10th and 11th divisions on their achievements. When he reported to Hamilton on the 8th it was with the extraordinary message, 'I consider Major-General Hammersley and the troops under his command deserve great credit for the results obtained against strenuous opposition and great difficulty'.[14] Hamilton replied that Stopford and his troops had indeed done splendidly. He was too much of a gentleman to observe that IX Corps outnumbered the 'strenuous opposition' by fifteen to one, that many troops had done little other than sit on the beach or go for a swim, or indeed, had he known it, that Hammersley had lost his nerve completely on the 7th and had achieved nothing worthwhile.

Admiral Robeck sent a cable to Hamilton urging him to come to Suvla personally but the message was lost without trace. Then Hamilton, despairing of hearing anything, decided to go himself but found that there was no transport available to take him. At 11.30 a.m. on the 8th he ordered his destroyer, the *Arno*, an Italian-built Portuguese craft, to be made ready, only to be told that there was trouble with her boilers. The Commander-in-Chief was therefore stranded 19 miles from the battlefront and was totally out of communication with it. Hamilton's frustration can be understood but not his response to the delay; there were many destroyers, sailing within a few miles of Imbros, which he could have ordered to take him to Suvla. It was not until 4.30 p.m. that Hamilton managed to obtain transport in the yacht *Triad*, more usually employed on pleasure cruises, which took a further ninety minutes to reach Suvla.

Aspinall and Hankey had meanwhile been investigating the situation at Suvla. On their arrival they were both struck by the relaxed atmosphere that reminded them of an 'August Bank Holiday in England'. 'The whole bay was at peace, and its shores fringed with bathers.'[15] Both assumed that the heights must have been taken and that everyone was relaxing after their endeavours. It was not until Aspinall was stopped on the beach by an officer who told him not to walk any further or he would be in the front line that the truth began to emerge. Aspinall asked where the Corps HQ was, only to be told that it was on board the *Jonquil* and that Stopford had not been ashore yet. Hankey reported to the Prime Minister.

Hardly any shells. No Turks. Very occasional musketry. Bathing parties round the shore. An entire absence of the expected bustle of a great disembarkation.

There seems to be no realisation of the overwhelming necessity for a rapid offensive, or the tremendous issues depending on the next few hours.[16]

The two men hurried on to 11th Division HQ, where they found Hammersley lying full-length on the ground, with his head in his hands, in a state of shock. His nerves had given way under the stress of the previous day's bombardment of his HQ and he was frankly unable to cope with the confusion. There seemed no point in continuing this conversation and so Aspinall and Hankey set off to meet Stopford on board the *Jonquil*. Further delays meant that they were unable to see the Corps commander until 3 p.m.

On boarding the *Jonquil*, Aspinall found Stopford on deck and in excellent spirits. He warmly welcomed both men saying, 'Well, Aspinall, the men have done splendidly and have been magnificent'.

'But they haven't reached the hills, sir', Aspinall replied.

'No, but they are ashore', Stopford continued.[17]

Aspinall could scarcely believe what he was hearing and exercised the greatest restraint in not bringing home to Stopford what a farce was being enacted ashore. He commented instead that Hamilton would be disappointed that the hills had not yet been taken and suggested an immediate assault, which Stopford replied would be impossible until the men had been rested. He intended to order a fresh advance the next day. Aspinall knew that he could do no more to press so senior an officer and joined Keyes and Robeck. They persuaded him to send off a message to Hamilton emphasising the great opportunity that was being missed. In spite of the obvious urgency of this message it did not arrive at Imbros HQ until the following morning.

GHQ had meanwhile received news that Turkish troops were approaching Suvla by forced marches. A message was sent immediately to Stopford to 'push on' as quickly as possible. Completely undismayed, Stopford passed this message on to his divisional commanders but with the proviso, 'In view of the want of adequate artillery support I do not want you to attack an entrenched position held in strength'.[18] Receiving this order Hammersley and Mahon decided to stay exactly where they were. Admittedly there was nothing to fire at, no real trench formations, no enemy guns or troop concentrations, yet clearly Stopford saw an advance without artillery cover as impossible, and who were they to argue with this? Fortunately Hamilton was now on his way to Suvla. At 6 p.m. he arrived aboard the *Jonquil* and hurried to see Stopford. What then took place had more to do with 'polite usage and good manners' than with military management. Hamilton seemed unable to convince Stopford of the urgency of the situation. When he pointed out that no ground had been gained since yesterday Stopford merely replied that he had ordered his brigadiers to gain what ground they could but without heavy fighting. The men, he said, were tired, the water supply unreliable and the guns were not being landed quickly enough to cover a major advance. He told Hamilton that he had decided to delay the occupation of the ridge until the next morning as this might involve heavy fighting. Hamilton knew from aerial reports that unless the ridge was occupied soon there would be some very heavy fighting indeed, as Turkish reinforcements were only hours away. He concluded by telling Stopford that Tekke Tepe and Ismael Oglu Tepe must be taken immediately. Stopford wished him luck in trying to inspire the brigade commanders but declined to follow him ashore as his leg was giving him trouble.

Hamilton went to visit 11th Division HQ to discuss matters with Hammersley, even though that officer was clearly far too ill to give worthwhile advice. Why Mahon, the senior officer present, was not consulted by either Aspinall or Hamilton is a mystery. His Xth Division had carried the bulk of the fighting so far at Chocolate Hill and Green Hill, his men were on the high ground at Kiretch Tepe, and he was at least fit and able to lead his men, which Hammersley certainly was not.

When Hamilton found Hammersley he met with the same kind of inertia already encountered in Stopford. Hammersley said that any attack would have to wait until the next morning as it would take too long to circulate orders. Hamilton fumed inwardly: 'There was one huge danger rapidly approaching us, already casting its shadow upon us, which, to me as Commander-in-Chief, outweighed every secondary consideration. We might have the hills at the cost of walking up them today; the Lord only knew what would be the price tomorrow.'[19]

Hamilton at last persuaded Hammersley to send 32nd Brigade to dig in on the crestline but this only caused more confusion. Two battalions had already occupied Scimitar Hill and Abrikjar on their own initiative, though no-one in authority apparently knew this, and so these troops were recalled to dig in on a line behind their earlier positions. Scimitar Hill was thus given up and had to be bloodily fought for later.

On the 9 August, Hamilton found Stopford at last ashore at Suvla Bay. However, he was discussing with engineers the siting of bomb-proof shelters for himself and his staff, believing that he would be there for some time. Perhaps nothing more completely illustrates Stopford's failure to understand the plan behind the Suvla landing than this incident. While he stood there on the beach, five British battalions were being held off by 800 Turks with no machine guns. In one area a young officer remarked to Hamilton that 'we are being held up by three men. There is one little man with a white beard, one man in a blue coat, and one boy in shirt sleeves'.[20] Elsewhere it was later discovered that troops in some bushes on the left of the front line, who had been holding up the British advance, were in fact British themselves.

At dawn on 9 August the British advance from Suvla resumed. An attempt was made to occupy the high ground from Kuchuk Anafarta on the left to Ismail Oglu Tepe on the right. However, the British had waited too long and Turkish reinforcements had at last arrived. The Turks at once occupied Scimitar Hill, so recently relinquished by men from the 6th East Yorkshire Battalion, and the British were obliged to try to recapture this position as it overlooked Ismail Oglu Tepe. Heavy fighting now took place in which the British lost nearly eight thousand officers and men and still failed to reach the ridges which they could have taken without bloodshed on the 7 and 8 of August.

After just nine days in command of IX Corps, Stopford was relieved of his command and replaced by Major-General de Lisle. His failure had been just one in a line stretching from Kitchener who, as Minister of War, had failed to equip the Suvla expedition with the kind of commanders it needed, to divisional commanders like Mahon and Hammersley who in spite of every opportunity failed to rise to the occasion. But it was in the relationship between Hamilton and Stopford that the most complete breakdown occurred. Hamilton was too much of a gentleman to give Stopford the peremptory orders needed to stir the old gentleman out of his torpor. Failing this, Hamilton at least had the option of taking command himself. On the Turkish side it is interesting to note that when one divisional commander, Feizi Bey, tried to tell von Sanders that his orders were impossible and that his troops were too tired he was instantly dismissed and replaced by Mustafa Kemal, for whom nothing was impossible. But Hamilton lacked the ruthlessness necessary to motivate Stopford or to supersede him, even though he knew him to be incompetent. In the final analysis, Hamilton must bear a heavy burden of blame for the failure of the Suvla Bay landings.

—8—
The Admiralty and Convoys (1917)

During the First World War, Britain's naval strategy was based on the maintenance of her supremacy at sea. Though the population may have been prepared by the media for a repeat of naval successes from the glorious past, and have expected victory in a great battle in the North Sea, a new Trafalgar, the men entrusted with command of the fleet were far more cautious. They realised that the nation's war effort depended on their capacity to remain strong at sea. The destruction of the German fleet was less important to them than that Britain should continue to be able to feed herself, transport troops from distant parts of the Empire, supply herself with raw materials and ship the 'tools of war' to her armies in France and the Middle East. When Churchill spoke of the Commander-in-Chief of the Grand Fleet, Sir John Jellicoe, as being 'the only man on either side who could lose the war in an afternoon', he was saying no more than many felt. Yet, even in 1914, such thinking was already outdated. At its moment of greatest power the Dreadnought battleship was to show itself terribly vulnerable to a far less expensive and far more humble weapon of war: the submarine. And by ignoring the potential of the submarine the Admiralty was exposing Britain to defeat far more certainly than if Jellicoe had risked and lost a 'second Trafalgar'.

In 1913 Lord Fisher, with the help of Captain S.S. Hall, produced a memorandum on submarine warfare, which forecast that in the event of war the Germans would employ submarines for commerce raiding. But it was rejected by the Admiralty on the grounds that a civilised power would never sink merchantmen without warning and without paying attention to the welfare of the crew.[1] In fact, at the outbreak of war Germany had no plan for a full-scale campaign against merchant shipping. Anticipating military victories on the Western Front she did not think in terms of a long conflict or the need for attrition on land and at sea. Yet the Germans had noted the extraordinary panic produced among British naval leaders by the idea of the submarine, not as a threat to merchantmen but to the battle fleet. In 1914 Sir Percy Scott had written in *The Times*,

Submarines and aeroplanes have entirely revolutionized naval warfare; no fleet can hide itself from the aeroplane eye, and the submarine can deliver a deadly attack even in broad daylight.[2]

The torpedoing of the three armoured cruisers *Aboukir*, *Hogue* and *Cressy* by U-9 created a sense of panic in the Grand Fleet. 'Periscopeitis' was a general affliction, and pursuits and battles with seals or bow-waves added an absurd element to a serious problem.

The Germans had regarded their surface raiders as the main weapon against British commerce worldwide. However, by Christmas 1914, they had all been hunted down and sunk by British forces. It was at this point, with the war in the west settling down into a long drawn-out struggle and with their capacity to attack British possessions virtually removed, that Germany decided to strike at British merchant shipping through a deliberate U-boat campaign. The old civilities were gone and international law was about to be flouted in a way that Churchill and the Admiralty had declared 'unthinkable' in 1913. On 4 February 1915, Germany declared a war zone around Britain in which ships would be sunk without warning. The German Chancellor, Bethmann-Hollweg, was concerned over the effect this might have on neutral opinion, particularly in the United States. Nevertheless, the German admirals were strongly backed by the Kaiser, claiming that they were merely reacting to the illegalities of the British blockade.

At the outset of the U-boat campaign Germany had just 20 submarines in action, some of them small and outdated coastal vessels. Yet this tiny force sank some 39 vessels in the first ten weeks, and on 7 May 1915, U-20 sank the liner *Lusitania* off the coast of Ireland, with the loss of 1198 lives, including 128 Americans. World opinion was outraged and the German campaign was swiftly halted. The British Admiralty became complacent. Offensive measures of many kinds had been developed, including nets, sweeps carrying explosive charges, underwater acoustics and depth charges. Moreover, the British system of patrols had achieved some success, with 7 submarines sunk, including two by ramming (one by the battleship *Dreadnought* herself). Churchill, First Lord of the Admiralty, was convinced that the U-boats had been beaten.[3]

Germany, however, had been building new and better submarines and was convinced that, by attacking British merchant ships, she could ruin Britain in six months. On 11 February 1916 a new 'conditional' campaign began by which only merchant ships in the war zone would be attacked. Again it was American opinion that brought the campaign to a halt when the French ship *Sussex* was torpedoed, with the loss of some American lives. However, this time the Germans could hardly afford to sheath their sharpest sword. On the Western Front the tremendous attritional battles of Verdun and the Somme had convinced Germany that unless her navy could play a more prominent part in the war it would be lost. The effects of the British economic blockade were bringing Germany close to starvation. The Commander of the High Seas Fleet, Admiral Scheer, and the Chief of Naval Staff, Admiral von Trotha, were convinced that a half-hearted submarine campaign was a serious mistake. They were fortunate in the fact that the new commanders of the Army, Ludendorff and Hindenburg, alarmed at the consequences of the 1916 battles in France, were willing to support an unrestricted U-boat attack on British trade. As a result, on 1 February 1917, a new U-boat campaign was launched in the North Sea, the Channel, the Mediterranean, the Western Approaches and on the Eastern seaboard of the United States. This time Germany was fully prepared and had 154 U-boats of a superior type, of which 70 could be at sea at any one time.[4] Now the figures for shipping losses rose alarmingly. In February 86 ships were sunk, in March 103 and in April 155. The total tonnage lost in April for Allied and British ships reached a staggering 869,103 tons.[5] Britain faced defeat in a matter of months unless an answer could be found to the U-boat menace. The First Sea Lord, Admiral Jellicoe, believed that Britain would soon need to seek peace, while the Secretary for War, Lord Derby, announced, 'We have lost control of the sea'.[6] In Colonel Repington's words, the war had resolved itself into a question of 'whether our armies could win the war before our navies lost it'.[7]

Figures of shipping losses, alarming as they were, were only part of the picture. Ships reaching harbour seriously damaged by U-boat attack were unable to sail again until substantially repaired, while others were prevented from sailing by reports of U-boats in the area. A sign of the stagnation that was descending on British trade is shown by the fact that in February and March of 1916, 1149 vessels entered British ports while in the same period in 1917 the figure was just 300.[8] Against the sudden impact of such losses the Admiralty seemed confused. They believed that their counter-measures were proving effective, yet their patrols were enormously wasteful in terms of manpower and ships. By the end of 1916 over 3000 vessels were being employed on submarine patrol, yet in the second half of 1916 only 15 U-boats were destroyed from all causes.[9] The 'Q' ships, which were armed merchantmen manned by volunteer crews, had been quite successful in the earlier part of the war, but now U-boats had grown suspicious and usually shot on sight.

Though the Admiralty had no clear policy it possessed weapons which, if more suitably employed, could have proved decisive. In favourable weather conditions the hydrophone gave warning of the presence of a submarine and its approximate position. Also, the introduction of the depth charge in 1916 was a really important step forward. On 6 July 1916 the motor-boat *Salmon* achieved a kill by the combined use of hydrophone and depth charge.[10] As David Divine points out, however, the Admiralty were lax in exploiting this new development. As late as July 1917, the weekly output of depth charges was a mere 140 against a demand for 500 by escort vessels.

This memorandum to the War Council in November 1916 illustrates the failure of the Admiralty to counter the U-boat threat.

Of all the problems which the Admiralty have to consider, no doubt the most formidable and most embarrassing is that raised by the submarine attack on merchant vessels. No conclusive answer has as yet been found to this form of warfare, perhaps no conclusive answer will be found. We must for the present be content with palliation.[11]

Admiralty efforts had been enormous but totally misplaced. Their philosophy had been that they must destroy U-boats faster than Germany could build them, rather than that they should prevent U-boats sinking British merchant ships. In the vastness of the seas it was infinitely more difficult to find a single U-boat than it was to defend a merchant ship. This is illustrated by the farcical 'Second Battle of Beachy Head' fought over a week in September 1916. Three U-boats, operating between Beachy Head and the Eddystone, an area commanded by the naval bases of Portsmouth, Portland and Plymouth, were hunted by 49 destroyers, 48 torpedo-boats, 7 'Q' ships and 468 armed auxiliaries. Yet, in seven days, the U-boats sank 30 merchant ships and escaped unscathed.[12]

It was to counter the U-boat threat that Jellicoe was brought from Scapa Flow to the Admiralty as the First Sea Lord, on 29 November 1916. However, for many reasons he was an unfortunate choice. His health was poor and as a hypochondriac he was weighed down by a deep pessimism. Rather than instilling energy into an ailing Admiralty, he seemed to lend it his own negative qualities. One of his first actions was to appoint Admiral Duff as Director of a new Anti-Submarine division to co-ordinate existing measures and to seek new weapons and policy in the fight against the submarine. Duff was a poor choice for such a difficult job. In February 1915, while commander of the 4th Battle Squadron, Duff had noted, 'With submarines alone she (Germany) cannot hope to inflict any serious damage to our merchant shipping'.[13] Like so many men at the Admiralty, Duff could not come to terms with a novel concept that was changing the nature of warfare. Like the others he had been brought up in a period where offensive gun-power and speed had been the vital elements in naval warfare. The German submarines had taken the initiative away from the British battlefleet. The only answer must be an offensive against them carried out by hundreds, indeed thousands, of small ships ranging from destroyers to small motor vessels.

To Jellicoe, 'there was no single way of defeating the U-boat'.[14] Victory would only come when it was suffocated by weight of numbers. The Admiralty was not in favour of the oldest method of protecting merchant ships at sea from attack, the convoy. They perpetuated the fallacy that escort vessels needed to be twice as numerous as the merchantmen they escorted. They also believed that

1. Convoys would require vast numbers of escort vessels better employed in search-and-kill patrol operations.
2. Convoys with the delays entailed in collecting the vessels in port, in organising merchantmen skippers and crews untrained for station-keeping, in the imposition of slow speeds on faster vessels, the alternating congestion and slackness in loading and discharging cargoes, would lead to a greater loss of trade than the U-boats could ever accomplish.
3. The greater the number of ships forming a convoy, the more vulnerable it must be to U-boat attack.[15]

However, as John Winton writes,

This view of convoy went in defiance of all the Navy's previous history. . . . The Navy had indeed been first formed specifically for convoy protection. The nation's prosperity and security had depended upon the safe passage of ships carrying troops and merchandise, in convoy, ever since the Middle Ages. . . . Yet, astoundingly, incredibly, by the end of the nineteenth century this priceless piece of naval knowledge had been lost by the Royal Navy.[15]

The fact remained that Britain was losing the war because of the U-boat campaign and the Admiralty was wrong in thinking that, whatever the costs of convoys, they could be any more heavy than those already being incurred. Though convoys were complex to organise, one had already been set up for the Channel coal trade to France, without which French industry would have collapsed. It was a great success and the Welsh colliers achieved almost complete immunity. Unofficially, a convoy system had been operated by the Harwich Force for the Dutch Trade to the Hook of Holland and in February 1917 Beatty had investigated ways of reducing losses in the Scandinavian trade, then running at 25 per cent, and came to the conclusion that convoys were the only answer. For once Jellicoe was forced to agree. Once instigated, the losses on this trade route fell to 0.24 per cent, a hundred-fold improvement.[16]

The national press was not slow to take up the argument in favour of convoys. The Navy's offensive against German submarines was not working; figures for U-boats constructed exceeded those of losses. The Admiralty was forced to defend its position and its most authoritative voice was that of the First Sea Lord. However, not everyone at the Admiralty was against convoys. The opposition to Jellicoe and Duff tended to be from junior officers like Captain Herbert Richmond and Commander Reginald Henderson. Richmond was particularly scathing about Jellicoe, commenting that 'Having missed two chances of destroying the German Fleet he is busy ruining the country by not taking steps to defeat the submarine'.[17] The fact that Admiralty opinion was hardening against convoys is shown in this pamphlet of January, 1917:

Whenever possible, vessels should sail singly, escorted as considered necessary. The system of several ships sailing together in a convoy is not recommended in any area where submarine attack is a possibility. It is evident that the larger the number of ships forming the convoy, the greater is the chance of a submarine being enabled to attack successfully, the greater the difficulty of the escort in preventing such an attack. In the case of defensively armed merchant vessels, it is preferable that they should sail singly rather than that they should be formed into a convoy with several other vessels. A submarine could remain at a distance and fire her torpedo into the middle of a convoy with every chance of success. A defensively armed merchant vessel of good speed should rarely, if ever, be captured. If the submarine comes to the surface to overtake and attack with her gun the merchant vessel's gun will nearly always make the submarine dive, in which case the preponderance of speed will allow of the merchant ship escaping.[18]

As John Winton remarks,

It would be difficult to find, even in the long record of Admiralty bureaucracy, a more stupid document and one which more pigheadedly ignored all the lessons of past naval history. It was all the more dangerous because it was not obviously the work of a lunatic. It sounded a reasonable measured judgement, taken after all the circumstances had been brought to account. Nor was it the product of a single deranged mind. As far as can be judged, it represented collective opinion in the Admiralty at the time.[19]

Rear Admiral Duff at the Anti-Submarine Division, charged with examining the current problems and practices of anti-submarine warfare, prepared statistics of all inward and outward voyages from British ports. He informed the Admiralty that there were 2500 movements each way each week, an astronomical figure which, if true, would have made convoys impossible for lack of escort vessels.[20] However, these figures was unreliable to say the least. As David Divine remarks,

To accuse the Admiralty of the falsification of statistics is a grave matter, yet under Duff figures were produced which wholly obscured the issues and for which it is difficult to find logical explanation.[21]

In fact, the figures were inflated by including all movements of ships over 300 tons, small coasters, short-haul trading vessels making repeated calls, as well as the daily movements of the Isle of Wight ferries. None of these needed to concern convoy planners. The result was that compared to weekly figures of 5000 ship movements, the losses to U-boat attack seemed insignificant.[22]

The first officer to question the figures was Commander R.G.H. Henderson, in charge of the French coal-trade 'controlled sailings'. When he investigated the origins of the figure of '5000' he found that no Admiralty department could explain it. Apparently the information had been supplied by Norman Leslie at the Ministry of Shipping. Approaching Leslie, Henderson found that the Admiralty figures had no basis in fact. The Admiralty 'had made a supreme ass of itself'.[23] The correct weekly figure for ocean-going merchant vessels was approximately 130 each way, well within the capacity of the Navy to escort.[24]

Lloyd George could hardly believe the extent of Admiralty incompetence: 'What an amazing miscalculation. The blunder on which their policy was based was an arithmetical mix-up which would not have been perpetrated by an ordinary clerk in a shipping office.'[25] If one believed that there were sailings of 2500 vessels each week, the loss of 20 to 40 a week to U-boat attack would seem insignificant. If, however, one judged the losses against the true figure of 120 to 140 the matter became desperate.[26] A quarter of all ships leaving Britain were being sunk by German submarines, and could not be replaced soon enough. During April 1917 losses reached a high point of ten vessels a day. Within weeks there would be insufficient shipping for British needs and the war would be lost.

Fortunately for the British war effort, junior officers at the Admiralty, including R.G.H. Henderson, were feeding information on the true state of affairs to Lieutenant-Colonel Maurice Hankey, Secretary to the War Cabinet.[27] They were helped in this by Norman Leslie, liaison officer between the Ministry and the Admiralty. Using the leaked information, on 11 February 1917 Hankey wrote a memorandum for the Cabinet proclaiming the virtues of convoys. The Prime Minister, Lloyd George, invited Hankey to a working breakfast at 10 Downing Street at which he was questioned by First Lord of the Admiralty Carson, First Sea Lord Jellicoe and the Director of Anti-Submarine warfare, Duff. Clearly, they were not pleased to be 'taken to task' by someone they regarded as a junior

Lieutenant-Colonel of Marines.[28] The outcome was disappointing, though Lloyd George was not immediately discouraged. In the next six weeks he visited Admiral Beatty at Scapa Flow and learned of the Commander-in-Chief's support for convoys. Moreover, the entry of the United States into the war was likely to solve any problem of a shortage of escort vessels. Nevertheless, in his diary entry for 30 March, Hankey was becoming despondent about the negative attitude of the Admiralty.

Personally I am much worried about the shipping outlook owing to submarines and the inability of the Admiralty to deal with it, and their general ineptitude as indicated by their stickiness towards any new proposal. I have many ideas on the matter, but cannot get at Lloyd George in regard to it as he is so full of politics. I am oppressed by the fear I have always held that, while moderately successful on land, we may yet be beaten at sea. Something like a million tons of the world's shipping have been lost in the last two months – and that takes a lot of replacement.[29]

Lloyd George was becoming increasingly unhappy with Jellicoe as First Sea Lord. The latter was pessimistic and quite unwilling to listen to arguments on the subject of convoys. As a result, on 25 April 1917, at a meeting of the War Cabinet, Lloyd George warned Jellicoe that he intended to visit the Admiralty in person on 30 April, to investigate 'all the means at present in use in regard to anti-submarine warfare'.[30] This was an unprecedented action and carried an obvious threat. Whether in consequence of this meeting or coincidentally, the following day Duff presented the First Sea Lord with a memorandum suggesting there was 'sufficient reason for believing that we can accept the many disadvantages of large convoys with the certainty of great reduction in our present losses'.[31] This was a complete – but welcome – *volte-face*.

The importance of Lloyd George's intervention, according to Stephen Roskill, has been much exaggerated.[32] Hankey had been recommending that he take action on convoys for some three months but to no avail. On the subject of the dangers of the U-boat campaign, Hankey records the Prime Minister as commenting on 22 April, 'Oh well, I have never regarded that matter as seriously as you have'.[33] The published accounts of Lloyd George's descent on the Admiralty on 30 April, written by Beaverbrook, Churchill and Lloyd George himself, all give the impression that it was. he who through force of personality converted an unwilling Admiralty to the idea of convoys. This was far from being true. It seems that Duff and Jellicoe had slowly and painfully come round to the inevitability of introducing them. The much heralded meeting at the Admiralty on 30 August was thus something of an anti-climax. In fact, Hankey records that he and Lloyd George spent their time 'pleasantly lunching with Adl. Jellicoe and his wife and four little girls – Ll G. having a great flirtation with a little girl of three'.[34]

Nevertheless, by whatever means, convoys were introduced and not a moment too soon. They immediately proved to be the major factor in overcoming the U-boat threat. During July and August only five convoyed ships were sunk out of 800 and by the end of September the U-boat was mastered. It would be wrong to suggest that losses dropped off altogether. The Admiralty continued to allow independent sailings as well as refusing to establish convoys for outward-bound ships. They also believed that the success of the convoy system would be seen in the number of U-boats sunk rather than the number of merchant ships safely delivered. By August 1917 almost the only ships being sunk were outward bound and Admiral Duff now recommended that outward-bound convoys be attempted, not for the obvious reason that they would cut shipping losses but for the specious one that they would 'give as many ships as possible experience of sailing in Convoy before the bad weather sets in'.[35] Lloyd George's frustration was immense:

The High Admirals had at last been persuaded by the 'Convoyers' not perhaps to take action, but to try action. But there was a reluctance and a tardiness in their movements. They acted as men whose doubts were by no means removed, and who therefore proceed with excessive caution and with an ill-concealed expectation that their forebodings will be justified by the experience. When anything went wrong with convoyed ships, it was reported with an 'I told you so' air to the War Cabinet.[36]

The Prime Minister was clearly dissatisfied with Admiral Jellicoe as First Sea Lord and on Christmas Eve, 1917, he was dismissed. His depression and poor health had made him a liability in so senior a position. Lieutenant-Commander Richmond commented that, 'one obstacle to a successful war is now out of the way'.[37]

The failure of the Admiralty to introduce a policy of convoying merchant shipping was one of the greatest errors of the First World War and brought Britain closer to defeat than any other single factor. The refusal to accept evidence which conflicted with their own preconceived ideas cost the country 3 million tons of shipping, countless tons of valuable food and war materials, and the loss of thousands of lives. Their ineffectual strategy of 'hunt and kill' was based on an outdated offensive philosophy which failed to take account of new technology. Senior officers in the Admiralty proved themselves personally incompetent through stupidity and obstinacy. As First Sea Lord, Admiral Sir John Jellicoe, who 'could have lost the war in an afternoon', took his natural caution to the level of inertness. Faced by an enemy he could not understand he virtually abandoned the struggle and could see only defeat. It was through the efforts of men like Hankey, Henderson and Leslie that the truth at last reached the Prime Minister and vital war-saving decisions were taken.

—9—
The Battle of Anual (1921)

The 'Scramble for Africa' in the late nineteenth century carried with it great prizes for the European powers, but these were sometimes won at considerable cost from the better organised African tribes. Military disasters were not new to the British Army, which was the most experienced European force in colonial warfare. Nevertheless, such experience did not always save British commanders from making the most elementary errors. At Isandhlwana, for example, during the Zulu War in 1879, Lord Chelmsford divided his command and, though the Boers had warned him of the need to laager his wagons when fighting the Zulus, he left his camp unfortified. Experience had shown that only concentrated fire-power could hold back the Zulus yet the British had their troops dispersed over a wide area. When the Zulus attacked, in overwhelming numbers, the British found that their reserve ammunition boxes were screwed down and, in the absence of screwdrivers, their fire slackened.[1] This was what the Zulus had been waiting for and they overran the camp, killing some 1300 European and native troops. It may be admitted that the Zulu 'impi' numbered over 20,000 warriors against the British force of a mere 1800. However, better reconnaissance by Chelmsford would have warned him of the presence of this formidable force and perhaps have prevented him from dividing his command.

At Adowa in 1896 the Italians fought, in Roberto Battaglia's words, 'the most incredible and absurd battle that has ever taken place in modern history'.[2] General Baratieri, with an army of 10,620 Italian troops and 10,083 native soldiers, attacked the army of the Ethiopian Emperor Minilik, numbering perhaps 100,000, and armed with 70,000 to 80,000 rifles. Baratieri was under intense political pressure from Prime Minister Crispi and felt unhappy at having to fight at all.[3] To the normal confusion of war the Italians added inaccurate maps, faulty reconnaissance, and vague and misunderstood orders so that the separate Italian brigades were soon lost in the hills, and cut off completely from each other and the commander-in-chief. The result was a massacre more than a battle. Of the Italian army, perhaps 6000 to 7000 were killed, with 8000 more wounded.

In the defeats at both Isandhlwana and Adowa the 'native' enemy had outnumbered the European troops by between 5 and 10 to 1. The European commanders, in each case, had underestimated their enemies and had divided their forces so that the various parts could be 'eaten up' piecemeal. In both cases reconnaissance had been poor and had not alerted the commanders to the dangerous proximity of enemy forces. However, at Anual in 1921, the Spanish Army was to suffer a defeat every bit as complete as that suffered by the British and the Italians, and yet against an enemy scarcely one-seventh their size.

At the beginning of the present century there was a strong movement in Spain for the establishment of a protectorate in Northern Morocco. As a result of the Franco-Moroccan Treaty of 1912, Spain held a zone in Northern Morocco on a lease from France, yet the area was totally dependent on money from Spain which was supplied by businessmen interested in the Rif iron mines in the interior. Militarily the region was extremely difficult to defend. The interior was roadless, unexplored and had unmapped mountain regions where lived fierce, independent tribes who would not submit to Spanish dominion.

The chief obstacle to Spanish ambitions in the Rif was the Caid of the Beni Urriagali, Abd el Krim, who succeeded his father in September 1920. Krim had been educated in Spain and became first an adviser to the Bureau of Native Affairs and later Professor of the Berber Chilha dialect at the Arab Academy at Melilla.[4] Krim was determined to prevent any European expansion, either French or Spanish, into his tribal territory. Helped by a very able brother, Si Mohammed, who was a mining expert, Abd el Krim continued his father's work of building up a sizeable arms cache in case Spanish troops tried to push deeper into the Rif.[5] In 1920 the High Commissioner for Morocco, the energetic General Damasco Berenguer, began to do just this, assisted by General Silvestre from Melilla.

Silvestre was renowned for being a courageous, 'fighting' general, who had been wounded no less than 16 times during the fighting in Cuba in 1898. Famous as a lady's man and a master of the social graces, Silvestre was a close confidant of King Alphonso XIII.[6] However, his temper occasionally overcame his reason, and his dislike of 'Moors', of diplomacy and of Abd el Krim in particular made it unlikely that he would achieve a peaceful settlement with the Rif leader. Conscious that the eyes of the Court at Madrid were on him, Silvestre was determined to teach the Rifs a lesson.

THE BATTLE OF ANUAL (1921)

By May 1921 the Spanish position looked good, at least on paper. General Silvestre's advance westwards from Melilla towards the central Rif had brought more territory under Spanish control than during the previous twelve years. He held an area 35 miles to the south and 80 miles to the west, and with an army of 25,700, made up of 20,600 Spaniards and 5,100 Moroccan Regulares, he outnumbered Abd el Krim's 3000 or so Rifian warriors.[7] However, Silvestre's troops were scattered about 144 outposts, blockhouses and forts, and this was to have considerable repercussions for the Spaniards. The usual garrisons of Spanish blockhouses were a mere 12 to 20 men, though centres like Batel, Dar Drius, Buy Meyan and Anual each had a garrison of 800.

The Spanish were optimistic that they would be able to subjugate the entire Rif and reach their target of Alhucemas Bay. Berenguer had been pleased when he visited Melilla in March and surprised to find the impulsive Silvestre behaving so moderately. He had been surprised also at the cordial reception he received from the Rifians, supposing this to represent some kind of acceptance of Spanish rule. Unfortunately he was mistaken. Their moderate behaviour reflected the fact that poor harvests had driven many tribesmen to migrate temporarily into Algeria in search of work. The tribes would only tolerate Silvestre's occupation as long as they were too weak to resist.[8]

The condition of the Spanish Army in Morocco was apparent to men like Abd el Krim. He knew that its morale was poor and that if he could raise the tribes to 'Jihad' – holy war – Spanish resistance would be minimal. How much of this was clear to the Spanish High Command is less easy to say. Berenguer had reported to the Minister of War in February 1921 that there were profound problems facing the army.[9] Ordinary soldiers were underpaid, underfed and poorly equipped. There were deficiencies in supply of war materiel and sanitary services were deplorable. Barracks and hospitals were filthy throughout the Protectorate, and losses from malaria were unnecessarily high. This report was presented to the Cortes, the Spanish Parliament, with the rider that though conditions were bad the 'martial spirit' of the troops was good.

Far from the 'martial spirit' of the troops being good one would have to say that in some units it was almost non-existent. The general level of leadership was low, many officers being incompetent, undisciplined and owing their position to nothing more than family connexions. Army pay was so low that some officers took second jobs. In Morocco, they spent much of their time away from garrisons and cared little for the welfare of their troops. For the common soldier army life was abysmal. Poor equipment, training, food and hospital services and an almost complete lack of medical supplies eroded morale.[10]

When he heard that Krim was preparing to fight, Silvestre, enraged, declared

This man Abd el Krim is crazy. I'm not going to take seriously the threats of a little Berber Caid whom I had at my mercy a short while ago. His insolence merits a new punishment.[11]

Even though warned by some tribal chiefs not to provoke Krim by crossing the Amerkran River, Silvestre scornfully dismissed their fears and did so. On 1 June, a Spanish detachment of 250 men besieged Abarran. However, the native policemen with them mutinied and attacked the Spanish troops, killing 179 including the commander. On the same day, Rifian tribesmen attacked the base of Sidi Dris.

Berenguer was worried by this news and sailed from Ceuta to see Silvestre at Melilla. When the High Commissioner ordered Silvestre to halt his advance in the Rif, the volatile commander went beserk and tried to throttle him, only being forcibly restrained by his staff officers.[12] Berenguer left, believing that his orders were clear enough, but Silvestre was determined that one further small advance would not do any harm. He therefore ordered the establishment of a new base at Igueriben, three miles south of Anual.

Abd el Krim now decided on a pre-emptive strike against the Spanish positions. The feeling against the Spanish had never been stronger amongst the ordinary tribesmen, and when Krim declared 'Jihad' he had willing listeners:

Oh, Muslims, we have wanted to make peace with Spain, but Spain does not want it. She only wants to occupy our lands in order to take our property and our women, and to make us abandon our religion. Do not expect anything good of Spain. . . . The Koran says, "Who dies in Holy War goes to glory."[13]

In spite of the emotional nature of his appeal, Abd el Krim did not act rashly but built up his strength by stealth. By probing the Spanish defences in a series of 'hit-and-run' attacks he came to the conclusion that the Spanish forces could be beaten in detail. With an army – or 'harka' – made up of his own Ben Urriaglis, Abd el Krim attacked suddenly on 17 July 1921.

The half-constructed base at Igueriben was first to be attacked. Incredibly it had been built three miles away from the nearest water supply and the Spanish soldiers were soon suffering from thirst.[14] As the fighting went on they were reduced to drinking the juice from pimiento and tomato tins, then 'vinegar, cologne, ink and finally sweetened urine'. A relief column was sent from Anual but it dared not advance to Igueriben through a narrow gorge, which was strongly held by the tribesmen. It

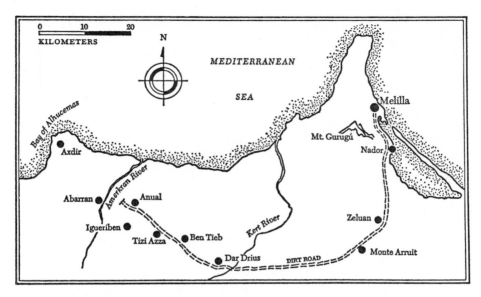

14. The Spanish position in the Rif was based on their occupation of isolated strong points. However, these were badly built and poorly sited. When Abd-el-Krim succeeded in capturing Anual, Spanish resistance collapsed and their forts were captured one after another.

eventually withdrew, having lost 152 of its own men, and left the base to its fate. On 21 July, Silvestre had tried to lead a cavalry charge through the gorge to rescue the garrison but was driven back by machine-gun fire from the hills. Igueriben was finally overrun and its garrison massacred.

Silvestre returned to Anual, a camp spread over three small slopes and overlooked by the surrounding hills. The previously confident general now began to panic. He had difficulty sleeping or digesting his food. When a telegram arrived from the king calling on him to reach Alhucemas Bay by 25 July, the king's birthday, Silvestre knew he was trapped by his own reputation as a 'fire-eater' and a man who got things done.[15] It was apparent to him that the local situation was hopeless and that even Anual, the main Spanish base in the Rif, could not be held. On the morning of the 22 July, after convening an officers' meeting, he ordered a full-scale retreat. No plans were made and the Spanish forces were simply told to pull out 'by surprise'.[16] The shock of this order, from the Commander-in-Chief himself, seems to have broken the nerve of many of the conscript troops, who broke ranks and fled in panic. Their officers did nothing to halt the stampede, while Silvestre, who seems to have had no idea how to handle the situation, simply shouted at his retreating troops, 'Run, run, the bogeyman is coming'.[17] In fact, he was already there, and few of the Spanish troops avoided death at the hands of the Rifs. How Silvestre died is uncertain but stories tell of Abd el Krim personally cutting off his head and later wearing the general's brilliantly coloured sash, though another report speaks of suicide.[18]

The Spanish forts and bases collapsed like dominoes. As survivors from the western and southern areas rushed east they only increased the panic by spreading stories of horrible massacre. Moreover, news of the Spanish disasters at Igueriben and Anual spread through the tribes who had so far remained quiet. Now they rose against the hated invaders. The collapse of the Spanish position and the rout of an army of over 20,000 by so few tribesmen was disgraceful. Here and there, some troops stood and tried to rally the others but they were overwhelmed by both the enemy and their own deserters. The fact was that the Spanish had prepared no fortified positions in the rear to which an orderly retreat could be made. All that stood between Anual and Melilla were dozens of tiny block-houses, whose roofs could be blown off by hand grenades.

General Navarro, Silvestre's second-in-command, tried to rally two or three thousand survivors and fall back on Melilla to link with the relief column he was sure must come. However, he was forced to halt at Monte Arruit because he refused to abandon his wounded men. Here he decided to try to defend the old adobe fort, built almost two-thirds of a mile from the nearest water. Again the Spanish had made this incredible mistake. At Monte Arruit there were no medical supplies of any kind and 167 men died from gangrene. Planes from Melilla tried to drop food and supplies to Navarro and his beleaguered garrison but most of the parcels were captured by the Rifs. Eventually, Berenguer signalled to Navarro permission to surrender, but after he had done so the Rif tribesmen rushed into the fort and killed everyone there except Navarro and a few others.

Monte Arruit had been less than twenty miles from Melilla and yet no attempt had been made to relieve the fort. The fact was that the garrison of Melilla was only 1600 strong and consisted of poor quality conscripts. Had Abd el Krim known it he could have taken Melilla as well and thereby denied Spain her only base in the North-East of Morocco. It is doubtful if the Spanish would have been able to re-take the city and re-establish their position in the Rif. But Krim's tribesmen were not trained soldiers. They had enjoyed the victory and the loot but now they were tired and wished to return home. In any case, the harvest was not far off and was far more important to these rural tribesmen than killing a few more Spaniards.[19]

When Berenguer heard the news he rushed reinforcements to Melilla and announced to the press, 'All is lost, including honour'. Perhaps Berenguer was right. The defeat of the Spanish army at Anual was the greatest defeat suffered by a European force at the hands of an 'uncivilised' army for centuries. For Spain the loss was enormous, not only in prestige, but in lives, materiel and territory. The figures for casualties vary widely but even the Cortes admitted to over 13,000 dead; the likely figure may be as high as 19,000, for the Rif took few prisoners. Materiel lost included 20,000 rifles, 400 machine guns and 129 cannon, while the whole Spanish investment in eastern Morocco – railways, mines, agricultural equipment, schools, military posts and so on – was lost in a matter of days.

It is easy to criticise the commander, Silvestre, or his conscript troops, or the planners, who built forts and bases and scattered their troops like seed about the desert. Yet, the politicians too had much to answer for in allowing the army to disintegrate from lack of supplies and money. Corruption had become a part of everyday Spanish life and was to be found in politics, professions, church and army. It took a disaster like Anual to make people take stock of their own actions, and the revelations which emerged about the behaviour of the Spanish army in Morocco make astonishing reading.

The findings of the Commission set up under General Picasso to investigate the disaster revealed the full extent of the corruption. While not every officer was either incompetent or corrupt, many were. During 1920, eleven captains who had served as bursars for their Corps had resigned to avoid being accused of embezzlement, and one had committed suicide. Money voted by the Spanish Cortes for road-building found its way into the pockets of senior officers. Junior officers pilfered what they could from army stores and sold it privately to supplement their own salaries. Officers spent much time away from their troops, senior ones either on leave in Spain or 'gambling and whoring' in Melilla. Soldiers and their wives bartered guns to the Rif tribesmen in market places in return for fresh fruit and vegetables.[20]

The quality of the Spanish conscript soldier was probably lower than anywhere in Europe. Eighty per cent of them were illiterate and they represented the least able of all those conscripted, as they had lacked the intelligence, education or money to find substitutes.[21] They were poorly trained and poorly armed, many having rifles that had been used in the 1898 War against the United States, which had not been used or cleaned since. One report spoke of a command of 30 men, 19 of whom had guns in such poor condition that they could fire a bullet no more than a hundred yards.[22]

The average Spanish soldier had little to give him pride in his profession. Paid less than a third of what the tribesmen earned as labourers on the road-building, and forced to subsist on coffee, beans, rice and bread, they learned to give as little as they got. They practised ways of avoiding front-line duty, eating tobacco to create the effect of jaundice or deliberately contracting venereal disease. They put nettles in minor wounds to make them fester or produced ulcer-like sores on their legs with red-hot coins.[23] In the face of such demoralisation the collapse at Anual becomes more understandable.

The leadership these men received was deplorable. At Melilla it was discovered that many officers had hidden in the cellars during the fighting, only to re-appear later claiming they had been prisoners. Other officers went on leave rather than face the Rifs and did not bother to return to their posts. One officer at Monte Arruit, on hearing the alarm, seized the only car and drove straight back to Melilla. At the height of the emergency, when the warehouses and military stores at Melilla were opened they were found to be empty, their contents having been sold to smugglers.[24]

The policy of building between 130 and 150 posts and blockhouses haphazardly around Melilla was also difficult to defend. Few bases had doctors or medical supplies and most of the soldiers had to wear summer uniforms all through the cold Moroccan winters because nothing else was available. Fifty trucks had been sent to Melilla to ease the transport problem but of these only five were ever seen in the Rif! At Anual the troops had been issued with just 40 cartridges each and there were only 600 shells altogether for the cannon. In such a situation what hope had the common soldier? The French commander, Marshal Lyautey, himself a master of colonial campaigns, remarked on hearing the news of Anual, 'The Spanish soldier, who is as brave as he is long-suffering, can, under another command, know better days'.[25]

One is finally left with Silvestre, the General who disobeyed orders and brought disaster on himself, his troops and his country. Certainly he was impulsive but it is just possible that like Baratieri at Adowa, he was under considerable pressure, in his case from King Alfonso, to achieve 'a decisive victory'. The Picasso Inquiry apparently discovered a letter to Silvestre, urging him to advance further into the Rif. 'Do as I tell you, and pay no attention to the Minister of War, who is an imbecile', said the king.[26] Silvestre's failings as a commander are clear but the disaster at Anual cannot be blamed on him alone. Abd el Krim's victory was over the decades of corruption and neglect that had been a substitute for policy in Morocco.

—10—
The Fall of Singapore (1942)

No other example in this book so completely illustrates the range of factors which contribute to military incompetence as the Fall of 'Fortress Singapore' to the Japanese on 15 February 1942. There were serious errors by politicians, planners and, at tactical level, by military commanders. It is impossible within the confines of a single chapter to do justice to the enormity of the failure, yet in fairness to the commanders to whom fell the unenviable task of defending the 'undefendable' I have chosen to concentrate on the strategic failures of a generation and in particular on the errors of Winston Churchill, Prime Minister and Supreme Warlord, whose political interference turned defeat into disaster in the Far East. In doing so I am not attempting to disregard the serious failings of individual commanders, but merely to point out that much of what happened resulted from political decisions taken years before the Japanese invasion. In this way Percival, for all his failings, was 'more sinned against than sinning'. A more able commander would have undoubtedly made more of what few advantages Percival had, but even a great leader of men would have found it difficult to correct the effect of decades of neglect and parsimony.

Before 1914 the development of the German navy had meant that Britain no longer enjoyed the luxury of being able to employ the best units of her fleet far from home. As a result, in the Far East, she relied on diplomacy rather than military strength to defend her interests and her alliance with Japan meant that she could rely on Japanese naval strength to combat German surface raiders. However, even during the First World War, there were developing signs of Anglophobia in Japan and after 1918 it was obvious that she could no longer be relied on as an ally. On the contrary, it was apparent that the rising power of Japan would pose the most serious threat to British interests in the Far East.

With the previously friendly Japan emerging as a potential enemy, Australia and New Zealand wanted assurances that they could rely on

Britain to provide a fleet powerful enough to deter any would-be aggressor. This presented Britain with two problems: she needed to build a major fleet base in the Far East and then to supply a fleet to occupy it. This meant that Britain would now need two fleets: one to be kept in British waters to counter the threat from any European power, and the other to be stationed in the east to counter any extra-European power.

There was no shortage of possible naval bases in the east but eventually the choice rested between Sydney and Singapore. In 1921 the decision was taken to build the base at Singapore, as it was thousands of miles closer to both Britain and to Japan, the likeliest future enemy. However, the 1920s was a period of financial stringency in Britain and it was quite beyond her resources to build a new fleet base in the east and a new fleet to go with it. The fact that her own battleships were ageing fast meant that there would need to be a huge programme of rebuilding if the British fleet was to match developing Japanese and American naval power. The Washington Treaty, which fixed British, American and Japanese naval strength in the ratio 5:5:3, offered a temporary respite, but it also meant that Britain could never match the Japanese fleet in the east while still retaining a fleet in British waters.

Faced by the inevitable collapse of her position as a world power Britain chose to ignore the problem and seek solace in her own propaganda. For a nation whose empire had been gained by naval power, maintained by the strength of her fleet, and whose strategy had emphasised the mobility that maritime power gave her, the knowledge that she now faced rivals whose potential power was greater than hers was difficult to accept. The result was that Britain chose not to face the problem squarely and try to find the best solution to it, but instead resorted to a policy which was strategically unworkable and politically dishonest. In order to placate Australian opinion it was declared that though the main fleet would be kept in European waters, in the event of trouble it would be sent east, arriving in no more than 70 days. This became an article of faith in British planning between the wars.

The defence of British interests in the east came to depend on the 'myth of the fleet' at a time when the resurgence of German naval power in the 1930s was making even the home fleet seem barely adequate. In quantity the British ships were still impressive but the new ships that were built in Germany outclassed their British opposite numbers in almost every respect. It soon became apparent that the British would have no ships to release for service elsewhere while the danger from Germany was so great.

A credibility gap was developing between what Britain promised and what she could possibly deliver. The time it would take for the main fleet to reach Singapore was extended to 90 days, then to six months, and eventually, in May 1939, it was admitted that it was no longer possible to say how long it would take the fleet to reach the east nor how strong it woud be. This was some way from the idea of the main fleet on which Australians, New Zealanders and Malays had come to depend.

The tardy recognition that it would be impossible to send a fleet to the east threw the strategy of defence into confusion. There could be no more sheltering behind the myth of an invincible fleet which would come from the Motherland to rescue her imperial children. The defence of Malaya and Singapore would have to be left to the Army and the RAF, and they would not simply be holding on until a relieving fleet arrived, they would need to be able to sustain an indefinite siege. This was a new situation. Previous planning had always postulated a naval defence of the Malayan peninsula, with the other two services occupying very much a secondary role. As a result there were no clear defence guidelines for Singapore.

The building of the naval base at Singapore, which began in 1921, was dogged by inter-service disputes. The immediate problem was where on the island to site it. In February 1923 the Navy decided against building the base on the seaward side as it would be too near the commercial harbour. However, a location east of the causeway from Johore imposed certain military needs. One immediate requirement was for a perimeter defence on the mainland which would place the base out of artillery range. There was ample evidence of how the Japanese were prepared to attack harbour fortresses. In 1904–5 they had besieged Port Arthur from the land, while in 1914 they had seized Tsingtao.[1] Nevertheless, in spite of this it was decided that Singapore needed to be defended from the sea not the land. There was a fallacious belief that the jungle of Johore and the south-east of Malaya would protect the base from any landward attack.[2] In any case it was believed that a land attack from the north would take too long. From the outset the defence of Singapore was to be based on a dangerous misconception.

The question of permanent fixed defences for the naval base resolved itself into a struggle between guns and planes. The Army was convinced that heavy artillery was the most effective weapon while the RAF, through Trenchard, argued in favour of a force of torpedo bombers, fighters and reconnaissance aircraft. In the context of the 1920s the argument was more real than it might seem to us today. The capability of airpower was an emotional issue. The RAF rightly pointed out that planes had a far greater range than artillery and could deal with an invasion force further out to sea than could fixed guns. They pointed out that no system of rigid linear defence on land could be effective against the mobility of a seaborne invasion. As a naval power, with experience of amphibious operation, Britain ought at least to have understood this point. The RAF explained that because of the speed of planes rapid reinforcement of Singapore would be possible. However, Admiral Beatty was the exponent of the big-gun theory and his arguments carried a lot of weight. In the end, the RAF's arguments failed to convince the planners, who claimed that there was no evidence that planes could sink warships.[3] It was certainly true that the planes of the 1920s were slow and poorly armed, yet as planes improved in quality they could be designed to improve their capacity to bomb ships. The naval base was intended to last for many years and thus an attempt needed to be made to anticipate technological developments. If aviation experts predicted that planes would soon be built that could sink warships at sea, it was foolish for planners to reject this argument simply because ships had not been sunk by planes at that time. It presupposed a stasis in military technology. The second argument against defence by planes was more valid. In the event of a crisis it might be impossible to spare them to be sent to the east, rather as it would be to spare ships. The outcome was that Singapore was to be defended by artillery until the late 1930s.

During the 1930s British thinking on Singapore came under pressure. The steady improvement in aircraft performance showed that advanced air bases and reconnaissance far out to sea were in fact essential to the defence of the naval base. This meant that airfields would need to be set up in the north and on the east coast of Malaya, and the RAF built them at Kuantan, Kahang, and three around Kota Bahru. The Army was furious because it has not been consulted, and some of the airfields had been built in indefensible places. In any case, now that they were there they would have to be defended and this meant a forward deployment of troops which would make it necessary to defend much of the Malayan peninsula.[4]

Perhaps the greatest shock to the concept of 'Fortress Singapore' came from the findings of the first staff assessment of a possible attack on Malaya and Singapore by the Japanese, which was carried out by Lieutenant-General Sir William Dobbie in 1937. Ironically, his Chief of Staff was Brigadier A.E. Percival, to whom would fall the defence of Singapore in 1942. Their findings were not very reassuring. They asserted that the Japanese would capture the airfields of Southern Thailand, then make a landing in Northern Malaya and Southern Thailand and advance on Singapore down the Malayan peninsula. They concluded that the long-held view that the jungle would prove an insurmountable obstacle to infantry was incorrect and that Singapore was vulnerable to a land attack from the north. Their recommendations included the defence of both Northern Malaya and Johore, the strengthening of the RAF to prevent amphibious landings, and the need for tanks.[5]

The reaction from the War Office in January 1938 was familiar, depressing and totally unconvincing:

1. The British Main Fleet would sail for Singapore no matter what the situation in European waters.
2. The Japanese were heavily involved in China – this had been underestimated.
3. The Chief of the Imperial General Staff did not consider provision of a tank unit justified.
4. There was little money for rearmament.[6]

The first statement was absurd. No-one can really have believed that the fleet would be committed to defending Singapore even at the cost of the homeland. By 1938 the threat from Germany – and that included her growing navy – was real enough for Britain to realise she needed every item in her armoury.

When war came in Europe it was necessary to exaggerate strengths and minimise weaknesses in order to maintain the myth of 'Fortress Singapore'. This task was well-suited to Winston Churchill's rhetorical style. The Japanese could not strike directly at Singapore, it was suggested, because their way was blocked by the Americans in the Philippines and the French in Indo-China. As Churchill insisted.

Singapore is a fortress armed with five 15-inch guns and garrisoned by nearly 20,000 men. It could only be taken after a siege by an enemy of at least 50,000 men. . . . As Singapore is as far away from Japan as Southampton is from New York, the operation of moving a Japanese Army with all its troopships and maintaining it during a siege would be forlorn. Moreover, such a siege, which should last at least four or five months, would be liable to be interrupted, if at any time Britain chose to send a superior fleet to the scene.[7]

There was dangerous complacency in this, especially in the unfounded assertion that Britain could interrupt the siege if she decided to send a superior fleet to the scene. The assumption here was that Britain possessed a superior fleet to Japan in 1939. In fact, this was far from being the case and Churchill knew it.

In 1939 Britain had 15 capital ships against 10 Japanese. However, of the British total three were World War One vintage battlecruisers, which had few advantages over those that had succumbed so disastrously at Jutland. None was capable of facing a modern enemy battleship. The fate of the

Hood was to be a clear illustration of that. Of the twelve British battleships, all but two had been built before or during the First World War, and many had done duty at Jutland. Only three of them had been modernised since 1936. In contrast, all ten of the Japanese capital ships had been modernised. Moreover, the *King George V* Class, which was being built in Britain at the outbreak of the war, was hopelessly outclassed by the two leviathans, *Yamato* and *Musashi*, that were being built in Japan. A simple comparison will suffice:

	Completion	Displacement	Armament	Speed	Armour
King George V	11/1941	38,000 tons	Ten 14 inch	29 knots	16 inch
Yamato	12/1941	64,170 tons	Nine 18 inch	27 knots	20 inch[8]

The Japanese were not slow to realise that in modern war the new capital ships were not battleships anyway, but aircraft carriers. In 1939 the British navy had seven aircraft carriers, with four being built. Against this the Japanese had six, with 11 being built. The demands of warfare in the Mediterranean would in any case ensure that Britain could never send carriers to the Far East.

In April 1940 General Bond, Percival's predecessor in Singapore, insisted on the need to build a formidable air strike capacity to compensate for limitations in the ground forces, particularly the absence of tanks. The troops he did have would be tied up in the defences of fixed positions, like airfields, with the result that the British defences would nowhere be strong. London now accepted the notion that air defence must be the cornerstone of the defence of Malaya. But having admitted this they did nothing about it, deferring the strengthening of airpower in Malaya until the end of 1941 and promising instead to send more troops. During the whole of 1940 they sent just one division. As H.P. Willmott writes,

In the whole of military history there can seldom have been a series of strategic decisions that reached such a nadir as did those of the British at this point. For the defense of Malaya the British had placed their faith in warships. When they realised the bankruptcy of this notion they turned to air power in order to economize on troops, and in the end they sent troops to economize on aircraft.[9]

The British had been depending on the French in Indo-China to supplement their limited force of aircraft. However, since the fall of France in 1940 the situation in the French colonies had become unclear. The Chiefs of Staff had estimated that the defence of Malaya required 22 squadrons of planes, consisting of 336 aircraft. This was a modest enough figure in view of the 700 or so that the Japanese would have at their disposal. In any case the RAF rejected this figure as too low and believed that 556 would be needed to enable them to defend Malaya against invasion, deny air bases in Borneo to Japan and also defend merchant ships. Even this number was barely enough.

During 1941 there were minor attempts to strengthen the RAF and the Army, yet both remained severely under-strength. The Chiefs of Staff had estimated that Singapore and Malaya needed 48 infantry brigades and two armoured brigades, whereas in November 1941 there were just 33 infantry battalions, including many semi-trained Indian units, and no tanks. On the airfields, in defence of which most of the troops were employed, stood a total of 141 second-rate aircraft, 17 Hudson, 34 Blenheim bombers, 27 Wildebeeste torpedo-bombers, 10 Blenheim night-fighters, 3 Catalina flying boats, 4 Swordfish, 5 Sharks and 41 Brewster Buffalos, the best of the bunch, but hopelessly outclassed by the Japanese Zeros.[10] Why, it may be asked, was the situation allowed to reach this deplorable state? For an answer one must turn to the interference of the Prime Minister, Winston Churchill.

The German invasion of Russia in June 1941 caused Churchill to divert to the aid of his new ally aircraft that were desperately needed in Malaya. Between June and December 1941, 53 British merchant ships sailed to Russia carrying war equipment, including at least 200 Hurricanes.[11] In view of their estimate of 336 planes for Malaya the Chiefs of Staff protested to the Defence Committee that the aircraft would 'pay a better dividend if sent to the Far East'. The figure of 336 became known to the Japanese who assumed it represented Britain's Far-Eastern air-strength, which it did not, because Churchill objected to so large a force. On 13 January 1941 he wrote to the Chiefs of Staff:

I do not remember to have given my approval to these very large diversions of forces. On the contrary, if my minutes are collected they will be seen to have an opposite tendency. The political situation in the Far East does not seem to require, and the strength of our Air Force by no means warrants, the maintenance of such large forces in the Far East at this time.[12]

As a result, when war broke out in the east, British forces in Malaya had, not 566 planes as requested in 1940, nor 336 as promised by the Chiefs of Staff, but a total of just 158 very low quality aircraft. Even this fact failed to bring a sense of reality to some of the commanders in Singapore, whose ethnocentrism blinded them to Japan's martial qualities. Percival wrote many years later:

Although it was apparent to most of us, including apparently the C-in-C, Far East and the AOC, that our Air Force was too weak to do much damage to a seaborne expedition before it could establish a bridgehead, yet at a Joint Staff Defence Conference held, I think, about August 1941, the view was officially expressed by the C-in-C's Air Representative (Gp.Capt.Darvall) that we could rely on the Air Force destroying, I think, about 70 per cent of the ships of an invading force before it landed. The trouble all along was that most of the Naval and RAF senior officers were far too optimistic as to what they would be able to do.[13]

British losses in the ill-fated Greek campaign, combined with the drain of planes and equipment sent to Russia meant that some 600 first-rate planes, which could have altered the strategic balance in the east substantially, were not available. Now the only way in which Singapore could be reinforced was by the Navy. It was proposed that by early 1942 there should be a fleet of three battleships and two or three aircraft carriers stationed at Ceylon, while four old battleships of the *Revenge* class would be used as escorts in the Indian Ocean. This may have looked good on paper but there was no disguising the fact that these old ships were no match for the Japanese. They were slow and relatively lightly armoured and would have succumbed easily to aerial attack. Winston Churchill was not in favour of this idea and felt more was to be gained by a gesture, which would be understood by friend and foe alike. British power in the east had for so long depended on her prestige, and it needed to be upheld by a display of naval might. Old World War One battleships would not do; it had to be the latest British battleship to show Britain's commitment to her eastern possessions. In fact this showed nothing of the sort. The Japanese would hardly be impressed by the curious strategy of sending capital ships unprotected by a carrier's air cover. Where Churchill saw the dispatch of the new battleship as an act of deterrence, the Japanese saw only a futile gesture. If they were prepared to assault the entire American Pacific Fleet at Pearl Harbour they were not going to be deterred by two lone British warships, however prestigious their pedigree.

The choice of the *Prince of Wales* was an obvious one, although she had not had a successful career up to then. Her early encounter with the *Bismarck* in company with the ill-fated *Hood* had nearly ended in disaster for her. Quite unprepared for an encounter with probably the strongest vessel afloat at that time, with workmen still aboard and with little opportunity for working up to peak efficiency, she suffered heavy damage before striking her opponent a damaging blow. Her captain's decision to break off the fight had won her an unenviable reputation. Nevertheless, she was the best Britain had, and possessed staying power in battle, even if she was under-gunned, with 14 inch in contrast to the American preference for 16 inch and the amazing 18 inch guns of the Japanese super-battleships.

The old battlecruiser *Repulse* was of First World War design, though she had been substantially modernised in the 1930s. She carried 15 inch guns and was a fast ship, but relatively lightly armoured. Even had she not succumbed to aerial attack she could not have faced Japanese battleships in a surface encounter and might even have struggled against two of the *Mogami* class heavy cruisers, which carried ten 8 inch guns. She might have served as a fast raider but it is doubtful if she would have been allowed this maverick role.

The original plan for Force Z, as the two capital ships were to be known, was that they would be accompanied by the aircraft carrier *Indomitable*. Unfortunately she ran aground in the West Indies and was unable to travel east. The outcome was that *Prince of Wales* and *Repulse* continued on the voyage to Singapore, unescorted by a carrier, carrying their fate in their own guns. They arrived at Singapore on 4 December and had the effect that Churchill had hoped on the garrison and local population of the island. Unfortunately what everyone took to be a symbol of British naval might was in fact an admission of its weakness. Britain had no carrier available and thus Force Z lacked an integrated air arm, nor could it even depend on a powerful RAF force in Malaya to provide cover. The two warships were more in the nature of a blood sacrifice for the ineptitude of a generation of British strategists and planners.

The British position in the Far East was based on prestige and moral power rather than military strength. This had been so in 1919 and little had happened since to change the situation. Unfortunately, British military planners had reached the conclusion that their best chance of thwarting a Japanese invasion of Malaya was to make a pre-emptive strike to capture Singora and Patani before the Japanese could do so. This was the essence of 'Operation Matador', but to be effective it needed two conditions: firstly Britain needed an absolute certainty of a Japanese intention to invade Malaya and, secondly, Britain needed to be willing to violate Thai neutrality. The situation was similar to that facing France in 1940. Although the French knew that the Germans would violate Belgian neutrality, being a guardian of the rights of small nations France was at a disadvantage because she could not violate Belgian neutrality herself, even to protect Belgium. Moreover, the violation of Poland's territory by Germany had been the *casus belli* in 1939 so it would be invidious for Britain to be seen to be doing the same in 1941. Where power was based on morality rather than military strength this proved an insoluble problem. In any case, Britain was still trying to avoid a war against Japan and needed to be careful not to do anything that might bring it about.

On 6 December 1941 Japanese transports were sighted off Cape

Cambodia, but where were they going? It was difficult to be certain and so nothing was done to put 'Matador' into operation. The result was that the Japanese landed unopposed at Singora and Patani. It was not until they began landing inside Malaya at Kota Bharu that British troops began to resist them. The Japanese had done exactly what so many British observers had expected and yet they had been allowed to get away with it.

In the first day's fighting the enormous gap in quality between British and Japanese planes was illustrated by the heavy British losses. However, at this point the Navy decided to intervene. Having failed to deter the Japanese from attacking Malaya and having failed to stop the invasion fleet, Admiral Tom Phillips decided to take his ships out and fight. Even a high-speed dash to the invasion area was bound to be dangerous, particularly as the Japanese had complete control of the air. Unfortunately, Admiral Phillips had a low opinion of air power and believed that capital ships, well-handled and well-fought, could easily overcome an attack from the air. He hoped by his dash to Singora to take the Japanese by surprise, but his ships were spotted by a reconnaissance plane from the cruiser *Kumano* and he was forced to call off the mission and prepare to return to Singapore. However, news of a landing at Kuantan gave him a new opportunity and so he headed there, maintaining radio silence to mask his approach but also making it impossible for the RAF to offer any air cover. When the two great ships arrived at Kuantan they found that the report had been false and the port was peaceful. Some four hundred miles from Singapore Phillips's ill-fated squadron was attacked by 88 bombers and torpedo-bombers from Indo-Chinese land bases. Although the British gunners fought desperately Phillips now saw the limitations of anti-aircraft fire as a defence against air strikes. The question which had occupied naval thinkers throughout the inter-war years was now to be finally settled in favour of the bomber. Without air cover the day of the battleship was over. Both ships were sunk with the loss of 840 lives. Only the presence of two destroyers enabled as many as 2072 of the crew to be rescued.

The loss of the *Prince of Wales* and the *Repulse* struck a devastating blow to British morale, quite out of proportion to the value of the ships themselves.[14] Churchill's bluff had been called and it was shown to have been a very shallow one. The effect on the ground troops in Malaya was very bad, for they had hoped that the two warships would be able to sever communications between the Japanese troops in Malaya and their High Command, perhaps ever preventing supplies, ammunition and reinforcements being brought in. Now that hope had gone their minds turned to the epic evacuations for which the Navy was famous, like Narvik, Dunkirk and Crete. How would it be possible for them to escape when the

Japanese controlled both air and sea?

News of Japanese landings at Kota Bharu made 'Operation Matador' redundant and even though the British forces still outnumbered the Japanese three to one, morale declined alarmingly. Preconceptions about Japanese equipment and the fighting quality of their soldiers were now proving to be terribly wrong. The British had underestimated their enemy, always a dangerous mistake in war. Louis Allen records two examples of this:

I was amused by one battalion commander, Brooke-Popham wrote to General Ismay, 'who while we were standing together looking at his men said "Don't you think they are worthy of some better enemy than the Japanese?" . . . I also got a similar remark from the Colonel of the Argyll and Sutherland Highlanders yesterday; he had trained his battalion to a very high pitch for attacking in the type of country one gets near the coast and said to me, "I do hope, Sir, we are not getting too strong in Malaya, because if so the Japanese may never attempt a landing."[15]

Allen comments pointedly that the colonel who feared himself too strong was, within a year, to lose his entire brigade to a single Japanese tank column. A further shock to British prestige came in the realisation that in their military technology the Japanese had advanced beyond the Allies. It had been a popular belief that Japanese pilots and planes must inevitably be inferior to those of the western powers. This was ethnocentrism perfectly expressed. When the Japanese A6M2 Zero-sen naval fighter appeared over Malaya and promptly cleared the skies of the Allied planes it aroused a feeling of psychological shock. Surely only white men could build and fly such a plane? The pilots must be Germans and the plans based on those of a western power. Such attitudes were an attempt to bolster the belief in white supremacy and to discredit everything Japanese. However, far more than the United States, Britain refused to face the truth about the Japanese and by doing so ensured the destruction of her own position in the Far East.[16]

The naval base at Singapore had been built for a Far Eastern fleet which Britain would never again be in a position to command. Thus the naval base ceased to have strategic value and became instead that 'most fateful of military phenomena – a symbol whose moral value outstripped all political and strategic significance'.[17] Singapore became for Britain a matter of pride and, in wartime, pride can be an expensive commodity. It was no Verdun, which had strategic as well as symbolic importance and did at least have the virtue of draining German as well as French manpower. For ten weeks a large British army defended a naval base which had been bereft of naval vessels for all but one day of the war. In Willmott's words it was 'a British virility symbol' which would demonstrate to the world British resilience.[18] Its value was entirely political. Promises made to Australia and New Zealand to keep a major British presence in Malaya now assumed greater significance than military or strategic considerations.

Before the war Churchill had believed that the Japanese could be deterred from attacking Malaya. He even believed that a weak naval force like Force Z could have this effect. Far from doing so, it acted instead as a pointer to British weakness rather than strength. However, never lost for an argument, Churchill now spoke of Singapore as being a fortress, which it never was or could have been. How an island with a civilian population of half a million (swollen to a million during the siege) could operate as a fortress, particularly as it had no land defences to the north, is difficult to imagine. H.P. Willmott writes:

One of the major difficulties that always confronts reasoned discussion of fortresses is the fact that in literature their sieges are invariably epic and until they fall they are always considered to be impregnable. The British public out of ignorance, and leaders out of stupidity or dishonesty or both, had failed to appreciate the glaring deficiencies of Singapore and the true functions of a fortress in the conduct of war. A fortress is a fortified position, the prime purpose of which is to cover a route or territory coveted by a possible enemy. In denying the enemy uncontested access, the fortress serves to tie down disproportionately large numbers of enemy forces and to buy time for the defense to build up and concentrate resources for counter-offensive operations.[19]

Without naval and air strength there was an obvious need for a strong garrison. However, although there were many troops available these were badly deployed in 'penny packets', defending airfields and installations. The very fact that Singapore was not a fortress served to tie down large numbers of British troops rather than those of the enemy.

At the start of the war Britain had a total of 90,000 troops in Malaya and Singapore, of whom 20,000 were British, 15,000 Australian, 37,000 Indian and 17,000 or so local Asian.[20] Altogether this was 40 per cent under strength, or 17 Battalions light. However, it was not simply a question of numbers. Malaya Command was something of a backwater and the troops there were poorly trained and had many second-rate officers. A particular problem was to be found in the Indian units, which comprised the largest single element in the Command. A century or more of experience had shown that the key to the effectiveness of Indian units was a close relationship between the troops and their officers, many of them white, who were fluent in native dialects. At the outbreak of war in Europe in 1939 the best Indian troops were sent to North Africa and the Middle East. The result was that the less good units were stationed in Malaya and the Far East. Moreover, the talented white officers were not left in a backwater but were moved to active service or staff positions in the theatres of war, while their places were taken by inexperienced, conscripted white junior officers, who were unfamiliar with the troops and their ways. The consequent decline in standards was inevitable. In fact, many of the Indian units were at best half-trained and had no experience at all in armoured warfare (there was not a single tank in the whole of India). The Australians were no better placed. Noel Barber records that

All except one battalion had been 'made up' with many untrained reinforcements. Some had sailed from Australia within two weeks of enlistment. Many hardly knew how to handle a gun. The decision to select these untrained Australian reinforcements for Malaya was unfortunate.[21]

The failed policy of deterrence towards Japan had meant that troops found themselves in the front line, where they had never been intended to be, against a well-equipped and professional enemy, whose capabilities had been seriously underestimated. The result was that the troops in Malaya lacked adequate training in anti-aircraft defence and had no anti-tank experience. Rather than sending anti-tank guns, London sent instead manuals on how to combat tanks without guns. Through an oversight on someone's part these were kept in an office cupboard and never issued until discovered by Brigadier Ivan Simpson.[22] This able and energetic officer personally devised a system of opposing enemy armour, specifically for the Indian troops, but was forbidden to circulate it by Malaya Command. Simpson's reports on the state of defences in Malaya make depressing reading. He found no evidence of any coherent policy of defence for the whole of the Malayan peninsula. When he suggested to the C. in C. General Percival that something should be hurriedly constructed, he was told that defensive positions would be bad for morale and would be an admission that some areas of Malaya could not be defended.[23] This attitude is quite remarkable: the fact that the truth was unpleasant did not make it any less the truth.

It is ironical that the Britsh anticipated almost every aspect of Japan's strategic intentions and yet were unable to do anything about thwarting them. The reason was that Malaya Command did not make the most of what advantages it did have. The British deluded themselves into thinking that Japan would not attack during the Northern monsoon, even though in their 1937 Report, Dobbie and Percival had said that this was possible and even likely, and since that time the Japanese had invaded China during the monsoon.[24]

Japanese infantry tactics also came as a shock to the British. Their mobility, many of them using bicycles, made light of the difficulties the

British had anticipated they would face in advancing through Malaya. At the head of their forces was a 'shock group' of light armour. Even though their tanks were relatively feeble in comparison with the best British, German or American tanks, they were supremely effective because they were the only tanks in Malaya. Japanese tactics consisted of using the roads to advance until they made contact with British forces, whereupon they moved into the jungle at the side of the roads to infiltrate, outflank and encircle their enemy. The British were tactically outclassed.

Just as the whole of the British army in Malaya was defending a naval base that was useless to Britain, so on a smaller scale her troops were defending airfields which were only as good as the planes that used them. The inferiority of British planes made it pointless to leave troops scattered throughout the countryside. The Jitra line that was supposed to hold for three months broke in 15 hours because of feeble resistance. Clearly only brilliant generalship and an influx of experienced reinforcements could save the whole of the peninsula. Of brilliant generalship there was absolutely no sign, but London decided to send more troops as if, at this eleventh hour, it was really possible to turn back the tide. It was decided to send the 18th British Division and the 17th Indian Division, which had been earmarked for North Africa, to Malaya instead, as well as an armoured brigade and 18 air squadrons. It was remarkable how troops who had been unavailable when they could have been of some use were suddenly 'discovered' in time to swell the number of prisoners-of-war. In fact, they only served to bring the garrison up to its full strength of 48 battalions. Had they been in Malaya at the time of the Japanese landings they could have been used for counter-offensive operations, but now it was too late. In any case, the quality of the new troops left much to be desired. The official historian, Major-General S. Woodburn-Kirby, comments:

A physically unfit British division, two untrained Indian brigades, a number of partially trained Indian and Australian reinforcements, and aircraft which could only be a wasting asset.[25]

With refugees fleeing from the fighting and crossing the causeway into Singapore to swell the civilian population, these new troops presented problems of feeding, billeting and even discipline. They were not acclimatized; the 18th British division had been at sea for eleven weeks and had, in addition, been trained in mechanized warfare, which none of them were to experience in Singapore. Their arrival, as the last troops were pulled back across the causeway, was a strategic absurdity. They were leaving their ships in order to become Japanese prisoners-of-war and Churchill and his Chiefs of Staff must have known this. Britain was facing humiliation, yet was it more humiliating to lose Singapore without making an effort or to fight to the last man and still lose it? The answer belonged to the world of politics.

In January 1942 the British Government was facing a certain disaster in Singapore. The decision to send substantial reinforcements to a garrison which could hold out for weeks at the most was a serious mistake. Politicians, particularly from Australia, stressed the fact that to abandon Singapore was to renege on promises made in the inter-war period. However, Churchill should have had the moral courage to withstand such pressure and emphasise that the security of Australia was better served by using the troops elsewhere rather than letting them be captured by the Japanese. Instead, Churchill resorted to exhortation and demanded that Malaya Command fight to the last man and yield the Japanese nothing but 'scorched earth'. No doubt this sounded splendid when spoken by a great orator to a receptive audience, but in practice it was a nonsense. As Willmott observes,

This typically Churchillian bombast illustrates the limitations, some would say shallowness, of the prime minister's political and strategic thinking. An army cannot devastate the ground on which it is ordered to stand and fight to the last man; it simply cannot destroy the means by which it lives if it is ordered to continue operations for as long as possible. The orders were strategically contradictory, while politically they were inane. It was inconceivable that a parliamentary democracy, even though an imperialist power, could consider fighting a battle of annihilation inside a city inhabited by a million subjects whom it was pledged to protect.[26]

The problem was of Churchill's own making. As in Greece he was preparing to squander his forces in pursuit of unrealistic political aims.

Considerations of space prevent a detailed account of the fighting in Malaya, the retreat to the island of Singapore and the final surrender. Much has been written on the subject and on the generalship of Percival.[27] Louis Allen, for example, comments:

Percival, the British Army commander, on whom fell the onerous burden of an impossible battle and a humiliating capitulation, was a skilful, knowledgeable and compassionate soldier, and a man of outstanding physical courage. But the circumstances called for leadership that went beyond bravery and competence.[28]

The events of 1941–2 were very much a postscript to the political and strategic blunders of the previous two decades. In the words of C.A. Vlieland, the Malayan Secretary for Defence, 'No failure of anyone in Malaya at the time, combatant or non-combatant, contributed to the disaster, which was the inevitable consequence of the policy of His Majesty's Government.[29]

—II—
The Suez Operation
(1956)

For both observers and participants the Suez operation of 1956 was a puzzling phenomenon. Masquerading as a peace-keeping action, it was a war in everything but name. Yet it was a war which lacked a clearly defined military object and in which the political object was never explicitly stated to the military commanders. The result was that the operation began in chaos and ended in fiasco. A contemporary mess-room joke conveys the feelings of the men who had to prepare the operation: 'Of the twelve different invasion plans prepared, Eden chose the thirteenth'.[1]

The Western withdrawal of financial aid for the building of the Aswan Dam prompted President Nasser of Egypt to nationalise the Suez Canal Company on 26 July 1956. In future, he declared, the canal would be run by Egyptians for the benefit of Egypt. In strategic terms this decision seriously affected Britain's interests in the Middle East. In the context of the 'Cold War', Britain saw Nasser as a pawn of Russia and the nationalisation of the Suez Canal as a means by which Russia could achieve a foothold in the Middle East, a region where British influence had always been paramount. British oil interests in the Persian Gulf could be endangered as could British allies in the region like Nuri es-Said of Iraq and King Hussein of Jordan. In fact, the maintenance of Hashemite rule in Iraq and Jordan, against the rising power of Arab nationalism as seen in the shape of Nasser's 'Young Officers' Revolt' in Egypt in 1952, was a prime consideration of British policy.

Britain and France were united in their attitude to Nasser's take-over of the canal by their view of the Egyptian president himself. In Britain, Prime Minister Eden, for so long an opponent of the Fascist dictators of the 1930s, saw Nasser as a new Hitler who must not be appeased. However absurd and misdirected this opinion was, there is no doubt that it was at the heart of Eden's reaction to the takeover of the canal. The French premier, Guy Mollet, a member of the French Resistance during World War Two, took much the same line as Eden, believing Nasser to be a dictator who was, moreover, aiding the Algerian rebels in their struggle against France. Eden and Mollet were agreed: Nasser must go.

However, the problem was to make a bald political aim acceptable to a world suspicious of colonialism. The Anglo-French perception was rooted in the nineteenth century and failed to take account of the shift since 1945 towards settlement of disputes by UN action. World opinion counted for more than ever before and in the finely balanced Russo-American struggle for influence in neutral and Third World countries such a blatant action as invading an independent country and toppling its political leaders would be resisted by friend and foe alike. In particular, Eden miscalculated the reaction of the United States, traditionally suspicious of Anglo-French colonialism. Such a strategic miscalculation can only have stemmed from a confused mind. Eden's health, never strong, played a significant part in the events which followed.

Fullick and Powell clearly state the problems the military leaders faced in not knowing the political aim of the proposed operation:

If the two allies had agreed a clear political aim and communicated it to their service chiefs, much time would have been saved. . . . The choice of landing places to a large extent depended on what the politicians were trying to achieve. A landing at Port Said was enough if the aim were no more than to return the Canal to international control, but to remove Nasser would probably require the occupation of Cairo with a consequent assault through Alexandria.[2]

Eden gave little thought to whether Britain had the military capacity to achieve his political aims. After all, Egyptian nationalist resistance had made it difficult for Britain to retain her control on the Canal Zone up to 1956. Did Eden really believe that within months the same British troops could return not merely to seize the Canal Zone but to overthrow the Egyptian government and hold down the entire population of a hostile country? It was Eden's failure to answer the question of what came after Nasser that most clearly reveals the incompetence of his strategy. Field-Marshal Montgomery, soon after he had heard that Eden planned a strike against Egypt, asked him what was his object. Eden apparently replied that it was to 'knock Nasser off his perch'. Montgomery says that he told Eden this was not good enough and that his generals would need to know what the political aim was after Nasser was toppled, in order to plan the right kind of operation.[3]

In 1956 there were many men who could have advised Eden on the likely consequences of his decision to overthrow Nasser. Senior civil servants and military experts, ambassadors throughout the world and Foreign Office officials, possessed the economic, political and military information which was at the disposal of any government in forming its policies. Eden's decision to keep these men in the dark robbed him of vital information. Yet their views, by conflicting with his preconceptions, might have made it impossible for him to win cabinet support. Hugh Thomas writes that at one stage the Joint Planners presented the cabinet with a paper which forecast quite accurately the likely repercussions of the proposed British action, including American hostility, condemnation in the United Nations, pressure on the pound and the eventual withdrawal. Apparently Eden called in the paper and destroyed it.[4]

On the day that Nasser nationalised the canal, 26 July, Britain alerted her commanders in the Mediterranean to the possibility of military action. The Chiefs of Staff were ordered to draw up a plan for seizing the canal, but whether this should be by a *coup de main*, carried out immediately by airborne troops, or by a full amphibious landing, was not made clear. In fact, the option of a *coup de main* did not really exist. Although probably the plan likeliest to have succeeded and least offensive to world opinion, neither Britain nor France had trained parachute troops available. Moreover, as the French were to discover, the British were dominated by their experiences at Arnhem and unwilling to commit troops to a large-scale airborne operation, unless they could be supported. At the suggestion of such an operation the Chiefs of Staff threatened to resign. The absence of a mobile strategic reserve made the idea of a pre-emptive strike unrealistic, and planning was now based on a six-week schedule.

In planning a seaborne invasion of Egypt there were two possible landing points, Port Said and Alexandria. The latter was far more suitable both tactically and strategically, and if the aim of the operation was to overthrow President Nasser and defeat the Egyptian Army then Alexandria became the obvious choice, being only 125 miles from Cairo. However, if the strategic aim was to control the Suez Canal Zone as a preliminary to establishing an international body to run the canal, then Port Said was the better choice, particularly if it was decided not to seek an encounter with the main Egyptian forces and so minimise casualties.

However, strategic considerations apart, Port Said was a difficult place to land troops. Its beaches were shallow and its port facilities very limited. An army landing there would have to pass down a causeway 25 miles long and only three hundred yards wide, along which ran two roads, a railway and the Sweet Water Canal. The causeway was connected to Port Said by two bridges, only one of which was strong enough to carry Centurion tanks. In addition, it was 50 miles to the nearest airport, whereas at Alexandria there were good beaches, excellent port facilities and an airfield.[5]

Since 1955 Egypt had been supplied with Russian arms through Czechoslovakia, and though it was difficult to assess how skilfully Egyptian pilots and tank commanders would use the Soviet equipment the British planners were understandably cautious. There was always the danger that advanced equipment might be operated by Soviet 'advisers' or by Eastern European 'volunteers'. These fears were reflected in the decision to assemble a force of 80,000 men, with the British supplying two-thirds and the French the remaining one third of the complement. Between them Britain and France were supplying 60 squadrons of aircraft and as large a fleet as was required. The planning was certainly on the grand scale, influenced, said the French, by British memories of 'Overlord', the invasion of Normandy in June 1944.[6]

On 3 August Lieutenant-General Sir Hugh Stockwell arrived from Germany to take command of the operation. His immediate deputy, and commander of the French forces, was to be Major-General André Beaufre. On his arrival Stockwell was presented with a Joint Planning Staff paper authorising him to mount operations against Egypt with a view to restoring the Suez Canal to international use. The paper stated that troops should land at Port Said after the Egyptian air force had been neutralised by Allied bombing. Stockwell was not impressed with the idea of a landing at Port Said. Instead, by 6 August, he had drawn up a plan code-named 'Musketeer' for a landing at Alexandria. This plan was presented to the Chiefs of Staff and then to Eden himself and by the 10 August it had been accepted and the date of 15 September set for the landing.[7]

From the outset there were clear differences in outlook between the British and French commanders. The French, fresh from their grim battles in Indo-China and Algeria, were far less concerned than their British counterparts about the need to minimise casualties. Moreover, the French were frustrated by the tedious complexity of British planning. But the true reason for the slow build-up of British forces was the rusty condition of the mechanism.

It may be asked why a country spending 10 per cent of its GNP on defence was not able to launch an immediate strike to seize the canal once Nasser had nationalised it. The answer was that in spite of the likelihood of small wars throughout her far-flung possessions, Britain had no capacity for prompt action. She had no 'flexible, mobile, well-trained and versatile' force and her troops lacked professionalism.[8] A third of her army was made up of conscripts and many of her regular soldiers were employed in the task of training the conscripts or in administrative work. The result was that at the 'sharp end' of the military stick there was to be found a considerable majority of conscripts. Artillery and infantry units had a particularly high percentage of conscripts, while the few regular privates and NCOs were generally those considered unsuited to promotion. Infantry section leaders and even some sergeants were relatively inexperienced conscripts, while subalterns were often 18 and 19-year-old National Servicemen. Towards the end of the war in 1944–5, too many regular commissions had been awarded, with the result that promotion became very difficult and good soldiers became disillusioned. By 1956 many captains and majors were old for their rank and had become cynical as their own prospects had declined. They were a generation in age away from the young conscripts they commanded and this contributed to weakening morale.

When Anthony Head, the Secretary of State for War, announced that Britain had the best equipped, trained and prepared army it had ever had in peacetime, he was unconsciously reflecting the appalling neglect that had generally been the fate of the British army in the past.[9] His comment conveyed a wholly inaccurate idea of the strength of British military capacity in 1956. In the first place, much of Britain's military equipment was obsolete and of World War Two vintage and had not even been very good when it was originally made, hardly matching the German, American or even Russian equivalents. British anti-tank guns were outranged by enemy tanks, the standard infantry sub-machine gun jammed and was dangerous, while all too often British lorries carried no spares. In NATO exercises it was known that the British forces frequently had to borrow equipment from other armies taking part.[10]

The idea of a *coup de main* attack on the canal had been impossible from the start. If Eden had ever thought in these terms it was because he was poorly informed of Britain's military capabilities. The Royal Air Force had just five squadrons of Hastings and Vickers Valetta troop-carrying planes, enough to carry just one parachute battalion. The Hastings was of a 1939 design and was incapable of carrying the Champ motor vehicle. In contrast, the Americans and the French had the Noratlas, which allowed the loading of heavy equipment through the tail, and was the envy of the British. However, even if the planes had been available it is doubtful if suitable troops could have been assembled in time. Two battalions of 16 Parachute Brigade were fighting EOKA in Cyprus and had had no parachute training for a year. The pilots themselves were out of practice. When it was realised that the Champ was too heavy to be carried by the Hastings an immediate search was undertaken to repurchase the jeeps that had been disposed of for next to nothing to Arab farmers in Middle Eastern Command. When re-possessed these vehicles were rushed to repair shops in preparation for their return to active service.[11]

In other respects British equipment caused grave concern. The capacity of the Egyptian Soviet-built tanks was something of an unknown quantity, particularly if driven by Egyptian crews. Although there was confidence in the capacity of the BAT (recoilless anti-tank gun), to take on the Soviet tanks, it had not been tested in tropical conditions and there was a fear that its mechanism might jam in a sandy atmosphere. The result was that BAT ammunition was not passed for service in Egypt and American 106mm RCLs had to be withdrawn from NATO stocks to cover the shortfall. Problems of a similar kind occurred with the new FLN self-loading rifles, which had to be withdrawn from the parachute regiments as the reloading mechanism might jam in the sandy conditions. The result was a return to the discarded No.4 rifle which had been used in the 1940s. In view of all of these problems, Anthony Head's comments appear as nothing more than political rhetoric.

If the Suez operation seemed to be in the tradition of British strategy, with a mobility based on sea-power enabling her troops to strike at her enemy's weakest point, it must also be remembered that it has been in precisely these operations that the least successful aspects of British military capacity have been revealed. A long list of disasters and fiascoes pre-date Suez, from Cadiz in 1625, through Pitt's abortive raids on the French coast in the mid-eighteenth century, to Walcheren, the Crimea, Gallipoli, Narvik and Dieppe. There can be no doubt that amphibious operations are difficult to stage but the Suez operation got off to the worst possible start by lacking the materials to do the job. In 1956 the Royal Navy was short of specialist landing ships, assault landing-craft and tank landing-craft. In fact there were just two LSTs at Malta, each capable of carrying eight LCAs and 2 LCTs. This was hardly enough to transport a single infantry battalion with a troop of tanks at the same time. There were other craft in 'mothballs' but half of these were found to be rotten. Some, which had been sold as pleasure steamers or ferries, were commandeered and put back into service.[12]

The preparation was amateurish. Insufficient thought had been given to the invasion base. Cyprus was the nearest British possession from which to launch the assault on Egypt, a mere 250 sea miles, but in every other way it was unsuitable. It had poor airfields, lacked workshops and an adequate harbour, and was in short a poor reflection on eighty years of British occupation. Moreover, it was not politically secure and EOKA was still operational. Malta, which had good airfields and an excellent harbour, was 1000 miles away, a six-day journey by slow convoy. Nevertheless, Malta was the choice, and the next problem was that of transporting the men and their equipment to the Mediterranean.

The movement of the two Centurion tank regiments, 1 and 6 Royal Tanks, to Southampton took on elements of farce which dogged the whole operation. At the end of July 1956 the officers and men of the tank regiments were scattered around the country helping the Territorial Army in their summer camps. When the news arrived that they were bound for Egypt the first task was to make the tanks operational. Some vehicles were decrepit and many needed spare parts. The store depots, however, were manned by civilians who took weekends off and so delays were common. The major task, though, was to transport the tanks from Tidworth to Southampton. The shortage of tank-transporters presented the planners with a headache, but with true British improvisation they thought of Pickfords, and the removal firm was called in to help. Safety, security but not speed marked the next four weeks. With Pickfords' men governed by union regulations each of the massive transporters took a week over a journey the army thought should take three days, and behind each group of vehicles there trailed a number of spares in case of breakdown, as required by the Regulations of British Road Services. It eventually took four weeks to load the 93 tanks at Southampton.

Any hope of a *coup de main* had gone but the publicity given to the massive preparations, both in Britain and France, served a purpose in applying psychological pressure to the Egyptian government. To add more weight to the invasion fleet the French sent the battleship *Jean Bart*, as if to symbolise that the Anglo-French action belonged to another era. Of the French fleet, most of the ships looked good but were in need of repair, while the *Jean Bart* herself had just one turret which was functional.

By the beginning of September the Allied forces were ready to sail for Alexandria, but so long had been the delay since Nasser took over the canal that the Egyptian leader had been able to demonstrate that he could operate it efficiently. Whereas an immediate occupation of the Canal Zone within the first few hours of Nasser's take-over would have won Britain support from at least her NATO and Commonwealth friends, now the world at large could see no justification for British and French interference in Egypt. With President Eisenhower of the United States making it quite clear that he was firmly opposed to the use of force, Eden and Mollet lacked a *casus belli*. They needed to find an excuse for setting sail in the first place. It would have been easier, perhaps, had opinion in Britain favoured the sending of the task force. Far from that being the case, the Labour party was united in opposition to Eden's actions and many members of his own party doubted him. Resignations from within the government should have convinced the Prime Minister that the expedition was not fated to succeed.

Problems of grand strategy now presented themselves. Britain and France were entering into an operation which would achieve the unusual effect of bringing the United States and the Soviet Union together at the height of the Cold War and at a time when Russian troops were suppressing Hungarian liberties. The world had eyes only for the two arch-colonial powers attempting to behave as if two world wars had never happened; as if decolonisation was not a growing force; as if Arab nationalism counted for nothing; and as if world opinion expressed through the United Nations was as impotent as it had been in the League of Nations between the wars. If the canal had been vital to Britain in the past, was not the support of the United States also vital, was not the opinion of her European allies and her Commonwealth friends vital? To use force against Nasser might create the very situation which Eden feared: it might force Egypt into the arms of Russia and give her the foothold in the Middle East which she wanted. Eden's assessment of Nasser overlooked the fact that the Egyptian president hoped to remain on the fence in the Cold War, getting what he could from both sides without committing himself to either. Once he fell into the arms of the Russians he would lose his only bargaining counter. Moreover, what made Eden believe that a regime in Egypt imposed by Britain and France could survive once the forces of those two powers were withdrawn? Nasser was a representative of a new, vigorous movement in the Arab world, which had overthrown the corrupt Farouk and replaced him with something more representative of the people. There were many British experts who expressed these views to Eden but he was not prepared to listen.

Clearly a landing at Alexandria was no longer a possibility. A major battle in a large port, followed by an occupation of Cairo, would have involved casualties on a scale which would have outraged world opinion. The landing would have to be transferred to Port Said, with the Suez Canal as the goal. This change of plan just before the fleet was due to sail amazed the military commanders. Both Stockwell and Beaufre were victims of their political masters and knew it.[13] They spent a week devising a completely new plan which bore the title 'Musketeer Revise'. Beaufre cynically described it as 'a second-rate copy of the Normandy landings, applied in a nineteenth-century colonial context'.[14]

'Musketeer Revise' consisted of three main elements: in the first place the neutralisation of the Egyptian airforce, then a programme of psychological warfare combined with an air offensive to disrupt Egypt's economy, army and morale, and finally occupation of the Canal Zone after land, sea and air operations.

The military commanders were rightly suspicious of psychological warfare. Their experience from World War Two was that dropping leaflets was a complete waste of time and that a prolonged bombing campaign might actually stiffen resistance rather than weaken it. Beaufre, in particular, could not understand how a bombing campaign could destroy Egyptian morale if it avoided the unpleasant necessity of killing civilians. In any case, in the 8 to 14 days allowed for this period of bombing, world opinion would have ample time to mobilise against Britain and France. Nevertheless, the psychological phase was considered an essential part of the Allied plan and would, it was hoped, prevent heavy civilian casualties.

Bernard Fergusson was appointed to the unenviable position of Director of Psychological Warfare and set about his task with great energy. He and his assistants were given the use of the Sharq al-Adna broadcasting station in Cyprus, as well as printing presses for the leaflets which the RAF were to drop. To spread the word there were 24 men in trucks with loud-hailers as well as the curious 'voice-aircraft' which had seen service in Kenya attempting to convince the Mau Mau of the error of their ways. Fergusson was soon in difficulties. The device designed to explode at a thousand feet, and scatter the leaflets gently over a wide area, in fact exploded at about head height and was a more potent weapon against the Egyptian civilians than much of the outdated equipment the army carried. The 'voice-aircraft' was silenced by thieves at Aden airport who, during a stop-over for refuelling, stole the loud-hailing device. Perhaps the most whimsical incident concerned the Palestinians whom Fergusson had appointed to broadcast anti-Nasser programmes in Arabic. Apparently their accents were mistaken by the mass of the Arab population for Jewish ones, which rather reduced their impact![15]

According to the plan of 'Musketeer Revise', British troops were given the task of taking Port Said by combined sea and air assault, while the French landed to the east of the town and concentrated on Port Fuad. Once the initial targets had been attained both forces were to advance, on either side of the canal, with the British turning west at Qantara to take the Abu Sueir airfield and the French crossing the canal lower down to take Ismailia and Suez. Then, if necessary, there would be a combined advance on Cairo. However, there were problems, some foreseen and others not. In the first place it was known that poor port facilities at Port Said would prevent a speedy build-up of forces. In fact, it might take up to two weeks to land all the troops and vehicles. In addition, the advance along the Causeway was fraught with danger. It was assumed that this would be defended by Russian SU-100 anti-tank guns, which would present a great threat to the advancing British Centurion tanks.

The biggest planning error concerned the French landing at Port Fuad. With so much recent experience of Egypt it is scarcely credible that the British planners could base their work on an out-of-date map, but the French advance from Port Fuad down the east side of the canal was in fact impossible. There was no longer a road there.[16] When the canal had been widened the road had been destroyed and to all intents and purposes Port Fuad was now an island. There was no option now other than to ferry the French across the canal after they had secured Port Fuad, so that they could advance down the Causeway behind the British.

The Israelis, allies of France, were puzzled by the enormous Allied build-up. They had their own dispute with Nasser but they could not see how, after so long had passed since he had nationalised the canal, Britain and France could suddenly find an excuse for starting their operation. Also, what was its real aim? Did the Allies believe that merely occupying the Canal Zone would topple the Egyptian president? Far from doing so, it would only serve to sting him into action and to increase the inflow of Russian aid to Egypt. The British Defence Minister, Walter Monckton, was similarly perplexed. He found the planning impressive but how was Britain to justify starting a war? As Fullick and Powell comment,

. . . it is hard to avoid the conclusion that the British and the French politicians never made up their minds as to what was to happen, so avoiding thinking the stages of the operation through to a logical but internationally unacceptable conclusion.[17]

The solution that Britain and France found to their dilemma was anything but internationally acceptable. The collusion with Israel, decided on 24 October at Sévres, was to have the most serious consequences for both nations, particularly for Britain. Her position in the Middle East was to be permanently damaged. At Sévres Britain, France and Israel agreed to the following programme which, it was assumed, would provide the Allies with the *casus belli* they were seeking. On the 29 October, Israel was to launch an attack in the direction of the Suez Canal. The following morning Britain and France would appeal to both Egypt and Israel to withdraw their forces ten miles from the canal and cease fighting. Egypt would be asked to allow a temporary occupation of key areas in the Canal Zone by Anglo-French troops. If Egypt refused to agree to the Allied ultimatum within twelve hours the Allies would launch their assault on 31 October. Israel, meanwhile, was free to pursue her own policy by attacking Sharm el-Sheikh and the Straits of Tiran. This was in everyway a remarkable agreement. As Christian Pineau observed, 'Even today, I wonder how Eden could have thought for one moment that the Arab world would swallow such a story'.[18]

On 29 October Israel duly launched her invasion of Sinai, and the following day, at 4.15 p.m., Britain issued an ultimatum to both sides to keep away from the canal. The French were less concerned with the subterfuge which the British seemed to need to square their consciences, and had already stationed 72 Mystére and F84F Thunderstreak fighters at Israeli airfields to counter any threat from Egypt's Russian bombers. Even before the ultimatum expired a French destroyer had attacked an Egyptian ship.

No one really believed that Egypt would accept the Allied ultimatum, particularly as she was involved in fighting Israel. Nasser could not have accepted such an insult and retained his personal standing in the Arab world. In any case, he was still convinced that Britain and France were bluffing and their threats were designed to weaken his position in the struggle with Israel. Nevertheless, at the end of twelve hours Britain prepared to bomb the Egyptian airfields. Her caution in not allowing her Canberras to conduct a daylight raid was unjustified as the standard of Egyptian fighter pilots and anti-aircraft defence was low. Yet the realisation that Britain intended to become militarily involved came as a profound shock. Nothing in the ultimatum had prepared public opinion at home for the reality of British bombing raids. Eden's claim to be keeping the two warring sides apart was shown to be an obvious lie. How could one be seen as an 'honest broker', representing the values of international law, by bombing one of the participants into submission? There was universal condemnation of the British action and the loudest complaints were heard from the United States.[19]

The French commander, André Beaufre, was particularly frustrated at the pedestrian pace of the whole operation. In contrast to the speed and efficiency of the Israelis, the Allies were ponderous and weighed down by the lessons of past encounters. The first forty-eight hours of the operation were allocated to the destruction of the Egyptian airforce. This was a ridiculously long time in view of the poor quality of the opposition. Eventually it took 44 squadrons of Allied planes 36 hours to destroy 260 Egyptian planes on the ground. In contrast, in 1967, on the first morning of the Six Day War, the Israelis destroyed 300 Egyptian planes in just three hours. One of the jokes going around at the time was that the Egyptian planes would be obsolescent before the British destroyed them.

The second phase of the operation was to take 8 to 10 days and was designed to destroy Egyptian willpower. An amphibious landing straight after the bombing would have been more likely to achieve this, but there was a technical reason why such a lengthy delay was necessary. The French convoy, having further to travel than the British, could hardly set sail on the day before the Israel invasion or else the entire cover story would be destroyed.[20] An interval was therefore necessary to allow the French forces to arrive and this was to be filled by the activities of Bernard Fergusson's Psychological Warfare department.

The third phase of the operation, involving the landing of Allied troops, was set to begin on D-Day, 6 November. After a naval bombardment, there would be a landing by two Royal Marine Commandos at Port Said, supported by tanks, while at Port Fuad three French Marine Commandos would come ashore. Thirty minutes later a parachute battalion would land at Gamil airfield, while a helicopter assault was taking place on the bridges leading to the Causeway. This plan exaggerated Egyptian strength and was based on a misreading of the terrain. If the Egyptians were as strongly entrenched on the Causeway as the British believed them to be, how was an advance down such a narrow funnel possible? The Causeway was impossible to outflank, as there was the canal on one side and marshy ground on the other, quite unsuited to tanks. Why were the French, who had the capacity to drop behind the Egyptian defenders from their Noratlases, not directed to do so? This would naturally have given them pre-eminence in the early part of the campaign, but their experiences in Indo-China gave them a combat-readiness that was missing from the British units. At all stages it was the undue caution of the British planners that frustrated French initiative. At one stage it appeared possible that France would act in conjuction with the Israelis and not wait for the British.

If military planning was slowing down the operation this was an indication of the confusion among the political leaders. The British commanders basically did not understand the Israeli role in the proceedings. Nor, as late as four days after the Allied ultimatum, could the high command on Cyprus obtain from London the date or even the precise point for the landings. As Fullick and Powell explain,

Isolated as the senior commanders were by a Cabinet which denied to them any knowledge of its political aims and subterfuges and left them to pick up what scraps of information their allies might let fall, it was little wonder that they were reluctant to take risks.[21]

As Eden began to appreciate the full strength of the opposition to him, led in the United Nations by the United States, and in the Commonwealth by Prime Minister Nehru of India, his health began to weaken. He realised that there could be no question of taking Cairo now and that civilian casualties must be kept to an absolute minimum. He therefore ordered his commanders to concentrate entirely on the Canal Zone and to limit the naval bombardment prior to the landings. It was all very well to say this but by removing the cover for his invasion forces he was apparently prepared to sacrifice British soldiers rather than risk the opprobrium of killing Egyptian civilians. It was obvious now that Eden had in mind purely a 'police action' rather than a war to overthrow Nasser.

'Cold feet' appeared to be the order of the day even in the air over Egypt. Britain had issued warnings to Egyptians, ordering them to keep away from areas to be bombed, namely the airfields near Cairo, plus Kabrit and Abu Seir. This must be one of the few occasions in war when the enemy has been given prior warning of the target of an attack. Had the Egyptians possessed any of the strength the British feared they would have been able to make the air-raids extremely costly for the attackers. As it turned out, Cairo West, where the Ilyushin bombers were stationed, was not bombed as there were American civilians being evacuated in that area. The purpose of the raids had now changed. The need to protect Israeli cities had been replaced by the need to protect the invasion fleet. The bombing was carried out by Canberras and by the huge new Valiants, but the order was given to limit the size of bombs to 1000 lbs to avoid casualties. The result of high level bombing with such tiny weapons was that though the runaways were pitted few Egyptian planes were damaged. Many escaped, the MIGs to Syria and Saudi Arabia and the Russian bombers to a base in the south of Egypt, at Luxor.

Fear of causing civilian casualties led to the decision not to bomb Radio Cairo. However, this enabled the Egyptian government to use the propaganda weapon against the Allies by issuing a continuous stream of exaggerated accounts of bombing stories, civilian deaths and other atrocities. It was not until 2 November that Cyprus informed London that the transmitting station for Radio Cairo was nowhere near any civilians, but fifteen miles out of Cairo in the desert. It was bombed and silenced but not until it had done much to undermine the British effort. The psychological war was in other ways not going well. Bernard Fergusson could not persuade the RAF to risk their pilots' lives in distributing leaflets which were so obviously pointless.

It was Allied morale which was in danger of erosion rather than Egyptian. British soldiers en route for Egypt were distressed by the obvious lack of support from their countrymen for their efforts. The BBC broadcast clear evidence that many people at home were strongly opposed to military intervention in Egypt. Seldom in British history can soldiers have gone into battle so uncertain about the rightness of their cause. Were they even at war? And if not how would they justify taking life. It was impossible to conceal the confusion into which the whole operation had slipped.

The planning of the naval bombardment was particularly difficult as it was subject to continual interference from political sources in London. After it had been finalised a message was received by the invasion fleet to the effect that no gun larger than a 4.5 inch could be used. This immediately precluded all the cruisers from taking part and their targets had to be re-allocated to the destroyers. No sooner had this been done than another signal arrived cancelling the bombardment altogether. A 'collective somebody' in London had basically lost his nerve and was prepared to see British troops land on a hostile shore without naval support. In fact, the naval planners decided to leave everything as it was and replace the notion of a bombardment with 'naval gunnery support', which had not been specifically forbidden. Nonetheless, it was appalling that troops and their commanders should be so confused in the last few moments before an operation by such vacillation on the part of politicians.

The parachute landings had now become almost pointless. They were to have no support from a naval bombardment, which was to be used to support the landings the next day, nor were they to have any support from tanks which were due to land the next day. Thus, for no apparent reason, the parachute troops were to be exposed to twenty-four hours of fighting without support. It was just as well that Egyptian resistance was so feeble. By the afternoon of the 5 November the Egyptian commander at Port Said was tentatively suggesting a surrender of the city. However, although the news was flashed prematurely to London and announced in the House of Commons by Eden, the Egyptians on advice from Cairo changed their minds. At 0900 on the 6th, Stockwell and Beaufre heard from Port Said and Port Fuad that the Egyptians were at last ready to surrender. Now occurred an extraordinary and almost comic event. A launch, containing Stockwell, Beaufre and the Air and Sea Task Force Commanders, entered the outer harbour of Port Said. Fighting was clearly still going on. The launch approached the offices of the Canal Company and came under fire from Egyptian troops. The Admiral turned to Stockwell and said drily, 'I don't think, General, they are quite ready to receive us yet!' As Beaufre observed, had the Egyptians held their fire they could have captured the entire high command of the Allied task force.[22]

Meanwhile Eden was facing a difficult dilemma. As C.L. Cooper writes,

His military establishment, powerful MPs from his own party, and his French ally were insisting that the operation proceed until at least some concrete military results were achieved. On the other hand, there was strong pressure, both in Britain and abroad, in favour of his announcing an immediate cease-fire. Unless he took the former course, all the political losses he had incurred would have been for naught, all the military preparation that had been made since late July would have to be written off. Unless he took the latter course, he would have to face the wrath of the United Nations, the United States and even of the Commonwealth.[23]

In addition Eden's health was failing fast. The Russian threat to use missiles against London and Paris may have been for the benefit of Arab public opinion but it served to worry many servicemen in Egypt. This feeling was reinforced by political and military officials in London who, on transmitting the order to cease fire at midnight, added the warning that if the troops did not do so 'there was a risk of Russian nuclear attacks on London and Paris'.[24]

At dusk on 6 November, a mere 36 hours since the landings had begun the military commanders learned that their governments had agreed to comply with the UN demand for a cease-fire. The French, in particular, were furious at the opportunities missed; the British were merely resigned to a dismal end for a thoroughly incompetent operation. In Beaufre's words, 'Our mountain was giving birth to a mouse'.[25]

On one thing everyone was agreed: the Suez operation was a failure on the grand scale, with incompetence as the most recognisable theme running through its every aspect. To C.L. Cooper

The British-French-Israeli alliance was, from its outset, an artificial one. It was born in conspiracy, but sired by men who had neither heart for nor gift of conspiracy. In part because of the nature of the alliance, there was little communication or trust between Britain and Israel from the beginning, and between Britain and France toward the end. And from beginning to end, Eden, Mollet, and Ben-Gurion had divergent perceptions of what the operation was supposed to achieve. Even worse, they were not aware until much too late that such differences existed. Add to this a gross miscalculation about international, especially American, reaction. Add, also, for Britain and France, a language problem, individual weapons systems, an excess of prudence by the planners and a dearth of panache by the commanders. A recipe for disaster certain.[26]

As a military operation Suez demonstrates the problems that can occur between military commanders and their political masters. It is easy to blame Eden for everything and see the soldiers as victims of an indecisive and ill Prime Minister. On the other hand, the military commanders were slow, cautious and uncertain in following the strategic dictates of the politicians. The Army was thoroughly rusty and revealed itself as incapable of reacting swiftly to a threat to British interests.

In retrospect one has to judge Eden's government as unrealistic in its response to the nationalisation of the Canal. As early as 26 July there were no adequate and trained troops for this difficult mission, transport aircraft were unavailable, there was no suitable base close to Egypt and there were no follow-up troops who could be organised in time. In every way the idea was unworkable. In view of the state of Britain's armed forces it was wrong for Eden to issue threats to Nasser without having the means to back them up. After all, the Suez Canal Zone had been evacuated by Britain in the first place because of the difficulty and expense of keeping a large-scale military force in Egypt in the face of local antagonism. How likely was it, therefore, that if British troops returned they would be seen other than as invaders? If their aim was to topple the Egyptian government – and Nasser was a popular and charismatic leader – how much greater resistance would they have faced than they had when merely confined to the Canal Zone? Moreover, if Nasser had been overthrown, leadership in Egypt would have devolved on terrorist groups of the kind which had troubled Israel for so long. Any government imposed by Britain would have been unpopular in the face of the rising power of Arab nationalism. As Fullick and Powell remark, 'The manner in which Eden and the French avoided the issue of what was to follow Nasser is a measure of a lack of foresight which was equalled only by their scant understanding of the new coherence of Arab nationalism'.[27]

The government was also at fault in the treatment of its military commanders. Stockwell was not informed of the part that Israel was playing in the plan and was left to pick up snippets of information from his better-informed French colleagues. Stockwell rightly said that soldiers need to be given a clear idea of what they are being sent to do and why. It was quite wrong that junior commanders should have had to do the politicians' job for them and justify the action to their men. The lack of a clear military objective bedevilled the whole operation: Eden's conflicting political aims – first, to topple Nasser and capture Cairo and, second, to take the Canal and guarantee freedom of navigation – meant that too much time was wasted in planning the wrong operation. Eden should have realised that in the context of world opinion in 1956 he was never going to be able to justify an amphibious assault on Alexandria, a full-scale battle against the Egyptian army and a triumphant march on Cairo.

To say that Stockwell did not known whether he was coming or going is hardly an exaggeration. He heard the news of the cease-fire while his troops were wading ashore and telegraphed London sarcastically, 'We've now achieved the impossible. We're going both ways at once.'[28] C.L. Cooper shows just how much Eden interferred in the planning of the military operations and how, as the domestic and international pressures grew, he became more hesitant and vacillating, communicating his indecision to the military.[29]

Nevertheless, the military commanders and planners cannot be absolved from guilt for the Suez fiasco. The British commanders were prisoners of the strategy and tactics of World War Two. They regarded Egypt as a formidable military power because of the Soviet hardware she had. Her Czech semi-automatic rifle was better than anything the British had (most were armed with breech-loading rifles of 1943 vintage). However, the assumption that Eastern European volunteers would be operating anti-tank guns and piloting planes was quite mistaken and based on intelligence errors. RAF instructors should have remembered the low quality of Egyptian pilot cadets at their training courses. The outcome of this overestimation of Egyptian potential was that the Chiefs of Staff insisted on assembling a huge invasion force, out of all proportion to the task ahead. The lesson of Arnhem showed them the dangers of attempting an airborne attack without follow-up troops being available. The difference, of course, was in the quality of the opposition. The Egyptians were not the Germans, and the Israelis were aware of this more than anyone. They blamed British planning errors and lack of daring for the failure of the Suez operation. Moshe Dayan described the eventual Allied landings in these words, 'After a lengthy incubation, two chicks had finally burst through';[30] while General Harkavi, Chief of Israeli Military intelligence, commented, 'Who did the British think they were invading? The Soviet Union?'[31]

Notes

PART ONE

1 The Commanders pp. 19–75

1 M. Howard, 'Use and Abuse of Military History' in *The Causes of Wars*, p. 191
2 A. Vagts, *A History of Militarism*, p. 28
3 W.C. Church, *Ulysses S. Grant*, pp. 188–9
4 P. Contamine, *War in the Middle Ages*, pp. 250–1
5 ibid., p. 251
6 E.S. Turner, *Gallant Gentlemen*, p. 152
7 ibid., p. 152
8 Contamine, op. cit., p. 259
9 N. Dixon, *On the Psychology of Military Incompetence*, p. 28
10 ibid., p. 32
11 H. Delbruck, *Geschichte des Kriegskunst in Rahmen der politischen Geschichte*, vol. II, p. 272
12 ibid., p. 283
13 B. Tuchman – *A Distant Mirror*, p. 553
14 ibid., p. 558
15 ibid., p. 559
16 ibid., p. 561
17 Dixon, op. cit., p. 55
18 See J.W. Fortescue, *A History of the British Army*, vol. V, book 8, ch. 13
19 C. Oman, *A History of the Art of War in the Middle Ages*, vol. II, p. 76
20 H. Freytag-Loringhoven, *The Power of Personality in War*, p. 36
21 C. Oman, *A History of the Art of War in the Sixteenth Century*, p. 406
22 M. Howard, *The Franco-Prussian War*, p. 173
23 Vagts, op. cit., p. 25
24 M. Cervi – *The Hollow Legions*, p. 33
25 ibid., p. 68
26 ibid., p. 72
27 ibid., p. 73
28 ibid., pp. 73–4
29 M.C.C. Adams, *Our Masters the Rebels*, p. 98
30 ibid., p. 94
31 T.H. Williams, *Lincoln and his Generals*, p. 142
32 T.H. Williams, 'The Military Leadership of North and South' in *Why the North Won the Civil War*, ed. D. Donald, p. 37
33 J.D. Cox, *Military Reminiscences of the Civil War*, vol. I, pp. 370–1

34 Thucydides. *The History of the Peloponnesian War*, book VII, p. 51

35 J.F.C. Fuller, *The Decisive Battles of the Western World*, vol. I, p. 72

36 R. Hough, *The Fleet that Had to Die*, p. 13

37 ibid., p. 32

38 ibid., p. 91

39 ibid., p. 115

40 ibid., p. 128

41 ibid., p. 162

42 D. Walder, *The Chanak Affair*, p. 169

43 ibid., p. 169

44 ibid., pp. 169–70; Lord Kinross, *Ataturk: The Rebirth of a Nation*, p. 314

45 Vagts, op. cit., p. 142

46 ibid., p. 267

47 F.F. Cartwright, *Disease and History*, p. 104

48 F. Richardson, *Napoleon's Death: An Inquest*, p. 88

49 ibid., p. 89

50 A. Bryant, *The Great Duke*, p. 440

51 H.L'Etang, *The Pathology of Leadership*, p. 210

52 C. Dowdey, *Robert E. Lee*, p. 238

53 Dixon, op. cit., p. 73

54 P. Macrory, *Signal Catastrophe*, p. 136

55 ibid., p. 166

56 L'Etang, op. cit., p. 160

57 Dixon, op. cit., pp. 162, 221

58 See Oman, op. cit., I, pp. 33–5

59 D.G. Chandler, *The Campaigns of Napoleon*, p. 455

60 Dixon, op. cit., p. 37

61 N. Stone, *The Eastern Front*, p. 50

62 C. Duffy, *The Army of Frederick the Great*, p. 172

63 A. Bryant, *Years of Victory*, p. 313

64 M. Glover, *Wellington as Military Commander*, pp. 74–5

65 J.W. Wheeler-Bennett, *Hindenburg: The Wooden Titan*, p. 22

66 Stone, op. cit., p. 226

67 Vagts, op. cit., pp. 267–8

68 A. Horne, *To Lose a Battle*, p. 155

69 Fortescue, op. cit., vol. II, p. 505

70 R. Hough, *The Great War at Sea, 1914–1918*, p. 70

71 G. Bennett, *Naval Battles of the First World War*, p. 15

72 Hough, op. cit., p. 79

73 ibid., p. 84

74 ibid., p. 86

75 B. Tuchman – *The Guns of August*, p. 184

76 Vagts, op. cit., p. 113

77 Dixon, op. cit., pp. 22–3, 159

78 Farwell, *The Great Boer War*, p. 159

79 ibid., p. 161

80 Dixon, op. cit., p. 62

81 Farwell, op. cit., p. 165

82 A. Horne, *The Price of Glory*, p. 125

83 ibid., p. 134

84 J.K. Fynn, 'Ghana-Asante', in *West African Resistance*, ed. M. Crowder, p. 32

85 Contamine, op. cit., p. 67

86 Oman, op. cit., vol. II, p. 141

87 ibid., vol. II, p. 139

88 Froissart, *The Chronicles of England, France and Spain*, book I, p. 44

89 ibid., I, p. 45

90 Oman, op. cit., vol. II, pp. 142–3
91 ibid., vol. II, p. 172
92 ibid., vol. II, p. 250
93 H. Talbot, *The English Achilles*, pp. 165–71
94 See arguments of Sir John Smyth in C. Oman, *Warfare in the Sixteenth Century*
95 Oman, op. cit., vol. II, p. 278
96 F. Parkman, *Montcalm and Wolfe*, p. 427
97 Fortescue, op. cit., book II, p. 335
98 J. Haswell, *The Battle for Empire*, p. 242
99 Dixon, op. cit., p. 81
100 A. Clark, *The Donkeys*, p. 164
101 ibid., p. 166
102 ibid., p. 167
103 ibid., p. 169
104 ibid., p. 171
105 ibid., p. 173
106 Plutarch, *Life of Crassus*, translated Rex Warner, p. 19
107 ibid., p. 20
108 B. Farwell, *Queen Victoria's Little Wars*, p. 272
109 Oman, op. cit., vol. II, p. 240
110 R. Browning, *The Byzantine Empire* pp. 130–1; S. Runciman, *A History of the Crusades*, vol. II, pp. 412–3
111 Chandler, op. cit., p. 697
112 ibid., p. 699
113 ibid., p. 700
114 ibid., p. 707
115 B. Liddell Hart, *A History of World War One*, p. 330
116 ibid., p. 330
117 ibid., p. 330
118 Hibbert, op. cit., p. 174
119 ibid., p. 175
120 ibid., p. 175
121 ibid., p. 176
122 Hough, op. cit., p. 128
123 ibid., p. 127
124 ibid., p. 128
125 ibid., p. 134
126 ibid., p. 138
127 Vagts, op. cit., p. 16
128 Dixon, op. cit., p. 155
129 Vagts, op. cit., p. 212
130 D. and P. Warner, *The Tide at Sunrise*, p. 351
131 Vagts, op. cit., p. 231
132 Dixon, op. cit., p. 80
133 C. Duffy, *Frederick the Great: A Military Life*, p. 130
134 ibid., p. 124
135 R.E. Dupuy and T.N. Dupuy, *The Compact History of the Civil War*, p. 232
136 F. Pratt, *Ordeal by Fire*, pp. 321–2
137 H.S. Commager, *The Blue and the Grey*, vol. II, p. 1002
138 J. Laffin, *Damn the Dardanelles*, p. 42
139 ibid., p. 97
140 ibid., p. 202
141 M. Middlebrook, *The First Day on the Somme*, p. 263
142 ibid., p. 266
143 J. Keegan, *The Face of Battle*, pp. 229–30
144 ibid., p. 240
145 Middlebrook, op. cit., p. 99
146 ibid., p. 250
147 Keegan, op. cit., p. 260
148 ibid., p. 261

2 The Planners pp 76–112

1 Dixon, op. cit., p. 399
2 ibid., p. 172
3 D.C. Watt, *Too Serious A*

Business, p. 20

4 ibid., p. 21

5 D. Divine, *The Blunted Sword*, p. 19

6 ibid., p. 19

7 A.J. Marder, *The Anatomy of British Sea Power*, p. 384

8 ibid., pp. 384–5

9 ibid., p. 385

10 ibid., p. 385

11 S. Bonnett, *The Price of Admiralty*, p. 141

12 R. Hough, *The Great War at Sea, 1914–1918*, p. 149

13 ibid., p. 141

14 ibid., p. 155

15 G. Bennett, *Naval Battles of World War One*, p. 224

16 G. Bennett, *Naval Battles of World War Two*, p. 146

17 T.H.E. Travers, 'The offensive and the problem of innovation in British military thought, 1870–1915', p. 532

18 ibid., p. 533

19 ibid., p. 538

20 ibid., p. 540

21 ibid., p. 544

22 A.J.P. Taylor, *English History, 1914–45*, p. 35

23 D. Divine, op. cit., p. 90

24 ibid., p. 147

25 ibid., p. 146

26 Stone, op. cit., p. 49

27 ibid., p. 49

28 Divine, op. cit., p. 148

29 ibid., p. 149

30 Dixon, op. cit., p. 116

31 ibid., p. 114

32 Divine, op. cit., p. 156

33 Dixon, op. cit., p. 117

34 Divine, op. cit., p. 157

35 ibid., p. 152

36 ibid., p. 181

37 ibid., p. 181

38 Cervi, op. cit., p. 60

39 ibid., p. 80

40 ibid., p. 67

41 ibid., p. 68

42 ibid., pp. 68–9

43 C. Hibbert, *Benito Mussolini*, p. 165

44 Cervi, op. cit., pp. 108–9

45 ibid., p. 178

46 ibid., p. 190

47 D. Mack Smith, *Mussolini*, p. 264

48 Cervi, op. cit., p. 192

49 Dixon, op. cit., p. 30

50 Horne, op. cit., pp. 221–2

51 ibid., p. 231

52 W. Lord, *Day of Infamy*, p. 18

53 ibid., p. 61

54 C. Ryan, *A Bridge Too Far*, p. 142

55 C. Wilmot, *The Struggle for Europe*, pp. 521–2

56 Divine, op. cit., p. 100

57 J. Lukacs, *The Last European War*, pp. 255–6

58 ibid., p. 60

59 Divine, op. cit., p. 188

60 ibid., p. 188

61 ibid., p. 189

62 Lukacs, op. cit., p. 259

63 ibid., p. 259

64 Divine, op. cit., pp. 190–1

65 ibid., p. 190

66 A.J.P. Taylor, op. cit., p. 519

67 Divine, op. cit., p. 184

68 ibid., p. 185

69 T. Wilson, *The First Summit*, pp. 134–5

70 Lukacs, op. cit., p. 260

71 ibid., p. 260

72 Divine, op. cit., p. 206

73 ibid., p. 207

74 ibid., p. 208

75 Vagts, op. cit. p. 80
76 Tuchman, op. cit., p. 55
77 J. Laffin, *Tommy Atkins*, p. 51
78 ibid., pp. 51–2
79 H. Haape in *The War 1939–45*, ed D. Flower & J. Reeves, p. 222
80 ibid., p. 229
81 H. Strachan, *European Armies and the Conduct of War*, p. 115
82 G.E. Rothenberg, *The Army of Franz Joseph*, p. 64
83 Strachan, op. cit., p. 113
84 Rothenberg, op. cit., p. 66
85 ibid., p. 66
86 Hough, op. cit., p. 277
87 ibid., p. 278
88 Divine, op. cit., p. 203
89 ibid., pp. 202–3
90 ibid., p. 204
91 T.H. McGuffi, 'The Walcheren Expedition and the Walcheren Fever', p. 195
92 ibid., p. 195
93 ibid., p. 196
94 ibid., p. 196
95 ibid., p. 198
96 ibid., p. 202
97 J. Ellis, *The Sharp End of War*, p. 304
98 ibid., p. 305
99 ibid., pp. 306–7
100 J. Steinbeck, *Once there was a War*, p. 8
101 G. Callender, *The Naval Side of British History* in Hough, op. cit., p. 55
102 Hough, op. cit., p. 56
103 ibid., p. 57
104 ibid., p. 62
105 ibid., p. 63
106 ibid., p. 64
107 ibid., p. 64

3 The Politicians pp. 113–144

1 M. Howard, 'The Relevance of Traditional Strategy' in *The Causes of Wars*, p. 85
2 S. Runciman, *A History of the Crusades*, vol. I, pp. 12–13
3 R. Lewin, *Hitler's Mistakes*, p. 132
4 ibid., p. 132
5 C. Layne, 'British Grand Strategy, 1900–1939', p. 319
6 ibid., p. 320
7 ibid., p. 321
8 ibid., p. 324
9 W. Murray, 'Munich 1938: The Military Confrontation', p. 286
10 R.S. Stolfi, 'Equipment for Victory in France in 1940', p. 8
11 ibid., p. 2
12 Murray, op. cit., p. 287
13 ibid., p. 288
14 ibid., p. 288
15 A. Horne, *To Lose a Battle*, p. 112
16 Murray, op. cit., p. 292
17 ibid., p. 296
18 G. Hopple, 'Intelligence and Warning Lessons', in *Military Lessons of the Falklands War*, ed., B.W. Watson and P.M. Dunn, p. 100
19 ibid., p. 98
20 R.K. Betts, *Surprise Attack: Lessons for Defense Planning* in Hopple, op. cit., p. 99
21 W.J. Ruhe, 'Submarine Lessons', in Watson and Dunn, op. cit., p. 7
22 G. Hopple, op. cit., p. 105
23 ibid., p. 105
24 ibid., p. 105
25 ibid., p. 105
26 ibid., p. 106
27 ibid., pp. 107–8

28 J. Connell, *Wavell*, vol. I, p. 269
29 ibid., p. 256
30 B. Liddell Hart, *History of the Second World War*, p. 114
31 ibid., p. 115
32 A.J.P. Taylor, op. cit., p. 525
33 J. Connell, op. cit., p. 307
34 ibid., p. 308
35 ibid., p. 308
36 J. Kennedy, *The Business of War*, pp. 74–6
37 A. Bryant, *The Turn of the Tide*, pp. 247–8
38 ibid., p. 248
39 A.J.P. Taylor, op. cit., pp. 525–6
40 W.G.F. Jackson, *The North African Campaign, 1940–3*, p. 75
41 ibid., p. 106
42 R.E. Dupuy and T.N. Dupuy, *The Encyclopaedia of Military History*, pp. 190–1
43 B. Catton, *Reflections on the Civil War*, p. 150
44 M. Hastings and S. Jenkins, op. cit., p. 266
45 ibid., p. 292
46 ibid., p. 274
47 ibid., p. 278
48 H.G. Summers, 'Ground Warfare Lessons' in Watson and Dunn, op. cit., p. 72
49 Hastings and Jenkins, op. cit., p. 362
50 H. Trevor-Roper (ed), *The Goebbels Diaries*, p. XX
51 Tuchman, op. cit., p. 199
52 C. Roetter, *Psychological Warfare*, p. 46
53 Tuchman, op. cit., p. 348
54 ibid., p. 358
55 ibid., p. 358
56 ibid., p. 359
57 ibid., pp. 359–60
58 Roetter, op. cit., p. 13

PART TWO

1 Cadiz pp. 147–165

1 R. Lockyer, *Buckingham*, p. 251
2 C.E. Penn, *The Navy under the Early Stuarts*, p. 141
3 S.J. Stearns, 'Conscription and English Society in the 1620s', p. 8
4 ibid., p. 10
5 C. Dalton, *Life and Times of Sir Edward Cecil, Viscount Wimbledon*, vol. II, p. 102–3
6 Penn, op. cit., pp. 145–6
7 Dalton, op. cit., p. 129
8 ibid., pp. 132–3
9 Penn, op. cit., pp. 141–2
10 ibid., p. 142
11 ibid., p. 145
12 Dalton, op. cit., p. 226
13 ibid., p. 143
14 S.R. Gardiner, *History of England from the Accession of James I to the outbreak of the Civil War, 1603–42*, p. 316
15 J. Glanville, *The Voyage to Cadiz in 1625*, p. 23
16 ibid., p. 28
17 Dalton, op. cit. p. 161
18 Penn, op. cit., p. 151
19 Gardiner, op. cit., p. 321
20 Dalton, op. cit., p. 178
21 ibid., p. 179
22 Penn, op. cit., pp. 156–7
23 Gardiner, op. cit., p. 323
24 J.J. Keevil, C. Lloyd and J.L.S. Coulter, *Medicine and the Navy, 1200–1900*, p. 168
25 Gardiner, op. cit., p. 324
26 Dalton, op. cit., pp. 194–5
27 Penn, op. cit., p. 164
28 Dalton, op. cit., p. 195

2 Marston Moor pp. 166–179

1 C.V. Wedgwood, *The King's War, 1641–1647*, p. 49
2 Peter Young, *Marston Moor: The Campaign and the Battle*, p. 73
3 ibid., p. 88
4 ibid., p. 87
5 ibid., p. 87
6 ibid., p. 73
7 ibid., p. 92
8 Wedgwood, op. cit., p. 314
9 Young, op. cit., p. 111
10 ibid., p. 111
11 Wedgwood, op. cit., p. 316
12 ibid., p. 316
13 ibid., p. 316
14 Young, op. cit., p. 122
15 J.S. Clark (ed), *Life of James II*, vol. I, in P. Newman, *The Battle of Marston Moor, 1644*, p. 73
16 Young, op. cit., p. 95
17 Wedgwood, op. cit., p. 318
18 Young, op. cit., p. 117
19 J.S. Clark (ed), op. cit., I, p. 22 et seq
20 Young, op. cit., p. 123
21 P. Newman, *The Battle of Marston Moor, 1644*, p. 92
22 Wedgwood, op. cit., p. 320
23 ibid., p. 321
24 A. Woolrych, *Battles of the English Civil War*, p. 77
25 Young, op. cit., p. 144
26 ibid., p. 71

3 Braddock at the Monongahela pp. 180–191

1 D.S. Freeman, *George Washington*, vol. 1, p. 82
2 H.C.B. Rogers, *The British Army of the Eighteenth Century*, pp. 70–1
3 P.E. Russell, 'Redcoats in the Wilderness: British Officers and Irregular Warfare in Europe and America, 1740 to 1760', p. 629
4 S. Pargellis, 'Braddock's Defeat', p. 253
5 P.E. Kopperman, *Braddock at the Monongahela*, p. 14
6 J.A. Houlding, *Fit for Service*, p. 357
7 F. Parkman, *Montcalm and Wolfe*, p. 149
8 ibid., p. 149
9 L. Maccardell, *Ill-Starred General*, p. 240
10 ibid., p. 244
11 ibid., p. 244
12 J.W. Fortescue, *A History of the British Army*, vol. II, p. 275
13 Kopperman, op. cit., p. 83
14 Maccardell, op. cit., p. 252
15 ibid., p. 251
16 Freeman, op. cit., p. 76
17 Pargellis, op. cit., p. 260
18 ibid., p. 264

4 The Commissariat in the Crimean War pp. 192–208

1 H. Strachan, 'Soldiers, Strategy and Sebastapol', p. 321
2 J. Sweetman, *War and Administration. The Significance of the Crimean War*, p. 44
3 Strachan, op. cit., p. 320
4 C. Hibbert, *The Destruction of Lord Raglan*, p. 251
5 Sweetman, op. cit., p. 46
6 ibid., pp. 46–7
7 Hibbert, op. cit., p. 247
8 C. Woodham Smith, *Florence Nightingale*, p. 155
9 Hibbert, op. cit., p. 248
10 Sweetman, op. cit., p. 51

11 Sir J. McNeill and A. Tulloch, *Report of the Commission into the Supplies of the British Army in the Crimea*, p. 6
12 ibid., p. 3
13 Hibbert, op. cit., p. 281
14 McNeill and Tulloch, op. cit., p. 5
15 ibid., p. 12
16 A. Tulloch, *The Crimean Commission and the Chelsea Board*, p. 100
17 ibid., p. 101
18 Hibbert, op. cit., p. 246
19 McNeill and Tulloch, op. cit., p. 6
20 Hibbert, op. cit., p. 242
21 ibid., p. 281
22 ibid., p. 278
23 McNeill and Tulloch, op. cit., p. 14
24 ibid., p. 17
25 McNeill and Tulloch, *Second Report*, p. 23
26 Tulloch, op. cit., p. 35
27 McNeill and Tulloch, *Second Report*, p. 25
28 ibid., p. 27
29 Hibbert, op. cit., p. 287
30 ibid., p. 287
31 ibid., p. 287
32 ibid., p. 287
33 Tulloch, op. cit., p. 14
34 ibid., p. 31
35 Sweetman, op. cit., pp. 55–6
36 ibid., p. 56
37 ibid., p. 56
38 ibid., p. 57
39 ibid., p. 58
40 Hibbert, op. cit., pp. 255–6

5 The Crater pp. 209–220

1 W.H. Powell, 'The Battle of the Petersburg Crater', in Bradford N. (ed), *Battles and Leaders of the Civil War*, p. 559
2 ibid., p. 559
3 ibid., p. 560
4 S. Foote, *The Civil War: A Narrative*, p. 532
5 ibid., p. 532
6 Powell, op. cit., p. 560
7 Foote, op. cit., p. 532
8 Powell, op. cit., p. 562
9 B. Catton, *A Stillness at Appomattox*, p. 239
10 ibid., p. 240
11 ibid., p. 240
12 Foote, op. cit., p. 535
13 ibid., p. 536
14 Catton, op. cit., p. 244
15 Powell, op. cit., p. 564
16 Foote, op. cit., p. 536
17 Powell, op. cit., p. 566
18 Catton, op. cit., p. 246
19 ibid., p. 249
20 Foote, op. cit., p. 537
21 Catton, op. cit., p. 251
22 ibid., p 252
23 Foote, op. cit., p. 537
24 ibid., p. 538
25 C.R. Fish, in *The Dictionary of Biographical Quotation*, ed. J. Wintle and R. Kenin, p. 122

6 San Juan Hill pp. 221–231

1 Frederic Louis Huidekoper, *The Military unpreparedness of the United States*, p. 154
2 Sargent, *The Campaign of Santiago de Cuba*, vol. I, pp. 79–80
3 Huidekoper, op. cit. pp. 158–9.

4 D.F. Trask, *The War with Spain in 1898*, p. 180
5 Hudiekoper, op. cit., p. 170
6 ibid., p. 170
7 Department of the Army ROTC Manual, *American Military History, 1607–1953*, p. 307
8 Hudiekoper, op. cit., p. 177
9 ibid., p. 177
10 W. Millis, *The Martial Spirit*, p. 271
11 ibid., p. 274
12 Trask, op. cit., p. 228
13 Millis, op. cit., p. 282
14 Trask, op. cit., p. 239
15 Millis, op. cit., p. 283
16 ibid., pp. 285–6
17 ibid., p. 288
18 ibid., p. 189
19 ibid., p. 290
20 Stephen Bonsal, *The Fight for Santiago: The Story of the Soldier in the Cuban Campaign*, p. 141

7 Suvla Bay pp. 232–244

1 A.J. Smithers, *The Man Who Disobeyed*, pp. 260–1
2 A.J. Smithers, *Sir John Monash*, p. 122
3 J. Laffin, *Damn the Dardanelles*, p. 129
4 ibid., p. 129
5 J. Hargrave, *The Suvla Bay Landing*, p. 151
6 C.F. Aspinall-Oglander, *The Official History of the Great War. Military Operations, Gallipoli*, II, p. 140
7 Laffin, op. cit., p. 142
8 ibid., p. 130
9 ibid., p. 131
10 ibid., p. 133

11 Hargrave, op. cit., p. 121
12 ibid., p. 131
13 ibid., p. 131
14 Laffin, op. cit., p. 136
15 Hargrave, op. cit., p. 145
16 Laffin, op. cit., p. 136
17 ibid., p. 136
18 A. Moorehead, *Gallipoli*, p. 180
19 Laffin, op. cit., p. 138
20 ibid., p. 137

8 Convoys pp. 245–254

1 D. Divine, *The Blunted Sword*, pp. 75–6
2 R. Hough, *The Great War at Sea, 1914–18*, p. 30
3 ibid., p. 175
4 ibid., p. 302
5 ibid., p. 302
6 J. Terraine, *White Heat: The New Warfare, 1914–18*, p. 256
7 ibid., p. 256
8 Hough, op. cit., p. 303
9 ibid., p. 303
10 Divine, op. cit., p. 77
11 J. Winton, *Convoy*, pp. 42–3
12 ibid., p. 40
13 Hough, op. cit., p. 169
14 ibid., p. 306
15 Winton, op. cit., pp. 12–16
16 Hough, op. cit., p. 308
17 ibid., p. 307
18 Winton, op. cit., p. 47
19 ibid., p. 47
20 Divine, op. cit., p. 80
21 ibid., p. 80
22 Winton, op. cit., p. 55
23 ibid., p. 56
24 Divine, op. cit., p. 80
25 Winton, op. cit., p. 56
26 ibid., p. 57
27 S. Roskill, *Hankey: Man of Secrets*, p. 357

28 Lord Hankey, *The Supreme Command*, vol. II, p. 648
29 ibid., p. 648
30 Hough, op. cit., p. 308
31 ibid., p. 308
32 Roskill, op. cit., pp. 381–2
33 ibid., p. 379
34 Hankey, op. cit., p. 650
35 Winton, op. cit., p. 78
36 ibid., p. 72
37 Hough, op. cit., p. 312

9 Anual pp. 255–262

1 D. Morris, *The Washing of the Spears*, p. 374
2 R. Battaglia, *La Prima Guerra d'Africa*, pp. 736–7
3 S. Rubenson, 'Adowa 1896: The Resounding Protest', p. 120
4 W.B. Harris, *France, Spain and the Riff*, p. 162
5 ibid., p. 163
6 ibid., pp. 164–5
7 D. Woolman, *Rebels in the Riff*, p. 83
8 ibid., p. 85
9 ibid., p. 85
10 ibid., p. 86
11 ibid., p. 88
12 ibid., p. 88
13 ibid., p. 89
14 ibid., p. 90
15 Harris, op. cit., p. 166
16 ibid., p. 167
17 Woolman, op. cit., p. 91
18 Harris, op. cit., p. 167; Woolman, op. cit., p. 91
19 Woolman, op. cit., p. 95
20 ibid., pp. 97–8
21 ibid., p. 98
22 ibid., p. 98
23 ibid., p. 99
24 ibid., p. 99

25 ibid., p. 101
26 ibid., p. 101

10 Singapore pp. 263–277

1 H.P. Willmott, *Empires in the Balance*, p. 103
2 ibid., p. 103
3 ibid., pp. 103–4
4 ibid., p. 104
5 ibid., pp. 104–5
6 L. Allen, *Singapore, 1941–2*, p. 45
7 ibid., pp. 41–2
8 G. Bennett, *Naval Battles of World War II*, pp. 39, 47
9 Willmott, op. cit., p. 105
10 N. Barber, *Sinister Twilight*, p. 42
11 Allen, op. cit., p. 50
12 ibid., p. 51
13 ibid., p. 52
14 Willmott, op. cit., p. 169
15 Allen, op. cit., p. 53
16 Willmott, op. cit., pp. 172–4
17 ibid., p. 218
18 ibid., p. 219
19 ibid., p. 219
20 ibid., p. 220
21 Barber, op. cit., p. 125
22 ibid., p. 23
23 ibid., p. 69
24 Willmott, op. cit., p. 227
25 S. Woodburn-Kirby, *The Chain of Disaster*, p. 184
26 Willmott, op. cit., pp. 236–7
27 See for example N. Dixon, *On the Psychology of Military Incompetence*, chapter 11
28 Allen, op. cit., p. 186
29 ibid., p. 243

11 Suez   pp. 278–293

1 C.L. Cooper, *The Lion's Last Roar*, p. 173
2 R. Fullick and G. Powell, *Suez: The Double War*, p. 22
3 ibid., p. 185
4 H. Thomas, *The Suez Affair*, pp. 158, 243
5 Fullick and Powell, op. cit., p. 18
6 ibid., p. 103
7 ibid., pp. 20–1
8 ibid., p. 30
9 ibid., p. 32
10 ibid., p. 34
11 ibid., p. 35
12 ibid., p. 37
13 ibid., p. 57
14 ibid., p. 57
15 ibid., p. 59
16 ibid., p. 61
17 ibid., p. 74
18 ibid., p. 86
19 Cooper, op. cit., pp. 174–5
20 Fullick and Powell, op. cit., p. 101
21 ibid., p. 104
22 K. Love, *Suez: The Twice-Fought War*, p. 621; Fullick and Powell, op. cit., p. 151
23 Cooper, op. cit., p. 190
24 ibid., p. 197
25 ibid., p. 203
26 ibid., p. 203
27 Fullick and Powell, op. cit., p. 188
28 Cooper, op. cit., p. 204
29 ibid., p. 204
30 Fullick and Powell, op. cit., p. 141
31 Cooper, op. cit., p. 207

Select Bibliography

ADAMS, M.C.C, *Our Masters the Rebels*, Harvard University Press, Cambridge, Mass, 1978.

ADCOCK, F.E., *The Roman Art of War Under the Republic*, Harvard University Press, Cambridge, Mass, 1940.

ADAMTHWAITE, A.P., *The Making of the Second World War*, Allen and Unwin, 1977.

ALGER, R.A., *The Spanish-American War*, Harker, New York, 1901.

ALLEN, L., *Singapore 1941–1942*, Davis-Poynter, 1977.

ASHLEY, M., *Rupert of the Rhine*, Granada, 1976.

ASPINALL-OGLANDER, C.F., *The Official History of the Great War. Military Operations, Gallipoli*, Heinemann, 1929.

BAILES, H., 'Patterns of Thought in the late Victorian Army', *Journal of Strategic Studies*, vol. 4, no. 1 (1981), pp. 29–46.

BARBER, N., *Sinister Twilight*, Collins, 1968.

BAREA, A., *The Track*, Fontana, 1984.

BARKER, A.J., *Townshend of Kut*, Cassell, 1967.

BARNETT, C., *Britain and Her Army, 1509–1970*, Allen Lane, 1970.

——, *The Desert Generals*, Kimber, 1960.

——, *The Swordbearers*, Eyre and Spottiswoode, 1963.

BEAUFRE, A., *1940, The Fall of France*, Cassell, 1967.

——, *The Suez Expedition 1956*, trans. R. Barry, Faber, 1969.

BEELER, J., *Warfare in Feudal Europe, 730–1200*, Cornell University Press, Ithaca, 1971.

BELLER, E.A., 'The Military Expedition of Sir Charles Morgan to Germany, 1627–9', *English Historical Review*, 43 (1928) pp. 528–39.

BENGTSSON, F.G., *The Life of Charles XII*, Macmillan, New York, 1960.

BENNETT, G., *Naval Battles of the First World War*, Batsford, 1968.

——, *Naval Battles of World War II*, Batsford, 1975.

BENTLEY, R., 'Weather in War-Time', *Quarterly Journal of the Royal Meteorological Society*, vol. 33, no. 142 (1907), pp. 81–138.

BETTS, R.K., *Surprise Attack: Lessons for Defense Planning*, Brookings Institution, Washington D.C., 1982.

BIDWELL, R.G.S., *Modern Warfare*, Allen Lane, 1973.

BIRNIE, A., *The Art of War*, Nelson, 1942.

BLOND, G., *Admiral Togo*, Jarrolds, 1961.

BOND, B., *The Victorian Army and the Staff College, 1854–1914*, Eyre Methuen, 1972.

——, (ed.) *Victorian Military Campaigns*, Hutchinson, 1967.

BONNETT, S., *The Price of Admiralty*, Hale, 1968.

BONSAL, S., *The Fight for Santiago: The Story of the Soldier in the Cuban Campaign*, Doubleday & McClure, New York, 1899.

BOYNTON, L.O.J., *The Elizabethan Militia 1558–1638*, Routledge and Kegan Paul, 1967.

——, 'Martial Law and the Petition of Right', *English Historical Review*, 79, (1964), pp. 255–84.

——, 'Billeting: The Example of the Isle of Wight', *English Historical Review*, 74, (1959), pp. 23–40.

BRADDON, R., *The Siege*, Cape, 1969.

——, *Suez: Splitting of a Nation*, Collins, 1973.

BRADFORD, N., (ed.), *Battles and Leaders of the Civil War*, Appleton Century, 1956.

BRETT-SMITH, R., *Hitler's Generals*, Osprey, 1976.

BROWNING, R., *The Byzantine Empire*, Weidenfeld and Nicolson, 1980.

BRYANT, A., *Years of Victory 1802–1812*, Collins, 1944.

——, *The Turn of the Tide*, Collins, 1957.

——, *Triumph in the West*, Collins, 1959.

——, *The Age of Chivalry*, Collins, 1963.

——, *The Great Duke*, Collins, 1971.

BURNE, A.H., *The Crécy War: A Military History of the Hundred Years War from 1337 to the Peace of Bettigny, 1360*, Oxford University Press, New York, 1955.

——, *The Agincourt War: A Military History of the Latter Part of the Hundred Years War from 1369 to 1453*, Oxford University Press, New York, 1956.

——, *The Battlefields of England*, Methuen, 1973.

BUSH, E., *Gallipoli*, Allen and Unwin, 1975.

CAFFREY, K., *The Lion and the Union*, André Deutsch, 1978.

——, *Out in the Midday Sun*, André Deutsch, 1974.

CALDER, A., *The People's War*, Panther, 1971.

CALLWELL, C.E., *Small Wars. Their principles and practices*, HMSO, 1906.

CALVOCORESSI, P. and WINT, G., *Total War*, Allen Lane, 1972.

CARTWRIGHT, F.F., *Disease and History*, Hart-Davis, 1972.

CARVER, M. (ed.) *The War Lords*, Weidenfield and Nicolson, 1976.

CASSAR, G.H., *Kitchener*, Kimber, 1977.

CATTON, B., *A Stillness at Appomattox*, Doubleday, New York, 1954.

——, *Glory Road*, Doubleday, New York, 1952.

——, *Mr Lincoln's Army*, Doubleday, New York, 1949.

——, *This Hallowed Ground*, Doubleday, New York, 1956.

——, *Reflections on the Civil War*, Doubleday, New York, 1981.

CERVI, M., *The Hollow Legions*, Chatto and Windus, 1972.

CHANDLER, D.G., *The Campaigns of Napoleon*, Weidenfeld and Nicolson, 1966.

CHALLENER, R.D., *The French Theory of the Nation in Arms 1866–1939*, Columbia University Press, New York, 1955.

CHRISTIANSEN, E., *The Northern Crusades*, Macmillan, 1980.

CHURCH, W.C., *Ulysses S. Grant*, Putnams, New York, 1897.

CLARK, A., *The Donkeys*, Hutchinson, 1961.

CLARK, J.S. (ed.), *Life of James II*, 1816.

CLAUSEWITZ, C. VON, *On War*, ed. Anatol Rapoport, Penguin, Harmondsworth, 1968.

COLLIER, R., *1940: The World in Flames*, Hamish Hamilton, 1979.

COLVILLE, J.R., *Man of Honour*, Collins, 1972.

COMMAGER, H.S., *The Blue and the Gray*, 2 vols., Bobbs-Merrill, Indianopolis, 1950.

CONNELL, J., *Auchinleck*, Cassell, 1959.

——, *Wavell, Scholar and Soldier*, Collins, 1964.

CONTAMINE, P., *War in the Middle Ages*, trans. M. Jones, Basil Blackwell, Oxford, 1984.

COOPER, C.L., *The Lion's Last Roar*, Harper & Row, New York, 1978.

COX, J.D., *Military Reminiscences of the Civil War*, New York, 1900.

CRAIG, G.A., *The Battle of Königgrätz*, Weidenfeld and Nicolson, 1965.

CREVELD, M. van, *Supplying War. Logistics from Wallenstein to Patton*, Cambridge University Press, Cambridge, 1977.

——, 'The German Attack on the U.S.S.R: the destruction of a legend', *European Studies Review*, vol. 2, no. 1 (1972), pp. 69–86.

CROWDER, M., (ed.), *West African Resistance*, Hutchinson, 1971.

CRUICKSHANK, C.G., *Elizabeth's Army*, 2nd edn., Clarendon Press, Oxford, 1966.

DALTON, C., *Life and Times of Sir Edward Cecil, Viscount Wimbledon*, 2 vols, Sampson Low, Marston, Searle and Rivington, 1885.

DELBRUCK, H., *Geschichte der Kriegskunst im Rahmen der politschen, Geschichte*, 7 vols., Berlin, 1900–36.

DICKS, H.V., *Licensed Mass Murder*, Heineman, 1972.

DIVINE, D., *The Blunted Sword*, Hutchinson, 1964.

DIXON, N., *On the Psychology of Military Incompetence*, Cape, 1976.

DOWDEY, C., *Robert E. Lee*, Gollancz, 1970.

DUFFY, C., *The Army of Frederick the Great*, David and Charles, 1974.

——, *The Army of Maria Theresa*, David and Charles, 1977.

——, *Russia's Military Way to the West*, Routledge and Kegan Paul, 1981.

——, *Frederick the Great. A Military History*, Routledge and Kegan Paul, 1985.

DUPUY, T.N., *A Genius for War, The German Army and General Staff 1807–1945*, Macdonald and Jane's, 1977.

——, *The Evolution of Weapons and Warfare*, Jane's 1982.

——, *The Military Life of Hannibal: Father of Strategy*, Franklin Watts, New York, 1969.

DUPUY, R.E & DUPUY, T.N., *The Encyclopaedia of Military History*, Macdonald and Jane's, 1970.

——, *The Compact History of the Civil War*, Hawthorn, New York, 1960.

——, *The Compact History of the Revolutionary War*, Hawthorn, New York, 1963.

EARLE, E.M., (ed.) *Makers of Modern*

Strategy, Princeton University Press, 1971.

ELLIS, J., *The Sharp End of War*, David and Charles, 1980.

ERLANGER, P., *George Villiers, Duke of Buckingham*, Hodder and Stoughton, 1953.

FAIR, C., *From the Jaws of Victory*, Simon & Schuster, New York, 1971.

FALLS, C., *A Hundred Years of War*, Duckworth, 1953.

——, *The Art of War*, Oxford University Press, 1961.

FARWELL, B., *Queen Victoria's Little Wars*, Allen Lane, 1973.

——, *The Great Boer War*, Allen Lane, 1977.

FEATHERSTONE, D., *Colonial Small Wars 1837–1901*, David and Charles, Newton Abbot, 1973.

FLOWER, D. and REEVES, J., *The War 1939–1945*, Cassell, 1960.

FOOTE, S., *The Civil War: A Narrative*, Random House, New York, 1958.

FORTESCUE, J.W., *A History of the British Army*, 13 vols., Macmillan, 1902–30.

FRASER, A., *Cromwell: Our Chief of Men*, Weidenfeld and Nicolson, 1973.

FREEMAN, D.S., *Lee's Lieutenants*, 3 vols., Scribner, New York, 1942–4.

——, *R.E. Lee, A Biography*, 4 vols, Scribner, New York, 1934–7.

——, *George Washington*, 7 vols, Eyre and Spottiswoode, 1948–54.

FRENCH, D., 'The military background to the "shell crisis" of May 1915', *Journal of Strategic Studies*, vol. 2, no. 2 (1979), pp. 192–205.

FREYTAG-LORINGHOVEN, Baron F.H.,

The Power of Personality in War, Berlin, 1905.

FROISSART, J., *The Chronicles of England, France and Spain*, Everyman Library, Dent, 1906.

FULLER, J.F.C., *The Decisive Battles of the Western World*, 3 vols, Eyre and Spottiswoode, 1954–6.

FULLICK, R. and POWELL, G., *Suez: The Double War*, Hamish Hamilton, 1979.

GARDINER, S.R., *History of England from the Accession of James I to the Outbreak of the Civil War*, 10 vols., Longmans, 1883.

GEYL, P., *Napoleon: For and Against*, Cape, 1949.

GLANVILLE, J., *The Voyage to Cadiz in 1625*, ed. Alexander Grant, Camden Society, 1883.

GLOVER, M., *Wellington as Military Commander*, Batsford, 1968.

GOOCH, B.D., *The New Bonapartist Generals in the Crimean War*, Nijhoff, The Hague, 1959.

GOOCH, J., *Armies in Europe*, Routledge and Kegan Paul, 1980.

GOULD, R.T.V., *Enigmas*, MacLehose, 1946.

GUDERIAN, H., *Panzer Leader*, Michael Joseph, 1952.

GUEDALLA, P., *The Duke*, Hodder and Stoughton, 1931.

——, *The Two Marshals*, Hodder and Stoughton, 1943.

HACKETT, Sir J., *The Profession of Arms*, Sidgwick and Jackson, 1983.

HANKEY, Lord M., *The Supreme Command*, vol. 2, Allen and Unwin, 1961.

HARGREAVE, J., *The Sulva Bay Landing*, Macdonald, 1964.

HARRIS, W.B., *France, Spain and the Riff*, Arnold, 1927.

HASTINGS, M., *The Oxford Book of Military Anecdotes*, Oxford University Press, Oxford, 1985.

HASTINGS, M. & JENKINS, S., *The Battle for the Falklands*, Michael Joseph, 1983.

HASWELL, J., *The Battle for Empire*, Cassell, 1976.

HEATHCOTE, T.A., *The Afghan Wars*, Osprey, 1980.

HENDERSON, G.F.R., *Stonewall Jackson*, Longman, 1932.

HERZOG, C., *The Arab-Israeli Wars*, Arms and Armour Press, 1982.

HIBBERT, C., *Mussolini*, Longman, 1963.

——, *The Destruction of Lord Raglan*, Longman, 1961.

HITTLE, J.D., *The Military Staff. Its History and Development*, Harrisburg Military Service, Penn, 1949.

HIGGINS, T., *Winston Churchill and the Dardanelles*, Heinemann, 1963.

HOPPLE, G., 'Intelligence and Warning Lessons' in Watson B.W. and Dunn P.M., *Military Lessons of the Falkland Islands War*, Arms and Armour, 1984.

HORNE, A., *The Price of Glory*, Macmillan, 1962.

——, *To Lose a Battle*, Macmillan, 1969.

HOUGH, R., *Admirals in Collision*, Hamish Hamilton, 1959.

——, *The Fleet that had to Die*, Hamish Hamilton, 1958.

——, *The Hunting of Force Z*, Collins, 1963.

——, *The Great War at Sea 1914–1918*, Oxford University Press, Oxford, 1983.

HOULDING, J.A. *Fit for Service. The training of the British Army, 1715–1795*, Oxford University Press, Oxford, 1981.

HOUSE, J.M., 'The Decisive Attack: a new look at French infantry tactics on the eve of World War I', *Military Affairs*, vol. 40 (Dec. 1976), pp. 164–9.

HOWARD, M., *The Franco-Prussian War*, Hart-Davis, 1961.

——, *The Mediterranean Strategy in the Second World War*, Weidenfeld and Nicolson, 1968.

——, *War in European History*, Oxford University Press, Oxford, 1976.

——, 'Use and Abuse of Military History' in *The Causes of Wars*, Allen and Unwin, 1984.

HUIDEKOPER, F.L., *The Military Unpreparedness of the United States*, Macmillan, New York, 1916.

IRVING, D., *The War Path*, Michael Joseph, 1978.

——, *The War Between the Generals*, Allen Lane, 1981.

JACKSON, W.G.F., *The North African Campaign, 1940–43*, Batsford, 1975.

JAMES, D., *Lord Roberts*, Hollis and Carter, 1954.

JANIS, I.L., *Victims of Groupthink*, Houghton Mifflin, Boston, 1972.

JANOWITZ, M., *The Professional Soldier*, Free Press, New York, 1960.

JOHNSON, R.U. and BUELL, C.C., *Battles and Leaders of the Civil War*, 4 vols., Century, New York, 1887.

JONES, R.V., *Most Secret War*, Hamish Hamilton, 1978.

JUDD, D., *Someone Has Blundered, Calamities of the British Army, in the Victorian Age*, Arthur Barker, 1973.

KARNOW, S., *Vietnam: A History*, Penguin, Harmondsworth, 1984.

KEEGAN, J., *The Face of Battle*, Cape, 1976.

KEEVIL, J.J., LLOYD, C. and COULTER, J.L.S., *Medicine and the Navy, 1200–1900*, 4 vols., Livingstone, 1958.

KENNEDY, J., *The Business of War*, Hutchinson, 1957.

KINROSS, LORD, *Ataturk: The Rebirth of a Nation*, Weidenfeld and Nicolson, 1964.

KON, D., *Los Chicos de la Guerra*, New English Library, 1983.

KOPPERMAN, P.E., *Braddock at the Monongahela*, Feffers, 1977.

LAFFIN, J., *Americans in Battle*, Dent, 1973.

——, *The French Foreign Legion*, Dent, 1974.

——, *Tommy Atkins*, Cassell, 1966.

——, *Links of Leadership*, Harrap, 1966.

——, *Damn the Dardanelles*, Osprey, 1980.

LAYNE, C., 'British Grand Strategy, 1900–1939: Theory and Practice in International Politics', *Journal of Strategic Studies*, vol. 2., no. 3 (1979), pp. 303–330.

L'ETANG, H., *Pathology of Leadership*, Heinemann, 1969.

——, *Fit to Lead*, Heinemann, 1980.

LEWIN, R., *Hitler's Mistakes*, Leo Cooper/Secker and Warburg, 1984.

LIDDELL HART, B., *History of the First World War*, Cassell, 1970.

——, *History of the Second World War*, Cassell, 1970.

——, *The Other Side of the Hill*, Cassell, 1951.

LIDDLE, P., *Men of Gallipoli*, Allen Lane, 1976.

LOCKYER, R., *Buckingham*, Longman, 1984.

LONGFORD, E., *Wellington. The Years of the Sword*, Weidenfeld and Nicolson, 1969.

LORD, W., *Day of Infamy*, Henry Holt, New York, 1957.

LORENZ, K., *On Aggression*, Bantam Books, New York, 1963.

LOVE, K., *Suez: The Twice-Fought War*, Longman, 1970.

LUKACS, J., *The Last European War*, Routledge and Kegan Paul, 1977.

LUVAAS, J., *The Education of an Army*, Cassell, 1965.

MACCARDELL, L., *Ill-Starred General*, University of Pittsburgh Press, Pittsburgh, 1958.

MCGOWAN, A.P., 'The Royal Navy under the First Duke of Buckingham,' London University Ph.D., 1967.

MCGUFFIE, T.H., 'The Walcheren Expedition and the Walcheren Fever', *English Historical Review*, 62, (1947), pp. 191–202.

MACINTYRE, D., *The Naval War Against Hitler*, Batsford, 1971.

——, *Narvik*, Evans, 1959.

MACK SMITH, D., *Mussolini*, Weidenfeld and Nicolson, 1982.

MCNEILL, Sir J. and TULLOCH, A., *Report of the Commission into the Supplies of the British Army in the Crimea*, 1856.

MACRORY, P., *Signal Catastrophe*, Hodder, 1966.

MCWHINEY, G., (ed.), *Grant, Lee, Lincoln and the Radicals*, Harper and Row, New York, 1960.

MAGNUS, P., *Kitchener: Portrait of an Imperialist*, Murray, 1958.

MARDER, A.J., *The Anatomy of British Sea Power*, Knopf, New York, 1940.

MARSHALL, S.L.A., 'Men against Fire. The Problem of Battle

Commanders in Future War,'
Washington Infantry Journal, 1947.

MASSIE, R.K., *Peter the Great*,
Gollancz, 1981.

MELLENTHIN, F.W. von, *Panzer
Battles 1939–1945*, Cassell, 1955.

MESSENGER, C., *Bomber Harris and
the Strategic Bombing Offensive
1939–45*, Arms and Armour, 1984.

MIDDLEBROOK, M., *The First Day on
the Somme*, Allen Lane, 1971.

MILLIS, W., *Armies and Men. A
Study of American Military
History*, Cape, 1958.

——, *The Martial Spirit*, Houghton
Mifflin, Cambridge, Mass, 1931.

MONTGOMERY, Viscount., *A History
of Warfare*, Collins, 1968.

MONTROSS, L., *War through the Ages*,
3rd edn., Harper, New York, 1960.

MOOREHEAD, A., *Gallipoli*, illustrated
edition, Macmillan, 1975.

MORRIS, D., *The Washing of the
Spears*, Cape, 1966.

MURRAY, W., 'Munich 1938: The
Military Confrontation', *Journal of
Strategic Studies*, vol. 2, no. 3
(1979) pp. 282–97.

——, 'The Luftwaffe before the
Second World War: a mission, a
strategy?', *Journal of Strategic
Studies*, vol. 4, no. 3 (1981),
pp. 261–70.

——, 'The Strategy of the "Phoney
War': A Re-evaluation', *Military
Affairs*, vol. 45, no. 1 (1981),
pp. 13–17.

NEWARK, T., *Medieval Warfare*,
Jupiter, 1979.

NEWMAN, P., *The Battle of Marston
Moor 1644*, Bird, 1981.

NICHOLS, F.T., 'The Organisation of
Braddock's Army', *William and
Mary Quarterly*, 3rd series, vol. 4,
1947, pp. 124–47.

NICOLSON, N., *Alex*, Weidenfeld &
Nicolson, 1973.

NICHOLSON, R.G.N., *Edward III and
the Scots*, Oxford University Press,
Oxford, 1965.

NORTH, J., *Gallipoli: The Fading
Vision*, Faber and Faber, 1936.

NUTTING, A., *No End of a Lesson*,
Constable, 1967.

OMAN, C., *A History of the Art of
Warfare in the Middle Ages*, 2
vols., Methuen, 1978.

——, *A History of the Art of War in
the Sixteenth Century*, Methuen,
1937.

OPPENHEIM, M., *History of the
Administration of the Royal Navy*,
Lane, 1896.

PACKENHAM, T., *The Boer War*,
Weidenfeld and Nicolson, 1979.

PADFIELD, P., *Tide of Empires, vol 1,
1481–1654*, Routledge and Kegan
Paul, 1979.

——, *Tide of Empires, vol. 2, 1654–
1763*, Routledge and Kegan Paul, 1982.

PALMER, A., *Napoleon in Russia*,
André Deutsch, 1967.

PARET, P., 'Colonial Experience and
European military reform at the
end of the eighteenth century',
*Bulletin of the Institute of
Historical Research*, vol. 37, no.
95, (1964), pp. 47–59.

PARGELLIS, S., 'Braddock's defeat',
American Historical Review, vol.
41, no. 2 (1936), pp. 253–269.

PARISH, P., *The American Civil War*,
Eyre Methuen, 1975.

PARKMAN, F., *Montcalm and Wolfe*,
Eyre and Spottiswoode, 1964.

PEMBERTON, B.W., *Battles of the
Crimean War*, Batsford, 1962.

PENN, C.D., *The Navy under the early
Stuarts*, Cornmarket, 1970.

PLUTARCH, *Fall of the Roman*

Republic, trans., R. Warner, Penguin, Harmondsworth, 1958.

PORCH, D., 'The French army and the spirit of the offensive', in *War and Society*, ed. Brian Bond and Ian Roy (1975), pp. 117–43.

PRATT, F., *Ordeal By Fire*, The Bodley Head, 1950.

PRESTON, R.A., WISE, S.F. and WARNER, H.O., *Men in Arms*, Thames and Hudson, 1962.

PROCOPIUS, *The Vandalic War*, trans. H.B. Dewing, Heinemann, 1916.

RICHARDSON, F., *Napoleon's Death: An Inquest*, Kimber, 1974.

ROBERTS, M., *The Military Revolution, 1560–1660*, University of Belfast, Belfast, 1956.

ROETTER, C., *Psychological Warfare*, Batsford, 1974.

ROGERS, H.C.B., *The British Army of the Eighteenth Century*, Allen and Unwin, 1977.

ROSKILL, S., *Naval Policy between the Wars*, Collins, 1968.

——, *Hankey. Man of Secrets*, 3 vols., Collins, 1970–74.

DEPARTMENT OF THE ARMY, WASHINGTON, ROTC MANUAL, *American Military History 1607–1953*, Washington, 1956.

ROTHENBERG, G.E., *The Army of Franz Joseph*, Purdue University Press, West Lafayette, 1976.

——, *The Art of Warfare in the Age of Napoleon*, Batsford, 1977.

——, *Napoleon's Great Adversaries. The Archduke Charles and the Austrian Army*, Batsford, 1982.

RUBENSON, S., 'Adowa 1896: The Resounding Protest', in Rotberg, R.I. and Mazru, A.A., *Protest and Power in Black Africa*, (eds.) Oxford University Press, Oxford, 1970.

RUHE, W.J., 'Submarine Lessons' in Watson, B.W. and Dunn, P.M., (eds.) *Military Lessons of the Falkland Islands War*, Arms, and Armour Press, 1984.

RUNCIMAN, S., *A History of the Crusades*, 3 vols., Cambridge University Press, Cambridge, 1951.

RUSSELL, P.E., 'Redcoats in the Wilderness: British officers and irregular warfare in Europe and America, 1740 to 1760', *William and Mary Quarterly*, 3rd series, vol. 35, no. 4 (1978), pp. 629–52.

RYAN, C., *A Bridge Too Far*, Hamish Hamilton, 1974.

SACHER, H.M., *The Emergence of the Middle East 1914–1924*, Allen Lane, 1969.

SARGENT, W., *History of an Expedition against Fort Duquesne in 1755*, Historical Society of Pennsylvania, 1855.

SCHLESINGER Jr., A.M., *A Thousand Days*, André Deutsch, 1965.

SEATON, A., *The German Army. 1933–45*, Weidenfeld and Nicolson, 1982.

SEYMOUR, W., *Battles in Britain, vol. 1, 1066–1547*, Sidgwick and Jackson, 1975.

SHEPPARD, E.W., *A Short History of the British Army*, Constable, 1926.

SIXSMITH, E.K.G., *British Generalship in the Twentieth Century*, Arms and Armour Press, 1970.

SMITHERS, A.J., *The Man Who Disobeyed*, Leo Cooper, 1970.

——, *Sir John Monash*, Leo Cooper, 1972.

SMYTHE, Sir J., *Leadership in War 1939–45*, David and Charles, 1974.

——, *Before the Dawn*, Cassell, 1957.

SPAULDING, O.L., NICKERSON, H. and

WRIGHT, J.W., *Warfare: A Study on Military Methods from the Earliest Times*, Infantry Journal Press, Washington, 1939.

SPEARS, E., *Assignment to Catastrophe*, Heinemann, 1954.

STEARNS, S.J., 'Conscription and English Society in the 1620s', *Journal of British Studies*, vol. II, 1972, pp. 1–23.

STEINBECK, J., *Once there was a War*, Corgi, 1961.

STEPHENS, R., *Nasser: A political biography*, Allen Lane, 1971.

STOLFI, R.H.S., 'Equipment for victory in France in 1940', *History*, vol. 52, no. 1 (1970), pp. 1–20.

STONE, N., *The Eastern Front*, Hodder and Stoughton, 1975.

STRACHAN, H., *European Armies and the Conduct of War*, Allen and Unwin, 1983.

———, 'Soldiers, Strategy and Sebastapol', *Historical Journal*, vol. 21, no. 2 (1978), pp. 303–25.

STRAWSON, J., *Hitler as Military Commander*, Batsford, 1971.

SUMMERS, H.G., 'Ground Warfare Lessons' in Watson, B.W. and Dunn, P.M. (eds.), *Military Lessons of the Falkland Islands War*, Arms and Armour Press, 1984.

SWEETMAN, J., *War and Administration*, Edinburgh, 1984.

SYMONS, J., *Buller's Campaign*, White Lion, 1974.

TALBOT, H., *The English Achilles*, Chatto and Windus, 1981.

TAYLOR, A.J.P., *English History 1914–45*, Oxford University Press, Oxford, 1965.

———, *The Second World War. An illustrated History*, Hamish Hamilton, 1975.

TERRAINE, J., *White Heat: The New Warfare 1914–18*, Sigwick and Jackson, 1982.

THOMAS, H., *The Suez Affair*, Weidenfeld and Nicolson, 1967.

THOMPSON, G.M., *The First Churchill*, Secker and Warburg, 1979.

THOMPSON, R.W., *Montgomery: The Field Marshal*, Allen and Unwin, 1969.

THUCYDIDES, *The History of the Peloponnesian War*, trans. R. Warner, Penguin, Harmondsworth, 1963.

TIGER, L., *Men in Groups*, Panther, 1971.

TOLAND, J., *Adolf Hitler*, Doubleday, New York, 1976.

———, *No Man's Land*, Eyre Methuen, 1980.

TOMASON, K. and BUIST, F., *Battles of the '45*, Batsford, 1962.

TRASK, D.F., *The War with Spain in 1898*, Macmillan, New York, 1981.

TRAVERS, T.H.E., 'The offensive and the problem of innovation in British military thought 1870–1915', *Journal of Contemporary History*, vol. 13, no. 3 (1978), pp. 531–53.

TREVOR-ROPER, H., (ed.) *The Goebbels Diaries*, Secker and Warburg, 1978.

TULLOCH, A., *The Crimean Commission and the Chelsea Board*, Harrison, 1880.

TURNER, E.S., *Gallant Gentlemen, a portrait of the British Officer 1600–1956*, Michael Joseph, 1956.

TUCHMAN, B., *A Distant Mirror*, Macmillan, 1979.

———, *The Guns of August*, Constable, 1962.

VAGTS, A., *A History of Militarism*,

revised edn., Meridian Books, New York, 1959.

VALENTINE, A., *Lord George Germain*, Oxford University Press, Oxford, 1962.

WALDER, D., *The Chanak Affair*, Hutchinson, 1969.

WARNER, D. & P., *The Tide at Sunrise*, Angus and Robertson, 1975.

WATSON, B.W., & DUNN, P.M. (eds.), *Military Lessons of the Falkland Islands War*, Arms and Armour Press, 1984.

WATSON, P., *War on the Mind*, Hutchinson, 1978.

WATT, D.C., *Too Serious a Business*, Temple Smith, 1975.

WEDGWOOD, C.V., *The King's War 1641–1647*, Collins, 1958.

WEIGHLEY, R.F., *History of the United States Army*, Batsford, 1968.

WENHAM, P., *The Great and Close Siege of York*, Roundwood, Kineton, 1970.

WHEELER-BENNETT, J.W., *Hindenburg: The Wooden Titan*, Macmillan, 1936.

WILLIAMS, K.P., *Lincoln Finds a General*, 4 vols., Macmillan, New York, 1949–56.

WILLIAMS, T.H., *Lincoln and His Generals*, Knopf, New York, 1952.

——, 'The Military Leadership of North and South', in Donald, D. (ed.), *Why the North won the Civil War*, New York, 1962.

WILLMOTT, H.P., *Empires in the Balance*, Orbis, 1982.

WILMOT, C., *The Struggle for Europe*, Collins, 1952.

WILSON, T., *The First Summit*, Macdonald, 1969.

WINTER, D., *Death's Men*, Allen Lane, 1978.

WINTON, J., *Convoy*, Michael Joseph, 1983.

——, *Jellicoe*, Michael Joseph, 1981.

WOODBURN-KIRBY, S., *Singapore, the Chain of Disaster*, Cassell, 1971.

WOODHAM SMITH, C., *Florence Nightingale*, Constable, 1950.

——, *The Reason Why*, Constable, 1953.

WOODWARD, D., *Armies of the World 1854–1914*, Sidgwick and Jackson, 1978.

WOOLMAN, D., *Rebels in the Riff*, Oxford University Press, Oxford, 1969.

WOOLRYCH, A., *Battles of the English Civil War*, Batsford, 1961.

WRIGHT, Q., *A Study of War*, University of Chicago Press, 1964.

YAPLE, R.L., 'Braddock's defeat: the theories and a reconstruction', *Journal of the Society for Army Historical Research*, XLVI, 1968.

YOUNG, P., *A Dictionary of Battles 1816–1976*, Mayflower, New York, 1977.

——, *Marston Moor: The Campaign and Battle*, Roundwood, Kineton, 1970.

YOUNG, R.J., 'Preparations for defeat: French war doctrine in the interwar period', *Journal of European Studies*, vol. 2, no. 2 (1972), pp. 155–72.

ZULFO, I.H., *Karari*, Frederick Warne, 1980.

Index

is due

NOV. 1993

-7. SEP. 2003